War and Childhood in the Era of the Two World Wars

The histories of modern war and childhood were the result of competing urgencies. According to ideals of childhood widely accepted throughout the world by 1900, children should have been protected, even hidden, from conflict and danger. Yet at a time when modern ways of childhood became increasingly possible for economic, social, and political reasons, it became less possible to fully protect children in the face of massive industrialized warfare driven by geopolitical rivalries and expansionist policies. Taking a global perspective, the chapters in this volume examine a wide range of experiences and places. In addition to showing how the engagement of children and youth with war differed according to geography, technology, class, age, race, gender, and the nature of the state, they reveal how children acquired agency during the twentieth century's greatest conflicts.

Mischa Honeck teaches US and transatlantic history at the Humboldt University of Berlin. He was a research fellow at the German Historical Institute Washington and is the author of *Our Frontier Is the World: The Boy Scouts in the Age of American Ascendancy* (2018).

James Marten was one of the founders of the Society for the History of Children and Youth and its president from 2013 to 2015. He edited the *Journal of the History of Childhood and Youth* from 2013 to 2018. His book *The Children's Civil War* (1998) was named an "Outstanding Academic Title" by *Choice*.

Publications of the German Historical Institute

Edited by

Simone Lässig

with the assistance of David Lazar

The German Historical Institute is a center for advanced study and research whose purpose is to provide a permanent basis for scholarly cooperation among historians from the Federal Republic of Germany and the United States. The Institute conducts, promotes, and supports research into both American and German political, social, economic, and cultural history; into transatlantic migration, especially during the nineteenth and twentieth centuries; and into the history of international relations, with special emphasis on the roles played by the United States and Germany.

A full list of titles in the series can be found at:
www.cambridge.org/pghi

War and Childhood in the Era of the Two World Wars

Edited by

MISCHA HONECK
German Historical Institute, Washington, DC

JAMES MARTEN
Marquette University, Wisconsin

German Historical Institute, Washington, DC,

and

CAMBRIDGE
UNIVERSITY PRESS

CAMBRIDGE
UNIVERSITY PRESS

University Printing House, Cambridge CB2 8BS, United Kingdom

One Liberty Plaza, 20th Floor, New York, NY 10006, USA

477 Williamstown Road, Port Melbourne, VIC 3207, Australia

314–321, 3rd Floor, Plot 3, Splendor Forum, Jasola District Centre,
New Delhi – 110025, India

79 Anson Road, #06–04/06, Singapore 079906

Cambridge University Press is part of the University of Cambridge.

It furthers the University's mission by disseminating knowledge in the pursuit of
education, learning, and research at the highest international levels of excellence.

www.cambridge.org
Information on this title: www.cambridge.org/9781108478533
DOI: 10.1017/9781108671965

First published 2019

Printed in the United Kingdom by TJ International Ltd. Padstow, Cornwall

A catalogue record for this publication is available from the British Library.

Library of Congress Cataloging-in-Publication Data
NAMES: Honeck, Mischa, 1976– editor. | Marten, James Alan, editor.
TITLE: War and childhood in the era of the two world wars / edited by Mischa Honeck
(German Historical Institute, Washington DC), James Marten (Marquette University,
Wisconsin).
DESCRIPTION: Cambridge ; New York, NY : Cambridge University Press, 2018. |
Series: Publications of the German Historical Institute | Includes bibliographical
references and index.
IDENTIFIERS: LCCN 2018042041 | ISBN 9781108478533 (alk. paper)
SUBJECTS: LCSH: Children and war – History – 20th century. | Youth and war – History
– 20th century. | World War, 1914–1918 – Children. | World War, 1914–1918 –
Youth. | World War, 1939–1945 – Children. | World War, 1939–1945 – Youth.
CLASSIFICATION: LCC HQ784.W3 W295 2018 | DDC 303.6/6083–dc23
LC record available at https://lccn.loc.gov/2018042041

ISBN 978-1-108-47853-3 Hardback

Contents

Figures

Contributors

Valentina Boretti, Department of History, School of History, Religions and Philosophies, SOAS University of London

Julie K. deGraffenried, Department of History, Baylor University

Antje Harms, Collaborative Research Centre "Otium. Boundaries, Chronotopes, Practices," University of Freiburg

Mischa Honeck, Historical Seminar, Humboldt University Berlin

Robert Jacobs, Hiroshima Peace Institute, Hiroshima City University

Kate James, St. Antony's College, University of Oxford

Esbjörn Larsson, Department of Education, Uppsala Univerity

Nazan Maksudyan, Centre Marc Bloch, Berlin

James Marten, Department of History, Marquette University

L. Halliday Piel, Department of History, Lasell College

Manon Pignot, Center for the History of Societies, Sciences, and Conflicts, University of Picardy Jules Verne

Karl D. Qualls, Department of History, Dickinson College

Patricia Heberer Rice, The Jack, Joseph and Morten Mandel Center for Advanced Holocaust Studies, United States Holocaust Memorial Museum

Kara L. Ritzheimer, Department of History, Oregon State University

Birgitte Søland, Department of History, The Ohio State University

Acknowledgements

Essay collections, even more than other books, require a lot of work by many people. The studies gathered here were inspired by a conference held at the German Historical Institute (GHI), Washington, DC, in 2014; the editors thank our co-conveners Andreas Gestrich (GHI London) and Arndt Weinrich (GHI Paris) as well as the directors of GHI Washington, Hartmut Berghoff and Simone Lässig, and of the GHI Paris, Thomas Maissen. Lemlem Meconen, Bryan Hart, and Susanne Fabricius provided logistical support for the conference.

For their contributions to the long process of making this into a book, we would like to thank David Lazar, staff editor at the GHI in Washington, and the editors and staff at Cambridge University Press.

But most of all we would like to thank our authors, for their patience, for their responsiveness to what must have seemed countless editorial suggestions, and for their fine work, which, unfortunately, never loses its relevance in a world wracked by conflict.

INTRODUCTION

More than Victims: Framing the History of Modern Childhood and War

Mischa Honeck and James Marten

By the dawn of the twentieth century, wars were no longer fought with sword and shield. Yet, despite their declining utility, these ancient tools of war remained potent symbols. Both figured prominently in Joseph Leyendecker's 1918 poster in support of the Third Liberty Loan Campaign, which urged Americans to buy more war bonds (Figure 0.1). What makes this piece of propaganda from World War I stand out, however, is not the association of sword and shield with a nation in arms or the towering, flag-draped Miss Liberty, bearing a shield with the seal of the United States of America. Rather, the most striking element in the scene is a kneeling Boy Scout, in full uniform, who looks up at the stern Miss Liberty and presents her with a mighty sword engraved with the words "Be prepared." Quite effectively, the poster ascribes a crucial role in war-making to this boy, and by extension to millions of other American boys. Rather than seeking shelter behind Miss Liberty's shield, the boy provides the "weapons for victory," thus serving as a metaphor for how children were not only enhancing the nation's combat readiness, but also enabling it to wage war in the first place.[1]

Leyendecker's allegorical poster opens a fascinating window onto the complex and seemingly contradictory relationships between children and armed conflict in the era of the world wars. According to contemporary ideals of childhood, children should have been protected, even hidden, from conflict and danger, yet they were also called on to contribute to the

---

[1] Leyendecker's illustration first appeared on the front page of the March 2, 1918, issue of the *Saturday Evening Post* and was reprinted in the April 15, 1918, issue of the magazine *Scouting*.

FIGURE O.1 Joseph Leyendecker, poster for the Third Liberty Loan Campaign (1918). Library of Congress, Prints and Photographs Division.

welfare of their families, the stability of their communities, and even the survival of their states in times of crisis. Children sold war bonds, grew victory gardens, worked in coal mines, collected rubber and scrap metal, sang patriotic songs, played war games, marched in parades, wrote letters to soldiers, made drawings, volunteered in hospitals, engaged in war relief, campaigned for peace, and fought and died in combat.

At the same time, people began to regard the determination and ability of societies to shield their young ones from the destructive forces of war as a measure of civilization.[2] Writing a history of war and childhood in the first half of the twentieth century thus means coming to grips with a fundamental paradox: How was it possible for modern societies to imagine childhood as a space of sheltered existence while at the same time accepting the need to mobilize children for war? How could it be, to draw on Leyendecker's imagery, that children were asked – forced, in some instances – to carry the sword when they should have been sheltered behind the shield? Unraveling and historicizing the paradox of these competing urgencies – to protect children from harm but also to integrate them into the body politic – is the purpose of this volume.

Children have been caught up in war since the dawn of humankind, but the scope of their engagement soared with the scale of the global conflicts that dominated the first half of the twentieth century. The period from 1914 to 1945, which Winston Churchill famously described as "another Thirty Years War," witnessed dramatic and mutually reinforcing transformations in the histories of war and childhood.[3] Both were shaped by converging forces, including nationalism, imperialism, capitalism, social Darwinism, and the global competition for resources and influence. First articulated by Enlightenment philosophers and developed by nineteenth-century bourgeois educators, budding ideals of a protected childhood,

---

[2] For overviews of the subject of childhood and war, see James Marten, ed., *Children and War: A Historical Anthology* (New York, 2002); and Elizabeth Goodenough and Andrea Immel, eds., *Under Fire: Childhood in the Shadow of War* (Detroit, 2008). Studies with a national or regional focus include William M. Tuttle, *"Daddy's Gone to War"*: The Second World War in the Lives of America's Children (New York, 1993); Nicholas Stargardt, *Witnesses of War: Children's Lives Under the Nazis* (New York, 2005); Christoph Schubert-Weller, *Hitlerjugend: Vom "Jungsturm Adolf Hitler" zur Staatsjugend des Dritten Reiches* (Weinheim, 1993); Ulrich Herrmann and Rolf-Dieter Müller, eds., *Junge Soldaten im Zweiten Weltkrieg: Kriegserfahrungen als Lebenserinnerungen* (Munich, 2010); Olga Kucherenko, *Little Soldiers: How Soviet Children Went to War, 1941–1945* (New York, 2011); and Yeeshan Chan, *Abandoned Japanese in Postwar Manchuria: The Lives of War Orphans and Wives in Two Countries* (New York, 2011).

[3] Winston Churchill, *The Gathering Storm* (London, 1948), xiii.

which reinforced the romantic view that youth was endowed with precious innocence and purity, were accompanied by the socially and politically motivated institutionalization of childhood, which brought the youngest members of society into direct encounters with all kinds of civic and state institutions. Policymakers in industrialized nations proclaimed that the implementation of child labor laws, public health reforms, compulsory education, and organized leisure time, as well as calls for less authoritarian forms of parenting, would improve the lives of children and their families. Yet these reforms occurred against the backdrop of modern nation-states trying to turn children into loyal young citizens ready to share the burden of sacrifice in times of crisis. Schools, child-rearing movements, and youth organizations designed in peacetime to bring order and discipline to children – to instill proper values, loyalties, and behavior – proved easily adaptable to the task of mobilizing young people once nation-states and empires began marshaling their material and human resources to compete with their enemies over territory, resources, ideology, and influence.[4] Just as children represented the futures of their families, they ensured the biological survival of their countries, ethnic groups, and religious denominations. Therefore, at a time when modern ways of childhood became increasingly possible for economic, social, and political reasons, it became less possible to fully protect them in the face of industrialized warfare on a massive scale.

This volume defines childhood broadly. It samples the lives of young people from elementary school age through adolescence and beyond as they struggled to survive in, adapt to, form bonds of community in, remember, and make sense of worlds torn asunder by the upheaval of war. This wide lens allows us to see how societies bent on regulating the transition from childhood to adulthood likened the process of growing up to a gradual evolution from higher to lower stages of dependency. This

---

[4] The literature on child welfare and youth work at the turn of the century is vast and growing. See, for example, Paula S. Fass, *Children of a New Word: Society, Culture, and, Globalization* (New York, 2007); Jon Savage, *Teenage: The Prehistory of Youth Culture, 1875–1945* (London, 2007), 64–73; and Sonya Michel and Eszter Varsa, "Children and the National Interest," in Dirk Schumann, ed., *Raising Citizens in the Century of the Child: The United States and German Central Europe in Comparative Perspective* (New York, 2010), 27–49. On the susceptibility of organized youth to militarism and war, see David I. Macleod, "Socializing American Youth to Be Citizen-Soldiers," in Manfred F. Boerneke, Roger Chickering, and Stig Förster, eds., *Anticipating Total War: The German and American Experiences, 1871–1914* (Cambridge, 1999), 137–66; and Arndt Weinrich, *Der Weltkrieg als Erzieher: Jugend zwischen Weimarer Republik und Nationalsozialismus* (Essen, 2013).

meant that, with the rise of developmental psychology in the late nine-teenth century, young people entering puberty were increasingly sub-sumed under modern conceptions of youth, commonly defined as a transitional period in which young people had ceased to be dependent children but had not yet been entrusted with all the privileges of adult-hood. Adults' frequent association of youth with dynamism, flexibility, and vitality set adolescents apart from children, yet the discourse of youth also became an important tool in the hands of adult elites who promul-gated the theory that nations and empires lacking in youthfulness were bound for extinction.[5] As both an age-based social cohort and an ideolo-gical construct detached from age, youth is integral to a multigenerational and multisited study of how children and adolescents affected, and were affected by, local, national, and transnational communities radically transformed by war.

Of course, although the history of modern childhood and war has to be framed globally, war was never a unifying global experience. War pedago-gues had to contend with peace educators over the hearts and minds of children and their parents in many industrialized societies.[6] The engagement of children and youth with war differed according to geography, technol-ogy, class, age, race, gender, and the nature of the state in which they lived. In fact, one of the key findings of this volume is that ideological disparities often mattered less than regional outlooks, social locations, and military capacities when it comes to explaining the different levels of exposure to armed conflict that young people experienced. Take as an example Julie deGraffenried's discussion of US and Soviet alphabet books generated dur-ing World War II (Chapter 5), which anchors the higher frequency of war-related themes in Soviet primers not in simplistic democracy–dictatorship binaries but in the relative absence of the physical horrors of war in American children's lives. Whether children and youths wound up as vic-tims, eyewitnesses, willing executioners, or subversive actors depended on local circumstances and contingent forms of socialization. In Antje Harms's chapter on the schism within the German youth movement during World

---

[5] See, for example, Joseph F. Kett, *Rites of Passage: Adolescence in America, 1790 to the Present* (New York, 1977); Mischa Honeck and Gabriel Rosenberg, "Transnational Generations: Organizing Youth in the Cold War," *Diplomatic History* 38(2) (2014), 233–39; and Richard Ivan Jobs and David M. Pomfret, "The Transnationality of Youth," in Jobs and Pomfret, eds., *Transnational Histories of Youth in the Twentieth Century* (New York, 2015), 1–20.

[6] See, for example, Andrew Donson, *Youth in the Fatherless Land: War Pedagogy, Nationalism, and Authority in Germany, 1914–1918* (Cambridge, MA, 2010), 59–90.

War I (Chapter 10), some young Germans can be found marching enthusiastically to the trenches, while others deplored the mass slaughter of
industrialized warfare. Comparing the lives of children from North
America, Europe, Turkey, and East Asia demonstrates that reconciling the
practices and ideals of childhood with the idea of war became a truly
transnational phenomenon, far more profound than conventional political
narratives can suggest. As described in Valentina Boretti's account of war
toys in China (Chapter 1) and Esbjörn Larsson's analysis of defense training
in Swedish schools (Chapter 6), children may not have actually experienced
war, but the cultural imaginary of war provided a nearly limitless reservoir
of values, practices, and identities for young people trying to master the
conflicting demands of self and society.

Historians of children and youth have brought to the field at least two
methodological distinctions that are important for the task at hand. Most
agree that childhood is a relational category that can be grasped, at any
time or place, only if one recognizes that childhood is bound up with
(though not bound by) adult expectations. Most scholars also underline
the culturally and ideologically constructed character of childhood by
emphasizing that the boundaries of what it means to be a child are not
demarcated by biological age and thus forever fixed, but evolve out of
dynamic, contested, and historically specific exchanges involving young
and old people alike. Appropriately, these historians stress the need to
differentiate between constructions of childhood and the lives of actual
children, even as these two dimensions are interwoven.[7] Understanding
children as historical actors with their own ideas, intentions, and identity-
forming experiences fulfills the critical function of refuting older
approaches that treated young people as mere objects of adult design.
Rejecting the idea that children are intrinsically passive and vulnerable
victims of war, the chapters collected here stress the agency of children
and youth in the face of adults' attempts to adjust their methods of
controlling young people's behavior to wartime exigencies. At the same

---

[7] Philippe Ariès, *Centuries of Childhood*, transl. Robert Baldick (New York, 1962);
Steven Mintz, "Reflections on Age as a Category of Historical Analysis," *Journal of the
History of Childhood and Youth* 1 (Winter 2008), 91–94; and Jay Mechling, "Children in
Scouting and Other Organizations," in Paula Fass, ed., *The Routledge History of
Childhood in the Western World* (New York, 2013), 419–33. On children as subaltern
actors, see Kristine Alexander, "Can the Girl Guide Speak? The Perils and Pleasures of
Looking for Children's Voices in Archival Research," *Jeunesse: Young People, Texts,
Cultures* 4 (Summer 2012), 132–45.

time, public authorities proved quite adept at sparking moral outrage by utilizing images of brutalized children in wartime propaganda, which was growing more effective due to advances in technologies of mass communication.

War obviously threatened conventional constructions of childhood and youth and introduced new ones; it also inspired an outpouring of sources unavailable to historians of peacetime childhoods, who are generally limited to one of two approaches. Some emphasize the ways that adults shape and define childhood, while others seek to provide the points of view of young people. The latter can often be difficult; children produce few documents, fewer still of which are preserved in archives. Yet wars offer an opportunity for historians to explore not only the ways in which adults considered the places of children and youth in wartime society but also the myriad responses of young people to war.

The chapters in this volume sample the many ways in which the documents produced during wars enable us to see into the lives of children and youth. They range from government reports to school curricula, textbooks to alphabets, letters from absent fathers to commercially produced war toys, from school essays to art projects, and from stories and novels explaining children's responsibilities in wartime to newspaper articles that for the first time recognized children's role in public life. These documents, which might not have been produced if war had not exploded into the lives of twentieth-century families and communities, provide extraordinary insights not just into the ways in which adults constructed young people's roles on the home front, or worried about their futures when confronted with the sharp end of war. They also shed light on how children and youth eagerly sought to participate in – or resignedly submitted to participating in – what might be the most awful or most thrilling event of their time.

Taking advantage of this abundance of evidence, this book integrates and expands on at least five bodies of scholarship. First, it joins what Dominic Sachsenmaier has summarized as "the global history trend," in particular the move toward privileging larger scales of analysis and embedding local findings in broader spatial and temporal horizons.[8] The individual chapters mostly revolve around a group of people, a region, a nation, or a certain cultural space, and only a few, such as Karl Qualls's essay on child refugees from Civil War Spain in Russia (Chapter 4) or Nazan Maksudyan's essay on Ottoman orphans in

---

[8] Dominic Sachsenmaier, *Global Perspectives on Global History: Theories and Approaches in a Connected World* (Cambridge, MA, 2011), 3.

Germany during World War I (Chapter 11), are explicitly devoted to probing cross-border interactions. Taken together, however, the chapters presented here offer a mosaic of experiences that invites reflection on global interdependencies and regional particularities as they pertain to the nexus of childhood, youth, and war in the age of the world wars.

Second, focusing on children and youth allows for a reevaluation of the total war paradigm so prominent in twentieth-century military, political, and social history. Scholars of total war have crafted typologies of total warfare that usually encompass the following key elements: the ability of states to mobilize all available resources for the purpose of war-making, the belligerents' disregard for morality and international law, the erosion of boundaries between soldiers and civilians, and the magnitude of destruction.[9] Despite its implicit acknowledgement of the increased vulnerability of noncombatants – women, children, and the elderly – the concept of total war hardly conveys the multiple ways in which war affected children and youth in the first half of the twentieth century. This is not to deny that under conditions of total warfare more and more children were asked to take on adult responsibilities, from joining the workforce to assuming military and paramilitary duties. But not all the wars in the period from 1914 to 1945 were total wars, nor were the total wars total to the same degree. Furthermore, children's militarization in times of peace and their centrality to postwar reconciliation, as Robert Jacobs documents in his chapter on child survivors of the atomic bombing of Hiroshima and Nagasaki (Chapter 14), suggest that the potentials that lie in a global-comparative history of war and childhood exceed total war framings.

Third, this volume builds on works that treat the social spaces where politics and play intersect with the seriousness they deserve. One of the ways that children integrate war into their lives is, naturally enough, through play. All children "practice" for adulthood by reenacting grownups' behavior, and war play is no different. Play allows children to process their fears and their burgeoning patriotism, and it helps them reduce the terror and excitement of war into manageable scenarios. Children can be

[9] See, for example, Roger Chickering and Stig Förster, eds., *Great War, Total War: Combat and Mobilization on the Western Front, 1914–1918* (Cambridge, 2000); Chickering, Förster, and Bernd Greiner, eds., *A World at Total War: Global Conflict and the Politics of Destruction* (Cambridge, 2005); Alan Kramer, *Dynamics of Destruction: Culture and Mass Killing in the First World War* (New York, 2007); and Niall Ferguson, *The War of the World: Twentieth-Century Conflict and the Descent of the West* (New York, 2007).

absolutely unflinching in what they choose to act out. Even in concentration camps, Jewish children played war games, taking on the roles of guards and prisoners, while children in Northern Ireland played "soldiers and terrorists" with street patrols and fake blood. A comprehensive analysis of play and modern warfare, however, cannot be confined to the activities of children alone but needs to investigate how adults sought to manipulate the play impulse of their young ones to prepare them for war. As part of their effort to participate in war and to absorb as much information about it as possible, children eagerly consumed war culture in the era of the world wars. They read books and stories about war, crowded movie theaters, avidly followed military campaigns in newspapers, and cheered at political and fundraising rallies. Indeed, educators, publishers, and other creators of the cultures of children and youth – inspired by pedagogical innovations and aided by technological changes – produced lessons, books, and toys that, with little subtlety, tried to shape the political opinions and attitudes of young students and consumers. Among other things, they showed children supporting their families, joining the home front war efforts, and accepting the hardships thrust upon them by war.[10]

Fourth, writing a history of modern war and childhood means paying attention to how children acted on the home front as well as on the battlefield. An extension of mobilizing children politically is mobilizing them for combat. Boys as young as ten or twelve often served in early modern armies, and the use of "boy soldiers" in the modern period, particularly in revolutionary and civil wars, has been well documented.[11] The nineteenth century saw the average age of soldiers in most armies rise significantly. Yet the world wars also saw significant mobilizations of youthful soldiers, especially in Germany and the countries it occupied, where Hitler Youth-style organizations proved easily adaptable to paramilitary purposes, and in the Soviet Union. By the last year of the war, for instance, 70 percent of German sixteen-year-olds had enlisted. Even in countries where youth did not serve on the front lines, many were formed into paramilitary units, and some took over home guard

---

[10] George Eisen, *Children and Play in the Holocaust* (Amherst, 1990); Morris Fraser, *Children in Conflict* (New York, 1973), 105. Tuttle's *"Daddy's Gone to War"* is still the most useful account of the war culture experienced by American children.

[11] See, for instance, Caroline Cox, *Boy Soldiers of the American Revolution* (Chapel Hill, 2016). UNICEF tracks the sobering fact that the use of child soldiers remains a significant facet of modern warfare. See more at www.unicef.org/media/media_pr_childsoldiers .html (accessed February 15, 2017).

duties.[12] Many scholars have studied the deployment of underage soldiers in dictatorial regimes; what is less well known, however, is that this practice was not foreign to Western nations, as Kate James demonstrates in her chapter on boy soldiers in the British Army and Royal Navy (Chapter 8). Studying the ways in which the wartime youth mobilization of liberal states resembled fascist youth organizations points to a much more complex, even sinister, interpretation of those states and their methods of militarizing children.

Fifth, in heeding the calls of scholars to prioritize the voices of children when writing about childhood, the chapters featured here do not simply add another social group to an already existing canvas of past events but repaint that canvas altogether. Considering children the "true missing link" for understanding modern warfare, they disprove the notion that adulthood is the requirement of meaningful historical action.[13] They follow in the footsteps of other historians who have shown how children exerted "agency" in choosing how to engage war on both the home front and the battle front. Many children, to be sure, were drawn into conflict against their will, but many also sought to be involved in war on their own terms.[14] As much as political leaders and educators might have commended young people's enthusiasm and held them up as models of self-sacrifice for their elders to emulate, the desire of elites to channel youthful behavior frequently clashed with the desire of children and youth to exercise as much autonomy as possible. As Mischa Honeck's essay on the Boy Scouts of America reveals (Chapter 7), youths' war fervor, which adult organizers had hoped to incite, often proved difficult to control. A similar story emerges from Kara Ritzheimer's essay (Chapter 2), which details the efforts of state censors in Wilhelmine Germany to curtail youths' consumption of wartime "trash" literature. A devastating trial and locus of socialization, modern war disrupted the lives of young people, sometimes with devastating consequences, at the same time that it empowered them. Acknowledging that children were struggling to

---

[12] Stargardt, *Witnesses of War*, 114, 242. For recent accounts of Soviet children's experiences during the war, see Kucherenko, *Little Soldiers*; and Julie K. deGraffenried, *Sacrificing Childhood: Children and the Soviet State in the Great Patriotic War* (Lawrence, 2014).

[13] For the quote, see Steven Mintz, "Why the History of Childhood Matters," *Journal of the History of Childhood and Youth* 5(1) (January 2012), 15.

[14] Among the historians who pioneered the study of children's agency in wartime are Tuttle, "*Daddy's Gone to War*" (1993), James Marten, *The Children's Civil War* (Chapel Hill, 1998); David M. Rosen, *Armies of the Youth: Child Soldiers in War and Terrorism* (New Brunswick, 2005); Stargardt, *Witnesses of War* (2005).

shape their destinies even in the most dire of circumstances calls into question the victimization discourse of earlier works, as children were reinventing the meaning of childhood for themselves and the societies they inhabited. Manon Pignot's analysis of children's drawings of war scenes during World War I (Chapter 9) provides a powerful reminder of children's ability to create semiotic spaces that helped them structure experiences of mass upheaval and violence. So, too, does Patricia Heberer Rice's story of young ghettoized Jews (Chapter 12), who were building hopeful cultural and intellectual communities as the horrors of the Shoah were unfolding around them.

As these examples indicate, the study of children and youth rather naturally – if tragically – meshes with the study of war in all of its military, political, and cultural contexts. At the most basic level, the narrative of children's experiences in wartime elicits emotional responses: horror, admiration, and sadness. We are impressed by the resiliency of children who endure sacrifices and shortages, contribute to family survival and community economies, and exert agency by choosing to take part in their countries' conflicts. They may be inspired by what Anna Freud once called a "primitive excitement" sparked by the chaos, danger, and opportunities for change provided by war, or by a deeper sense of political engagement, as Robert Coles argued in his classic *The Political Life of Children*.[15]

Inevitably, wars shift, fracture, and destroy family relationships and dynamics. The millions of refugees dislocated from their communities and homes during the world wars suffered many hardships and indignities, among them a disruption in the capacity of family members to fulfill their traditional roles and responsibilities. Child migration in times of war took on many forms, from the young Spanish evacuees highlighted by Karl Qualls to the fervent colonizers that Halliday Piel rescues from oblivion in her chapter on Japanese boy soldier-settlers who descended on Manchuria in the 1930s and 1940s (Chapter 3). Although they were safe from invading armies and falling bombs, hundreds of thousands of American children were uprooted as families moved to areas with war industries and military bases. Even in families who remained in their homes, the absences and even deaths of fathers and other loved ones forced teenagers to take on adult roles, leaving school to manage farms, work in factories, and raise younger siblings. More than half a million underage British children went to work in factories and mines during World War I, while two million

[15] Anna Freud and Dorothy Burlingham, *War and Children* (London, 1943), 23–24; Robert Coles, *The Political Life of Children* (New York, 1986).

German boys and girls were sent to the country to bring in the 1942 harvest, and almost that many American youth quit high school to go to work.[16]

Wars end and children grow up. Yet the lives of all who live through armed conflict – whether they witnessed the sharp end of war or watched it from a safe distance – are forever changed. The politics and culture of a country are inevitably shaped by the ways that its children respond to war and its aftermath. Shame and anger could turn the German youth of World War I into the Nazis of the 1940s, while the triumphalist narrative that quickly developed in the United States after 1945 helped create Cold Warriors out of the children of the "Greatest Generation." Children found ways to locate their contributions, however small, in the larger national history. Children can also become part of a nation's collective war memory, as honored survivors of Stalingrad, as steady contributors to family stability, or as scarred, somber victims of Hiroshima and Nagasaki. As such, they come to represent in their nations' memories the causes for which the wars were fought, even as the contributions of children like those discussed in Birgitte Søland's essay on American orphans who had become subjects of medical experimentation during the Second World War had left physical and psychological scars (Chapter 13). Children, then, become an audience for the lessons imposed by war. Those lessons have varied dramatically over time and place, from the jingoistic empire-building that dominated British textbooks in the late nineteenth century to the anti-imperial narrative in Japanese schoolbooks after their defeat in World War II.[17]

Another particular kind of war memory depends on children for its power: the efforts to provide relief for displaced victims of war and to promote reconciliation and reunification through such efforts. Drawing on some of the same motivations and methods exerted by early twentieth-century child welfare reformers, organizations such as Britain's Save the Children Fund and the American Red Cross mobilized during both world

---

[16] Arthur Marwick, *The Deluge: British Society and the First World War* (New York, 1965), 43, 224–45; Jay Winter and Jean-Louis Robert, eds., *Capital Cities at War: Paris, London, Berlin 1914–1919* (Cambridge, 1999), 442–44; Tuttle, *"Daddy's Gone to War,"* 82.

[17] See, for instance, Stephen Heathorn, *For Home, Country and Race: Constructing Class, Gender and Englishness in the Elementary Classroom* (Toronto, 2000), and Aya Matsushima, "A Japanese History Textbook and the Construction of World War II Memory," in Heather Snell and Lorna Hutchison, eds., *Children and Cultural Memory in Texts of Childhood* (New York, 2014), 67–86.

wars to provide food and shelter to refugees, many of whom were children. One of the noble but failed efforts to prevent future conflagrations that grew out of World War I, the League of Nations, issued the "Declaration of the Rights of the Child" in 1924, which included among its five articles a mandate to care first for children in times of crisis. A generation later, in 1946, the United Nations created the United Nations International Children's Emergency Fund (UNICEF), which is still the leading organization providing relief to child victims of war. According to the cultural anthropologist Liisa Malkki, these initiatives inscribed children into the modern internationalist lexicon as "embodiments of a basic human goodness and symbols of world harmony; as sufferers; as seers of truth; as ambassadors of peace; and as embodiments of the future."[18]

Although the chapters in this collection end with the immediate aftermath of World War II, children and youth have continued to suffer because of armed conflict. Even as the capacity of most nations to build protected childhoods for their young steadily increased in the decades after 1945, and even though there have been no wars approaching the scale of either of the wars that dominate this volume, the world remains a very dangerous place for children. Civil wars in Africa and Asia, conflicts sparked by the Cold War between the great powers but fought in far-flung parts of the world, and the rise of terrorism (and the West's response to terrorism) have all contributed to disruption and death for countless children and youth. Indeed, according to the United Nations, during a single decade spanning the 1980s and 1990s, wars killed two million children and disabled at least another four million. One million young people were orphaned or separated from their parents, twelve million were made homeless, and untold millions suffered psychological trauma.[19] Worldwide conflicts might have characterized the war narratives of children in the first half of the twentieth century; the unfortunate epilogue to that story is the endless wars of liberation and repression and greed and ideology that succeeded them.

Childhood and youth are times of discovery and confusion, wonder and fear, dependence and frustration. Young people continued to pass

---

[18] Liisa Malkki, "Children, Humanity, and the Infantilization of Peace," in Ilana Feldman and Miriam Ticktin, eds., *In the Name of Humanity: The Government of Threat and Care* (Durham, 2010), 60.

[19] "The State of the World's Children, 1996," UNICEF, www.unicef.org/sowc96/1cinwar .htm (accessed February 15, 2017).

through the ages of childhood and youth during the wars of the twentieth century. For some, the usual markers of maturation remained more or less in place; for others, whatever expectations they might have had for a predicable path to adulthood vanished in blood and flames. The experiences of most children lay somewhere between these extremes, and although *War and Childhood in the Era of the Two World Wars* does not attempt to provide a complete history of children and war in the first half of the twentieth century, it does bring structure to this fascinating and awful topic. It reminds us that modern warfare would not have been possible without modern childhood. More than victims, children were seen as future citizens, as future defenders, as one of the objects about which wars were fought, and as one of the resources for fighting them.

PART I

INSPIRING AND MOBILIZING

Civilian casualties reached catastrophic levels in the age of industria-lized mass warfare, and contemporaries bemoaned the violent impact of war on children who succumbed to illness, malnutrition, and persecution, and who died in bombing raids, massacres, and geno-cides. We cringe at the ghastly spectacle of children becoming the victims of war, but many societies that wept over losing their young were also reaping what they had sown. The chapters in this section not only demonstrate how unreliable and fragile the ideal of a protected childhood was in times of total war. They also reveal the extent to which adult decision makers in goverments, corporations, schools, and youth organizations encouraged children to support the state's capacity to wage war in places ranging from the home front to the battlefield.

Armed conflict became an inescapable fact for children growing up in the first half of the twentieth century. Although children were mobilized for war in varying degrees across time and space, young people were militarized long before the actual fighting began. In China, war toys became an integral part of educating the nation's youth, and even neutral states such as Sweden established defense service training in public schools. In nearly all societies ravaged by war, representations of child victims were accompanied by images of children as model citizens pub-lished in newspapers, on posters, and in primers – to name a few outlets – that linked participation in the war effort to heroic duty and sacrifice. Adult propagandists in states as ideologically diverse as Wilhelmine Germany, imperial Japan, the Soviet Union, and the United States all deployed the trope of the patriotic child to bolster the fighting spirits of their respective nations.

While adults inspired and oversaw the mobilization of their young, the following chapters show that children embraced war on their own terms. War bred compliance but also independence as children adopted new civic roles, social identities, and (semi)military duties. With their fathers conscripted and their mothers drawn into the workforce, children played with war toys, consumed juvenile war literature, paraded the streets, volunteered in patriotic youth organizations, and looked for ways to join the armed forces irrespective of their young age. Youth's enthusiasm for war often clashed with the intention of their elders to limit their involvement to what adults considered appropriate wartime behavior along the lines of age and gender, and sometimes of race and class. In pursuing war, modern societies experienced intergenerational tugs-of-war over the proper boundaries separating childhood and adulthood. Even as children acted in accordance with the war aims of their goverments, their actions also reflected young people's search for meaningful spaces of self-realization, as well as their capacity to develop their own responses to the violent conflicts that engulfed them.

Patriotic Fun: Toys and Mobilization in China from the Republican to the Communist Era

Valentina Boretti

To celebrate Children's Day in 1932, Chinese boys and girls were encouraged to participate in a target-shooting competition. They were to try to pick off Japanese planes, tanks, and warships with bow and arrow, popguns, and balls. In 1951, the time had come to play "Executing the War Criminals"; with toy rifles or bows, children could take aim at targets with images of Chiang Kai-shek and Harry Truman.[1]

The use of politicized leisure to mobilize children is pervasive throughout the world, but its expressions in pre-Cultural Revolution China have attracted little attention so far. Focusing on prescribed leisure, this chapter traces a preliminary genealogy of play-training for activism in China and comments on youngsters' reactions. Looking at the deployment of toys to mobilize children from the 1910s to the early 1950s, it investigates the ways in which different regimes employed play and playthings as instruments to foster engagement in struggles of a political, commercial, or military nature.

Although it cannot be assumed that children followed the script closely, a study of how leisure was framed offers insights into notions of nationhood and ideal personhood. It can also provide a perspective on cultural continuities between the Republican and Communist eras, such as constant mobilization and normative opposition to nonpurposeful leisure. Examining the function of toys as instruments of mobilization highlights,

---

[1] Qian Gengzin, ed., "Ershiyi nian ertong jie huodong baogao (er xu)," *Zhejiang minzhong jiaoyu* 3 (1932), 47–52; Chen Heqin and Wu Chengqi, "Qiangbi zhanfan," *Xin ertong jiaoyu* 6(11) (1951), 31.

moreover, a range of porous boundaries: between toy and tool, fun and seriousness, child and adult, aggression and defense, peace and war.

In both Republican and Communist China, toys were employed to instruct children in what to do and what to be: to make them physically and morally healthy, curious about science, creatively productive, and militant, which did not necessarily signify militarized but rather committed to rallying for the nation. Militancy – or, perhaps more accurately, activism – had more to do with patriotic awareness and preparedness than warlike aggressiveness, although militaristic attitudes might emerge. Against the backdrop of recurring calls for assertive self-defense against actual or perceived besiegement, children were urged to cultivate non-puerility and participative responsibility. Crucial to this agenda was a discourse of mobilization, formulated by intellectuals, pedagogues, ideologues, and public officials – in short, the experts – and disseminated to urban and rural children, parents, and educators through publications, classroom instruction, and events or campaigns. With its reiteration of tropes and prescriptions that varied only slightly over the decades from one regime to the next, this discourse amounted to a choral enterprise, and it is as such that we shall explore it, rather than focusing on solo voices.

LEISURE AND THE MARTIAL SPIRIT FOR THE REPUBLICAN NEW CITIZENS

At the turn of the twentieth century, following several defeats and perceived humiliations, the fear was widespread in China that "extinction" – to use the evolutionary terminology then in vogue – was near. "Survival" would depend upon renewal. Like their counterparts in other countries, Chinese reformers maintained that national revival ought to start with children.[2]

This putative discovery of children as present and prospective "new" citizens located them in opposition to a (mostly imagined) tradition, construed as oblivious to the peculiarities of childhood and condemned as unable to produce "useful" citizens. Although some, like artist Feng Zikai or writer Lu Xun, did plead for the need to appreciate youngsters as

---

[2] Carl Ipsen, *Italy in the Age of Pinocchio: Children and Danger in the Liberal Era* (New York, 2006); Mark A. Jones, *Children as Treasures: Childhood and the Middle Class in Early Twentieth Century Japan* (Cambridge, MA, 2010). On China, see Andrew F. Jones, "The Child as History in Republican China: A Discourse on Development," *positions* 10(3) (2002), 695–727.

such, the dominant discourse, especially from the late 1920s onward, remained focused on the value of children to national rejuvenation. New children had to be self-reliant, robust, industrious, well educated, and aware of their responsibility to the nation: Youthfulness was no excuse for eschewing duty.[3] Because properly nurturing these crucial assets was vital, no aspect of children's lives escaped the interference of experts, who tended to accuse parents of incompetence.

Leisure became a serious matter. Play and toys were discursively recast as tools for nation- and citizen-building because of their capacity to unconsciously train and mold young citizens from infancy. Determination, courage, patriotism, creativity, and cooperativeness could all be fostered through play, if it were properly guided and if suitable toys were used.[4] In line with the claim that only now were children's inclinations appreciated, playthings were proclaimed a necessity and declared to be extremely influential. "Appropriate" toys, capable of producing the new child, should be not merely entertaining. Chinese experts, like their counterparts elsewhere, did not approve of amusement that served no discernible purpose.[5] Rather, playthings had to be educational and to help cultivate body and spirit, fostering qualities like love for science, manual inventiveness, and a martial spirit.[6]

Indeed, particular importance was attached to martial spirit. In 1935, the *Shanghai News Child's Companion* informed young readers that the unflattering "sick man of East Asia" sobriquet attributed to China was

---

[3] Liang Qichao, "Lun youxue" (1897), in Wu Song, et al., eds., *Yinbingshi wenji dianjiao* (Kunming, 2001), vol. I, 47–57; Lu Xun, "What Is Required of Us as Fathers Today" (1919), in Lu Xun, *Selected Works* (Beijing, 1980), vol. II, 56–71; Xian Baiyan, "Ertong de shehuihua," *Funü zazhi* 8(2) (1922), 23–27; Song Jie, "Ertong jiuji wenti," *Dongfang zazhi* 22(17) (1925), 50–69; Feng Zikai, "Ertong de darenhua," *Jiaoyu zazhi* 19(7 and 8) (1927), 1–3; Pan Shu, "Zenyang zuo yige yingfu guonan de ertong," *Xiao xuesheng* 5(5) (1935), 1–6; Zhang Yucai, "Xiandai jiating yu ertong jiaoyang," *Dongfang zazhi* 32(11) (1935), 91–97.

[4] Shen Buzhou, "Lun youyi," *Jiaoyu zazhi* 4(12) (1912), 215–27; Xi Zhen, "Rensheng zhi genben jiaoyu," *Funü zazhi* 3(8) (1917), 4–10; Chen Heqin, "Ertong xinli ji jiaoyu ertong zhi fangfa," *Xin jiaoyu* 3(2) (1920), 140–46; Chen Yongsheng, *Wan yu chi* (Shanghai, 1931).

[5] Gary Cross, *Kids' Stuff: Toys and the Changing World of American Childhood* (Cambridge, MA, 1997), ch. 5; Catriona Kelly, *Children's World: Growing Up in Russia 1890–1991* (New Haven, 2007), 125–26.

[6] Xu Fuyan, "Wanju yu youzhi jiaoyu zhi guanxi," *Funü shibao* 9 (1913), 24–27; Wei Shouyong, "Ertong wanju wenti," *Funü zazhi* 3(8) (1917), 4–6; Wang Muqing, "Ertong wanju de yanjiu," *Zhonghua jiaoyu jie* 16(7) (1927), 1–3; Chen Jiyun, *Wanju yu jiaoyu* (Shanghai, 1933); Qing Shan, "Ertong wanju jianghua: wanju shi yizhong zhongyao de jiaoyu gongju," *Xiandai fumu* 1(8) (1933), 28–29.

due to the weakness of its people, which had been caused by the respect traditionally enjoyed by literati to the detriment of military men. This had induced disdain for physical exercise, but the "weak" were to be "eliminated." A martial spirit was, therefore, indispensable if China was to "survive" and end its "humiliation."[7]

This discourse of martial spirit and physical robustness had originated well before the establishment of the Republic in 1912. It dated back to the late nineteenth century, when intellectuals – Liang Qichao being the most influential – had declared the Chinese and China to be unfit. Overlooking the importance of martial culture in the Qing empire as well as the fact that Chinese models of masculinity encompassed both literary ability and martial prowess,[8] reformers maintained that the prominence accorded to the former had begotten physical and spiritual weaklings. Liang advocated respect for martial qualities, which, he claimed, China had possessed in antiquity and ought to recover in order to avoid perishing.[9] This discourse echoed a much earlier tradition of blaming defeat on flawed masculinity.[10] It also possibly contained a measure of self-orientalization, that is, the reproduction of Euro-American constructs of "the Oriental" as effeminate and incompetent.[11] Although healthier empires like Britain also experienced apprehension over masculinity at this time, Chinese anxieties reflected a substantial national crisis.[12] Allegedly inept men and "crippled" women unable to raise vigorous offspring[13] had to be

---

[7] Guo Pinjuan, "Shangwu jingshen," in Shenbao ertong zhoukan she, ed., *Shenbao ertong zhi you* (Shanghai, 1935), vol. I, 15–16.

[8] Joanna Waley-Cohen, "Militarization of Culture in Eighteenth-Century China," in Nicola Di Cosmo, ed., *Military Culture in Imperial China* (Cambridge, MA, 2009), 278–95; Kam Louie, *Theorising Chinese Masculinity: Society and Gender in China* (Cambridge, 2002).

[9] Liang Qichao, "Lun shangwu" (1903), in *Yinbingshi wenji dianjiao*, vol. I, 615–21; James R. Pusey, *China and Charles Darwin* (Cambridge, MA, 1983), 260–73; Colin Green, "Turning Bad Iron into Polished Steel: Whampoa and the Rehabilitation of the Chinese Soldier," in James Flath and Norman Smith, eds., *Beyond Suffering: Recounting War in Modern China* (Vancouver, 2011), 156–57.

[10] Martin W. Huang, *Negotiating Masculinities in Late Imperial China* (Honolulu, 2006), ch. 4.

[11] Song Geng, *The Fragile Scholar: Power and Masculinity in Chinese Culture* (Hong Kong, 2004), 9.

[12] Stephanie Olsen, *Juvenile Nation: Youth, Emotions and the Making of the Modern British Citizen, 1880–1914* (London, 2014).

[13] Liang Qichao, "On Women's Education" (1897), in Lydia H. Liu, Rebecca E. Karl, and Dorothy Ko, eds., *The Birth of Chinese Feminism: Essential Texts in Transnational Theory* (New York, 2013), 189–203.

replaced by robust new citizens,[14] who were to cultivate a martial spirit or outlook.[15]

Fostering a martial spirit in children was meant to induce not militarism but rather physico-spiritual strength, unity, and the ability to *mobilize* in order to defend and reshape China, culturally, politically, militarily, and commercially. Beginning in the early Republican years, military toys were employed to help nurture a martial spirit so as to create citizens poised to fit into the modern world while infused with the spirit of a heroic past. In the 1910s and early 1920s, pedagogues praised swords and spears as testimonies to ancient soldierly virtues and commended toy soldiers, warships, and firearms as educational because they cultivated imagination, knowledge, awareness of the military, and a martial spirit.[16] Even foreign toys, like the American-made Daisy Air Rifle, were advertised in 1920 as tools to cultivate boys' "indispensable" martial spirit and to turn China into a strong nation.[17]

The appreciation of military playthings was not universal in China before the late 1920s, however, probably because of the association of military iconography with ravaging warlord armies.[18] Indeed, journalists expressed misgivings about promoting toy soldiers in educational exhibitions, and the widely read *Ladies' Journal* warned mothers that military toys could give a misleading impression of war as "fun" and also encourage destructiveness.[19] Children themselves showed mixed reactions. Some boys and girls did apparently enjoy playing with air pistols, arranging toy soldiers against fantasy enemies, and engaging in play battles with friends,[20] but surveys also revealed that some children ignored or

[14] Andrew D. Morris, *Marrow of the Nation: A History of Sport and Physical Culture in Republican China* (Berkeley, 2004).

[15] Paul J. Bailey, *Gender and Education in China: Gender Discourses and Women's Schooling in the Early Twentieth Century* (Abingdon, 2007), 98; Nicolas Schillinger, *The Body and Military Masculinity in Late Qing and Early Republican China* (Lanham, MD, 2016), ch. 6.

[16] Bao Qiong, "Ertong yu wanju zhi guanxi," *Zhonghua funü jie* 1(9) (1915), 6–7; Jia Fengzhen, "Jiaoyu shang zhi wanju guan," *Jiaoyu zazhi* 11(5) (1919), 33, 36, and 11(6) (1919), 45; Jiaoyu bu putong jiaoyu si, ed., *Ertong wanju shencha baogao* (Beijing, 1922), 18, 34, and list of toys: 3, 7, 18, 60–61; "Ertong wanju shencha baogao biao," *Xin jiaoyu* 7(5) (1923), 447–48, 452, 461.

[17] *Dongfang zazhi* 171(8) (1920), n.p.

[18] Arthur Waldron, "The Warlord: Twentieth-Century Chinese Understandings of Violence, Militarism, and Imperialism," *American Historical Review* 96 (1991), 1073–1100.

[19] "Kaimu hou Xinwenbao zhi jizai," *Xin jiaoyu* 9(5) (1924), 961; Jing Xun, "Ertong de youxi ji wanju," *Funü zazhi* 9(4) (1923), 123.

[20] Hua Zheru, "Wo zhi youtong shidai," *Shaonian zazhi* 8(3) (1918), 9–11; Chow Chung-cheng, *The Lotus Pool of Memory* (London, 1961), 22; Hsieh Ping-ying, *Girl Rebel:*

disliked toy weapons.[21] Children's magazines sometimes featured covers portraying boys (and, very occasionally, girls) playing with toy weapons, and drawings or photographs of guns sent by boys; sometimes they ran stories that deplored the "cruelty" of airguns or associated them with "homicidal battlegrounds."[22]

Attitudes began to change in the late 1920s after the Nationalist Party (GMD) gained nominal control of most of China and increasingly promoted militant – even militarized – nationalism. The Japanese seizure of Manchuria in 1931, followed by outright war in 1937, predictably reinforced the discourse of martial mobilization. With rare exceptions, such as Feng Zikai,[23] experts spoke approvingly of military toys, which frequently appeared in publications.

Children's periodicals praised cultivated yet martial boys who bravely trained to protect the nation. Previously anti-military authors penned stories that urged boys to "polish rifles and sharpen swords." Student poems sang of fearless resistance and willingness to shed blood for China.[24] Picture cards showed boys "studying military drills" as they played with their toy armaments on the lounge carpet.[25] While mentioning the potentially harmful effects of warlike games, texts for educators and parents argued that toy weapons could instill a "valiant" spirit along with initiative and attention.[26] According to experts, the Chinese lacked resoluteness, which ought to be cultivated from infancy. This may have been why kindergartens, before and after the war, were supposed to be equipped with military toys: Playing with bows and arrows or swords

The Autobiography of Hsieh Pingying (New York, [1940] 1975), 19; N. T. Wang, *My Nine Lives* (San Jose, 2001), 6; Yang Xianyi, *White Tiger: An Autobiography of Yang Xianyi* (Hong Kong, 2002), 8.

[21] Su Yishi xiao, "Jiangsu Yishi fuxiao di'er jie ertong wanju zhanlanhui jingguo baogao," *Jiaoyu zazhi* 14(4) (1922), 6–12; Zhang Jiuru, "Jiangsu Jiushi fuxiao ertong wanju ceyan baogao," *Jiaoyu zazhi* 14(8) (1922), 1–2, 9.

[22] See photographs in *Ertong shijie* 8(1)3 (1923), n.p.; *Ertong shijie* 18(20) (1926), n.p.; drawing by Chen Zhaoyu, "Qiqiang," *Ertong shijie* 14(1) (1925), n.p.; and stories by Zhuodai, "Qiqiang yu kouqin," *Ertong shijie* 12(10) (1924), 3–11; Boyou, "Wan," *Xiao pengyou* 157 (1925), 34.

[23] Feng Chenbao and Feng Yiyin, eds., *Feng Zikai manhua quanji: ertong xiang juan* (Beijing, 1999), vol. II, 172.

[24] Yu Cheng, "Aiguo nan'er," *Ertong shijie* 22(3) (1928), 2; Boyou, "Wuzhuang qilai," *Xiao pengyou* 553 (1933), 26; Zhang Ruxiu, "Zhonghua nan'er," *Xiao xuesheng* 7(3) (1937), 42–43.

[25] *Erge huapian* (Shanghai, 1930s), vol. I, series 4, n.p.

[26] Chen Jiyun, *Wanju yu jiaoyu*, 72; Yu Jifan, *Wanju yu jiaoyu* (Shanghai, 1933), 29, 50; Wang Guoyuan, comp., *Wanju jiaoyu* (Shanghai, 1933), 6, 24.

would "cultivate a martial spirit," and riding hobby-horses would promote bravery in boys.[27] Revising his earlier views, the influential pedagogue Chen Heqin affirmed that a good toy "must arouse children's martial spirit," and he approved of toy guns, cannons, and warships for fostering courageous and soldierly attitudes.[28]

The discourse on martial spirit centered on "children" and on boys specifically when toy weapons were involved. Its iconography featured boys predominantly. Girls were occasionally mentioned in connection with war toys and games, however, and they did engage in military play. Like the image of the ideal child, mobilization was coded as masculine but was nonetheless intended for both genders.[29] Military toys may not have been specifically recommended for girls, but the brave-cum-patriotic-cum-scientific attitude that informed the narrative of mobilization and martial spirit was. And so was anti-imperialist activism.

TOYS AND ANTI-IMPERIALIST MOBILIZATION

If toy-centered mobilization had focused mainly on the inner cultivation of courage and martial spirit before the early 1930s, it came to encompass external fronts as well – both commercial and military – during the 1930s and early 1940s. As the periodical *Children's World* instructed its young readers in 1933, national goods and national defense were the means to repel "the imperialists" who intended to "carve up" China.[30] Girls and boys were thus asked to protect China and their own Chinese-ness by mobilizing against two foreign armies: the toy army of imported playthings and the real army of Japanese invaders.

In China, as elsewhere,[31] foreign playthings had in fact long been seen as symbols and spearheads of economic and, above all, cultural encroachment. To cite but a few examples, already in 1912 the *Industrial Magazine of China* was arguing that imported toy soldiers

[27] Chen Heqin, "Youzhiyuan zhi shebei," *Jiaoyu zazhi* 19(2) (1927), 7–8; Su Wanfu, ed., *Youzhiyuan de shebei* (Shanghai, 1935), 19, 99, 131–32; Zou Dehui, comp., *Youzhiyuan de youxi* (Shanghai, 1937), 11–12; Wan Qiyu, *Zenyang banli youzhi jiaoyu* (Shanghai, 1947), 7.

[28] Chen Heqin, "Wanju" (1925) and "Ertong wanju yu jiaoyu" (1939), in *Wanju yu jiaoyu* (Kunming, 1991), 36–37 and 108–09.

[29] As seen, for instance, in the Girl Scouts: Margaret Mih Tillman, "Engendering Children of the Resistance: Models for Gender and Scouting in China, 1919–1937," *Cross-Currents: East Asian History and Culture Review* (e-journal) 13 (2014), 134–73.

[30] Lianghuan, "Guofang moxing zhizuo fa," *Ertong shijie* 30(1) (1933), 22–23.

[31] Michel Manson, *Jouets de toujours: de l'Antiquité à la Révolution* (Paris, 2001), 323–24.

sporting the flags of both the country of manufacture and China laudably cultivated a martial spirit but at the same time caused harm because they might encourage love for two flags or two countries. In 1926, the prominent pedagogue Zhang Zonglin deplored the predominance of foreign toys in kindergartens, expressing concern about their potential impact on the Chinese-ness of children.[32] Although experts reviled Chinese toys old and new, they repeatedly – but unsuccessfully – urged consumers to buy patriotically.

The crusade for national toys reached a climax after the invasion of Manchuria as Japanese toys became the main target of hostility. Children were reminded not only that opposing "enemy goods" was among their social duties[33] but also that they must not fund foreigners, as the Japanese were using the profits they earned from exporting toys to annihilate the Chinese. Children penned stories in which boys, patriotically instructed by their teachers, supervised their younger brothers' acquisitions, while girls rectified their mothers' negligent purchases by resolutely exposing dishonest toy sellers. Youngsters were also encouraged to urge their parents to carefully check where toys were made before making a purchase.[34] Vigilant (adultified) children were thus to police (infantilized) adults, including their own parents. Mobilization also involved manual work: Youngsters were urged to realize that toys could "sell the nation," to stop depending on foreign ingenuity (for Japanese imports were, in fact, still considerable), and instead to use their brains and hands to invent new toys for themselves and for China.[35]

Children unable to make their own toys could purchase playthings manufactured locally. Indeed, patriotism was used in advertising Chinese-made toys. Tanks could "arouse national consciousness." Tank-shaped candy purportedly capable of "cultivat[ing] children to be militant

---

[32] Li Wenquan, "Shuo wanju," *Zhongguo shiye zazhi* 5 (1912), 15–16; Zhang Zonglin, "Diaocha Jiang Zhe youzhi jiaoyu hou de ganxiang," *Zhonghua jiaoyu jie* 15(12) (1926), 2; Xu Yasheng, "Ertong wanju de yanjiu," *Funü zazhi* 15(5) (1929), 16; Susan R. Fernsebner, "A People's Playthings: Toys, Childhood, and Chinese Identity, 1909–1933," *Postcolonial Studies* 6(3) (2003), 282–85.

[33] Zhu Yanfu, *Ertong jie* (Shanghai, 1936), 22.

[34] Zhou Hui, "Yang wawa," *Ertong shijie* 30(11) (1933), 96–98; Wei Suzhen, "Gege he didi mai wanju," *Xiao pengyou* 595 (1934), 42–43; Jinxi, "Wanju jinkou he zizhi wanju," in Shenbao ertong zhoukan she, ed., *Shenbao ertong zhi you*, vol. I, 51.

[35] Dujuan, "Ertong he wanju"; Naichang, "Wanju keyi mai guo," in Shenbao ertong zhoukan she, ed., *Shenbao ertong zhi you*, vol. I, 39, 53.

citizens" prompted one boy to proclaim that he would use it to fight the enemy.[36]

Opposing a real foreign army became imperative in the 1930s and 1940s, and, as in Europe, toys were used to familiarize children with war.[37] New patterns for time-honoured tangram puzzles reproduced "modern weapons of war" like tanks and anti-aircraft guns. Kindergarten children, it was suggested, could use building blocks to make warships and armoured vehicles, and anti-Japanese "patriotic games" were designed for elementary schools.[38] The magazine *Modern Children* offered instructions and drawings for a puzzle featuring the collaborationist politician Wang Jingwei, his wife, and "a Japanese thief": The pieces could be recombined to make "many amusing monster figures," thereby ridiculing the enemy.[39] Texts offered instruction not only on how to fashion toy animals and figurines, but also on how to make cannons, crafted from thread spools and bamboo, and radish bombs.[40]

Possibly the most significant aspect of this call to miniature arms was the emergence in the mid 1930s of "national defense toys" (a term also used in the United States during World War II)[41] and, shortly afterward, of "war of resistance toys" ("war of resistance" was the term used for the Second Sino-Japanese War). These new discursive tags turned military playthings into training tools with little ludic significance. Some children did in fact assert that, with the Japanese invasion of Manchuria, the time for recreation was over, which dovetailed with adult invitations to "put toys down" and to focus on trying to support the nation in danger.[42] Children were apparently to relinquish play and move on to reproducing

[36] China Can advertisement in *Yong'an yuekan* 1 (1939), n.p.; Guanshengyuan advertisement in *Xiandai fumu* 1(1) (1933), n.p.; Lien Ling-ling, "From the Retailing Revolution to the Consumer Revolution: Department Stores in Modern Shanghai," *Frontiers of History in China* 4(3) (2009), 379.

[37] Antonio Gibelli, *Il popolo bambino. Infanzia e nazione dalla Grande Guerra a Salò* (Turin, 2005).

[38] Yuesheng, "Qiqiao xin tu," *Ertong shijie* 30(6) (1933), 51; Shen Baiying, et al., comp., *Youzhiyuan gongzuo yibailiushi zu* (Changsha, [1936] 1939), 52, 302; Morris, *Marrow of the Nation*, 133.

[39] Yang Wuzai, "Xiao wanyi," *Xiandai ertong* 5(5) (1942), 9.

[40] Lin Lübin, *Ertong shougong* (Shanghai, 1933), vol. III, 167–68; Lei Jiaxian, *Guoshi wanju zhizuo fa* (Shanghai, 1937), 51.

[41] Lisa L. Ossian, *The Forgotten Generation: American Children and World War II* (Columbia, MO, 2011), 56.

[42] Liu Huanming, "Shei he wo wan," *Xiao pengyou* 553 (1933), 41; Boyou and Xiyi, "Ertong nian de nuli," *Xiao pengyou* 666 (1935), 12; Sun Jie and Ming Min, "Shidai xiao xianfeng," *Kangzhan ertong* 2(1/2) (1940), n.p.

combat: Youthfulness may have shielded them from the battlefield but not from becoming acquainted with war. The Chinese may have been inherently peaceable, as textbooks argued, but the nation had to be protected.[43]

Children's periodicals, primary school handicraft textbooks, and materials for educators all addressed the issue of "defense training" or "war of resistance education," offering a playful introduction to arms. Some advocates of defense training did concede that weapons were used to kill but argued that reproducing them was crucial in helping children acquire the military knowledge needed to resist the foreign invasion. Detailed explanations were therefore provided on how to construct a wide array of military apparatus – from aircraft carriers and gas masks to machineguns and anti-aircraft artillery – out of scrap or other easily obtainable materials; these toys were sometimes referred to as "defense models" or even "teaching material."[44] Throughout unoccupied China, schoolchildren engaged in these modeling activities and had their achievements duly appraised and ranked.[45] Reproduction was also understood as the springboard to future invention: Toy- or model-making initiated children into labor, resourcefulness, technology, and warfare simultaneously.

In China, as in other theaters of war, basic knowledge of aviation was considered necessary to resist aggression. Thus, for example, kindergarten teachers in rural areas fashioned airplanes out of cigarette packets to introduce their young students to aviation. According to children's magazines, constructing toy airplanes would help train the young to defend China against its imperialist enemies.[46] However, a survey conducted in the mid 1930s found that few children in the countryside liked toy planes, to the disappointment of some commentators. Interest in "national defense education" toys like airplanes was imperative, they argued:

---

[43] Peter Zarrow, *Educating China: Knowledge, Society, and Textbooks in a Modernizing World, 1902–1937* (Cambridge, 2015), 68, 127.

[44] Lianghuan, "Guofang moxing zhizuo fa"; Zong Lianghuan, *Junxie moxing zhizuo fa* (Shanghai, 1933); Xu Jian'an and Yao Jiadong, eds., *Guofang xunlian xiaoxue gongyi jiaocai* (Shanghai, 1936); Wu Ding, "Kangzhan shiqi xiaoxue kecheng ji jiaocai zhi yanjiu," *Jiaoyu zazhi* 28(5) (1938), 43; Rui Xuanzhi, "Xiaoxue kangzhan jiaocai yi shu," *Jiaoyu zazhi* 28(6) (1938), 33; Jiang Xiangnan, "Kangzhan wanju," *Xiandai ertong* 6(4) (1942), 136–38. On the mobilization of orphans in wartime, see M. Colette Plum, "Lost Childhoods in a New China: Child-Citizen-Workers at War, 1937–1945," *European Journal of East Asian Studies* 11 (2012), 237–58.

[45] "Quanguo xiaoxue chuzhong xuesheng zizhi feiji gaoshepao moxing chengji pingpan biao," *Guangxi sheng zhengfu gongbao* 1138 (1941), 7–11.

[46] Sun Mingxun, *Laogong you'er tuan* (Shanghai, 1935), 153; Shenzi, "Feiji," *Xiao pengyou* 754 (1937), 23–25; Jiang Xiangnan, "Kangzhan wanju," *Xiandai ertong* 6(3) (1942), 100–02.

The absence of such interest could only be the result of unfamiliarity and could thus be easily remedied by encouraging aeromodeling in handicraft classes.[47] One suspects that children might sometimes have seen – and despised – making "defense toys" as homework, on account of their connection to school- and state-promoted activities.

Nonetheless, some youngsters did echo the association between toys and defense. One boy voiced regret that he was too small to kill the enemies with his airgun, for example. Some used improvised corncob "bombs" to play at bombing the Japanese.[48] Other boys, however, simply played war games out in the street or made their own toy pistols, water-guns, and broadswords, displaying perhaps a martial spirit but not necessarily militant defense-mindedness.[49] Military toys, toy-making, and play did not inevitably entail a *conscious* acceptance of the full anti-imperialist mobilization package, and of course toy-making was, to many, simply a necessity. Raising their "national consciousness" might, indeed, not have been the main reason why children engaged in play.

LEISURE FOR THE "SUCCESSORS TO THE REVOLUTION"

Internal military conflict might have come to an end in China by late 1949, but mobilization did not. Although the Communists claimed to be radically different from the Nationalists, their early 1950s discourse of childhood and play was rather similar to that of their predecessors, albeit with more emphasis on the collective and more extensive politicization and regimentation. Texts for educators and children's magazines disseminated the message that the young, as "successors" to a valiant cause, had to cultivate themselves to be "new" and "useful" people who would be able to construct and protect the motherland. Even more markedly than before, mere amusement was despised in favor of purposeful leisure: A "befuddled life"[50] was no longer tolerable.[51] If grown-ups were

---

[47] Luo Zixin and Wang Zhilu, "Xiaoxue ertong xingqu de diaocha yanjiu," *Jiaoyu zazhi* 26(8) (1936), 76.

[48] Yang Yijing, "Qiqiang," *Xiao pengyou* 555 (1933), 38; Henrietta Harrison, *The Man Awakened from Dreams: One Man's Life in a North China Village, 1857–1942* (Stanford, 2005), 162.

[49] Zhu Caipei, "Xinnian de youxi," *Xiao pengyou* 444 (1931), 69; Wang Meng, *Wang Meng zizhuan. Diyibu, bansheng duoshi* (Canton, 2006), 45; Fu Zhengyi, *Jianji rensheng: Fu Zhengyi zizhuan* (Beijing, 2007), 6.

[50] Fang Jianming, "Qingzhu liu yi ertong jie," *Xin ertong shijie* 45 (1950), 6.

[51] Fang Yuyan, "Liangge shijie de ertong shenghuo," *Renmin jiaoyu* 2 (1950), 27–30; Zhang Guofan, "Yinggai lizhi zuo ge xin ertong," *Xin ertong* 28 (1950), 2; Che Xiangchen,

infantilized and the young made adult in the People's Republic, as Jean-Pierre Diény rightly argued,[52] this was only an intensification of Republican attitudes.

Like their precursors, the Communists looked upon play as an educational tool. Play was supposed to teach children love of labor, collectivism, tenacity, discipline, and politeness.[53] And mobilization. Parents and educators were repeatedly advised to guide and supervise play, albeit without stifling children's creativity. Creativity was to be rechanneled, however, if it went in the wrong direction. Around 1950, for example, some primary school children in Beijing who had wanted to be the Americans in a play battle because they considered them to be more vigorous than their opponents were set straight by means of thorough "current affairs education" about the Korean War. Military games with toy weapons were fine for cultivating courage, vigilance, and hatred of imperialism, but only when carried out according to the script.[54] Posing as a People's Liberation Army (PLA) soldier or as a volunteer fighter against "American devils" in Korea was laudable, but impersonating "evil characters" could allegedly result in children taking on their bad ways. Bad characters could, however, be impersonated on occasion for reasons of expedience. For example, one player in "Cooperation Between the Army and the People," a game recommended for primary schools in 1949, was to take on the role of Chiang Kai-shek.[55]

Whether defined as children's "closest friends" or "tools to educate children," playthings remained catalysts of mobilization under the Communists, but increasingly in conjunction with "meaningful" group activities such as toy-making and collective play. Children were in fact soon expected to make toys rather than simply play with them like toddlers. Experts claimed that, in contrast to the previous regime's

"Haohao xuexi, jianshe zuguo," *Hao haizi* 81 (1953), 1; "Xingfu de xia yidai," *Renmin huabao* 6 (1954), 4–7; Zhongguo fulihui shaonian gong, "Shanghai shaonian gong gongzuo jingyan," *Renmin jiaoyu* 6 (1956), 48–51.

[52] Jean-Pierre Diény, *Le monde est à vous. La Chine et les livres pour enfants* (Paris, 1971), 7.

[53] Zhong Zhaohua, "Zenyang jiao xiao haizi youxi," *Xin ertong jiaoyu* 7(5) (1951), 16–17; Ya Su, "Xuexi Sulian dui you'er jiaoyu de fangfa," *Xin Zhongguo funü* 6 (1953), 12.

[54] Chen Dingxiu, "Jieshao 'ertong leyuan,'" *Xin jiaoyu* 2(6) (1951), 37; "Jieshao Beijing shi shaonian ertong dui de shishi jiaoyu huodong," *Renmin Ribao* (1951), in Jiaoyu ziliao congkan she, ed., *Xiao xuexiao de shaonian ertong dui* (Shanghai, 1951), 80–83.

[55] Zhong Zhaohua, "Zenyang jiao xiao haizi youxi," 16; Lüda shi minzhu funü lianhehui fuli bu, ed., *Zenyang jiaoyu haizi* (Dalian, 1953), 37; Kou Xiulan, "Youxi," *Xin Zhongguo funü* 1 (1955), 21; *Xiao xuesheng chang you ji* (Shexian, Henan, 1949), 37.

negligence, the government was now ensuring that all children had "new" and "appropriate" toys. Again, a good plaything should instruct, and foster a love of labor or an interest in science. Although some educators argued that dolls ought to look Chinese, the struggle against foreign toys subsided, most likely because the few available items hailed from socialist countries.[56]

Toy-related mobilization in the early 1950s could involve volunteerism, as when primary school children (were) rushed to create playthings for hastily established kindergartens. Or it could involve manual-intellectual mobilization, as when home- or school-made toy replicas of machines – defined as "models" – were held up as examples of children's engagement with science and technology, and of their eagerness to learn the productive skills needed to rebuild and protect China.[57] And, despite the fact that the martial spirit was no longer mentioned, toys could be instruments of martial mobilization for political and quasi-military struggle. In all its facets, the discourse of activism tended to address "children" – yet it was still a masculine-coded model that girls had to pursue.

TOYS AS AGITATION TOOLS: BETWEEN TANKS AND DOVES

Chinese children had to learn to be concerned with political affairs; they should be "always prepared."[58] In the early 1950s, the Taiwan question and the Korean War offered opportunities for them to (im)prove their preparation. Mobilization was promoted mainly through toy- or model-making, in a happy blend of creative labor, frugal resourcefulness, and political education. In such activities, youngsters were expected to display a remarkable fervor that reflected the intense gratitude they presumably felt for enjoying such happy lives. As in the Republican era, the mobilization of children involved ridiculing enemies and training to defeat them as well as the acquisition of basic scientific-technological skills.

---

[56] Fu Baochen, ed., *Ertong wanju zhanlan jiniance* (Chengdu, 1950); Beijing shi gongshang guanli ju, "Benju guanyu zhaokai ertong wanju zuotanhui de hanjian zuotanhui jilu ji juxing ertong wanju zhanlanhui wenti xiang shifu de baogao ji qi youguan cailiao," *Beijing Municipal Archives*, file 22-12-896, 1950–1952; Zhou Shufen, "Zenyang wei haizi xuanze wanju," *Xin Zhongguo funü* 1 (1954), 31.

[57] Yang Guang, "Meili de wanju," *Xiao pengyou* 1045 (1952), 12–13; Xinhua she, "Zhou zongli he re'ai kexue de xiao pengyou zai yiqi," *Xin shaonian bao* 408 (1955), 1.

[58] Feng Wenbin, "Shike zhunbei zhe," in Zhongguo xin minzhuzhuyi qingnian tuan Xinjiang sheng gongzuo weiyuanhui, ed., *Zhongguo shaonian ertong dui shouce* (Dihua, 1952), 7–8.

Children were expected to show support for the PLA's efforts to "liberate" Taiwan. They also had to be prepared to act, as did some primary school pupils who reportedly trained to help the army by devising makeshift parachutes with cloth doll dummies.[59] Youngsters were also supposed to develop a sound political awareness, in school and at home. Methods for cultivating it included the use of recreational "teaching aids" that primary school children could craft with their teachers. One such teaching aid, named "Blast the War Criminal," involved constructing figurines of "war criminals" such as Chiang Kai-shek and Dwight Eisenhower and then lighting firecrackers placed on their heads.[60] Toy-making manuals suggested that, to entertain themselves, children draw "the common enemy of the Chinese people, wretched Chiang" with the body of a dog, as he was "the running dog of American imperialism," and then shoot him with bamboo arrows tipped with suction cups.[61]

Patriotic education also involved participation in the campaign "Resist America, Aid Korea." Primary school students could apparently acquire a solid yet enjoyable anti-imperialist extracurricular education by fashioning "highly interesting" games as "War Criminal Enters the Coffin": Players threw balls at a figurine to try to topple it and make the "coffin" lid close over it.[62] Or children could craft toy planes – as a poem in the periodical *Good Children* suggested – to go first to bomb the American imperialists and then fly on to Beijing to see Mao Zedong.[63] Toy-making could also involve a fruitful combination of political and scientific competence. Optical illusions, manuals advised, could be investigated by making a thaumatrope that showed a dagger – the people's "peace-protecting armed forces" – piercing a "US-armed Japanese warlord" and the maneuvering hand of "an American warmonger" behind him. To comprehend the principle of gravity, children could produce the revamped, or rearmed, rendition of a tumbler toy in the shape of a fearless soldier, ever standing to safeguard the people, the motherland, and peace.[64]

---

[59] Guo Lin, "Women shi zheyang peiyang ertong de chuangzaoxing de," *Renmin jiaoyu* 2 (1950), 52.

[60] Xu Linshou, *Xiaoxue jiaoju zhizuo* (Shanghai, 1953), 169.

[61] Xiong Dafu and Fu Tianqi, *Ziji zuo wanju* (Shanghai, 1953), 84–86. "Wretched Chiang," which could also be rendered as "damned Chiang," is the translation of "Jiang gaisi," a pun on Chiang Kai-shek's name as pronounced in Mandarin, Jiang Jieshi.

[62] Xu Linshou, *Xiaoxue jiaoju zhizuo*, 170.

[63] Yin Zhenwu, Liu Ruiying, and Wang Minggang, "Zhizao xiao feiji," *Hao haizi* 71 (1953), 21.

[64] Xiong Dafu and Fu Tianqi, *Ziji zuo wanju*, introduction, 8–9, 51–52.

Hardly any mention of these activities can be found in contemporary accounts, although some children seem to have echoed the discourse of mobilization. Primary school boys purportedly made toy rifles for toddlers so that they could learn to protect the country as the Chinese Volunteer Army did. Student groups who engaged in learning about science and technology by crafting models out of scraps proudly reported that had their "Liberation tank" artillery been real, it would have "killed quite a few American devils."[65] Chinese boys played games such as "Resist America, Aid Korea." Even foreign boys living in China pretended that their siblings were spies for Chiang Kai-shek and, together with their Chinese playmates, attacked them with mudball "hand grenades." As before, children crafted toy weapons and played war without explicitly attaching militant significance to it.[66] That is, they apparently were not fighting for peace in their play.

Antithetical as this may seem, icons of both war and peace coexisted in prescribed leisure. Toy-making suggestions for children encompassed cardboard doves, and the periodical *Women of New China* alerted mothers to the ideological correctness of peace dove puzzles.[67] Revolving-horse lanterns, which youngsters were encouraged to construct in order to learn about the effect of heat on air, could be decorated with peace doves or images of the Chinese Volunteer Army pursuing American soldiers.[68] Education should apparently promote patriotism and internationalism. Like the Soviet Union, the "new China" and its children were striving for peace.[69] Very seldom did

[65] Liu Guanying, "You yiyi de liwu," *Xin shaonian bao* 253 (1952), 3; Lin Fuqi, "Wode 'jiefang hao' tanke," *Kaiming shaonian* 72 (1951), 44–45.

[66] Ralph Lapwood and Nancy Lapwood, *Through the Chinese Revolution* (London, 1954), 82; Zhou Zhangshi, "Women nage shihou de wanju," *Yuwen jiaoxue yu yanjiu* 7 (1997), 20; Ye Weili with Ma Xiaodong, *Growing Up in the People's Republic: Conversations Between Two Daughters of China's Revolution* (New York, 2005), 34; Cui Puquan, "Wo xiao shihou de ertong wanju," in Bian Jian, ed., *Chayu fanhou hua Beijing* (Beijing, 2006), 173–74.

[67] Zhou Shufen, "Zenyang wei haizi xuanze wanju," 31; Wen Quan, "Heping ge," *Hao haizi* 66 (1953), 28. On the peace dove icon, see James Z. Gao, "War Culture, Nationalism, and Political Campaigns, 1950–1953," in C. X. George Wei and Xiaoyuan Liu, eds., *Chinese Nationalism in Perspective: Historical and Recent Cases* (Westport, 2001), 180; on doves, and children as icons, see Chang-tai Hung, *Mao's New World: Political Culture in the Early People's Republic* (Ithaca, 2011), 191–98.

[68] Guo Yishi, "Zoumadeng," *Zhongguo shaonian ertong* 30 (1950), 13; Jinzhou shi Taihe wanquan xiaoxue, "Jiechuan kongqi de mimi," in Zhongguo xin minzhuzhuyi qingnian tuan zhongyang shaonian ertong bu, ed., *Shaonian ertong dui de huodong* (Beijing, 1951), 55–56.

[69] Mu Shaoliang, "Women de jieri," *Xin ertong shijie* 45 (1950), n.p.; Wang Jingpu and Zhang Zonglin, "Aiguozhuyi jiaoyu zai youzhiyuan," in Xu Teli, et al., *Lun aiguozhuyi*

experts recommend supplying children with toy tanks or guns, and playthings from socialist countries were extolled as nonviolent, as opposed to
American "warmongering" toys. Yet Chinese factories churned out toy
tanks and guns as well as peace doves, as peace-loving children in stories
were "provoked" to react against bullies who boasted about their American
toy bayonets.[70] And the military was a constant presence. Beginning in
kindergarten, children were taught to love and emulate the army, which
was represented as compassionate and protective.[71] Tanks appeared in
pictures that were used to decorate classrooms. Toy-making texts featured
sorghum stalk warships. Pedagogues still included artillery pieces among the
shapes suggested for assembling blocks.[72] The conciliatory attitude thus
went hand in hand with reminders of the necessity of vigilance, indicative
of an undercurrent of insecurity. Children's periodicals, too, reiterated that
lurking without and within were enemies – including imperialists, capitalists,
and Nationalists – who were eager to destabilize the new China and to
jeopardize world peace. Accordingly, permanent mobilization was
required.[73]

Leaving aside the point that doves (and even the army) can signify
militancy for peace, some of the assessments of playthings displayed at
a 1950 exhibition may help explain the seemingly incongruous coexistence of doves and armaments because they illuminate how the difference
between war and resistance was constructed and perceived. Planes and
tanks laudably fostered an interest in science, according to one observer,
but they had the downside of "arous[ing] the idea of warfare" in the
young. At the same time, a figurine of a Japanese soldier was commended
for "arous[ing] the idea of resistance war."[74] Warfare was judged to be
bad, but wars of resistance were good even if they, too, entailed combat

jiaoyu (Beijing, 1951), 106–14; Peter N. Stearns, *Childhood in World History*, 2nd edn.
(London, 2011), 107.

[70] "Zhongguo renmin duiwai wenhua youhao xiehui Shanghai shi fenhui guanyu Deyizhi
Minzhu Gongheguo ertong wanju zhanlanhui de wenjian," *Shanghai Municipal
Archives*, file C37-2-49, 1954–1955; Xi Jian, "Renqing diren," *Shaonian ertong* 18
(1950), 7–8.

[71] He Gongchao, "Haoren yao dangbing," *Xin ertong shijie* 44 (1950), 24–25; Ding Hua,
"Beihai you'eryuan san nian lai shi zenyang jiaoyu haizimen de," *Renmin jiaoyu* 6 (1953),
14.

[72] Xing Shuntian, *Jiaoshi buzhi tuhua* (Shanghai, 1950), fig. 10; Zhonghua quanguo minzhu
funü lianhehui ertong fuli bu, ed., *Shougong he tuhua* (Beijing, 1950), 29; Wu Chengqi,
"Chuanxin jimu," *Xin ertong jiaoyu* 8(2) (1952), 28.

[73] Fang Bai, "Xin Zhongguo de youxiu ernü," *Zhonghua shaonian* 6(22) (1949), 3–4;
Tang Yue, "Zenyang qingzhu women de jieri?" *Xin ertong shijie* 69 (1951), n.p.

[74] Fu Baochen, *Ertong wanju zhanlan jiniance*, 41, 44.

and violence. Criticizing war does not necessarily amount to rejecting confrontational mobilization, especially when it is associated with resistance to perceived aggression. Moreover, war and violence can be legitimized and rationalized as just, be it to repel invaders, as was the case in the Republican era, or for the sake of revolution or political goals, as in the Communist era.[75] The cohabitation of peace doves and antagonistic leisure can thus be situated within the paradigm of resistance versus war: Warmongers and criminals can be joyfully smashed by righteous resisters armed to preserve peace.

CONCLUSION

Taking children's toys as "a silent signifying dialogue between them and their nation,"[76] this chapter has explored an aspect of the top-down part of that dialogue, the impact of which is difficult to determine because most data on childhood tend to be "adult-generated or adult-controlled."[77] Sketchy impressions gathered from accounts suggest that children appropriated selectively from adults' efforts to mobilize them. Yet, high-handed as it may have been, the rhetoric of activism was acting on, and responding to, assumptions and urgencies (perceived humiliation, nationalism, belief in education and malleability) that made it intelligible to children and adults alike.

Whether in times of war or nominal peace, mobilization through leisure did not necessarily imply outright belligerence. Rather, it encouraged patriotism, discipline, political and technical competence, physical and moral strength, and determination: in other words, the capacity to resist rather than attack. Mobilization was constructed as defensive: It would save the nation from "extinction," repel invaders, or protect peace. Ludic fierceness was legitimated and simultaneously downplayed as just preservation and rightful opposition to real or perceived external encroachment.

---

[75] Sheldon Lu, "*Beautiful Violence*: War, Peace, Globalization," *positions* 12(3) (2004), 760, 763; Stephanie Donald, "Children as Political Messengers: Art, Childhood, and Continuity," in Harriet Evans and Stephanie Donald, eds., *Picturing Power in the People's Republic of China: Posters of the Cultural Revolution* (Lanham, MD, 1999), 80.

[76] Walter Benjamin, "The Cultural History of Toys" (1928), in *Walter Benjamin: Selected Writings, Volume II, part 1, 1927–1930*, ed. Michael W. Jennings, et al. (Cambridge, MA, 1999), 116.

[77] Thomas J. Schlereth, "The Material Culture of Childhood: Problems and Potential in Historical Explanation," *Material History Bulletin/Bulletin d'histoire de la culture matérielle* 21 (1985), 11.

Toys were sometimes called models or teaching aids. This might signify a wish to legitimate playthings by disavowing the play element, perhaps deemed frivolous when connected to grave national concerns. The name change, in other words, might have been meant to alter the perception of the object: You do not use trifles when playing for keeps. Alternatively, the name rectification might have signified a culture of imitation/emulation whereby toys became in fact and in name the props for rehearsing adult responsibilities. Conversely, calling war toys "defense toys" or expunging the martial spirit in name while cultivating it in fact might suggest the wish to downplay antagonism in favor of just resistance. The very concept of the military toy is in fact complex. Toys that are not inherently military (tangrams, revolving-horse lanterns) could be deployed to cultivate quasi-belligerent attitudes. Indeed, as Brian Sutton-Smith points out, knowing the context in which a plaything is used is key to identifying its effects.[78] Calling war toys "educational," as many experts did, was not necessarily an oxymoron: If playthings were tools for instruction, and if the goal of education was to produce useful people, a tool that conveyed military knowledge – knowledge that could be applicable in a time of perceived threat – could thus be educational.

The seemingly contradictory stances of cherishing children while acquainting them with the battlefield can, finally, be explained by referring to their role as national symbols. Ostensibly, the Republican and Communist regimes both set great store by children's wellbeing and accorded them high status. In return, children were asked to perform duties that included reciprocating the protection they received from the state. Trained by "toys," children were supposed to mobilize and struggle to preserve the renewed personhood, and nationhood, that they owed to the state.

---

[78] Brian Sutton-Smith, *Toys as Culture* (New York, 1986), 11, 251.

2

Forging a Patriotic Youth: Penny Dreadfuls and Military Censorship in World War I Germany

Kara L. Ritzheimer

In 1916, the year that German military leaders instituted the policies of total war to break the stalemate of the western front, Berlin teacher and anti-"trash" activist Paul Samuleit launched a salvo against the German pulp fiction industry. In a compact yet detailed study titled *Kriegsschundliteratur* (*Wartime Trash Literature*), Samuleit attacked publishers for transforming the war and soldiers' heroics into fictional grist for military-themed pamphlet stories. This commercialization of the front, he warned, was diminishing the likelihood that war might inspire selflessness, loyalty, and patriotism in the nation's youth. Certain that censorship was the most effective tool for combating this problem, he urged military authorities across Germany to use their expanded wartime powers to regulate pulp fiction retailers and thereby limit young people's exposure to this sensationalist trash.[1]

Samuleit premised this appeal for censorship on two important concepts. The first was the belief that children, adolescents, and teenagers were a communal resource whose physical, intellectual, and mental development was a matter of great national concern. After all, poorly socialized children might one day become criminals, degenerates, or unreliable soldiers. The second was a confidence in the capacity of public policy to positively shape the intellectual and emotional development of young people. In peacetime, these two concepts had supported an expansion of

---

[1] Paul Samuleit, *Kriegsschundliteratur: Vortrag, gehalten in der öffentlichen Versammlung der Zentralstelle zur Bekämpfung der Schundliteratur zu Berlin am 25. März 1916* (Berlin, 1916), 8, 30–34.

public youth welfare services.² During World War I, they provided military authorities with a rationale for curtailing young people's access to a number of supposedly harmful influences, including dance halls, movie theaters, taverns, alcohol, cigarettes, and pulp fiction.

These wartime restrictions benefited from peacetime precedents. For several decades prior to World War I, social reformers and public authorities had been extending the state's interventionist reach into young people's lives, particularly those deemed to be "wayward" or potentially "wayward." And, in the first years of the twentieth century, progressive social reformers began to speak of a child's legal right to education, a concept defined expansively to include not only academic instruction but also moral and civic education.³ Whereas the first approach framed intervention as a defensive measure intended to protect society from the juvenile delinquent, the second justified intervention by prioritizing the wellbeing of the child. Both concepts gave wartime authorities the confidence that policy could guide the maturation of young people and even compensate for the shortcomings of incompetent or absent parents.

Germany's mobilization in 1914 provided military officials with the legal means to put these theories into action. When the imperial government proclaimed a state of imminent war with Russia on July 31, 1914, it also activated the Prussian Law of Siege of June 4, 1851. According to historian Gerald Feldman, this law gave deputy commanding generals stationed throughout the nation's twenty-four army corps districts "virtually dictatorial power" at the same time that it lifted peacetime press protections. These military authorities were responsible for recruiting troops, making them ready, and deploying them to the front as well as for ensuring both order and public safety on the home front.⁴ By 1915, military authorities were using their expanded authority to intervene on behalf of overburdened mothers, restore the patriarchal authority of

² Larry Frohman, *Poor Relief and Welfare in Germany from the Reformation to World War I* (New York, 2008), 179–83.
³ Edward Ross Dickinson, *The Politics of German Child Welfare from the Empire to the Federal Republic* (Cambridge, MA, 1996), 11, 74–75; Larry Frohman, "The Break-Up of the Poor Laws – German Style: Progressivism and the Origins of the Welfare State, 1900–1918," *Comparative Studies in Society and History* 50 (2008), 990.
⁴ Roger Chickering, *Imperial Germany and the Great War, 1914–1918* (Cambridge, 2004), 33–34; Ernst Conrad, *Das Gesetz über den Belagerungszustand vom 4. Juni 1851 (mit dem Abänderungsgesetze vom 11. Dezember 1915* (Berlin, 1916), iii; Gerald D. Feldman, *Army, Industry, and Labor in Germany 1914–1918* (Princeton, 1966), 31; David Welch, *Germany, Propaganda and Total War, 1914–1918: The Sins of Omission* (New Brunswick, 2000), 30.

missing fathers, and more closely regulate how young people spent their free time.

This chapter examines these efforts through the lens of wartime regulations surrounding the sale and consumption of wartime penny dreadfuls. Hero-centered pamphlet stories had been thrilling German readers since 1905, when entrepreneur and Dresden publisher Adolf Eichler acquired the copyright for both the *Buffalo Bill* and the *Nick Carter* series.[5] When Germany entered into war in early August 1914, writers and publishers relocated the heroes of these pamphlet stories from the shores of North Africa, South America, and the Mediterranean to the trenches and battlefields of the western and eastern fronts. Wary observers labeled this new genre "wartime trash," or (*Kriegsschundliteratur*), and warned that these cheap stories could have a disastrous impact on the children and teenagers who so eagerly devoured them.[6] Most deputy commanding generals in Germany tended to agree. By 1917, twenty-two of twenty-four had imposed wartime controls on pulp fiction retailers.[7]

Censorship is, as Gary Stark rightly notes, "a form of social control employed by governing authorities to defend and secure conformity to the shared political, social, religious, and moral norms and values that . . . [are deemed] essential for communal integration, social cohesion, and civil order."[8] But this definition overlooks the degree to which censorship can also be aspirational. Authorities can employ censorship not only to entrench certain norms and values but also to coax desired behaviors or attitudes by restricting consumption choices and controlling visual and conceptual environments. During World War I, deputy commanding generals used censorship in this aspirational fashion to control young people's exposure to the war and thereby foster a culture among youth that embraced patriotism, duty, and morality.

The war created the extraordinary legal framework for precisely the sort of increased state intervention in the lives of young people that prewar

[5] Ronald Fullerton, "Toward a Commercial Popular Culture in Germany: The Development of Pamphlet Fiction, 1871–1914," *Journal of Social History* 12 (1979), 498; Christian Huck, "American Dime Novels on the German Market: The Role of Gatekeepers," in Huck and Stefan Bauernschmidt, eds., *Travelling Goods, Travelling Moods: Varieties of Cultural Appropriation (1850–1950)* (Frankfurt, 2012), 111.

[6] Samuleit, *Kriegsschundliteratur*, 8, 15; Wilhelm Tessendorff, *Die Kriegsschundliteratur und ihre Bekämpfung: mit einem Verzeichnis empfehlenswerter Kriegsschriften* (Halle, 1916), 2, 4.

[7] Dickinson, *The Politics of German Child Welfare*, 116.

[8] Gary D. Stark, *Banned in Berlin: Literary Censorship in Imperial Germany 1871–1918* (New York, 2012), xxii.

social reformers had championed. Indeed, since the late eighteenth century, public authorities had been assuming ever greater responsibility for minors. One of their first forays into youth welfare was the 1794 Prussian Allgemeines Landrecht. This legislation allowed state authorities to appoint and monitor legal guardians for illegitimate or fatherless children. This law also permitted, as Edward Ross Dickinson explains, "the institutionalization of children who were mistreated, starved, or turned to the bad by their parents." Soon after German unification, imperial authorities addressed the question of whether juvenile offenders or "wayward" children could be prosecuted or removed from the care of their parents and placed in foster care or reform school. While the National Criminal Code of 1871 did not allow for this possibility in the case of children aged twelve or under, revisions to the law adopted in 1876 made such intervention by state authorities possible. Furthermore, the Prussian Law on Compulsory Education of 1878 permitted guardianship courts to place child offenders between the ages of six and twelve in foster care or reform schools. Social reformers who were worried about purported increases in juvenile delinquency urged state authorities to go even further and intervene not just in the lives of those children who had already committed an offense but also to intercede in the lives of potential delinquents.[9]

German authorities pursued these incremental interventions at the same time that progressive social reformers on both sides of the Atlantic were rethinking the relationship between the family and the state as well as the relationship between social policy and the individual.[10] In Germany, historian Larry Frohman explains, reformers Hugo Appelius and Wilhelm Polligkeit maintained the naturalness of the parent–child relationship even as they asserted that parents had a "duty to ensure the proper physical, intellectual, and moral development of [their] offspring." Parents who failed to transmit an understanding of right and wrong, or what was moral and immoral, to their children were likely to raise nonproductive citizens, or worse, children who "would become a burden on or a danger to society." States therefore had a vested interest in families and what took place within the confines of the home. Given the state's interest in producing hard-working, law-

---

[9] Dickinson, *The Politics of German Child Welfare*, 18–20; Frohman, *Poor Relief and Welfare*, 183–84.

[10] Glenda Elizabeth Gilmore, "Responding to the Challenges of the Progressive Era," in Gilmore, ed., *Who Were the Progressives?* (New York, 2002), 11; Frohman, "The Break-Up of the Poor Laws," 983.

abiding citizens, Appelius further suggested that, instead of simply disciplining juvenile delinquents, authorities provide these children with the education they had previously lacked and thereby reduce the likelihood of recidivism.[11]

In the years immediately preceding the war, social reformers across the globe began to rethink the logic and delivery of youth welfare services. In the United States, progressive reformers advocated child labor laws, children's health and hygiene, children's access to recreational activities and playgrounds, juvenile courts, and moral protections for adolescents and teenagers. In France, activists took up the plight of the "morally abandoned child" and pushed for expanded educational opportunities and labor protections for adolescents. British campaigners tackled several issues, especially child abuse.[12] In Germany, reformers identified children as legal actors entitled to special protections. In a 1908 essay, Polligkeit contended that just as parents have a duty to educate their children, so too did children possess "an implicit legal right" to education. This legal right obliged the state to guarantee children's access to an education defined broadly to include instruction that would facilitate future employment as well as a civic and legal education. Two years later, Georg Schmidt, mayor of Mainz, asserted that children belonged both to their families and the state and that, consequently, states must intervene in situations in which children confronted "moral endangerment."[13] Collectively, these ideas about youth welfare helped to frame children and teenagers not only as impressionable creatures in need of shelter and guidance but also as a communal commodity whose physical, intellectual, and mental well-being was the legitimate target of state policy.

This understanding of youth as a resource, combined with concerns about the potential loyalty and readiness-to-serve among working-class teenagers, motivated officials in Prussia to institute the Youth Cultivation Edict in 1911. With this decree, Prussian authorities signaled their

---

[11] Frohman, *Poor Relief and Welfare*, 185–86.

[12] James Marten, *Childhood and Child Welfare in the Progressive Era: A Brief History with Documents* (Boston, 2005), 13–22; Mary E. Odem, *Delinquent Daughters: Protecting and Policing Adolescent Female Sexuality in the United States, 1885–1920* (Chapel Hill, 1995), 95–99; Sylvia Schafer, *Children in Moral Danger and the Problem of Government in Third Republic France* (Princeton, 1997), 5; Kathleen Alaimo, "Shaping Adolescence in the Popular Milieu: Social Policy, Reformers, and French Youth, 1870–1920," *Journal of Family History* 17 (1992), 426–30; George K. Behlmer, *Child Abuse and Moral Reform in England, 1870–1908* (Stanford, 1982), 1–16, 78, 97–98, 110.

[13] Dickinson, *The Politics of German Child Welfare*, 75; Frohman, *Poor Relief and Welfare*, 182.

willingness to play a larger role in both coordinating and funding recreational and educational activities for male youth. The edict's preamble outlined its purpose: to create patriotic, loyal, morally upright, and physically fit young men. For two years, reformers concerned about the lives and choices of teenaged girls lobbied Prussian authorities to modify the edict to extend its scope to encompass teenaged girls as well. In April 1913, Prussian authorities amended the decree so that it now included female youth.[14]

In the years leading up to World War I, both progressive social reformers and state authorities in Germany signaled their confidence that public institutions could stand in for absent or incompetent parents and exert positive influences on the development of children, adolescents, and teenagers. This new perspective on youth welfare and its purpose animated German society as it entered into a war that, according to Elisabeth Domansky, effectively "destroyed" the family unit.[15]

World War I was an intensely disruptive event that quickly altered the social universe in which children and youth lived and worked. Conscription and mobilization peeled away the fathers, mothers, teachers, and employers who, prior to the war, had constituted a protective layer around young people. Wartime production needs, in turn, drew more and more workers, especially teenaged boys, into the industrial labor force. As these processes intensified in 1916 when war turned total, military authorities adopted a series of restrictive regulations aimed at compensating for absent parents and, in their place, controlling young people's bodies, free time, and spending choices.

Many adolescents and teenagers first encountered the war through conscription and recruitment polices. Between August 1914 and July 1918, more than thirteen million German men served in the German army. As Richard Bessel notes, "Roughly one-fifth of the German population experienced wartime military service." Men between the ages of twenty-one and twenty-four consistently comprised the largest percentage of combat soldiers, but the demographic profile of the men

---

[14] Derek Linton, *"Who Has the Youth, Has the Future": The Campaign to Save Young Workers in Imperial Germany* (New York, 1991), 139–49; Derek Linton, "Between School and Marriage, Workshop and Household: Young Working Women as a Social Problem in Late Imperial Germany," *European History Quarterly* 18 (1988), 387–88, 395.

[15] Elizabeth Domansky, "The Transformation of State and Society in World War I Germany," in Amir Weiner, ed., *Landscaping the Human Garden: Twentieth-Century Population Management in a Comparative Framework* (Stanford, 2003), 58.

who either volunteered or were conscripted shifted as the war dragged on. By 1915, high casualty rates increased the military's reliance on older men, particularly those in their late twenties and early thirties. A significant number of these soldiers were husbands and fathers whose departure created noticeable absences. Historical appraisals suggest that by 1915 one-third of husbands had been conscripted. Contemporaries estimated that as many as six million families had a father serving in the army.[16] As Domansky argues, "One of the most immediate, drastic, and enduring results of German society's gendered mobilization for total war was the disappearance of men – of fathers, husbands, brothers, and sons – from their families."[17]

This disappearance of men changed women's roles in the home as well as in the wartime economy. Nearly overnight, anywhere from a third to half of all mothers became single parents responsible for supporting and caring for their families. Wives and children whose husbands and fathers were serving in the military were eligible for wartime separation allowances. Imperial authorities intended these payments to help offset the departure of a family's breadwinner. Yet separation allowances were inadequate on their own to support a family, particularly when local authorities failed to provide additional assistance.[18] These shortfalls served to deepen the importance of women's work. Although the war did not dramatically change the number of women who worked outside the home, it did alter the type of jobs they performed. Many female laborers moved out of domestic work and into factory jobs. After the military command's introduction of the Hindenburg Program in 1916, more shifted into jobs in heavy industry. By war's end, more than two million women worked in factories with ten or more employees.[19] When they were not heading off to work, many mothers were standing in food lines

[16] Richard Bessel, *Germany After the First World War* (New York, 1993), 5, 8–9; Ute Daniel, *The War from Within: German Working-Class Women in the First World War* (New York, 1997), 130; Andrew Donson, *Youth in the Fatherless Land: War Pedagogy, Nationalism, and Authority in Germany, 1914–1918* (Cambridge, MA, 2010), 138.

[17] Elisabeth Domansky, "Militarization and Reproduction in World War I Germany," in Geoff Eley, ed., *Society, Culture, and the State in Germany, 1870–1930* (Ann Arbor, 1997), 442.

[18] Donson, *Youth in the Fatherless Land*, 138–41; Frohman, *Poor Relief and Welfare*, 213–18.

[19] Ute Daniel, "Women's Work in Industry and Family: Germany, 1914–1918," in Richard Wall and Jay Winter, eds., *The Upheaval of War: Family, Work and Welfare in Europe, 1914–1918* (Cambridge, 1988), 273; Wilhelm Flitner, "Der Krieg und die Jugend," in Otto Baumgarten, et al., eds., *Geistige und sittliche Wirkungen des Krieges in*

or searching for items that were persistently in short supply, such as coal and clothing. In many cases, women could accomplish these tasks only by leaving their children alone, by relying on extended family networks for help with childcare, by placing their children in daycare, or by sending children to live with family members.[20]

The conflict also diminished the importance of teachers, schools, and apprenticeship programs for young people. Conscription and voluntary enlistments relocated teachers to the front. As the year 1916 began, for example, 1,700 of the 4,300 Protestant teachers working in the state of Württemberg had already been deployed. Of this number, 500 had been killed. War likewise drew teachers working in industrial continuation schools into trenches and battlefields. Institutions consolidated classes and hired more female teachers to offset shortages of male teachers. Despite these remedies, many schools had to close their doors in the last years of war as illnesses and epidemics swept through the population. Educators and administrators also had to contend with shortages of class-rooms and coal. Since the beginning of the war, the military had been requisitioning schools for military needs in part because, when the war started in early August, most schools were in the midst of a summer break.[21]

In addition to affecting home and school, mobilization impacted how young people, both those of working age and those still in school, spent their time. Over the course of the war, young people between the ages of fourteen and seventeen constituted a quarter of the total labor force. In 1916 alone, this age group accounted for approximately 40 percent of the industrially employed workforce. Youth employment continued to grow throughout the war. The most dramatic increases occurred in industries directly related to war needs, including mining, metal processing, and manufacturing chemicals, machines, and instruments.[22] Roger Chickering explains that these increases can be attributed to the

Deutschland (Stuttgart, 1927), 267; Chickering, *Imperial Germany and the Great War*, 113.

[20] For more on food shortages during World War I, see Belinda J. Davis, *Food, Politics, and Everyday Life in World War I Berlin* (Chapel Hill, 2000).

[21] Bessel, *Germany After the First World War*, 24; Donson, *Youth in the Fatherless Land*, 126; Flitner, "Der Krieg und die Jugend," 255–58; Linton, "*Who Has the Youth, Has the Future,*" 188–89, 200–01.

[22] Linton, "*Who Has the Youth, Has the Future,*" 197–200; Eve Rosenhaft, "Restoring Moral Order on the Home Front: Compulsory Savings Plans for Young Workers in Germany, 1916–1919," in Frans Coetzee and Marilyn Shevin-Coetzee, eds., *Authority, Identity and the Social History of the Great War* (Providence, 1995), 84.

"centrality of labor-intensive technologies to maintaining Germany's armies" and the enormous number of unskilled adult male workers that military conscription removed from the workforce. Even schoolchildren contributed to the war effort. Girls, for example, knitted socks and woolens for soldiers during school hours normally set aside for sewing instruction. During the Christmas season of 1914 and 1915, schoolchildren helped to prepare gift packages for the front. Schools also encouraged students to solicit donations and, in some regions, rewarded those who reached pre-set goals. Beginning in 1916, students helped to gather any food that might alleviate home front food shortages, such as wild berries, acorns, wild vegetables, and resin.[23]

Nineteenth-century liberal political theory identified the family as the principal agent for shielding and nurturing children, but mobilization and conscription deeply limited many families' ability to fulfill this function.[24] Fathers became soldiers, mothers became factory workers, schools closed, and, in many cases, children were left to fend for themselves. Families fractured as they struggled to survive. Many sent children to live with relatives located in the countryside, at first to help with the harvest and later, during intense food shortages, for the simple reason that there young people might find enough food to eat. In some cases, it was welfare authorities that relocated children.[25]

Amid extensive handwringing about the war's impact on the family, anecdotal stories of rising immorality inspired wartime concerns about a perceptible "unruliness" and "waywardness" among adolescents and youth. Wartime observers attributed much of this increasing waywardness to inflated wartime wages. Youth who labored in manufacturing jobs did in fact experience an increase in their wages, sometimes by as much as 200 or 300 percent. A common wartime lament among reformers and educators was that industrially employed youth, particularly young men, were earning wages that outstripped their maturity. One commentator noted that some eighteen-year-olds were earning as much as 70 marks a week. Although research has shown that inflation and the high cost of living offset these remarkable increases, with the costs of room and board in some cases increasing by as much as 225 percent, these wartime

---

[23] Roger Chickering, *The Great War and Urban Life in Germany: Freiburg, 1914–1918* (New York, 2007), 134; For more on persistent employment problems, see Bessel, *Germany After the First World War*, 12–21; Flitner, "Der Krieg und die Jugend," 259.

[24] Domansky, "The Transformation of State and Society," 58.

[25] Flitner, "Der Krieg und die Jugend," 258.

impressions were partially accurate. Although young male workers typically earned less than their adult male counterparts, they were frequently paid more than adult women.[26] These higher wages, commentators worried, when combined with absent fathers, translated into dangerous levels of autonomy. In Oftersheim, a small town situated close to Heidelberg, for example, Catholic officials complained that young workers were too independent, earned too much, and were frivolous with their money, buying as many as twenty cigarettes a day, gambling, and spending their time and cash in pubs.[27]

This waywardness, commentators repeatedly warned, was a matter of national concern, particularly if it generated increases in juvenile criminality. Albert Hellwig, a jurist and wartime commentator on youth criminality, explained that in the first months of war, rates of juvenile criminality had dipped, implying that the conflict was exercising a positive influence on young people. But by early 1915 a perceptible increase in the growing "unruliness" of both male and female youth had taken place, a shift that translated into higher rates of criminality among boys and elevated sexual promiscuity among girls. Between 1913 and 1918, he reported, the number of adolescents convicted of property crimes increased by 57.4 percent. Boys constituted a significant majority of these convicted juvenile offenders.[28] Although many juvenile crimes originated in wartime shortages, reformers and military authorities identified waywardness, in all of its forms, as a growing and national problem.

Beginning in 1915, military authorities revealed a willingness to use restrictive policies to combat perceived waywardness and unruliness among youth. Over the course of the war, nineteen deputy commanding generals limited young people's alcohol consumption, seventeen banned smoking for minors, fifteen restricted the types of movies young people could see, and twelve instituted curfews for young people.[29] And, as

---

[26] Dickinson, *The Politics of German Child Welfare*, 114–15; Rosenhaft, "Restoring Moral Order," 84; Wilhelm Bloch, "Die Wirkung des Krieges auf die Jugendlichen," *Zentralblatt für Vormundschaftswesen Jugendgerichte und Fürsorgeerziehung*, May 25, 1915, 38; Linton, "*Who Has the Youth, Has the Future*," 202; Donson, *Youth in the Fatherless Land*, 149.

[27] "Verführung der Jugend betr.," Erzbischöfliche Pfarrkuratie in Oftersheim to Erzbischöfliches Ordinariat, January 28, 1918, Erzbischöfliches Archiv-Freiburg, B2-48-4.

[28] Dr. Albert Hellwig, *Der Schutz der Jugend vor erziehungswidrigen Einflüssen* (Langensalza, 1919), 7; Daniel, *The War from Within*, 160–61.

[29] Dickinson, *The Politics of German Child Welfare*, 116–17.

previously noted, an overwhelming majority closely regulated the retail trade in pulp fiction and wartime trash.

When Germany went to war in 1914, so too did Heinz Brandt, Horst Kraft, and Konrad Götz, pamphlet-fiction protagonists who, week after week, engaged in frontline heroics and death-defying adventures. By 1916, according to contemporary estimates, eighteen different series with military themes were in circulation in Germany, with some series comprising as many as seventy separate installments.[30] Prominent titles from the era included *War Volunteer* (*Kriegsfreiwillig*), *War and Love* (*Krieg und Liebe*), *Our Men in Uniform* (*Unsere Feldgrauen*), *Spies* (*Spione*), *In the Storm of Bullets* (*Im Kugelregen*), *The Iron Cross* (*Das eiserne Kreuz*), *For Germany's Honor* (*Um Deutschlands Ehre*), *The War* (*Der Krieg*), and *In Enemy Territory* (*In Feindesland*).[31]

These wartime series were, on many levels, derivatives of the hero-centered pamphlet format that had been electrifying German readers since 1905. In the decade following the arrival of *Buffalo Bill* and *Nick Carter* pamphlets in Germany, entrepreneurial publishers had introduced readers to numerous protagonists who quickly became mainstays of the pamphlet industry, including Wanda von Brannburg, Captain Stürmer, Sitting Bull, Ethel King, Dick Turpin, Texas Jack, Sherlock Holmes, and Lord Lister. This genre proved to be lucrative. In the years preceding World War I, contemporaries estimated that publishers were selling as many as 300 million pamphlet stories a year and generating as much as 60 million marks in annual revenue. Publishers who were eager to capitalize on popular interest in the war quickly relocated popular prewar heroes into the trenches and theaters of the front line. As wartime critic Wilhelm Tessendorff noted in his 1916 study of the pulp fiction industry, in the eighty installments of the series *Heinz Brandt* published before the war, the titular hero served in the French Foreign Legion. Beginning with pamphlet number 81, Heinz and his brother Fritz turned "a new page" and became model soldiers in the German army.[32]

[30] Heinz J. Galle, *Groschenhefte: Die Geschichte der deutschen Trivialliteratur* (Frankfurt am Main, 1988), 93; Samuleit, *Kriegsschundliteratur*, 8–9, 15; "Kriegsschundliteratur," *Pädagogische Zeitung* 45 (April 20, 1916), 218.

[31] Tessendorff, *Die Kriegsschundliteratur*, 17.

[32] Donson, *Youth in the Fatherless Land*, 103; Fullerton, "Toward a Commercial Popular Culture," 498, 500; Huck, "American Dime Novels," 111; Hans-Friedrich Foltin, ed., *Lord Lister, genannt Raffles, der große Unbekannte: 10 Lieferungshefte in einem Band* (Hildesheim, 1979); Dr. Ernst Schultze, *Die Schundliteratur: ihr Wesen, ihre Folgen, ihre Bekämpfung* (Halle an der Saale, 1925), 20–29; Tessendorff, *Die Kriegsschundliteratur*, 2.

Critics complained that these wartime series shared several unfortunate similarities with their prewar counterparts. Both genres were mass-produced, cheaply made, and poorly written. Widely distributed through newsstands, shops, and peddlers, both were designed to generate massive profits by appealing to "base instincts" rather than by seeking to educate or ennoble readers. Consequently, both lacked any redeeming literary or cultural value. And both, unfortunately, proved to be wildly popular with adolescent and teenaged boys and girls.[33] The root cause of these similarities lay not only in the proven success of the pamphlet formula but also in the fact that the same "shabby publishing houses" that had manufactured penny dreadfuls before 1914, firms such as Mignon and Verlag Moderner Lektüre, became publishers of pulp fiction stories set against the backdrop of war. As Paul Samuleit lamented in his 1916 assessment, "the same swift quills" that had produced a nearly endless stream of adventure and criminal stories in peacetime had taken up the topic of war with "astonishing swiftness and unison."[34]

Most aggravating for critics was these stories' tendency to sensationalize the war. "The content of these stories is the same in every series," Tessendorff observed. In the space of thirty-two pages, "scoundrels [*Galgenvögel*]" and "quick scribblers [*Schnellschmierer*]" used the language and imagery of patriotism to turn the war into a profitable commodity. To illustrate his point, Tessendorff recounted the plot of an installment in the series *Um Deutschlands Ehre*. This particular pamphlet misappropriated the true story of Lieutenant Otto Weddigen, captain of the SM *U-9*, a submarine credited with sinking three British ships (HMS *Cressy*, HMS *Hogue*, and HMS *Aboukir*) on September 22, 1914. The fictional account featured Lieutenant Erich Hart and five other sailors who had been taken prisoner by British officials after surviving the sinking of their own ship, the SS *Königin Luise*. As the story develops, the six men escape British detention and connive their way onto the *Cressy*, a vessel preparing to transport British volunteers to France along with two other ships, the *Hogue* and the *Aboukir*. Hart quickly takes control of the ship's telegraph and signals nearby German ships with information about the three cruisers' departure. The dispatch reaches the *U-9*, and the German

---

[33] Samuleit, *Kriegsschundliteratur*, 5–13; Tessendorff, *Die Kriegsschundliteratur*, 3, 9; Dr. R. v. Erdberg, "Schundliteratur," *Volksbildungsarchiv: Zentralblatt für Volksbildungswesen* 5 (1917), 28–29.

[34] Tessendorff, *Die Kriegsschundliteratur*, 2; Donson, *Youth in the Fatherless Land*, 92; Samuleit, *Kriegsschundliteratur*, 9.

submarine swiftly sinks the three British ships. Hart and his fellow sailors are flung into the sea but the *U-9* quickly rescues them. Tessendorff objected to the way in which this and other stories manipulated, exaggerated, and thereby trivialized the actual event.[35]

Samuleit similarly criticized these cheap stories for their "ridiculous" content. He singled out the series *Feldgrau* to illustrate his point. This series repeatedly placed its hero, Cadet Officer Helmut Steinburg, in outlandish and unlikely scenarios intended to thrill readers rather than portray the war accurately. In one installment, von Steinberg encounters a dead soldier still clutching his horse, having been killed by a bullet wound that turned into quick-moving tetanus. In another pamphlet, Steinburg discovers an undamaged airplane sitting in a forest meadow. Despite never before having been in such a plane, he and a fellow soldier successfully fly a reconnaissance mission before enemy fire shoots them down. Steinburg survives uninjured although his companion is severely wounded. The hero must survive, Samuleit wryly noted, so that he can thrill readers in the next 145 installments.[36]

These stories' tendency to focus on a singular hero who accomplishes extraordinary feats, often on his own initiative, inflamed critics. The evidence for this frustration can be found in the distinction reformers and authorities drew between "wartime trash" and patriotic "wartime literature." Both genres located heroes at the front, provided young readers with "violent, graphic war stories," and glorified soldiers who, on their own or in small groups, accomplished amazing feats of bravery and cunning. And yet there were subtle and obvious differences between the two genres. On a basic level, "wartime trash" stories appeared in paperback while "war literature" was most likely to be published in hardback.[37] More glaring differences emerged when it came to plot and structure. According to its critics, wartime penny dreadfuls were more likely to celebrate the "individual hero" and mitigate the importance of the average soldier who steadfastly remained on the front line. These stories also ignored the contributions of the nation's military commanders. Tessendorff wrote, "While in actuality, the ingenuity of military

[35] Tessendorff, *Die Kriegsschundliteratur*, 4–6; Otto Weddigen, *Lieut. Otto Weddigen's Account of the U-9 Submarine Attack* (Ipswich, 2009); Bodo Herzog, "Vom 50 Jahren: der Erfolg von Weddigen am 22. September 1914," *Marine-Rundschau: Zeitschrift für Seewesen* 61 (1964), 271–75.

[36] Samuleit, *Kriegsschundliteratur*, 16–17.

[37] Samuleit, *Kriegsschundliteratur*, 5; Tessendorff, *Die Kriegsschundliteratur*, 3, 9; Erdberg, "Schundliteratur," 28–29; Donson, *Youth in the Fatherless Land*, 104.

leaders and the loyal service of every soldier determines the battle, [in wartime pamphlet stories] Heinz Brandt, Helmut von Steinberg, or some other hero determines the outcome. He discerns the advantageous opportunity, sees the enemy's failures and weaknesses, and designs the attack plan. In vain we might search for the names of the true heroes of our glorious victories. We will find neither the names of [Paul von] Hindenburg nor [August von] Mackensen; they are insignificant when compared with Heinz Brandt, Helmut von Steinberg, and others." Conversely, as historian Andrew Donson explains, "wartime literature" tended to depict the protagonist as "a monolithic, machine-like German soldier" who, while "loyal and fierce," "lacked all personality." These preferred stories were also more likely to celebrate national heroes such as Hindenburg. In spite of their inherent violence, or perhaps because the publishers of these stories had successfully persuaded military authorities that such stories were "beneficial to the war effort," deputy commanding generals were less likely to censor "wartime literature" while they targeted *Kriegsschundliteratur* with much greater zeal.[38]

The line between worthless pulp fiction and redeeming patriotic literature proved to be murky. Take, for example, the case of *Kriegsfreiwillig*, a popular wartime pamphlet series. The second installment in the series, subtitled "Kasernenleben," or "Life in the Barracks," told the story of young Heinz Hochberg and his sister Marta, both of whom had committed their energies and lives to the war effort. The story opens with Heinz's first days in the army and traces his evolution from new recruit to model soldier. His sister, meanwhile, joins the Red Cross to help care for wounded soldiers. While Heinz passes his days absorbing military life, Marta travels to the front lines of Belgium to provide medical care to injured men. Heinz learns how to march, make his bed, and patrol the front lines; Marta helps to repel a nighttime raid on the medical outpost. Both are ready to lay down their lives for Germany.[39] Some military censors identified the series as "wartime trash," perhaps because of its focus on these two characters, and included it in their trash index; others did not. Bavarian officials, for example, placed it on their registry, while military censors in Baden elected not to do so.[40] As Kaspar Maase notes,

---

[38] Tessendorff, *Die Kriegsschundliteratur*, 7; Donson, *Youth in the Fatherless Land*, 99–104.

[39] *Kriegsfreiwillig: Erlebnisse eines Primaners, Kasernenleben*, No. 2, 1915.

[40] Samuleit, *Kriegsschundliteratur*, 45; "Bekanntmachung: Die Bekämpfung der Schundliteratur betreffend," *Verordnungsblatt. Gr. Bad. Korps-Kommando der Gendarmerie*, July 29, 1918, 123–30, Generallandesarchiv Karlsruhe (hereafter GLAK), 235/35545.

the distinction between war trash and war literature was "absolutely arbitrary."[41]

Despite the subjectivity involved in categorizing texts, critics of wartime pulp fiction were certain that wartime trash was likely to undermine war's capacity to positively shape the nation's youth. If carefully cultivated, they asserted, this wartime generation might become the "seed of a new Germany," one being birthed in the "bitter contractions and pain" of war. War, Samuleit asserted, had the potential to function as a "spectacular" educator for the next generation and solidify an appreciation for the values of self-sacrifice and service.[42] Conversely, "wartime trash" signified, as Hellwig noted in his wartime study of juvenile criminality, an "adverse educational influence [*erziehungswidrigen Einfluss*]."[43] This "adverse" characteristic originated, in part, from the formulaic devices that publishers and authors used to captivate readers. Furthermore, greedy publishers supplied young people eager for news from the front with stories that sensationalized the magnificent feats of their soldier-fathers as the "most foolish and dangerous adventure fantasy." Civilians were not unique in their frustration. In a 1916 decree targeting "wartime trash," military authorities in Kassel similarly complained that these pamphlets presented young readers with ridiculous depictions of the German army's greatest feats.[44]

Wartime explorations of youth in this time of war provide an outline of the type of youth social reformers hoped might emerge from this national struggle. In his 1915 text *German Youth and the War* (*Die deutsche Jugend und der Krieg*), pedagogue Ludwig Gurlitt praised the nation's youth for the readiness they had shown at war's beginning to serve their nation. He described the young men who headed into war as possessing a special mixture of burning enthusiasm, modesty, self-sacrifice, boldness, selflessness, and stoicism. On their own initiative and out of devotion to the fatherland, they had committed their lives to this national struggle. (In fact, a 1915 report issued by Prussian authorities revealed that, of 37,000 male students over the age of seventeen, 20,000 were currently and voluntarily serving in the military.) Their impressiveness extended to the

[41] Kaspar Maase, "'Schundliteratur' und Jugendschutz im Ersten Weltkrieg: Eine Fallstudie zur Kommunikationskontrolle in Deutschland," 4, https://hdms.bsz-bw.de/frontdoor/in dex/index/docId/398 (accessed October 5, 2016).

[42] Samuleit, *Kriegsschundliteratur*, 8.

[43] Dr. Albert Hellwig, *Der Krieg und die Kriminalität der Jugendlichen* (Halle, 1916), 160–61; Samuleit, *Kriegsschundliteratur*, 8.

[44] Tessendorff, *Die Kriegsschundliteratur*, 3–4; Samuleit, *Kriegsschundliteratur*, 40.

battlefield. In contradiction to enemy propaganda detailing the brutality of the German soldier, he asserted, a spirit of camaraderie ruled the German army. "Every [soldier]," Gurlitt wrote, "shares his last piece of bread, his last cigarette [and] leaves his cover to help his wounded comrade." The war, he contended, had also elicited a spirit of harmony and cohesiveness among these young men.[45]

When Germany entered into total war in 1916, youth acquired greater symbolic significance. Friedrich Wilhelm Foerster, a pacifist, illustrated this shift in his book *German Youth and the World War* (*Die deutsche Jugend und der Weltkrieg*). Much of his text advised teenaged boys and girls on how they should comport themselves during the war. Boys, he advised, should be ready to step in as part of a home front "replacement army [*Ersatzreserve*]" and compensate for the temporary or permanent absence of a father or older brother. They should function as a pillar of support to their mothers and help to keep their families financially afloat through their own employment. Conversely, he advised girls to model selflessness and devotion. Instead of describing a youth capable of serving the nation, as Gurlitt had done, he portrayed a youth worthy of the nation's enormous sacrifices. Particularly those who had lost a father or a brother in the war must rescue, through their own actions, the "moral legacy [*sittliches Vermächtnis*]" bequeathed to them by these war dead. Although those who had given their lives would never return, a disciplined, honorable, and steadfast youth might help to compensate and provide solace for their deaths.[46]

The key to transforming the war into a positive educational experience, one that might nurture these types of values, activists asserted, lay in controlling how young people encountered and perceived it. If penny dreadfuls with military themes and content constituted a corrosive educational influence, one likely to tarnish young people's appreciation of their nation's struggle and the sacrifice of their fathers and brothers, then the solution lay in preventing their exposure to such stories. One strategy for doing so was simply to eliminate the appeal these stories exercised on young people by using the good to drive out the bad. Provide students with better alternatives, Tessendorff counseled, and teach them to discriminate quality from trash. Another and more immediate approach, and one

---

[45] Ludwig Gurlitt, *Die deutsche Jugend und der Krieg* (Greiz, 1915), 32–35; Flitner, "Der Krieg und die Jugend," 256.

[46] Friedrich Wilhelm Foerster, *Die deutsche Jugend und der Weltkrieg: Kriegs- und Friedensaufsätze* (Leipzig, 1916), 9–15.

endorsed by Samuleit, was to encourage deputy commanding generals to use their expanded wartime powers to impose consumption controls on the retail pulp trade.[47]

Starting in 1915, in fact, military authorities throughout Germany began to make use of their wartime powers to create trash registries designed to limit the purchase of prewar and wartime penny dreadfuls. The first to do so was the deputy commanding general located in Münster, who referenced Article 9 of the 1851 Prussian Law of Siege as he published an index of texts that were no longer to be sold, openly displayed, or publicly advertised. This wartime registry, announced in December 1915, was sweeping in its reach. It restricted sales of prewar favorites such as *Nick Carter, Ethel King, Buffalo Bill, Lord Lister*, and *Texas Jack* as well as wartime series such as *Unsere Feldgrauen, Kriegsfreiwillige, Der Krieg*, and *Das eiserne Kreuz*. One month later, in January 1916, military authorities in Kassel similarly published a registry of prohibited texts. In the preamble to this decree, officials explained that the State of Siege law and the wartime suspension of freedom of the press had provided them with the legal means to protect the nation's youth by extinguishing their access to stories that romanticized criminality, recounted outlandish heroics, and misrepresented the feats of both the army and the nation. In March of that year, military authorities in Munich introduced their own registry and described it as a measure intended to protect adolescent youth. Authorities in Berlin published their own registry two weeks later.[48] By war's end, nearly every deputy commanding general had instituted similar decrees regulating pulp fiction.[49]

Authorities working in the nation's War Ministry expressed doubts in January 1916 as to whether the military should be engaged in censoring pulp fiction and wartime penny dreadfuls. On the one hand, they noted, the military's top priority should be censoring items that contravened the nation's military interests. On the other hand, these temporary wartime measures were unlikely to have a lasting impact on the trash trade.[50] Even Karl Brunner, a long-time anti-trash activist and Prussia's civilian censor before and during World War I, agreed that military ordinances against

---

[47] Samuleit, *Kriegsschundliteratur*, 8, 31; Tessendorff, *Die Kriegsschundliteratur*, 8.
[48] Samuleit, *Kriegsschundliteratur*, 38–52.
[49] Dickinson, *The Politics of German Child Welfare*, 116.
[50] Kriegsministerium, doc. no. 430/1.16.z.1, January 24, 1916, GLAK, 235/35546; Elisabeth Süersen, "Die Stellung der Militär- und Zivilbehörden zur Schundliteratur," *Volksbildungsarchiv: Beiträge zur wissenschaftlichen Vertiefung der Volksbildungsbestrebungen* 4 (October 1916), 211.

trash were only provisional controls that would disappear when the war
ended.[51] The determination of an overwhelming majority of deputy commanding generals to control the retail trade in trash and wartime penny
dreadfuls, despite these ambivalent comments from the War Ministry,
suggests that they viewed censorship as a device for both controlling the
retail pulp trade and surrounding youth with influences likely to induce
useful qualities, namely patriotism, loyalty, and selflessness.

In his 1916 analysis of the wartime pulp fiction industry, Samuleit
juxtaposed his criticism of wartime penny dreadfuls with assurances
that, up to this point, the nation's youth had proven itself capable of
shouldering the demands of war. Complaints that the war was fueling
both neglect and delinquent behavior in young people lacked substantia-
tion, he explained, while ample evidence proved that teenaged boys and
girls were actively supporting the war and, even more importantly, trans-
figuring into a generation that, after war's end, would be equal to the
challenges of reconstruction. This great resource, he reminded his readers,
was not an incidental outgrowth of war. Rather, it was the product of
a decades-long and society-wide commitment to popular education and
a determination among educators to eliminate any "pests [*Schädlinge*]"
and to root out any "weeds [*Unkraut*]" that might damage young people's
intellectual growth. It was this commitment to replacing the bad with the
good, to surrounding youth with positive influences, he promised, that
would allow Germany to both persevere and win the war. One key
component, he explained, was the fight against "wartime trash."

---

[51] XIV Armeekorps Stellvertretendes Generaloberkommando, doc. no. 3065, May 22,
     1916, GLAK, 235/35546; Karl Brunner, "Der Kampf gegen die Schundliteratur im
     Kriege," *Deutsche Strafrechts-Zeitung* 3 (1916), 138–39.

3

Recruiting Japanese Boys for the Pioneer Youth Corps of Manchuria and Mongolia

L. Halliday Piel

In the decade before World War II, the Japanese government initiated a policy to underwrite the migration of thousands of Japanese farmers to Manchuria. As part of this policy, the Pioneer Youth Corps of Manchuria and Mongolia (Man-Mō kaitaku seishōnen giyūgun), hereafter referred to as the *giyūgun* or Pioneer Youth Corps, sent approximately 86,000 male adolescents between 1938 and 1945 to reclaim farmland in northern Manchuria and Inner Mongolia. Yet, for decades after the war, it remained forgotten by most Japanese citizens.

"The first time I heard of the existence of the *giyūgun* was ten years ago in 1997," wrote Arai Emiko in the preface of her historical novel *The Boys' Manchuria*. "At the time, I was writing a series 'Remembered War Songs' for *Tokyo Newspaper* [*Tōkyō shinbun*], when someone asked me to include Pioneer Youth Corps songs. It was Aoki Kunio, a first-generation graduate of the Vanguard Training Center [Kyōdō kunren-sho]. As I had never heard of the Pioneer Youth Corps, and did not know the songs, Mr. Aoki kindly sent me enough documents to fill a cardboard box."[1] Intrigued, Arai accompanied sixty former members of the Pioneer Youth Corps to visit Harbin in northeast China, where more than fifty years earlier they had lived in camps and attempted to cultivate the land.

"We stood on the wide plain where some 3,000 bodies were said to lie," recalled Arai. "There was no memorial, no gravestone. When

The research for this article was supported by the Arts and Humanities Research Council (UK) research grant AH/J004618/1.
[1] Arai Emiko, *Shōnentachi no Manshū: Man-Mō kaitaku shōnen giyūgun no kiseki* (Tokyo, 2007), 206.

I thought of the people discarded in the fields, I was choked with emotion." She points out that from the Chinese perspective the boys were at the forefront of the Japanese invasion, but from the postwar Japanese perspective they were minors, abused by the military state.[2] About 24,000 died or disappeared, mostly during and after the Soviet invasion of August 9, 1945. In the words of the Nagano Prefecture History Teachers' Association, "The promise of receiving 20 *chōbu* [49 acres] of farm land as a reward for reclaiming virgin grassland was betrayed by the reality that most of the children who trained in camps in the homeland and overseas ended up losing their lives while defending Manchukuo, or while being forced to settle in the Soviet Union" in Siberian prison camps.[3]

The Pioneer Youth Corps first began to reemerge in the public consciousness after 1972, once diplomatic relations between Japan and China were reestablished in that year, allowing Japanese officials and journalists to visit China and speak to Japanese widows and orphans still trapped there decades after Japanese forces had withdrawn. In the 1980s, *giyūgun* survivor Sugawara Kōsuke garnered visibility as a legal activist for their repatriation. Some of the "left-behind persons [*zanryū hōjin*]" had been wives and children of Youth Corps graduates.[4] Thus, the corps reemerged tangentially in the shadow of the "left-behind persons" issue. Its peripheral position in national memory may also be due to the lack of the kind of heroic "last stand" that brought fame to kamikaze pilots and others. The cohort of survivors who were repatriated from China and the Soviet Union to Japan in the 1950s had returned without fanfare to a society busy rebuilding itself.

Although the Pioneer Youth Corps was a keystone of colonial emigration to Manchuria, it was not distinguished from adult farm emigration in the scholarship on Manchuria until 1973, when historian Kami Shōichirō, who aimed to correct what he saw as the neglect of children in historical studies, positioned it as child abuse and its participants as children, distinct from adult farmers. Kami himself had been recruited as a boy, but the war ended before he could serve. Referring to the supporting role

---

[2] Ibid., 208.

[3] Nagano-ken rekishi kyōikusha kyōgikai, ed., *Man-Mō kaitaku seishōnen giyūgun to Shinano kyōiku kai* (Tokyo, 2000), iii.

[4] Sugawara wrote a series of articles in the *Asahi Newspaper*. He took the stand in a 2003 lawsuit against the Japanese government by 612 plaintiffs seeking compensation for its slowness to repatriate them along with their Chinese children. The ongoing politics of the "left-behind persons" issue has been reported in English by BBC News, the *Japan Times*, and *Japan Focus*.

the *giyūgun* played in Japanese military strategy, Kami called it an unprecedented use of boys as "armed colonists" with almost no historical counterpart other than the children's crusade of medieval Europe.[5] Kami's view of the *giyūgun* is based on postwar concepts of human rights and social responsibility. More recently, Shiratori Michihirō has criticized Kami's victim narrative, while acknowledging that the *giyūgun* was not an extension of the adult experience. Rather, it was a form of wartime public education, emphasizing patriotic service to the nation.[6]

The Pioneer Youth Corps still awaits a proper evaluation in the English-language scholarship. There are three reasons to distinguish it from adult farm emigration: First, its main architects, Katō Kanji (1884–1967) and Tōmiya Kaneo (1892–1937), viewed the results of their 1932 farm settlement experiment as a failure and proposed that youth settlers would succeed where adult settlers had failed. They viewed adolescence as distinct from and possibly superior to full-fledged adulthood. Second, the methods of recruitment were adapted for elementary school children, and therefore the program was not merely an extension of adult emigration. Third, the vision of adolescence expressed by Katō and Tōmiya, and implied in the recruitment methods, resonates with the wartime reformulation of children as *shōkokumin* ("little nationals") under the 1940 National Education Ordinance. This reformulation enabled policymakers to draw on the labor of children in ways that had been discouraged in the previous era of Taisho liberalism (1912–1926).

Besides illuminating wartime notions of childhood and adolescence, the recruitment data collected by the program managers give insight into the motivations of ordinary boys, yielding a more nuanced picture of the popular support for the imperial project than might be assumed on the basis of the nationalistic propaganda for farm emigration that has been studied by Louise Young, Annika Culver, and others.[7] The motivations of the boys can be contextualized in overlapping spheres of influence: patriotism at school and in the training camps; the pragmatic realism of farm

[5] Kami Shōichirō, *Man-Mō kaitaku shōnen giyūgun* (Tokyo, 1973), 2, 8. Despite Kami's influence on the field of children's history, the Pioneer Youth were omitted in the seminal 1977 seven-volume *History of Japan's Children* (*Nihon kodomo no rekishi*), edited by Hisaki Yukio, and the subsequent 2007 *Japanese Children's History* (*Nihon kodomo shi*) by Moriyama Shigeki and Nakae Kazue. These general histories focus on the home front when they mention the war.

[6] Shiratori Michihiro, *Man-Mō kaitaku shōnen giyūgun shi kenkyū* (Sapporo, 2008), 2.

[7] Louise Young, *Japan's Total Empire: Manchuria and the Culture of Wartime Imperialism* (Berkeley, 1998); Annika Culver, *Glorify the Empire: Japanese Avant-Garde Propaganda in Manchukuo* (Vancouver, 2013).

culture; pockets of rebellion in the form of regional tenant farmer strikes; family circumstances; and, finally, the larger opportunities of empire and the constraints of war.

THE PROPOSAL FOR YOUTH EMIGRATION

Katō Kanji's *Petition Regarding the Formation of the Manchurian Pioneer Youth Corps*, co-signed by five others on November 11, 1937, was approved by the Japanese Diet and went into operation in 1938. An agricultural science graduate of the prestigious Tokyo Imperial University, Katō was an influential proponent of *nōhonshugi* ("agriculture-as-the-essence-ism"), a movement seeking to restore the primacy of the farm village as the moral and economic basis of the nation, in opposition to urbanization and industrialization. Some leaders of this "agrarian fundamentalism," as Thomas Havens calls it, demanded economic protection for the small producer against the large (often absentee) landowner. But Katō was among those who thought mass emigration overseas would relieve overpopulation and channel food resources back to the homeland.[8]

The takeover of Manchuria by the Kantōgun (Kwantung/Guāndōng Army) in 1931 (the "Manchurian Incident") provided Katō with a pretext to propose large-scale farm emigration to Manchuria. Katō was well connected with the Kantōgun, which had been guarding Japanese assets in Manchuria, in particular, the South Manchurian Railways Company (Mantetsu), acquired during the Russo-Japanese War of 1904–1905. Many army officers came from rural areas, and a radical faction among them plotted to defy the Japanese government, which they blamed for rural poverty and other issues. One of their acts of defiance, the Manchurian Incident, dragged the government into a colonial venture. Captain Tōmiya Kaneo, a Kantōgun plotter responsible for the 1928 assassination of Manchurian leader Zhāng Zuòlín, helped Katō design his farm emigration program to complement the Kantōgun's strategic plan to populate a buffer zone on the Soviet border with people it could trust.[9] When the military gained political power in 1932, Katō obtained

---

[8] Thomas Havens, *Farm and Nation in Modern Japan: Agrarian Nationalism, 1870–1940* (Princeton, 1974), 22, 127; Sandra Wilson, "The New Paradise: Japanese Emigration to Manchuria in the 1930s and 1940s," *International History Review* 17(2) (May 1995), 258.

[9] Wilson, "The New Paradise," 250; Young, *Japan's Total Empire*, 385.

support to launch an adult emigration program. In 1937, he turned his attention toward youth, hoping to train a more resilient type of emigrant.[10]

His *Petition* begins by declaring that the recent "China Incident" (the formal start of war in 1937 between Japan and Chiang Kai-shek's Chinese nationalist government) is an emergency requiring patriotic emigrants to secure Manchuria by establishing farm villages there. "And as the most effective and appropriate practical means," he continues, "we hereby propose a Manchuria Pioneer Youth Corps, and call for immediate deployment."[11] Thus, youth colonists were presented as the "most effective" tool of imperialism.

The list of their functions seems a tall order for mere adolescents, aged fifteen to nineteen: land reclamation, farm establishment, village construction, paramilitary policing of rail lines, ideological support, immigration policy support, and, finally, village leadership, after completing a training program consisting of a two-month course in Ibaraki Prefecture, Japan, followed by a three-year course in camps in Manchuria. The responsibilities are justified as patriotic service, now expected of most citizens under the emerging "National Spiritual Mobilization Campaign [*Kokumin seishin sōdō undō*]."[12] The Ministry of Education had just released its March 1937 *Fundamentals of Our National Polity* (*Kokutai no hongi*), teaching schoolchildren that society was based on the unity of sovereign and subject, and that loyalty to the emperor would be "the sole way in which we subjects may live."[13] Government councils and mass organizations were examining how schoolchildren might be mobilized for the war effort. In the following year, schoolchildren would be deployed to farms during school vacations.

The Pioneer Youth Corps was therefore in the vanguard of a trend to enlist the labor of persons under the age of twenty (i.e., not full adults) for the war effort. In government circles, education advisors increasingly used

[10] Nagano-ken, ed., *Shinano kyōiku kai*, 26, 29.

[11] Katō Kanji, et al., "Man-Mō kaitaku seishōnen giyūgun hensei ni kansuru kenpakusho," reprinted in Shiratori Michihiro, ed., *Man-Mō kaitaku seishōnen giyūgun kankei shiryō*, 7 vols. (Tokyo, 1993), vol. I, 5–6.

[12] From later strategic plans and recruiting literature, we learn that about 300 youths were to be chosen from each graduating class in Manchuria to lead the adult settlers. These leaders were distinguished by the variant term *giyūtai* (volunteer corps) though some documents use the word *senkentai* (forward dispatch corps): Shiratori, *Giyūgun shi kenkyū*, 1–2, 6.

[13] Wm. Theodore de Bary, et al., eds., *Sources of Japanese Tradition: 1600 to 2000, Part Two: 1868 to 2000* (New York, 2006), 279.

the term *shōkokumin* ("little countrymen") instead of *jidō* ("child"), reflecting the wartime responsibilities expected of children. In the November 1940 issue of *Education* (*Kyōiku*), child psychologist Hatano Kanji (1905–2001) criticized "child's mind-ism" (*dōshin-shugi*, or child-centered romanticism), a phrase signifying the sentimental view of the child in the children's literature of the liberal Taisho era. He argued that it infantilized children, extending their childhood unnaturally. "Children today are consumers," he wrote. "You see them loitering, doing nothing, sponging off their parents." Yet, because they want to grow up, "children yearn to be included in the productive life of adults more than one expects." He believed that they should be allowed to do so with proper guidance from adults.[14]

Similarly, the *giyūgun* assumed that youngsters would happily volunteer to join without coercion. Although the total-war orientation of the militarists in power promoted children's inclusion in the war effort, it does not mean that children were uniformly viewed as little adults. Recent scholarship shows that the romantic image of the "innocent child" had not disappeared but continued to be employed in militaristic propaganda, in which, for example, children play soldier or interact with soldiers. For adult viewers, it sentimentalizes war, as Sabine Frühstück points out. For children, it "promises acceleration into adulthood."[15] During the war, Ogawa Mimei (1882–1961), one of the founders of the "child's mind" movement, advised children's authors to "join the energetic *shōkokumin*," whom he portrayed as passionately leading the way toward "a new beginning."[16] It is perhaps this romantic faith in the energy of the young that led the Kantōgun General Staff in July 1937 to envisage a plan to train "pure and innocent farm boys" to develop "the spirit necessary for true nation-building farm folk."[17] Katō's petition to the Diet drew on this plan. Kami believes that the idea of recruiting adolescents came initially from Katō's friend, army officer Tōmiya.

Between 1932 and 1935, hundreds of adult settlers in Manchuria gave up and returned to Japan. The first wave of settlers was overwhelmed by

---

[14] Hatano Kanji, "Jidō bunka no taisei," reprinted in Katō, et al., eds., *Jidō bunka to gakkō kyōiku no senchū sengo* (Kanagawa, 2012), 247.

[15] Sabine Frühstück, "On the Moral Authority of Innocence," conference paper presented at "Childs Play: Multi-Sensory Histories of Children and Childhood in Japan and Beyond," University of California at Santa Barbara, February 27, 2015.

[16] Ogawa Mimei, "Kaihō sen to hossoku no ketsui," in Nippon Shōkokumin bunka kyōkai, ed., *Shōkokumin bunka ron* (Tokyo, 1945), 36.

[17] Sakuramoto Tomio, *Man-Mō kaitaku shōnen giyūgun* (Tokyo, 1987), 31.

Chinese resistance. The second wave was beset by a mysterious mental illness that came to be called *tonkonbyō* (land reclamation camp disease), causing listlessness and extreme self-withdrawal. Tōmiya's evaluation concluded that three types of "weak character" were most susceptible to *tonkonbyō*: school dropouts without agricultural experience, relatively affluent persons seduced by "Manchuria fever" in the media, and "long-haired, high-collar" young men (a euphemism for stylish urbanites). He recommended recruiting graduates of higher elementary school (*kōtō shōgakkō*, a two-year optional program after the six years of mandatory elementary school) as well as economic immigrants, and "pure and innocent youngsters [*junsui no nenshōsha*]."[18]

Tōmiya died before he could see his idea fulfilled by the Pioneer Youth Corps, which Kami maintains was founded on the notion that youth were "flexible in mind and body."[19] In Sakuramoto Tomio's words, the youth were presented as "saviors" who would come to the aid of the adult farmers, men typically past military age (over the age of forty-four).[20] A photograph in *Manchuria Illustrated* (*Manshū gurafu*) of a woman working in the field with a baby on her back – a symbol of safety and fertility according to Culver – was accompanied by a caption promising that the corps of "picked youths" "has conquered every difficulty and has proved the possibility of Japanese emigration to Manchuria."[21] This optimism in the power of youth similarly informed Sampō, the Greater Japan Industrial Patriotic Association, which in 1941 expressed hope that youth brigades placed in Japanese munitions factories would police the morals and behavior of adult workers.[22]

At the same time there was anxiety about delinquent youth, as David Ambaras explains. Police regularly rounded up factory youth milling about the entertainment districts of Tokyo after work.[23] Katō appeals to this anxiety in the *Petition*, when, after providing a rough budget and listing the mass organizations that could be called on to provide support, he writes:

Based on the population census, there are about 1,500,000 farm boys between age fifteen and eighteen, of whom about 700,000 have to leave their villages and go

---

[18] Kami, *Man-Mō kaitaku*, 22, 25–26.
[19] Ibid., 84.
[20] Sakuramoto, *Man-Mō kaitaku*, 35.
[21] Culver, *Glorify the Empire*, 126.
[22] David R. Ambaras, *Bad Youth: Juvenile Delinquency and the Politics of Everyday Life in Modern Japan* (Berkeley, 2006), 180–81.
[23] Ibid., 170–71.

elsewhere for work. They congregate in the cities, where some remain unemployed, others attract the bad elements of society, or else they become the cause of social problems and thought crimes, thereby becoming a cancer for the future of the national people.[24]

Here, "thought crimes" was a euphemism for communism and other ideological threats to the imperial system. Katō's readers would have been aware of the history of tenant farmer strikes in impoverished rural areas, fueling the spread of political radicalism.

In Nagano Prefecture, for example, silkworm income collapsed during the Great Depression, and prefectural authorities estimated that the number of starving children in 1932 rose from 966 in June to 4,506 by September. Concurrently, the number of tenant-farmer strikes increased from 70 incidents in 1931 to 269 in 1934. With the formation of the Nagano Branch Teachers Union (Kyōrō Nagano shibu) in July 1932, local schools became centers of activism. In a government crackdown on Communists in 1933, known as the "February 4 Incident," police arrested 137 teachers and 56 school principals for opposing the Manchurian invasion and the extra-constitutional "Emperor System." The Ministry of Education took measures to tighten its grip on teachers, while Nagano's Shinano Education Association added emigration to Manchuria to its platform on combating the spread of communism in schools. Nagano Prefecture would contribute the greatest number of boys to the Pioneer Youth Corps. On the national level, the government launched the Rural Economic Revitalization Campaign in 1932, and by 1936 it was justifying emigration to Manchuria in terms of this campaign.[25] Hence, Katō's proposal to keep underemployed rural youth out of trouble by sending them to Manchuria already resonated with government policy.[26]

Katō also understood the need for economic incentives to persuade parents to let their sons move far away. He wrote that if the program "opens the door to a life that fulfills their hopes, and offers a more meaningful service to the nation, youth from around the country will spontaneously respond, and parents and elders will happily cooperate without reservations."[27] By "fulfill their hopes," he meant the possibility of

[24] Katō, et al., "Kenpakusho," 9.
[25] Mori Takemaro, "Colonies and Countryside in Wartime Japan: Emigration to Manchuria," *Asia-Pacific Journal: Japan Focus*, n.p., [2003], www.japanfocus.org/-Mori-Takemaro/1810 (accessed April 28, 2014).
[26] Nagano-ken, ed., *Shinano kyōiku kai*, 195–203.
[27] Katō, et al., "Kenpakusho," 10.

receiving an education and, after graduation, nine hectares of land. He and his readers understood that the household system based on primogeniture excluded younger sons from inheriting the family headship and property, and reduced their prospects for marriage. Thus, he specifically recommended that the program recruit "second and third sons." Katō had made the same promise of land to adults, who were likewise younger sons, so this aspect of the Pioneer Youth Corps was no different. The innovation was the promise of a training program that was presumably equivalent in value to middle school.

Since the 1910s, demand for postelementary school education had outstripped supply, leading to fiercer competition, as described by Mark Jones.[28] Postelementary education was financially inaccessible for many children. Recent scholarship on Japanese films of the 1930s reveals a rash of popular films with child protagonists depicting poor boys' aspirations for education.[29] Teacher and education researcher Kiyohara Michihisa wrote in *Education* in 1941 that boys and girls who left their rural elementary schools for industrial jobs in the city chose factories that offered continuing education. Quitting a job was usually related to disappointment with the education offered.[30] Katō's promise of free education in the Pioneer Youth Corps was surely calculated to appeal to the mindset of adolescents leaving home to find work.

However, there was a caveat: As Japan's leading ethnologist Yanagita Kunio (1875–1962) had pointed out in 1912, "book learning" could help boys become office clerks, but it would not turn them into farmers. Yanagita, who wished to preserve rural folk culture as the essence of Japanese spirit, criticized school education, as Melek Ortabasi explains, for "inspiring in its students a desire to *leave* the farm, not return to it."[31] To agrarian fundamentalists, leaving the farm meant the weakening of family and village ties, and the corrupting influence of modern Western ideas in the cities. Rural educators in the 1930s experimented with "home place studies [*kyōdo kyōiku*]" to foster local pride.[32] Agricultural "youth

[28] Mark A. Jones, *Children as Treasures: Childhood and the Middle Class in Early Twentieth-Century Japan* (Cambridge, MA, 2010).

[29] Harald Salomon, "Children in the Wind: Reexamining the Golden Age of Childhood Films in Early Showa Japan," conference paper presented at "Childs Play: Multi-sensory Histories of Children and Childhood in Japan and Beyond," University of California at Santa Barbara, February 27, 2015.

[30] Kiyohara Michihisa, "Kōba junkai ki," *Kyōiku*, 9(11) (1941), 49–59.

[31] Melek Ortabasi, *The Undiscovered Country: Text, Translation, and Modernity in the Work of Yanagita Kunio* (Cambridge, MA, 2014), 183–84.

[32] See Kären Wigen, "Teaching About Home: Geography at Work in the Prewar Nagano Classroom," *Journal of Asian Studies* 59(3) (August 2000), 550–74.

schools [*seinen gakkō*]," offering part-time and night classes to working youth, began to emphasize, in the words of two school directors, the "cultivation of character related to the land" and "the backbone or core of the village" rather than simply teaching skills for employment.[33] However, the severe labor shortage during the war accelerated the migration of youths to the cities for jobs in the munitions industry. Therefore Katō's *Petition* may be understood as an attempt to keep the idealized farm village intact by transposing it to Manchuria, where presumably there was enough land for everyone, while providing an education to maintain village integrity.

As outlined above, Katō presented the Pioneer Youth Corps as a way to serve the homeland, build the empire, defeat communism, combat rural poverty, and preserve farm culture. Implicit in his *Petition* is the idea that youth under the age of twenty, still too young for military conscription (at least in 1937 – the minimum age declined as the war went on), would be more effective than adults at eventually achieving these goals because of their purity, innocence, and eagerness to learn. This view accorded with the wartime reformulation of children as *shōkokumin* with responsibilities to the state. Youngsters' childlike innocence now signified malleability rather than immaturity.

RECRUITING PIONEER YOUTH

Survey questionnaires filled out by recruits in the main training center in Uchihara City, Ibaraki Prefecture, show that recruiters reached Katō's target audience. In 1938, most recruits were second or third sons aged fifteen or sixteen (70.2 percent) who came from farm villages (90.7 percent). The majority had completed youth school (33.5 percent) and almost half higher elementary school (47.5 percent).[34] Of those who answered the April 1940 survey, 13 percent were class leaders or assistant class leaders, talented youth who might be eager for more education.[35] Of the nine prefectures that contributed more than 2,000 recruits in 1942, four were in the sericulture region of central Japan, and two were in the Tohoku region, both areas severely affected by the Great Depression.[36]

---

[33] Henshū l'inkai, *Nagano-ken sangyō kyōiku 100 nen shi* (Nagano, 1986), 58–59.
[34] Sakuramoto, *Man-Mō kaitaku*, 138, 140; *Kaku shu tōkei zuhyō*, reprinted in Shiratori, ed., *Kankei shiryō*, vol. II, 176, 179.
[35] Sakuramoto, *Man-Mō kaitaku*, 137–38.
[36] Nagano-ken, ed., *Shinano kyōiku kai*, 8.

The Land Reclamation Bureau produced child-friendly pamphlets. They were written in simple sentences with fewer *kanji* (Chinese characters) and more *furigana* (pronunciation glosses) than found in a newspaper article of the period. One example, *You Too Can Become a Pioneer Youth* (*Anata mo giyūgun ni naremasu*), is produced almost entirely as a cartoon sequence, from the first scene, in which a boy asks his family for permission to join the *giyūgun*, to the last page, showing the promised lifestyle in Manchuria. The tone is light-hearted; the figures of the pioneer youths are childlike, smaller than the adults (parents and teachers), with round, neotenous heads.

Another way to attract the young was through popular music and fiction. The aforementioned legal activist Sugawara Kōsuke recalled falling in love with a fantasy of endless grassy plains, as portrayed by the "Song of the Mounted Bandit" ("Bazoku no uta").[37] The "mounted bandits" were Japanese right-wing outlaws of the 1910s, operating in defiance of the Taishō government to organize Manchurian rebels against the Chinese government. A famous bandit was the sixteen-year-old Kohinata Hakurō, a former newspaper boy who in 1916 ran away to Manchuria, where he joined the Gen'yōsha (Dark Ocean Society) led by ultranationalist Tōyama Mitsuru (1855–1944). His exploits inspired several adventure stories serialized in the children's magazines *Boys' Club* (*Shōnen kurabu*) and *Boys of Japan* (*Nihon no shōnen*) during the 1920s.[38]

Sugano Masao, who joined the first wave of Pioneer Youth when he was eighteen, was inspired by the agrarian vision of the farm educator, poet, and children's author Miyazawa Kenji (1896–1933). Sugano wrote his own inspirational Manchuria novel, *Battling the Soil* (*Tsuchi o tatakau*), receiving a prize in 1940 from the Ministry of Education for celebrating the ethic of hard work and the rough beauty of the frontier landscape. The ministry regularly arranged for letters and compositions by Pioneer Youth to be read in schools.[39] Sugano, however, was an unusual case, older than average, and unusually educated, having attended an agricultural high school. Interview subjects contacted by

---

[37] Kanegawa shinbunsha henshūkyoku hōdōbu, *Manshū rakudo ni kiyu: kenpei ni natta shōnen* (Yokohama, 2005), 27.

[38] Ueda Nobumichi, "Bazoku no uta, monogatari o kakeru bazoku," *Hōsho gekkan* (August 2002), n.p., http://nob.inernet.jp/note/note_23.html (accessed September 25, 2002).

[39] Itō Giichi, *Sugano Masao shōden*, quoted in Suzuki Keimori's blog, *Miyazawa Kenji no sato yori*, http://blog.goo.ne.jp/ (accessed May 26, 2014).

this author have relatively little memory of what they read as children compared to what they sang, and those raised in farm households said they had no children's books. After 1941, paper shortages limited extra-curricular reading materials, but children could still enjoy songs. As a boy, Kami was drawn to the *giyūgun* in part because of a catchy song, "We Are the Young Pioneer Corps." Written by an adolescent amateur (though professionally set to music), it became the most popular of several *giyūgun* songs solicited from the public for a radio contest.[40]

The power of popular music notwithstanding, survey results indicate that schoolteachers were the most effective recruiters. The majority of respondents claimed they joined because of a teacher (47 percent in 1941 and 56 percent in 1944). The media ranked second (13 percent) in 1944. Joining because of a parent was a distant third place (5 percent in 1941 and 8 percent in 1944).[41] It follows that recruitment efforts aimed at youth would focus heavily on schools. In 1941, Nagano's Shinano Education Association conducted a survey of homeroom teachers in charge of graduating seniors in higher elementary school, inquiring into successes and failures encountered during recruitment. The answers indicate that teacher enthusiasm and personal connections, such as knowing a *giyūgun* recruit, were helpful. Efforts include showing films about the *giyūgun*, letting Pioneer Youths address the class, and inviting the local emigration committee to answer questions from concerned parents.[42]

"Land reclamation teams" in the senior year of higher elementary school were not uncommon. Even elementary schools sometimes organized fifth- and sixth-graders into "Asia Development" brigades for boys (*Kōa shōnen tai*) and girls (*Kōa shōjo tai*).[43] The Shinano Association produced a *Manchurian Reader* to teach about the region's geography, its peoples, and the Japanese development projects there. According to the preface, the reason was, "So they will have the right attitude and a proper understanding of the mission ... and be a help in the development of Mongolia and Manchuria." The significance of such strategies is that children too young to join were being primed in advance for colonial emigration, regardless of whether or not they were planning to emigrate.[44]

[40] Kami, *Man-Mō kaitaku*, 45.
[41] Ibid., 141.
[42] Nagano-ken, ed., *Shinano kyōiku kai*, 88–89.
[43] Sakuramoto, *Man-Mō kaitaku*, 154, 180.
[44] Nagano-ken, ed., *Shinano kyōiku kai*, 16, 221.

Sakuramoto writes that, based on the success of land reclamation brigades in higher elementary school, the Land Reclamation Office and the Ministry of Education cooperated on a plan to expand the recruitment efforts to youth outside the public school system by establishing land reclamation brigades in twenty-six youth groups and youth schools in several prefectures. In this way, boys (and girls) in the workforce could be reached and exposed to pioneer farming, Manchurian development, and the spirit of service to the empire.[45] Not discussed here, though it was carried out concomitantly, was a program to prime farm girls to become future brides of graduates of the Pioneer Youth program.[46]

Kōsaka Masayasu (1881–1967), a co-signer of Katō's *Petition*, solicited the cooperation of local administrators and youth group leaders. He was the director of the Greater Japan League of Youth Groups (Dai Nihon rengō seinendan), an umbrella organization created to centralize the informal youth groups that had existed in Japan since the eighteenth century. The tradition of community service (such as patrolling for fires and running errands for the elderly) could now be used for the needs of the state. On December 21, 1937, youth group leaders from around the country gathered together for a conference about the Pioneer Youth Corps. On January 20, 1938, they formed an association, which would become responsible for producing promotional articles for newsletters, and for mobilizing children to collect donations, such as pens, towels, and soap for care packages.[47] Schools and youth groups were ideally suited for recruiting youth, and may be considered parent organizations in the sense that they cultivated an ethic of learning through service, shared by the Pioneer Youth Corps.

EXPECTATIONS VERSUS REALITIES

The Pioneer Youth program was meant to produce robust settlers, but the youth fared no better than adults when faced with the environmental challenges. Situated in the north on the Soviet border, the camps were plagued by a short growing season and bitterly cold, dry winters with areas of permafrost that were unsuitable for rice, the Japanese staple food.

---

[45] Sakuramoto, *Man-Mō kaitaku*, 154.

[46] For information on brides, see Yeeshan Chan, *Abandoned Japanese in Postwar Manchuria: The Lives of War Orphans and Wives in Two Countries* (New York, 2011), 18.

[47] Kumagai Tatsujirō, *Dai Nihon Seinendan shi* (Tokyo, 1942), 382–83.

Patrolling in winter temperatures dropping well below freezing could result in serious frostbite. Though promised nine hectares of land, settlers rarely received more than 2.9 hectares. Perhaps that is why few *giyūgun* graduates took up the offer, choosing instead to join the army or the colonial administration, or return to Japan.[48] They were no more committed to preserving Katō's vision of the traditional small cultivator than the older settlers, who resorted to renting out their land to Chinese tenants.[49] The number of Pioneer Youth recruits dropped from 24,365 in the first year of operation (1938) to 9,508 in the following year. Although the numbers rose again, between 1940 and 1944 they averaged 11,746, well short of the initial goal of 30,000 per year.[50] The numbers of adult farm emigrants never matched targets either.[51]

The rate of the so-called camp illness, *tonkonbyō*, in the youth camps in Manchuria was as high as it had been among adult settlers, if not higher, according to Kami. Camp administrators (*kanbu*) decided that a maternal touch might help and called for educated matrons over the age of thirty to supervise the dormitories. However, with only 1 matron per 400 boys, not to mention their additional kitchen and infirmary duties, the women made little difference. The idea of substitute mothers demonstrates that the *kanbu* viewed the boys as children, but ironically many women quit because of sexual harassment. They were not mother figures in the eyes of some of their charges.[52]

Demoralization manifested itself in other ways. In a single year (1939), there were 21 arsons, 12 shootings, 12 altercations, and 6 suicides; moreover, 177 boys tried to run away, and 137 were jailed.[53] An inspector's report of unknown date (but issued after the 1939 Nomonhan Incident referenced therein) reports a lack of discipline at the large training camp in Nènjiang. Being few in number, the *kanbu* apparently pandered to the boys out of fear of rebellion, thereby "allowing a few bad apples to misguide the majority." The report suggested that moral education and a family-style (rather than military-style) atmosphere would improve morale and behavior.[54]

---

[48] Wilson, "The New Paradise," 234; Suleski, *Manshū no seishōnen zō*, 49.

[49] Wilson, "The New Paradise," 267.

[50] These figures represent numbers of recruits, not the numbers sent to Manchuria. A portion of the recruits dropped out during their training in Japan: Sakuramoto, *Man-Mō kaitaku*, 143.

[51] Wilson, "The New Paradise," 282.

[52] Kami, *Man-Mō kaitaku*, 84–86, 95, 97–98.

[53] Ibid., 99–100.

[54] "Nonkō kunren sho," reprinted in Shiratori, ed., *Kankei shiryō*, vol. VI, 55.

But this recommendation was not acted on, it seems. When Nakamura Akio from Nagano Prefecture was sent to the Tetsurei training camp in Běi'ān in 1944, there was no family ambiance. Prison-like reformatories had been set up to punish delinquents, following an incident in the Shōto camp in Bìnjiāng, in which youths had been killed. In his autobiography, Nakamura wrote that he was sent to the Chōsui Special Training Camp for boxing the ears of a kitchen boy without apology while he was kitchen supervisor. He endured a living hell of harsh discipline that caused some of his fellow inmates to wet their beds at night from stress.[55] Suleski proposes that Pioneer Youth actually resisted adults and rebelled against "unfair" supervisors.[56] This is entirely possible, since many came from regions with a history of tenant-farmer strikes, and the *kanbu* were clearly worried enough to found reformatories. But Nakamura attributes incidents of thieving, bullying, and suicide among boys to hunger rather than rebellion per se.[57]

Restrictions on interacting with local Chinese added to the boys' isolation and alienation. Nakamura, who once sneaked off base to sell his *shinmaki* (night dress) for cash in a Manchurian village, had to communicate by hand gesture because he did not know the local language.[58] Meanwhile Sugano, like many settlers, looked down on the Chinese, writing in his diary after a visit to a village in 1939, "I felt their filthy odor enveloping my whole body."[59] Sugawara, as a seventeen-year-old corps leader, was allowed to regularly visit the house of a certain Chinese contractor Wang, who eventually offered a daughter in marriage. But he had to decline.[60] Youth Corps members were prevented from forming family and kinship networks with local Chinese that might have provided a sense of integration and security.

The youths were no less susceptible to disease than the adults. The inspection report states that two to three boys fell sick each day of the inspector's visit in July, possibly due to contaminated well water. The infirmary was too small to handle the high number of cases (788 out of a total of some 2,000 boys). Tuberculosis was a recurring problem, and meals were not nutritionally balanced.[61] Sugano died of pleurisy

---

[55] Nakamura Akio, *Aa Man-Mō kaitaku shōnen giyūgun* (Tokyo, 2007), 34–35, 39–41.
[56] Suleski, *Manshū no seishōnen zō*, 49, 35.
[57] Nakamura, *Aa Man-Mō*, 88.
[58] Ibid., 57.
[59] Mariko Asano Tamanoi, *Memory Maps* (Honolulu, 2009), 42.
[60] Kanegawa shinbunsha, *Manshū rakudo ni kiyu*, 92–93.
[61] "Nonkō kunren sho," 54, 56.

contracted in the Nènjiang camp. When Oohaba Hiroyuki from Nagano Prefecture arrived in Nènjiang at age fourteen in 1944, typhus or dysentery broke out, killing more than ten members of his Seventh Company. For this reason, they were evacuated to Xing'ān (Khingan) Province in Inner Mongolia. Perhaps because of the state of the war, food was in short supply, and Oohaba and his fellow troopers were reduced to eating mice and snakes. Yearning for home, they made up a song mocking the "idiots" who joined the *giyūgun*.[62]

Katō sought "young men of high purpose," in the words of Havens, who would "work for Yamato [*Yamatobataraki*]" instead of "looking for security and a comfortable life."[63] Yet, the recruitment literature dangled the promise of wealth, so, arguably, the motives of those who joined were not so different from their adult predecessors. This may be one reason why they did not always live up to Katō's dreams. The pragmatism of these economic emigrants is evident in the reasons they give for joining. Nakamura wanted "to make a household I would not be ashamed of" and avoid being commandeered for factory work. In view of the wartime food shortages in Japan, he added, "We were encouraged by the thought that in Manchuria we would be able to eat to our heart's content."[64] For Kami, being the third son of a member of "the farm village proletariat" in Saitama Prefecture, joining seemed like the best way to combine his duty to the nation with "realistic aspirations."[65] An editor's feedback in a collection of student essays highlights the gap between the state's agenda and the prosaic motivations of the economic emigrant: "Y-kun needs to reflect on his motivations." Going to Manchuria, the editor explains, was not the same thing as emigrating to South America or Hawaii for a better life. "The attitude of his mother, telling the boys to join in order to get the promised ten *chōbu* of land does not match the aims of the Pioneer Youth Corps." The aim was to "build the nation" in the same way that Japan grew by annexing Hokkaidō.[66]

---

[62] Oohaba Hiroyuki, interview with NHK (Japan Broadcasting Corporation), filmed on 10 March 2009 and 16 June 2010 for "Kyōsangun ni dōin chōsensō made," *Sensō shōgen*, NHK archives, http://cgi2.nhk.or.jp/shogenarchives/shogen/ (accessed May 16, 2014).

[63] Yamato is an alternate name for Japan: Havens, *Farm and Nation*, 292.

[64] Nakamura, *Aa Man-Mō*, 11, 19.

[65] Kami, *Man-Mō kaitaku*, 6.

[66] Momota Sōji, ed., *Bokura no bunshō, watashitachi no shi* (1940), quoted in Sakuramoto, *Man-Mō kaitaku*, 26.

When the promises in the recruitment literature were not delivered and rumors of dangerous conditions in Manchuria trickled back to Japan through informal channels (as the press and letters home were censored), farmers undoubtedly concluded that the risks were too great. It appears that family members were dissuading boys from joining up. The number of boys who joined without family approval rose to almost half by 1942. In a survey, 322 respondents said that their mothers objected, while 216 said that their fathers objected. After fathers came grandmothers, brothers, sisters, aunts, uncles, and finally grandfathers, in that order.[67] The Ministry of Education's 1941 moral primer, *The Way of Subjects* (*Shinmin no michi*), stressed Confucian respect for parents and elders (filial piety) as the key to social stability and loyalty to the emperor.[68] Ironically, officials did not hesitate to override parental objections as needed. Sugawara managed to join by stealing the family seal (*inkan*) to stamp the application form without family consent. When his father went to the school to protest, his teacher lied and said that the decision was final.[69] The drop in recruitment figures suggests that, unlike Sugawara, more boys were heeding their parents' objections.

Sugawara's mother feared that he was only thirteen and too slight of build for what was surely just another "army." Her words hint at a desire to protect her son from the dangers of military service. Trying to avoid it would have been treasonous but, at the time of Sugawara's application (1942), settlers were still being exempted from the draft. Some applicants possibly took this into consideration, in which case, they would have been demoralized to discover, in the words of Mimura Michio of Nagano Prefecture, who joined in the same year as Sugawara, that the *giyūgun* "was not a land reclaiming unit; it was like a preparatory army for the Kantōgun." As the war drained men and resources, the Kantōgun increasingly used Pioneer Youths to protect supply lines and military stores, until they were old enough to be drafted (once the exemption was lifted in 1943). "I had no sense of being a farmer reclaiming the land," Mimura writes. "In the domestic training center [Ibaraki], the training was to strengthen our bodies. I have no recollection of weeding a field. It was mostly marching, and rifle and sword practice."[70]

[67] Sakuramoto, *Man-Mō kaitaku*, 139, 142–43.
[68] De Bary, et al., eds., *Sources of Japanese Tradition Part Two*, 305.
[69] Kanegawa shinbunsha, *Manshū rakudo ni kiyu*, 24–27.
[70] Mimura Micho, "Giyūgun wa shō guntai," in Nagano-ken, ed., *Shinano kyōiku kai*, 104–05.

CONCLUDING THOUGHTS

On the same day that the Americans dropped the atomic bomb on Hiroshima, Soviet forces crossed the Siberian border into Manchuria. In the line of their advance, just south of the border, lay the Pioneer Youth camps and half of the civilian farm settlements. Though farm settlers made up just 14 to 17 percent of total Japanese emigrants to Manchuria, because of their location, they suffered 45 to 50 percent of the casualties.[71]

While this tragedy is the reason for the ultimate failure of the Pioneer Youth Corps, it is also clear that Katō had underestimated the challenges of life in the Manchurian outback, and overestimated the power of cultivating "Japanese spirit" among "pure boys" to overcome these challenges and preserve the traditional Japanese village in a foreign environment. The boys who joined were initially willing, eager, and patriotic, and they lived up to their role as *shōkokumin*. But they were not blank slates. Most had been raised in the same poverty that shaped the commonsense survival strategies of their parents and elders. So, despite their training, they retained a certain degree of opportunism, which made them as likely to retreat as to advance in the face of insurmountable difficulty, much like the adult settlers before them.

---

[71] Kami, *Man-Mō kaitaku*, 5; Young, *Japan's Total Empire*, 411; Wilson, "The New Paradise," 273.

4

Defining the Ideal Soviet Childhood: Reportage About Child Evacuees from Spain as Didactic Literature

Karl D. Qualls

During their 400-mile walk from Málaga to Valencia, the five Molinas children, ages six to thirteen, endured lethal attack from land and air. Having already lost one of her children to the war, their mother decided to send her remaining children to the Soviet Union, although France and Belgium were also possibilities. "Many [families] cried. My mom cried," one of the children told a Soviet reporter. "Me – no. I knew that in Russia it would be good." The story of Remedio, Alfredo, Carmen, Manuel, and Francisco, while extreme in some respects, shares much with the stories of other refugee children. In what was thought by most participants to be a short-term evacuation to avoid bombing, some children thought it could be an exciting getaway, an adventure. For others, it was a frightening leap into the unknown. There is little typical about evacuation stories except the assurance of change. The stories of the nearly 3,000 Spanish refugee children as they transitioned in 1937–1938 from Civil War Spain to the USSR became didactic tools for Soviet mythmakers. Journalists and authors narrowed the official public narrative about the children's experiences on arriving in the USSR so as to construct the children as heroic symbols and models of the ideal Soviet childhood to which they adapted.[1]

I would like to thank the Howard Foundation and the Research and Development Committee at Dickinson College for funding to support this ongoing project.
[1] Quote from A. Gudimov, "Gosti iz Ispanii," *Izvestiia*, April 8, 1937. This is not the first study to look at children and youth as heroic models and symbols, and the Spanish children were neither the first nor last example. Pavlik Morozov and Zoya Kosmodemianskaia are certainly the best-known. See Catriona Kelly, *Comrade Pavlik: The Rise and Fall of a Soviet Boy Hero* (London, 2007); Adrienne M. Harris, "The Lives and Deaths of a Soviet Saint in the Post-Soviet Period: The Case of Zoia Kosmodem'ianskaia," *Canadian Slavonic Papers*

Stories about Spain's Civil War and the intervention by Germany and Italy had filled Soviet newspapers and short films for nearly a year. Children born in the Second Spanish Republic (1931–1939) lived during a tumultuous time: The monarch was overthrown, political violence increased as successive socialist and conservative governments seized power, and private and public debt grew as the economy faltered. Daily briefs from the various front lines of the Civil War were usually front-page news and accompanied by stories of German and Italian collaboration with General Francisco Franco, and communications from Spanish leaders with the Soviet Union and international bodies about the plight of the people and the democratically elected government in Spain. Throughout 1936, daily columns in Soviet newspapers kept the public informed about the progress of the war. In addition, periodic campaigns to raise money and awareness brought the war to a personal level. During September 1936, for example, the pages of the Communist Party's newspaper *Pravda* carried stories about women's meetings and fundraising for the women and children of Spain, including articles about individuals, families, and groups giving money for the cause. Short films such as *Spanish Children in the USSR* (1937) portrayed "apocalyptic images of a darkened and terrorized Spanish Republic" followed by "daybreak in sunny and tranquil Moscow."[2]

As the Spanish children began to arrive in the USSR in 1937, they entered a country undergoing profound changes, which led writers to use the stories of the *niños* as a tool of persuasion. In the Soviet Union, the 1930s was a decade of Stalin centralizing power and industrializing the nation as the country turned inward and sought to create "socialism in one country." At the end of the decade, however, the Great Terror was at its height, and the search for enemies of the people left many children parentless when the secret police arrested their families. On top of the paranoia and fear caused by these internal convulsions, there was a growing fear that the war in Spain was only a prelude to a much larger conflict with Germany. Adolf Hitler had been stating for more than a decade that Germany and the Soviet Union could not coexist, and the

---

53(2–4) (2011), 273–304. Children continued to find resonance in Cold War culture. See, for example, Margaret Peacock, *Innocent Weapons: The Soviet and American Politics of Childhood in the Cold War* (Chapel Hill, 2014).

[2] *Pravda*, September 15, 16, 17, 18, 19, 20, 1936; Daniel Kowalsky, "The Soviet Cinematic Offensive in the Spanish Civil War," *Film History* 19 (2007), 13. See Gosudarstvennyi arkhiv Rossiiskoi federatsii (State Archive of the Russian Federation, Moscow; hereafter, GARF) f. 8009, op. 20, d. 45, ll. 1–22, for one of the first extensive reports on their arrival.

success of new German technologies and tactics in Spain caused a great deal of concern in the Soviet Union as it continued to industrialize and Stalin slaughtered much of his officer corps in the Great Terror.

There was also a fear, justified or not, that Soviet children were becoming more unruly. Therefore, in 1937, just as the *niños* were arriving, the Commissariat of Enlightenment introduced dramatic educational reforms to strengthen discipline and improve education. The foundation of many of the reforms came from the teachings of pedagogue Anton Makarenko and his calls for discipline, manual labor, and self-government. Soviet press reports and Elena Kononenko's book *Little Spaniards (Malen'kie ispantsy)* simplified the range of experiences the children reported and about which Soviet officials were aware. Because journalists and Kononenko operated under a censorship regime, scholars can also read their writings on the young Spaniards not only as reportage but also as a type of instruction manual for the ideal childhood. Soviet writers transformed the arrival experiences of the *niños* into tales of state oversight and accommodation that would lead to disciplined and happy children prepared to work hard for the greater good.[3]

RESPONSES TO EVACUATION AND RECEPTION

On March 22, 1937, the first Spanish children were evacuated to the Soviet Union. After German pilots bombed Guernica the following month, four more ships, the last in December 1938, carried nearly 3,000 children, mostly from leftist families, to various parts of the Soviet Union, the only country that had come to the aid of Spain's democratically elected republic. The Basque government's Department of Social Assistance and Culture, along with members of the Communist Party of Euskadi and International Red Aid, a Comintern-affiliated organization that aided Republican soldiers and citizens, secured safe passage out of the country for thousands of additional children. Unlike the other countries that received evacuated Spanish children – including France, Great Britain, and Belgium – the Soviet Union paid all costs during the children's residence in their new homeland. Moreover, the Soviet Union, fearing

---

[3] James Bowen, *Soviet Education: Anton Makarenko and the Years of Experimentation* (Madison, 1962); E. Thomas Ewing, *The Teachers of Stalinism: Policy, Practice, and Power in Soviet Schools of the 1930s* (New York, 2002): Chs. 5 and 6 detail the return to teacher-centered instruction with set curricula and the renewed importance of discipline in classrooms in the 1930s; Elena Kononenko, *Malen'kie ispantsy* (Moscow, 1937).

that their parents' political loyalties would put the children at risk, was the only European country not to send the children back to Spain after the Civil War concluded. Therefore, the USSR created a network of boarding schools exclusively for the Spanish evacuees and their adult caregivers; these closed only in 1951 as the youngest evacuees moved into higher education or work.[4]

Letters from the children and more recent oral histories show a wide range of responses to the displacement from Spain and resettlement in the Soviet Union. Loss and fear of the unknown punctuated stories of the 1937 evacuation, but many stories also carried a sense of hope in finding a safe place to live. The reception and treatment awed some children; others reported a sense of dislocation in a foreign culture.

Fear dominated many children's memories of their evacuation from Spain because the Republic's enemies had no intention of letting Spanish children leave the country. A child on the second expedition recalled, "I remember the day we had to leave they were constantly bombarding the port and we could not go. We left the next day escorted by a Soviet submarine." Adolfo Cenítagoya remembered bombs and shells from German Junkers falling near the old French ship that carried him from Spain. The voyages were arduous. Narrators remembered the dark of the cargo hold where they bedded down on mats to the sounds of crying children all around. Retching was frequent as people tried to overcome loss and seasickness. The ocean was "as bad as the Germans," an evacuee recalled. Unfortunately for Ana del Bosque Arín, who had just seen the

---

[4] For more on these boarding schools, see Karl D. Qualls, "From Niños to Soviets? Raising Spanish Refugee Children in House No. 1, 1937–1951" *Canadian-American Slavic Studies* 48 (2014), 288–307, and Qualls, "From Hooligans to Disciplined Students: Displacement, Resettlement, and Role Modeling of Spanish Civil War Children in the Soviet Union, 1937–1951," in Nick Baron, ed., *Displaced Children in Russia and Eastern Europe, 1915–1953: Ideologies, Identities, Experiences* (Leiden, 2017), 131–54. For scholarship on other countries, see J. J. Alonso Carballés, 1937. *Los niños vascos evacuados a Francia y Bélgica: historia y memoria de un éxodo infantil, 1936–1940* (Bilbao, 1998); G. Arrien, *Niños vascos evacuados a Gran Bretaña, 1937–1940* (Bilbao, 1988); Adrian Bell, *Only for Three Months: The Basque Children in Exile* (Norwich, 1996); Hywel M. Davies, *Fleeing Franco: How Wales Gave Shelter to Refugee Children from the Basque Country During the Spanish Civil War* (Cardiff, 2011); E. Labajos-Pérez, *Los niños: histoire d'enfants de la guerre civile espagnole réfugiés en Belgique, 1936–1939* (Brussels, 1994); P. Marqués, *Les enfants espagnols réfugiés en France (1936–1939)* (Paris, 1993); E. Payá Valera, *Los niños españoles de Morelia: el exilio infantil en México* (Lleida, 2002); D. Pla Brugat, *Los niños de Morelia: en estudio sobre los primeros refugiados españoles en México* (Mexico City, 1985); A. Sánchez Andrés, *Un capítulo de la memoria oral del exilio: los niños de Morelia* (Madrid, 2002).

film *The Mask of Fu Manchu*, the crew of the *Sontay* was mostly Chinese. Like others, Ana remembered the discomfort of the rolling waters, uncomfortable mats, and the feeling of being trapped below decks because the Chinese mariners frightened her too much to walk the corridors of the ship. One evacuee in the cargo claimed, "The treatment in the Chinese ship was horrible, we were all in the hold, everyone vomited. All the time they gave us rice to eat and the rats that were in the ship were like cats. Moreover, the whole way we could not change clothes or anything." Another remembered being "dizzy all the time" and asking to go home. Many simply could not eat in such conditions. The journey itself was often described in negative terms: "everyone sleeping on mats in the ship's hold," "throwing up on ourselves," going "without eating," "children crying."[5]

Other children narrated a sense of loss during evacuation and their journey to the USSR. Separation from parents was as disturbing as the war raging around the children. Unlike the willing departure of the Molinas children, one boy recalled "screaming and crying all the time because I did not want to leave anything. My mother would never forgive herself for sending me to the Soviet Union," while another stated, "Like many, I came here deceived. I did not want to come." The evacuation, punctuated by feelings of loss and fear, forced children to leave behind everything they knew. Family and friends usually remained in war-ravaged Spain, leaving these children initially with nothing but hunger and tears. "We missed everything," one child recalled, "we missed our homeland, we missed our parents, we missed our religion, we missed a Spanish education, we missed everything because we were very little."

---

[5] After the evacuations, Franco called for all children to be returned and even formed the Extraordinary Delegation for the Repatriation of Minors to forcibly seize children from nearby countries: Alicia Alted, "Le retour en Espagne des enfants evacués pendant le guerre civile espagnole: la délégation extraordinaire au rapatriement des mineurs (1938–1954)," in Centre d'histoire de l'Europe du vingtième siècle, ed., *Enfants de la guerre civile: vécus et representations de la génération née entre 1925 et 1940* (Paris, 1999), 53; Ricard Vinyes, Montse Armengou, and Ricard Belis, *Los niños perdidos del franquismo* (Barcelona, 2003). Quotations are from Immaculada Colomina, *Dos patrias, tres mil destinos: vida y exilio de los niños de la Guerra de España refugiados en la Unión Soviética* (Madrid, 2010), 24; Enrique Zafra, Rosalía Crego, and Carmen Heredia, *Los niños españoles evacuados a la URSS (1937)* (Madrid, 1989), 134, 44; Alicia Alted, et al., eds., *Los niños de la guerra de España en la Unión Soviética: de la evacuación al retorno (1937–1999)* (Madrid, 1999), 51–52; Colomina, *Dos patrias, tres mil destinos*, 25, 24; Marie José Devillard, et al., eds., *Los niños españoles en la URSS, 1937–1997: narración y memoria* (Barcelona, 2001), 79–80.

Separation was too much for some children who then tried to run away. Even though they were told it would only be a three-month evacuation, the Mezquita brothers hid on the *Havana*'s lifeboats hoping to return to Spain rather than carry on to their destination. Others, like Carlos Roldán Alcalde's brother, who was hospitalized in the USSR with measles and therefore separated from his brother, escaped (although briefly) from an institution so as not to be parted from a sibling.[6]

As traumatic as the fear and loss of evacuation and transport were for some children, other *niños* felt relieved to escape the violence, poverty, and hunger that had accompanied bombing and fighting in Spain. The fear of war and the arduous journeys across rough seas patrolled by German submarines made landfall in a peaceful town a pleasant change for many of the children. It was "like reaching paradise after being in hell"; the children lived "like princes and princesses, being educated in the best manner possible, like being in Paradise." Ángel Rodríguez remembered his mother insisting that her children go to the Soviet Union. Once she had made the decision and completed the paperwork, all that remained was the agonizing wait underground where "windows in the basement were shut with sandbags to protect us against the guns. We had to run to that basement five or six times a day, covering our ears not to hear the whistle of bombs that were dropping near our home." When Ángel finally boarded a French ship in Gijón, he was relieved because officials assured the children that they would return as soon as the war was over. Another former evacuee remembered that her parents had "sent all us children thinking that now we were on vacation for three months."[7] They did not know that three months would turn into a lifetime for most of them.

Although most children remembered their first days in the USSR much more positively than the evacuation and journey, some reported ill treatment on arrival. A few were not enamored with the USSR despite the large crowds, flowers, music, and treats that greeted them on their arrival. Some of the children even took exception to their treatment. The children were

---

[6] Colomina, *Dos patrias, tres mil destinos*, 21; Devillard, *Los niños españoles en la URSS*, 78; Alted, *Los niños de la guerra de España en la Unión Soviética*, 52, 80. An August 1937 report showed that 70 percent (1,053 of 1,498) of the children were placed in sanatoria because of illness: GARF f. 8009, op. 20, d. 45, ll. 14–22.

[7] Ronald Fraser, *Blood of Spain: The Experience of Civil War, 1936–1939* (London, 1979), 434; Dorothy Legarreta, *The Guernica Generation: Basque Refugee Children of the Spanish Civil War* (Reno, 1984), 166; Zafra, *Los niños españoles evacuados a la URSS*, 132; Colomina, *Dos patrias, tres mil destinos*, 20.

filthy and louse-ridden after the long journey, so showers and a change of clothes were the first priority for the Soviets. At this point, cultural differences sometimes came to a head. Before they even stepped on Soviet soil, one official called the *niños* "frighteningly undisciplined" when compared to Soviet children. Antonio Martínez remembered that a row of sorts started when the girls and boys, although only a few years old, were told to shower together, which was apparently scandalous to those raised in Catholic Spain. Children also complained that Soviet officials took material goods – sometimes the children's only tangible connection to home – from them. Although many children arrived in tatters and welcomed the crisp uniforms they were given on arrival, others wanted to keep their clothing. One woman reflected on her first experience by noting that her clothing "was made of ... smocking [*nido de abeja*], which was very fashionable then and I looked so good in it, and suddenly they give me the same as everyone else, and I never saw the other dress again ... where can it be? ... but oh well." She expressed a desire to keep her finery and individuality, but in the end she seemed resigned to her fate. For other children, clothes had an even more personal meaning. One woman recalled that her "mom made us a couple of little black dresses ... when my father died ... [W]e took very few things [to the USSR] but what bothered me most was that Mom bought us raincoats because we had no money for coats, and they took them away from us ... they made us tear up the only Bible we had." The dresses represented a connection with her father and the raincoats symbolized the family's financial sacrifice for the children. The disposal of the Bible was an immediate recognition that the girl's religious traditions and identity were no longer going to be part of her public life.[8]

For all the fear, loss, and outrage they displayed, numerous children expressed relief, hope, and wonder at their treatment and new opportunities in the USSR. Frequently children wrote, or remembered decades later, that their living conditions improved greatly once in caring Soviet hands. In a letter home just two weeks after landing in the USSR, Raimundo García reported that Soviet sailors had treated the children well. Other children focused on the good food the Soviets provided, which differed greatly from the hunger that they had felt in France while waiting to change ships. José and Pilar Fernández, like many others, wrote to their

---

[8] GARF f. 8009, op. 20, d. 45, l. 6; Alted, *Los niños de la guerra de España en la Unión Soviética*, 80. Many leftists in Spain were still Catholic, including members of the Basque Communist Party: Devillard, *Los niños españoles en la URSS*, 94.

father in Bilbao that their ship was not in the best condition for passage on rough and fog-obscured seas, but that music, flags, and excited crowds had greeted them at their destination, where they received new clothes. Another girl recalled that "on arrival we had chocolate cake and many gifts. Then they took us to a room full of toys. There we stripped and bathed, then came some doctors and they gave us a checkup."[9]

Food and material goods were most welcome. Isidro San Baudelio Echevarría's letter to his brother noted that after his arrival in Leningrad, where music and the "Internationale" greeted his group, he started fattening up on bread and butter, cheese, café con leche, and rice pudding. Fortunately, he was also able to swim in the "free air" unmolested by shells and bombs. Ángel Gutiérrez recalled the journey itself quite fondly: "We had good and abundant food, and the sailors treated us with exquisite care and generosity. Everything seemed too fantastic." Soviet elites often intervened personally. One *niño* recalled Marshal Aleksandr Yegorov's visit to his boarding school. Yegorov inspected the food, the toilets, and even the children's blankets. A few days after his visit, the children received new "beautiful, soft, and warm camel hair blankets" to replace their less-than-adequate ones. Carlos Roldán Alcalde noted more than six decades later that, each time he went to Leningrad, all he could remember was the music and sun greeting him as he walked down the gangplank.[10]

The initial days in the USSR were memorable and full of wonder for many of the children. One of the older boys, fourteen-year-old Daniel Monzó Carbonell, wrote to his father and siblings that his arrival was filled with young Pioneers and waving flags, a "building that looks like a palace" with gardens and trees all around, a loving Russian official, and "everything we want." The availability of toys also amazed fourteen-year-old Araceli Sánchez-Urquijo, but he was particularly impressed that at Leningrad's northern latitude there was enough natural light that there were only a few hours of darkness. Twelve-year-old Enrique Undiano

---

[9] AGC-Salamanca, PS Santander "o" 49/3, in *Alted, Los niños de la guerra de España en la Unión Soviética*, 59; Zafra, *Los niños españoles evacuados a la URSS*, 105; Colomina, *Dos patrias, tres mil destinos*, 27. Soviet officials reported children eating "colossal amounts" of vegetables and being troubled by repeated medical problems: GARF f. 8000, op. 20, d. 45, ll. 14–22.

[10] Zafra, *Los niños españoles evacuados a la URSS*, 107; Eduardo Pons Prades, *Los niños republicanos. El exilio* (Madrid, 2005), 105; José Fernández Sánchez, *Mi infancia en Moscú. Estampas de una nostalgia* (Madrid, 1988), 37; Alted, *Los niños de la Guerra de España en la Unión Soviética*, 52.

wrote a letter to his mother and sister six days after reaching Leningrad. In it, he voices his fascination with the Soviet submarines and warships he encountered in port, and the four meals per day with unlimited bread and butter; fruit, cheese, and chocolate (both to eat and drink, apparently) topped his list of favorite things about Russia. He also noted with pleasure the abundance of entertainment available to the children, particularly the "billiards, swings, balls, tennis courts, bicycles, and cars with big pedals."[11]

In addition to the abundant food, many novelties fascinated Enrique Undiano. Women's equality and technology were novel to many of the children from the poorer parts of Spain. Electric trams were as foreign to Enrique as the women he saw driving the trains and working on the roads. The suburban Moscow camp, which he described as a "wonderland [*jauja*]," was a launching pad for his hopes and dreams. He looked forward to field trips to Lenin's mausoleum and museum exhibits about the tsars and Republican Spain. In a month, he noted (probably mistakenly), he would begin training as an aviator. Whether he was correct or not, his brief letter detailed his hopes and dreams and the opportunities he saw in the Soviet Union, where even women could drive trains. The frequent and fond mention of food, entertainment, and exciting new opportunities both illuminate the *niños'* sense of expectations for a happy childhood and suggest the absence of such luxuries in wartime Spain.[12]

PRESENTING THE NIÑOS TO THE SOVIET PEOPLE

It is clear that the Spanish children had varied perceptions of their journeys and arrivals, yet Soviet media edited these responses and gave to the reading public a unified and homogeneous understanding of the *niños* and their lives. The crowds cheering the children's arrival were "sufficient to paint a sharp contrast between the sun-drenched, joyful arrival in Russia and the panicked departure from the shrinking Republican zone" in Spain. Although film shorts likely reached a wide audience, they were brief and did not tell a child-centered story nor allow viewers to "know"

---

[11] Vicente Ramos, *La Guerra Civil (1936–1939) en la provincia de Alicante* (Alicante, 1973), vol. II, 231; Prades, *Los niños republicanos*, 116; Zafra, *Los niños españoles evacuados a la URSS*, 101.

[12] Zafra, *Los niños españoles evacuados a la URSS*, 101. "*Jauja*" refers to a place where one's needs are met effortlessly. It would be equivalent to the Land of Cockaigne.

the subject. Written stories became a key vehicle for greater humanization of the children, and an elaboration of their stories sought to impart lessons as much as to distract from current problems in the USSR. Press coverage and film shorts simplified the many and varied experiences endured by the Spanish children into a more consistent and didactic narrative and created an impression much more positive than many Soviet officials discussed in private.[13]

In contrast to the mixed responses of Spanish children, however, the Soviet print media constructed an almost undifferentiated image of the children as escaping a dark life of fear, loss, and hopelessness and arriving in their new homeland comforted by abundance and good care and filled with hope, purpose, and opportunity. Journalists and writers painted a verbal picture, occasionally illustrated with photographs, that often told individual stories of the journey from darkness to light. In publications about the *niños*, we learn what the ideal childhood is supposed to be and, not surprisingly, it is the antithesis of everything the children had experienced in fascist-ravaged Spain, where exploitation and control by the landed elite (*señores*) and the Catholic Church continued. Soviet newspapers discussed the escape from the horrors of war and the children's personal experiences with death, fear, and exploitation. Journalists' accounts of the *niños'* first days in the USSR reflected the experiences of some of the *niños*: enjoying abundant food and recreation, finding new friends among the Soviet Union's many nationalities, exploring opportunities unheard of in Spain, and expressing a burning desire to learn and return to the fight in Spain. However, news stories omitted stories about disgruntled children.[14]

Unlike films, the written word provided implicit descriptions of an ideal Soviet childhood. Elena Kononenko's book *Malen'kie ispantsy* (*Little Spaniards*), published by Detizdat, the main state-run press for children's books, provided didactic lessons to young Soviet students about how the *niños'* stories illustrated ideal Soviet behavior. In the late 1930s, Kononenko was embarking on a career writing about children's behavior

[13] Kowalsky, "The Soviet Cinematic Offensive," 13.
[14] See, for example, "Rasskaz ispanskoi pionerki," *Pravda*, April 4, 1937; A. Gudimov, "Gosti iz Ispanii," *Izvestiia*, April 8, 1937; N. Tokarev, "Spanish Children at 'Artek,'" *Pravda*, April 3, 1937; V. Solov'ev, "Baskskie deti u leningradskikh pionerov," *Pravda*, June 25, 1937; "Parakhod 'Santai' priblizhaetsia k beregam SSSR," *Komsomol'skaia Pravda*, June 21, 1937; "Leningrad gotovitsia k priemu baskskikh detei," June 21, 1937; "Stolitsa zhdet detei geroicheskoi Ispanii," *Komsomol'skaia Pravda*, October 5, 1937; "Ispanskie deti pribyli v Leningrad," *Komsomol'skaia Pravda*, July 15, 1938.

and education. Her *Little Spaniards* was written in highly accessible prose for her young audience, and with more than 50,000 copies in print, the book would have been available for many children to read. She followed the lives of a diverse set of boys and girls – literate and illiterate, orphans and children sent abroad by their parents for safety's sake, urban and rural, from Communist and from (seemingly) apolitical families – who experienced personal trauma before the decision was made to leave on the first voyage of evacuee children.[15]

Writing during the Great Terror, when many Soviet children's family and friends were being arrested, Kononenko told her young Soviet readers about the *niños'* perseverance in the face of violence and loss. Remedio and her brother Francisco endured bombings and saw charred human legs and bloodied dogs amidst the rubble. José traveled with his father to the front, where a fighter with "blood oozing through the bandages" of an amputated leg confronted him on his arrival and where he found that his brother had been killed days before. Torres, the little orphan, became a grenade-thrower and was knocked unconscious in battle. Rosario lived among the orchards of Valencia, but, despite her poverty, she rarely ate any of the oranges because the orchards belonged to the *señores*. When her father lost his poorly paid factory job, they were evicted and forced to live in the forest. When Rosario's father went to the front, she went to a home run by abusive monks; fascists later bombed the monastery after Republicans had taken over and improved it. Even more tragic was the life of Madrid's children. Raphael had to become the man of the house when his father went to the front. Each day, the boy dodged bombs and bullets to get wood and food for a family so malnourished that his mother's breast milk had dried up. When a bomb killed Raphael, his mother sent little Antonio to the USSR. Emilia and other children built barricades from cobbles and lived in a basement for weeks; they heard stories of fascists cutting off children's fingers and burning them alive in the streets.[16]

In these stories, Kononenko informed her young readers about children who had suffered the violence of war but also poverty, capitalist

---

[15] Kononenko wrote articles about crudeness and egoism, for example, which were part of a turn toward discipline in the classroom precisely at the time the Spanish children were arriving. See, for example, "Egoisty," *Komsomol'skaia Pravda*, March 21, 1938; "Grubost'," *Komsomol'skaia Pravda*, January 3, 1938. *Sovetskaia pedagogika*, the regime's new pedagogical mouthpiece, even discussed the latter. See S. N. Belousov, "Ob otklikakh na stat'iu E. Kononenko – "Grubost'," *Sovetskaia pedagogika*, no. 8 (1938), 144–52.

[16] Kononenko, *Malen'kie ispantsy*, 12–60.

exploiters, and abusive clergy, none of which, of course, were to be found in the USSR after the Bolshevik Revolution. Children were in danger in other countries, she suggested, but in the Soviet Union they enjoyed the protection of the state and the party. Moreover, Kononenko showed the *niños* and their parents fighting for their freedom and against repression until it was time for them to leave home in order to be trained in the socialist motherland. Young Soviet readers were to take nothing for granted.

Little Spaniards, which focused on the first evacuees to the Soviet Union, also highlighted, among other things, the development of fraternal relationships, opportunities in the USSR unheard of in Spain, the abundance that greeted the new arrivals, and the courage of the children as they held back tears that flowed from memories of family and friends killed or left behind in Spain. The children arrived with no friends in the USSR, yet their heads swam with fantastic images of a snow-covered country where children went to school on skis and no trees existed. They "could not paint a picture of their future life." When they finally reached Yalta at 11:30 on March 30, 1937, it was as sunny "as in southern Spain. The children shrieked from happiness and surprise." They were warmly and immediately welcomed into their new families in a land full of sunshine, trees, and a happy childhood. A "throng [*tolpa*] of people" gathered at the pier. They were smiling and cheering and throwing white and pink flowers in the air and playing music. Saragossa, waving his hand, cried out in two languages: "*Viva Rusia. Da zdravstvuet Sovetskaia Rossiia!*" He was answered with: "Long live the children of heroic Spain." The Russian and Spanish children immediately formed a bond and "kissed and held each others' hands tightly." They spoke different languages, but the "children perfectly understood one another. They communicated with gestures, eyes, and smiles." Everyone understood four words: Lenin, Stalin, communism, fascist. On the "big holiday," the Spaniards learned about the friendship of peoples as Russians, Ukrainians, Tatars, Spaniards, Mongolians, and more led songs and dances.[17]

Kononenko's description matches many of the *niños*' letters and recollections about the outpouring of affection on their arrival, but she ignored the counternarrative of fear and loss. She instead showed children who could overcome trauma and quickly adapt to displacement; these were skills that were quite necessary at this time of the Great Terror. Despite language barriers, children were children, and the Soviets quickly put the

---

[17] Ibid., 68, 69, 70, 78, 109.

Spaniards at ease in their new homeland. Kononenko's story suggested that the Soviet Union was a land of opportunity where the state and the party would provide a happy life, abundant food, new friends, and many more gifts so that light could overcome darkness. Moreover, the insistence that happiness was a, if not *the*, goal of childhood mirrored the Western conceptions of the ideal childhood in the twentieth century.[18]

All the abundance we should expect from reading late 1930s Soviet literature marked the Spaniards' new lives. As several scholars have shown, Stalinist art and literature of the period began to portray consumption of goods as an aspiration for the new Soviet man and woman. Soviet fiction often commented on white table cloths and lamp shades as signs of material improvement in the 1930s. Kononenko listed numerous signs of abundance and state care enjoyed by the Spaniards: cocoa and hot pirozhki; volleyballs, bicycles, swings, toys, dolls, teddy bears, cars, and building blocks; beaches, fishing, flowers, nightingale songs, and the cypress and laurel trees most missed from home. Lest her readers think the Spaniards were interested only in material goods, Kononenko noted, "the young Spaniards especially liked to go to the children's technical station." Eating and playing were fine and part of a normal childhood, but a Soviet childhood also had to be practical. Here children learned about railroads, radio stations, needlework, and art. This recounting of the arrival story shows children who were grateful for the abundance of care and the gifts Stalin bestowed on them. They were impressed by all the food and toys and the beautiful surroundings. Yet, what did the "little heroes" like most? Practical learning and work that would prepare them to contribute to society in future years. In this year of displacement, fear, and chaos in the Soviet Union, Kononenko was assuring her young Soviet readers that the USSR would take care of them in return for their work for the collective. Even as families and schools began to be torn apart by the Great Terror, the state would protect and care for those who were willing to live according to Soviet principles.[19]

[18] On state-directed happiness, see Jeffrey Brooks, *Thank You, Comrade Stalin! Soviet Public Culture from Revolution to Cold War* (Princeton, 2001); Karen Petrone, *Life Has Become More Joyous, Comrades: Celebrations in the Time of Stalin* (Bloomington, 2000). For changing notions of childhood, see Peter N. Stearns, "Defining the Happy Childhood: Assessing a Recent Change," *Journal of the History of Childhood and Youth* 3(2) (2010), 165–86.

[19] On images of abundance under Stalin, see Katerina Clark, *The Soviet Novel: History as Ritual* (Bloomington, 2000), chs. 4–6; Vera Dunham, *In Stalin's Time: Middleclass Values in Soviet Fiction* (Durham, 1990). Kononenko, *Malen'kie ispantsy*, 85. On the economy of the gift, see Brooks, *Thank You, Comrade Stalin!*, ch. 5. On the Great Terror

Reports showed more than just happiness and abundance in a new fraternal environment; they also showed how the USSR helped the children adjust after their unhappy childhoods in Spain. "Spanish children are sleeping in their bedrooms," reported A. Gudimov, "Occasionally a frightened cry is heard – the children dream of home with shells, machinegun fire, with sirens warning of an air raid." Nightmares had an effect because the children were "frightened of noisy games" and, although they all drew well, they only sketched planes, fascist bombing, tanks, and shooting. All illustrations agitated them, and they were becoming nervous and not sleeping well. Soviet adults recognized the trauma (a word not used) and tried to distract the children from the horrors with play and by introducing them to new acquaintances. The art classes noted by Gudimov showed that Spanish and Soviet children did not share the same outlook. The Spaniards' art depicted death and war, things "they had seen not long ago in their homeland ... Our [Soviet] children drew trees, flowers, animals, passenger trains, the Metro, and the Arctic," where Soviet explorers were making front-page news. Kononenko implied that a Soviet child could depict beauty, human possibility, and achievement because that is what life in the Soviet Union represented. When a girl who had drawn burning homes was shown how to draw a flower, it was progress for her: "Their childhood, stolen by the fascists, is returning to them," wrote Kononenko. Soviet childhood was one of happiness and hopes. The Spaniards had to be taught how to become both happy and Soviet, which writers depicted as synonymous. A state could either steal childhoods or nurture children's development, and even traumatized children could be taught happiness.[20]

and schools, see Ewing, *The Teachers of Stalinism*, ch. 7. On children and the Terror, see Cathy Frierson, *Silence Was Salvation: Child Survivors of Stalin's Terror and World War II in the Soviet Union* (New Haven, 2015).

[20] A. Gudimov, "Gosti iz Ispanii," *Izvestiia*, April 8, 1937. For more on children's art in the Spanish Civil War, see G. R. Collins, *Children's Drawings of the Spanish Civil War: A Collection of 153 Drawings by Children Living in Refugee Colonies During the War* (New York, 1986); A. L. Geist, *They Still Draw Pictures: Children's Art in Wartime from the Spanish Civil War to Kosovo* (Urbana, 2002); Aldous Huxley, *They Still Draw Pictures! With Sixty Illustrations of Drawings Made by Spanish Children During the War* (New York, 1938). In her study of children after World War II, Tara Zahra noted, "One central goal of humanitarian workers after the war was to restore both children and adults to their traditional roles, to make children into children again." Only after the war did refugee agencies begin to think about children's psychological needs. See Tara Zahra, *The Lost Children: Reconstructing Europe's Families After World War II* (Cambridge, MA, 2011), 9 and ch. 3. See also Kononenko, *Malen'kie ispantsy*, 86–87 (drawings pp. 57, 65).

Current events and political education also helped the Spaniards learn to become Soviet. Reading the news from Spain to the children every day caused them to want to be "just as courageous as their parents." Pioneers from Dagestan wrote to the *niños* of their paramilitary training and readiness to fight. A Tatar Pioneer leader at the camp explained tsarist class oppression by noting that none of the palaces around Crimea had belonged to the people. The children, and the reader, were then to draw the connection to the *señores* of Spain mentioned in the story of Rosario's life in Valencia. Revolution in Spain, then, could bring equality and happiness just as it had in Russia, Kononenko suggested. Political freedom was a treasure, a gift of Soviet life, but one for which people had had to fight. Vincente, for example, beamed at the honor of carrying the red banner. He could finally "openly carry the red banner for which the fathers and older brothers were now dying at the front." Letters from home assured the children that the fascists would be crushed and urged the children to study hard so that they could be of use to society when the Republic won. To that end, "All the children," Kononenko reported, "promised teachers and Pioneer leaders that they would study hard." Kononenko's depiction defined childhood as happiness derived from state-supplied care and bounty, but also as requiring diligence and commitment to fulfill one's obligations to others. It was a happy childhood, but not one of carefree innocence.[21]

CONCLUSION

The Soviet Union, from its inception, viewed children as a precious resource. If properly raised, they would achieve the full realization of communism in the USSR. In the 1930s, as the USSR continued to grow into socialism and move closer to full communism, the Soviets stopped discussing the possibilities of reforming wayward children as they tried to ignore the ongoing problem. However, with the Great Purges removing more parents, teachers, and classmates from children's lives, Kononenko's discussion of the Spanish children in some ways served as a surrogate discussion about the role of the state and party in turning children into new Soviet men and women. As her young readers learned about their new Spanish comrades, they were also learning how to behave as Soviets and to view the state that sought to "fashion youths into productive, devoted members of a Communist society." Although Kononenko, journalists,

---

[21] Kononenko, *Malen'kie ispantsy,* 90, 91, 109.

and filmmakers deliberately ignored stories of trauma among the *niños*
after they arrived in the USSR so as to highlight Soviet care and concern,
we must not forget that many of the children remembered their time in the
boarding schools as a wonderful experience under the kind supervision of
the state. Numerous scholars have discussed the importance of families
replacing institutions in the 1930s, but the Spaniards had no nuclear
family in the USSR to which they could turn. The Soviet boarding schools
for Spanish children served as surrogate families without the threats of
counternarratives of ideal behavior that might often come from a nuclear
family.[22] Soviet authorities' largess toward the Spanish children was clear
to everyone; it even incurred the ire and jealousy of some Soviet citizens.

   The Great Purges and the parentless children they created necessitated
greater attention to rearing children in a more disciplined environment.
The pedagogical changes in 1937 could be seen as part of this turn, but so
too could *Little Spaniards* and its stories of Soviet care overcoming the
loss of parents and transforming children into hardworking, collectivist,
and happy builders of tomorrow. Unfortunately, no evidence has been
found about how readers used or received this book. Soviet readers knew
well the myth of boy-martyr Pavlik Morozov, who fulfilled his duty to
report his parents as enemies of the people only to be killed by relatives.
Tales of the little heroes of Spain provided a more positive ending in which
the Soviet state became a transformative agent, bringing children from
darkness to light and providing opportunities unavailable to most in
Spain. The reach and longevity of *Little Spaniards* did not match those
of Pavlik Morozov, but it likely had a similar effect. The stories of extraordinary children staged the norms of Soviet childhood in which the
regime's beneficence protected, guided, and provided for children and
brought happiness as they transformed into politically conscious and
active adults.

---

[22] GARF f. A-2306, op. 70, d. 5991; Catriona Kelly, *Children's World: Growing Up in
   Russia 1890–1991* (New Haven, 2007); Lisa Kirschenbaum, *Small Comrades:
   Revolutionizing Childhood in Soviet Russia, 1917–1932* (London, 2001); Ann Livshiz,
   "Growing Up Soviet: Childhood in the Soviet Union, 1918–1958" (Ph.D. diss., Stanford
   University, 2006). For a discussion of changing attitudes toward wayward children, see
   Alan Ball, *And Now My Soul Is Hardened: Abandoned Children in Soviet Russia,
   1918–1930* (Berkeley, 1994); Juliane Fürst, "Between Salvation and Liquidation:
   Homeless and Vagrant Children and the Reconstruction of Soviet Society," *Slavonic
   and East European Review* 86(2) (2008), 232–58. On the rise of the family as the unit
   of child rearing, see David Hoffmann, *Stalinist Values: The Cultural Norms of Soviet
   Modernity, 1917–1941* (Ithaca, 2003), 106–07.

5

Learning More than Letters: Alphabet Books in the Soviet Union and the United States During World War II

Julie K. deGraffenried

Even in the dark days of World War II, young Soviet children could enjoy a new edition of *Zhivye bukvy* (*Living Letters*) by esteemed children's writer Samuil Marshak. Published in 1944, Marshak's book correlated the letters of the Russian alphabet with adult professions, accompanied by illustrations of children dressed and acting in ways appropriate to the occupation. Among the variety of alphabet books available to American consumers at this time, one in particular shares Marshak's focus on professions to teach literacy. The Samuel Lowe Company of Kenosha, Wisconsin, published an untitled ABC book for young American children in 1943, featuring adult professions prominently, offering cheerfully colored vignettes of childlike figures at work for each letter of the English alphabet.

As a cultural artifact, the alphabet book provides a means to under-stand and compare constructions of children and childhood during World War II in the Soviet Union and United States. To be clear, this is not meant to be a binary comparative piece. Though I suggest comparisons between the two adult visions of childhood, the primary purpose is to contextualize these exempla of Soviet and American children's culture in the broader narrative of childhood and war in the 1940s. The project is source-driven; finding two alphabet books published at nearly the same time that fea-tured occupations in two languages accessible to me invited – begged for, really – simultaneous analysis. Because "the history of the child and the history of the alphabet have proceeded hand in hand," special attention will be paid to both text and images in the books as the words, ideas, and representations included in them reveal significant adult messages about mid-twentieth-century visions of Soviet and American childhood, social values, gender roles, and expectations about children's contributions to the war.[1] While the American book more directly engages the war as part of the child's world, the Soviet version prompts the child to imagine his or her participation in it. The two books demonstrate two societies grappling with the tension between ideals and reality, between the desire to safeguard the innocence of childhood and the need to mobilize the young. The invitation to literacy that was extended to small children simultaneously summoned them to war.

THE ABCS AS CHILDREN'S LITERATURE

Children's literature is one way to explore and interpret the attitudes, values, and cultural norms of a society; in it, we may see the significant, the accepted, and the hoped-for, concurrently. Acknowledging the importance of the young to the building of socialism, the Soviet Union sought from its inception to create a literature designed to shape, educate, and inform the Soviet child.[2] In far less state-directed fashion, twentieth-century American educators, parents, and experts, too, recognized the uses of literature to extol desired values and character traits for American children. Both countries saw the child, "'unwritten' [and] untainted," as "a natural figure upon which ... identities may be draped."[3]

The education of the young served as a dearly held and fiercely defended ideal in the twentieth-century Soviet Union and United States. For the Soviets, modernization, an ideology that provided the masses with that which had been reserved for the few, and political socialization necessitated education for children; for twentieth-century Americans, education provided knowledge essential to democratic citizenship, self-expression, and opportunities for self-advancement. Literacy, as the "embodiment of significant social ideals," both proved and guaranteed

---

[1] Quote from Patricia Crain, *The Story of A: The Alphabetization of America from* The New England Primer *to* The Scarlet Letter (Stanford, 2000), 12.

[2] Felicity Ann O'Dell, *Socialisation Through Children's Literature: The Soviet Example* (Cambridge, 1978); Evgeny Steiner, *Stories for Little Comrades: Revolutionary Artists and the Making of Soviet Children's Books* (Seattle, 1999); Catriona Kelly, *Children's World: Growing Up in Russia, 1890–1991* (New Haven, 2007); Marina Balina and Larisa Rudova, eds., *Russian Children's Literature and Culture* (London, 2008); Jacqueline Olich, *Competing Ideologies, and Children's Literature in Russia, 1918–1935* ([np], 2009).

[3] Julia L. Mickenberg and Lynne Vallone, "Introduction," in Mickenberg and Vallone, eds., *The Oxford Handbook of Children's Literature* (Oxford, 2011), 13.

a nation's success.[4] This task, begun in the home and completed at school, often started with the alphabet book.

Though not often considered a politically charged work, the abecedarium conveys far more than simply the building blocks of words. The letters (or signs) mean little in and of themselves, but they nonetheless carry layers of attached meaning. The presentation of the alphabet, according to Patricia Crain, "offers access to a broad range of cultural formations, including the contours of ideology."[5] First and foremost is the question of accessibility. By mass-producing alphabet books for children, both the United States and the USSR established that even the youngest members of their respective societies can – in fact, were expected to – learn to read and write.[6] Second, the alphabet chosen – English for the American book and Russian for the Soviet – conveys a message about cultural dominance and authority in both an immigrant-built "melting pot" and a multi-ethnic empire. Third, the text and images used to construct the alphabet book are laden with cues about everything from normative behavior to affective association to political ideals to gender expectations. In short, a children's ABC book teaches multiple literacies: grammatical, social, cultural, political. Finally, the interactive nature of the give-and-take between reader/ viewer and book should not be forgotten. The book presents literacies to the child who in turn activates those learned literacies through attitudes and behaviors.[7] The inherent didacticism of the ABC book allows the child-reader to consume, digest, and apply its lessons in the lifelong process of identity formation.[8]

Materials such as pictorial alphabets have existed since the fourteenth century. Though such books were originally designed for religious purposes and adult audiences, gradual changes in views on educational goals and childhood brought about concerted efforts to teach children the

[4] Cathy N. Davidson, *Reading in America: Literature and Social History* (Baltimore, 1989), 12.

[5] Crain, *The Story of A*, 5.

[6] See David Diringer, *The Alphabet: A Key to the History of Mankind*, 2nd edn. (New York, 1948), 17, for more on the art of writing and the decline of its exclusivity over time.

[7] Crain, *The Story of A*, 56. Annika Takala and Kerttu Vepsäläinen argue that the ABC book has a "greater influence on the child than other books" because, as one of the first books a child encounters, it conveys text-image lessons that linger: "Elements of World View Conveyed by ABC Books and First Readers in Different Countries," *International Schulbuchforschung* 7(23) (1985), 138.

[8] Ivan Illich and Barry Sanders, *The Alphabetization of the Popular Mind* (San Francisco, 1988), x.

alphabet through the entertaining use of image and text.[9] The "A was an Archer, who shot at a frog" verse, reproduced in the 1943 Samuel Lowe abecedarium, first appeared in print in *A Little Book for Little Children* in the early eighteenth century and was reprinted many times subsequently in English-language books.[10] Images of professions accompanying letters of the alphabet, while not as popular as images of animals or children, appeared regularly, beginning in the mid nineteenth century.[11] Modern author-illustrators "dressed up and decked out, animated, ornamented, narrated, and consumed" the alphabet.[12]

Like picture books, modern alphabet books use two different forms of communication – text and image – to narrate and describe or represent their contents, bidding the child-reader not only to learn to read, but also to learn to observe.[13] Modern alphabet books rely almost exclusively on the nexus between the visual and the textual, whereas earlier versions depended nearly entirely on the textual. While alphabet books often have no visual or verbal setting, the illustrations provide an affective experience, an aid to literacy as a verbal experience, and an aesthetic experience for the reader.[14] Soviet authorities in particular emphasized the "power of the image to convey social change not only as an obligation, but also as an object of individual desire and a source of individual fulfillment."[15] Together, the text and image create a real or imagined world for the child, offering opportunities for creation (by the author) and re-creation (by the reader). They provide scholars with a reflection not only of

[9] See Crain, *The Story of A*, 19, 33; Max J. Okenfuss, *The Discovery of Childhood in Russia: The Evidence of the Slavic Primer* (Newtonville, MA, 1980); Kimberly Reynolds, *The History of Children's Literature: A Very Short Introduction* (Oxford, 2011); Peter Hunt, *International Companion Encyclopedia of Children's Literature*, 2nd edn. (New York, 2004).

[10] Anne Rowe, "Learning the Letters," in Eve Bearne and Victor Watson, eds., *Where Texts and Children Meet* (London, 2000), 151.

[11] See, for examples, *Cousin Honeycomb's Alphabet of Trades* (c. 1856); *Picture Gift Book* (London, 1866); William Nicholson, *An Alphabet* (New York, 1898); V. V. Mayakovsky, *Soviet Alphabet* (1919). The first can be found in Ruari McLean, *Pictorial Alphabets* (London, 1969), 12–19. Mayakovsky's was not meant for children. See Anna Rapoport, "Russkii mir v russkikh azbukakh," *Papmambuk*, October 25, 2013, www.papmambook.ru/articles/746.

[12] Crain, *The Story of A*, 64.

[13] Maria Nikolajeva and Carole Scott, *How Picturebooks Work* (New York, 2001), 1; Crain, *The Story of A*, 7.

[14] Jane Doonan, *Looking at Pictures in Picture Books* (Woodchester, 1993), 7; on lack of setting, see Nikolajeva and Scott, *How Picturebooks Work*, 62.

[15] Robert Bird, *Adventures in the Soviet Imaginary: Soviet Children's Books and Graphic Art* (Chicago, 2011), 40.

contemporary artistic style and forms, but also of the values of the society that produced and used them.[16]

THE ALPHABET GOES TO WAR

These particular books, though, were created and published in the context of global conflict: World War II. They entered societies and, more specifically, childhoods in which war was affecting home life, education, and children's culture. Most American children neither experienced the war first hand nor lived in a family containing a member of the armed forces, yet the war effort permeated their daily lives.[17] Surging patriotism in the United States influenced everything from consumption to parenting to attitudes toward child labor, from radio programs to paper dolls to leisure activities.[18] American producers of children's culture, with the notable exception of book publishers, wove a war of "good versus evil" into cartoons, radio programs, comic books, and toys, manipulating patriotism both to inspire war bond, conservation, and collection campaigns and to sell products. Pleas to protect preschoolers from the effects of war abounded, but for children beginning formal schooling at the same age as political awareness emerges – age five or six – education was about imparting patriotism, democratic ideals, and support for the war as much as academics.[19]

Children in the Soviet Union faced related changes, intensified by the fact of Axis invasion. Nearly all children in the Soviet Union had a family member in the armed forces, and working parents lived largely at the factory rather than at home; millions of children lived in territory occupied by Axis forces, faced evacuation, or died at the hands of the enemy.[20] As in

---

[16] Doonan, *Looking at Pictures in Picture Books*, 8, applies these ideas solely to images, but I think they are applicable to text choices as well – even in terms of style and form, for fonts and representations of language (and alphabets themselves) change over time.

[17] Nearly a fifth (18.1 percent) of American families contributed one or more members to the armed forces: William J. Tuttle, Jr., *"Daddy's Gone to War": The Second World War in the Lives of America's Children* (Oxford, 1993), 31. See also Lisa Ossian, *The Forgotten Generation: American Children and World War II* (Columbia, MO, 2011).

[18] See Tuttle, *"Daddy's Gone to War,"* 119–20, 141, 151, 154, 158.

[19] On preschoolers, see Anna Wolf, *Our Children Face War* (Boston, 1942); "First Lady Urges Normal Child Life," *New York Times*, January 5, 1942. On the politicization of children in wartime, see James Marten, *The Children's Civil War* (Chapel Hill, 1998), 24–25, and Tuttle, *"Daddy's Gone to War,"* 45. On education, see ibid., 112–13.

[20] Julie deGraffenried, *Sacrificing Childhood: Children and the Soviet State in the Great Patriotic War* (Lawrence, 2014), ch. 1.

the United States, wartime education emphasized patriotism alongside academics, though Soviet schooling was often sporadic and interrupted by labor or conditions of war.[21] In children's culture, ideals of self-sacrifice and war-preparedness predated the war; a common theme was that the "land of the happy childhood" had to be defended from "enemies" who sought to take it away.[22] Once war began, that idea became reality: War saturated the state-produced Soviet children's culture – radio, magazines, literature, film – with attempts at amelioration via folklore, whimsical poetry, and art only appearing in later years of the war. The "us-versus-them" dichotomy present in Soviet children's culture throughout the twentieth century found a ready target in time of war: Much-publicized Axis atrocities affirmed a real, not simply imagined, enemy.[23]

Into such landscapes entered the two alphabet books in question. *Living Letters* by Marshak, illustrated by graphic artist and painter Adrian Mikhailovich Ermolaev, was in its second printing in 1944, having first appeared four years earlier from Detizdat, the state children's literature publishing house (Figure 5.1).[24] The book is tiny, only 7.5 cm by 10.5 cm, printed on low-quality, rough brownish-yellowish paper typical of war-era children's books. Only the cover is in color, limited to blue, yellow, black, and white; the remainder of the book is black and white. Each page features one letter, one drawing, and one verse using the letter presented. The 1943 Samuel Lowe booklet of sixteen full-color pages, untitled and coverless, is unattributed, a practice not unusual for mass-produced, low-cost works of that decade.[25] The large (25 cm by 30 cm) booklet is printed in double-spreads throughout, on rough ecru construction paper, with eight image sets presenting the alphabet to children: adult occupations, the "A was an Archer" traditional verse alphabet, military professions and items, children performing actions, animals, types of

---

[21] Kelly remarks on the static nature of primary education (with its mixture of academic skills and patriotic education) and similarities to Western educational objectives across the nineteenth and twentieth centuries: Kelly, *Children's World*, 531.

[22] Olga Kucherenko, *Little Soldiers: How Soviet Children Went to War, 1941–1945* (Oxford, 2011), ch. 3.

[23] On the dichotomous nature of children's culture, see Kelly, *Children's World*, 598. On enemies, see deGraffenried, *Sacrificing Childhood*, 64–66, 89–94, 122–25.

[24] In the 1940s, *Zhivye bukvy* was printed in 1940, 1944, 1947, and 1949, in print runs from 40,000 to 100,000, at a cost to consumer of 50 k. to 10 r.: A. Koshelev, *Russkie poety XX veka: materialy dlia bibliografii* (Moscow, 2007), 333.

[25] The omission of an author's name is fairly typical; the lack of a cover is found on a few other Lowe examples and is attributable to cost-cutting; the lack of a title is atypical, and has so far made finding publication information impossible.

FIGURE 5.1 *Living Letters* (1944), front cover.

buildings, fruits and vegetables, and flowers, in that order (Figure 5.2). Each page is edged in pink, with figures related to nursery rhymes scattered in the border. According to Crain's morphology of the alphabet, both books should be categorized as an alphabet array in that they

FIGURE 5.2 "A – Aviator … " Front cover of alphabet book, Samuel Lowe Company (1943).

"emphasize the alphabet's function of ordering and arbitrary arrangement," presenting the English and Russian letters as "a way of taking in the world," a world that is "knowable, graspable, and obtainable."[26] These were not the only alphabet books printed in the Soviet Union and

[26] Crain, *The Story of A*, 91.

United States during World War II, but selecting two works that use adult occupations to visually anchor the alphabets provides the most useful parallel for comparison.[27]

The books themselves tell us about adult constructions of children and childhood during the war. Marshak, the author of *Living Letters*, a poet, director of state children's publishing houses in Moscow and Leningrad, and translator, was one of the most influential figures in Soviet children's literature. His works, which ran the gamut from pure fancy to heroic socialist realism depending on the political climate, received several Stalin Prizes and a Lenin Prize and are still considered a beloved part of the literary canon of children's literature in Russia today.[28] Even during the war, when the state drastically reduced production of children's literature, nearly twenty of Marshak's works appeared.[29] Though Ermolaev illustrated *Living Letters* in its 1944 incarnation, it is famed artist Vladimir Vasilevich Lebedev who deserves credit for the style and design of the book. Ermolaev's drawings are highly derivative, clearly modeled on Lebedev's original 1940 images, in an obvious attempt to reproduce the illustrations in a far smaller format. Lebedev's work, like Marshak's, ranged from the avant-garde to the politically acceptable socialist realism, but tenets he established – borderlessness, lack of perspective (or flatness), the "floating" image in whitespace, simple forms and silhouettes, textured drawing – survived major shifts in artistic doctrines and influenced scores of illustrators.[30] In addition, his position as art director in the only state children's publishing house ensured that his style would be familiar to children across the USSR.

---

[27] Marshak himself penned two other alphabet books during the war: *Veselaia azbuka*, ill. N. Radlov (Moscow, 1943), and *Avtobus No. 26: smeshnaia azbuka v stikhakh* (Tashkent, 1946). These use animals and everyday items to illustrate the text: Koshelev, *Russkie poety*, 333–34. In the United States, see Leah Gale, *The Alphabet from A to Z*, ill. Vivienne Blake (New York, 1942), and Maud Petersham and Miska Petersham, *An American ABC* (New York, 1941). Gale's, one of the original Little Golden Books, uses everyday objects; the Petershams' book, a 1942 Caldecott Honor Book, uses images drawn from American history and legend.

[28] Elena Sokol, "Samuil Iakovlevich Marshak," in Neil Cornwell, ed., *Reference Guide to Russian Literature* (London, 1998), 545–46; Albert Lemmens and Serge Stommels, *Russian Artists and the Children's Book, 1880–1992* (Nijmegen, 2009), 94, 111, 114–15.

[29] Koshelev, *Russkie poety*, 328–34.

[30] Lebedev illustrated the very first children's book to be published after the October Revolution: Lemmens and Stommels, *Russian Artists and the Children's Book*, 77, 115, 172–73. Ermolaev was an accomplished children's book illustrator in his own right, including dozens of works by Marshak, Arkady Gaidar, Agniya Barto, and Lev Kassil'.

The assignment of a basic alphabet book to such a decorated pair was not unusual, given the Soviet authorities' emphasis on the book as the most "essential means for promoting the official worldview and instilling ... norms."[31] It also suggests the premium that Soviet authorities placed on children's literacy, especially in time of war, when formal schooling was utterly disrupted by displacement, lack of resources and personnel, and student absenteeism in the Soviet Union. At the same time, its size and quality indicate a broader wartime trend – the radical reduction in state resources for children. Not only production but also the quality of children's books, both physically and creatively, declined because of scarce resources, the relocation of many writers and artists to the front, and the reassignment of others, including Marshak and Lebedev, to the production of propaganda for adult audiences. Books for children tended to be about one-third the size of prewar editions so that sizeable print runs could be maintained.[32] Prices for books plunged, reflecting the cheaper materials and eliminating concerns about accessibility; if the books could be found, they could be purchased by anyone. The absence or change in appearance of children's literature, however, might have provided another indicator of the war's immediacy for Soviet children. The tiny *Living Letters*, with its "imitation" Lebedev illustrations, reflects wartime developments in the Soviet Union.

Samuel Lowe founded a publishing company in 1940 hoping to provide children's literature at low cost in enormous quantities. Having developed a line of affordable, high-quality books that he succeeded in having placed in five-and-dime stores like Woolworth's for Western Publishing in the 1930s, Lowe struck out on his own. Compared to the average children's illustrated book at $1.50, Lowe's 10-cent and 25-cent full-color, highly illustrated offerings extended a popular alternative to the masses.[33] Lowe's placement and pricing of books like the 1943 alphabet book sent a message that all children should and could read. Critics, ostensibly concerned about the regulation of literary and artistic standards, disparaged such books, decrying "the projection of mass-production methods and values into the picture book realm," yet the

---

[31] Kucherenko, *Little Soldiers*, 32.

[32] deGraffenried, *Sacrificing Childhood*, 186–89.

[33] Leonard S. Marcus, *Golden Legacy: How Golden Books Won Children's Hearts, Changed Publishing Forever, and Became an American Icon Along the Way* (New York, 2007), 6, 8, 10, 32, 36.

books sold millions of copies in the 1940s.[34] Compared to the Soviet example, Lowe's book says less about formal government intentions toward children's education, due to privatized book publishing; however, its appearance can highlight corporate decision making, social norms, or popular culture in the United States.

The placement of cheap children's books in the toy departments of stores suggested reading as an appropriate leisure activity for little ones. Because Lowe's book prioritizes image choice over language acquisition, it is likely that it was designed as a toy book.[35] The war facilitated the association; when a decrease in the availability of metals and rubber made toys scarcer, demand for children's books increased.[36] Paper rationing, which began in 1943, did influence production: Some publishers had difficulty filling orders, and repackaged backlists, in smaller sizes and abridged formats, became common.[37] Shortages, however, in no way approached those of their Soviet ally. Further, there is little difference in image quality or the number of colors used in printing compared to prewar books, nor was there an exodus among artists due to war: Writer Margaret Wise Brown, illustrators Tenggren and Wanda Gág, and author-illustrators Ingri and Edgar Parin d'Aulaire, Virginia Lee Burton, and Robert McCloskey all created a number of works in the early 1940s. Little about the Samuel Lowe book suggests a childhood of wartime deprivation.

Comparing the occupations chosen to embody and exemplify the letters of the Russian and English alphabets in the Soviet and American books requires a consideration of both text and images as well as of potential cumulative effects of the verbal–visual interaction on the child-reader. Further, the vocations must be considered in light of the war's

---

[34] Quote ibid., 58. Samuel Lowe's *Three Little Kittens*, for example, sold 1.5 million copies in its first six months.

[35] Alphabets privileging language acquisition focus on one letter sound at a time – i.e., "C is for cat" – rather than offering the reader the more complex (and confusing) "C is for Commando and Chair." My thanks to Clay Butler and Melisa Dracos for pointing this out. Alphabet books as toys date back to at least the mid eighteenth century with Mary Cooper's *The Child's New Plaything* (1742) and were common in nineteenth-century advertising. See James Mason, ed., *The Yearbook of Facts in Science and the Arts for 1877* (London, 1877), 28.

[36] See, for example, "Currents in the Trade," *Publishers Weekly*, March 27, 1943, 1339; see also, Marcus, *Golden Legacy*, 71.

[37] See, for example, "Currents in the Trade," *Publishers Weekly*, March 25, 1944, 1282; see also, Marcus, *Golden Legacy*, 72, 75. In fact, the two copies of the Lowe alphabet book that I have are printed on two different kinds of paper, suggesting some instability in the paper supply. Contents and color remain the same, however.

context: Why were these careers chosen instead of others? What were adults saying to children about their role(s) in the war? Finally, how does the message presented in these books fit in the broader role for young children imagined by each society during World War II?

Marshak's *Living Letters* offers the child reader twenty-eight letters of the Russian alphabet, one letter per page, with a verse that features a name beginning with the letter presented and, in twenty-seven of the twenty-eight cases, a profession that begins with the highlighted letter.[38] Most consist of a short sentence ("Borya is a drummer"/"*Boria – barabansh-chik*"), but twelve are two or more sentences ("Lyonya is the best skipper. He leads boats and ships through the rapids to the river."/"*Lenia – luchshii lotsman. On cherez porogi lodki, parokhody vodit po reke.*") The occupations chosen are, simultaneously, highly typical of an industrialized society and quite specific to the Soviet context. They are all adult roles with which Soviet children would have been familiar; none ventures out of time or place for the sake of creativity or novelty. Further, the variety of occupations demonstrates the classlessness characteristic of Stalin's 1938 proclamation of "socialism achieved."[39] There are military jobs – airplane pilot, drummer, grenade-thrower, engineer, soldier, sailor, engine drivers, border guards – and workers – miners, plumbers, electricians, builders – and a sprinkling of scientific, creative, and professional vocations, such as zoologist, artist, pediatrician, and teacher (Figure 5.3). Military positions predominate, comprising thirteen of the twenty-eight examples, while workers come in a close second at nine, mirroring the types of figures celebrated and held up for emulation in children's culture in the 1940s.[40] When Marshak penned the first edition of *Living Letters*, the Soviet Union was at war with Finland in the Winter War of 1939–1940, an event which heightened the sense of militarism apparent

---

[38] Of the thirty-three letters in the Russian alphabet, Marshak excludes the hard sign ъ, soft sign ь, and the letters ё, й, and ы. A complete listing of all thirty-three letters is included at the end of the book. An English translation of the text of Marshak's book can be found in the Appendix to this chapter.

[39] J. V. Stalin, "On the Final Victory of Socialism in the USSR" (first published in *Pravda*, February 14, 1938), quoted from www.marxists.org/reference/archive/stalin/works/1938/01/18.htm. In an open letter published in *Pravda*, Stalin declared that the bourgeoisie had been successfully liquidated by a triumphant proletariat, signaling that class struggle was at an end.

[40] For example, the August–September 1941 issue (no. 8–9) of *Murzilka*, the Soviet magazine for preschoolers, features poetry about soldiers defeating fascists, an entreaty for children to contribute to the war effort, a letter from a boy whose father is going to the front, a story about a heroic pilot who shot down enemy planes, instructions for air raids, and a letter from a collective farm about children's work there.

Т

Толя —
Тракторист.

20

FIGURE 5.3 "T – Tolya is a tractor driver." *Living Letters.*

in children's culture in the late 1930s. The gravity of the Great Patriotic War (June 1941–August 1945) only enhanced the relevance of Marshak's occupational choices, undoubtedly contributing to its publication. Any of the professions could be seen as essential to the war effort, or at least related, as the need for defense workers and medical personnel became critical. Even the two that seem most whimsical – Eva the horseback rider in the circus and the Charlie Chaplin imitator – can be seen as promoting much-needed physical fitness and proper opposition to fascism.[41] Perhaps surprisingly, literacy is affixed not to communist ideology but to modern Soviet society and the war it was fighting.[42]

Ermolaev's highly textured, charcoal drawings depict children acting out the verse. With the exception of two, the children are not drawn in frontal position – that is, they do not face or confront the reader – but instead are quarter-front, completely sideways, or even turned away from the viewer (Figure 5.4). This implies children in action or intent on their activities, rather than a self-conscious performance for the reader. The two exceptions affirm this: One is a child imitating Charlie Chaplin (so, a performer) and the other is a zinc-engraver who presents his finished product for inspection (again, a performance). The verticality of the images denotes motion, activity, and energy.[43] The figures are surrounded by negative space; nothing grounds where they walk, dance, ride, and stand or suggests a setting in which they act. This is not altogether unusual for an alphabet book and has a longstanding precedent in Soviet book illustration as well.[44] The issue of class having been settled by the aforementioned victory of the proletariat, these children could be anywhere in the Soviet Union, accomplishing deeds in any environment. The negative space allows the reader to fill in the setting with his or her imagination, personalizing or universalizing the venue of achievement. Additionally, the absence of framing invites the viewer into the picture; in other words, Borya the drummer seemingly could march right off the page and into the child-reader's world.

The world of the American child, according to the Lowe alphabet, was far larger than that of the Soviet, accommodating a number of occupational options for the young to consider. As mentioned earlier, this

[41] Chaplin's film *The Great Dictator* was released in 1940. Chaplin was a favorite at the movies in the USSR.

[42] There is no "S is for Stalin" or "L is for Lenin," as might be expected by those unfamiliar with Soviet children's culture. This is not unusual for Marshak's work, or for the 1940s in general. Support for the war and Soviet society indicated political loyalty as sufficiently as hero-worship.

[43] Molly Bang, *Picture This: How Pictures Work* (San Francisco, 2000), 44.

[44] See Bird, *Adventures in the Soviet Imaginary*, 12, on negative space in early Soviet book illustrations.

Костя — краснофлотец,
Клим — красноармеец.
Кто из них вернее попадает
в цель?

12

Леня —
Лучший лоцман. Он через
пороги
Лодки, пароходы водит по реке.

13

FIGURE 5.4 Left: "K – Kostya is a Red Navy sailor. Klim is a Red Army soldier. Which of them more truly judges the target?" Right: "L – Lyonya is the best skipper. He leads boats and ships through the rapids to the river." *Living Letters.*

alphabet book offers a variety of text/image combinations to actualize the letters; three of the eight use adult professions for a total of sixty-seven examples.[45] In the three that feature professions, the text varies from simple labeling in the first alphabet ("aviator," "barber," "carpenter") to a personified alphabet in verse form ("A was an Archer, who shot a frog/B was a Butcher who had a little dog") to a repetitive, representative alphabet ("F is for Flyer," "G is for General").[46] The occupations selected for use include the historical or traditional, the modern, and the World War II-specific. Simply placing a version of the "A was an Archer" alphabet in the book ensured the presentation of adult roles dating back at least two centuries – esquire, gamester, tinker – imparting new vocabulary to child-readers. The labeled alphabet offers a number of familiar,

[45] The military page in the Lowe alphabet combines military items – a dive bomber, a howitzer, a jeep – with military personnel. A list of the three alphabets featuring professions can be found in the Appendix to this chapter.
[46] Of the other five alphabets, two are simple labels, one is representative, one is personified, and the remaining is an active alphabet that uses children's names and tasks, such as "Frank goes Fishing" or "Helen feeds the Hen."

twentieth-century professions, with an odd dash of Old World elite culture: "dentist," "engineer," "fireman," and "glass blower" keep company with "hackman"; "upholsterer" and "wood carver" sandwich "valet." The integration of new and old, high and low, may have been intended to suggest the alleged classless nature of American democracy or perhaps to highlight the European roots of North American culture; whatever the intent, the hodgepodge has a leveling effect, hinting at the professional equality of monarch and barber that is mirrored in the book's illustrations. In the military-themed alphabet, thirteen types of personnel coexist, including "admiral," "quartermaster," and "lieutenant" (Figure 5.5). Another seven use martial terminology but include a human agent: A soldier blows a trumpet in "R is for Reveille" while a sailor mans a "Y Gun." Nearly all are dressed in World War II-era uniforms, emphasizing their contemporaneity, and the vocabulary would have been familiar from popular culture. The choice to include military roles had precedents in the early twentieth century, and may have been based on children's positive responses to wartime pop culture.[47] Taken as the whole, however, the text suggests that the war effort is simply one part of a much larger world upon which the child is invited to gaze. The same number of (directly) military professions are featured in the Soviet and American alphabet books but in far different proportions: thirteen of twenty-eight professions illustrated in the Soviet book as opposed to thirteen of seventy-eight in the American. The American text, mirroring the society in which it was created, recognizes both the immediacy and distance of the war in the "land of opportunity."

Part of this distance is created by the images designed to accompany the Lowe alphabet. As in the Soviet book, each letter is illustrated by a figure acting out the occupation introduced by the text. The figures interact with the letters rather than being placed apart from them, in a tableau format reminiscent of Kate Greenaway's work of the nineteenth century (Figure 5.6). For example, the Parson sits on the loop of the capital letter P while the Quaker grasps the sides of the Q and leaps through it. Like the positioning of text choices, the tableau format has the effect of "leveling" the figures; no size cues suggest greater or lesser significance of occupation to the viewer.[48] The alphabets are presented in double-spreads; that is,

---

[47] Other examples of military-themed alphabet books include *Little Soldier Boys ABC* (New York, 1900) and L. Frank Baum, *The Navy Alphabet and The Army Alphabet* (Chicago, 1900).

[48] Crain, *The Story of A*, 112–15.

A is an
Admiral

B is for
Bombs

C is for
Commando

D is for
Dive Bomber

I is for
Infantry

J is for
Jeep

K is for
Kitchen Police

L is for
Lieutenant

M is for
Machine Gunner

R is for
Reveille

S is for
Sergeant

T is for
Tank

U is for
U-boat

V is for
Victor

FIGURE 5.5 "A is an admiral ... " Alphabet book, Samuel Lowe Company.

a line of alphabet letters runs from the left side of the verso to the right side of the recto. Any sense of being drawn into the book's world, however, is undone by the framing which borders each alphabet. Framing creates detachment by telling our brains that we are observers, looking at a picture.[49] This particular frame, colored in a soothing light pink,

---

[49] Nikolajeva and Scott, *How Picturebooks Work*, 62.

R is for	S is for	T is for	U is for	V is for
Reveille	Sergeant	Tank	U-boat	Victor

FIGURE 5.6 Tableau format, Alphabet book, Samuel Lowe Company.

decorated with nursery rhyme figures – Jack and Jill, the cat and the fiddle, the three bears – softens the entire book's effect: Language acquisition is associated with playfulness, and fictional characters stand in direct contrast with the "real" world of adult roles that they frame.

The tableau figures are clearly the work of a single artist. Unlike the hand-sketched, realist figures of the monochromatic *Living Letters*, all in the American examples are cartoon-like in colors ranging from pastels to primaries to military khaki, perhaps in an effort to appeal to children by imitating the wildly popular comic book.[50] Overlapping is the primary method used to create depth, though a light touch of modeling is apparent in some figures.[51] Each figure, however, is grounded, whether by a specific environment or by the letter itself. The lumberjack, for example, stands on grass chopping a log, with a blue sky and tall forest in the background; the sergeant is surrounded by negative space, but is confined by his interaction with the letter S. These images are contained. Certain professions can only occur in certain locations – a forest, the ocean, a city, an office – thus, the reader must work harder to visualize him- or herself in such roles. Personalization is made even more difficult by the artist's choice to draw the figures, for the most part, as miniature adults. The roundedness of the figures' bodies and heads as well as most of their facial expressions, reminiscent of Rose O'Neill's Kewpies, suggest childishness and docility.[52] Receding hairlines,

[50] The vast majority of children – 95 percent of boys and 91 percent of girls, starting at age five – read comic books during the war: Tuttle, *"Daddy's Gone to War,"* 158.
[51] Overlapping means that foreground objects obscure the view of background objects, which creates the illusion of depth. Modeling is the use of light and shading to make a figure appear solid and three-dimensional.
[52] See Bang, *Picture This*, 71, on curved shapes and their effects.

clothing, and posture, however, imply adultness: The cherubic iceman wears a fedora and has anchor tattoos on his forearms! The military personnel smile in fun – even the figure on kitchen duty peeling potatoes – reflecting a predominant American memory of World War II "as a time of rewarding adventures" among those who were children during the war.[53]

Both the Soviet and American books seek to teach vocabulary related to the adult world and specific to the context of war. The Lowe alphabet goes further in presenting terminology of war, offering twenty-six examples of war-related words or phrases, but the effect is tempered by its inclusion among dozens of other lexical opportunities. The American child had the ability to turn the page and escape the war whereas the Soviet child encountered ongoing, consistent reminders of the war throughout Marshak's book. The verbal–visual images in the two books differ dramatically. Ermolaev's are clearly children acting in ways more appropriate for adults: A boy in a singlet – PE or camp clothing – is caught in the act of throwing a hand grenade; a boy in shorts wields a flashlight and rifle, playing border guard (Figure 5.7). The viewer is not allowed to question the age of the figures; they thrust solidarity upon the child-reader. Lowe's artist, however, creates a distance between the reader and the adult occupations by visual cues, framing, and image overload.

Both books reflect mainstream, though flawed, adult views of the working and fighting world as male and Caucasian. Only five of Marshak's characters are female (18 percent), while only four of the sixty-some figures (6 percent) in the Lowe alphabet are female. Most of the female figures work at traditionally female jobs, such as nurse (both), teacher (Soviet), and quilt-maker (American), though Marshak allows for a girl-architect and a girl-agricultural worker (Figure 5.8). Considering the number of women working in agriculture during the war, this is realistic; yet Marshak perpetuates a society-wide disgrace in ignoring the 800,000 women in the Soviet armed forces. One might expect the proportion of women workers to be higher in the Soviet book because of the egalitarian rhetoric present in Soviet ideology, yet Marshak's work reflects the limited nature of this promise and its realization in Soviet life. Lowe's alphabet, too, dismisses the dramatic rise in the female labor force occurring during World War II, reflecting conventional gender-typed behaviors.[54] Neither does Lowe's artist recognize minorities in the workforce or the army. There are no African Americans, Latinos, or Asian

[53] Tuttle, "*Daddy's Gone to War*," 234.
[54] Ibid., 143.

Г

Глеб —
Гранатометчик. Драться он
идет.

6

FIGURE 5.7 "G – Gleb is a grenade-thrower. He is off to fight." *Living Letters.*

Americans among these toilers, typical for war-era American children's culture.[55] Ermolaev's drawings depict representative "Slavic" children, and Marshak's choice of names only includes two nods to the more than

[55] See ibid., ch. 10, for discussion of the racial prejudices common to children's culture.

100 ethnic groups residing in the USSR.[56] On the whole, both books present the dominant ethnic group as the only ethnic group.[57] The books propose societies not entirely consistent with either reality or ideology.

CONCLUSION

The Marshak book intimated to Soviet children that they were expected to participate in the defense of their country, whether through military, civilian, or support roles. Text, image, and design invited the child-reader into the adult world of war through this introduction to literacy. The book's tiny size made manifest the scarcity and deprivation caused by war, and perhaps only the novelty of a new book in wartime made it attractive to preschoolers. The images retain elements of innocence beyond the realism of the child figures: The pediatrician practices medicine upon a doll, the engine driver rides a child-sized locomotive, the nurse treats a fuzzy teddy bear. These, however, appear side by side with more jarring images of children brandishing guns and grenades. Affectively, the child-reader might enjoy the luxury of a book and the amusement of Marshak's verse; but the war looms over this encounter with the alphabet. *Living Letters* demonstrates the physical and psychological proximity of war for Soviet children, as was characteristic of contemporary Soviet children's culture, and foregrounds adult expectations of children's participation in the war effort.[58]

The book's message was reinforced by a system that encouraged children to appreciate labor, value self-sacrifice, and find meaning in the collective.[59] Heroism could be attained through acts of loyalty to that system, which in wartime meant active participation in the war effort even for the youngest of children. Official children's culture provided little respite or haven from the realities of war, depicting the war in great detail, through art, narrative, and poetry that mirrored adult wartime culture. Soviet childhood was mobilized to meet the needs of war. While invasion necessitated such mobilization, ideology laid the groundwork for it.

---

[56] "Khariton" is a Greek name, and "Iakov" a Jewish one.
[57] The US population was 89.8 percent "white" in 1940; the USSR's population was more than 75 percent East Slavic in 1940: Frank Hobbs and Nicole Stoops, US Census Bureau, Census 2000 Special Reports, Series CENSR-4, *Demographic Trends in the 20th Century* (Washington, DC, 2002), 75; Demoskop Weekly, Institut demografii Natsional'nogo issledovatel'skogo universiteta "Vysshaia shkola ekonomiki," http://demoscope.ru/wee kly/ssp/ussr_nac_26.php.
[58] On children's culture during the war, see deGraffenried, *Sacrificing Childhood*.
[59] Kucherenko, *Little Soldiers*, 39, 45, 105.

C

Соня —
Санитарка.

19

FIGURE 5.8 "S – Sonya is a nurse." *Living Letters.*

In contrast, the Lowe alphabet was designed to elicit a positive emotional response from the child-reader, who could choose whether to engage in a war that is presented as entertaining rather than dangerous.

Because of the image–text interaction, not only are the lettered occupations cast as something to be pursued later in life but participation in the war itself as an adult task. Yet Samuel Lowe's decision to include military terms and personnel in a book for children was out of character for American children's literature on the whole.[60] Though war pervaded other aspects of children's culture, authors, illustrators, and publishers eschewed it in favor of soothing or fanciful narratives such as McCloskey's *Make Way for Ducklings*, Burton's *The Little House*, and the Curious George adventures.[61] In fact, the World War II era saw fewer references to death in children's literature than any other period between 1721 and 1975.[62] While American children lived, watched, learned about, worked for, and played war, they did not have to read about it in their books. Whether responding to the popularity of war-themed culture among children out of disdain for the literary elite or in the hopes of increasing profits, Lowe introduced a taboo subject to the youngest of readers; yet he cushioned the blow. His book demonstrates that, despite popular culture and children's interests, an adult conception of white, middle-class childhood as a haven of innocence separate from the harsh adult world predominated in the wartime United States.[63] Adults maintained that the war, ideally, remained "over there."

On the whole, then, these two abecedaria provide evidence of differing adult constructions of childhood, reflective of divergent wartime needs, preexisting ideologies, and systems of cultural production. They affirm that the acquisition of literacy, in all its forms, is a practice fraught with political, social, economic, cultural, and national undertones. Conflict complicated, disrupted, and intensified this process. The scale of World War II resulted in messages to children from adults that directly engaged the war as part of the child's world – albeit to different degrees – but defined that world and the significance of the child's literacy itself through the use of normative, politicized text and images. Learning the ABCs had always been about more than learning letters but, in this context, it also made children participants in the war. What these books indicate in microcosm, world war revealed on a grand scale: The line between child

[60] Tuttle, "*Daddy's Gone to War,*" 156; Marcus, *Golden Legacy*, 71.

[61] Even Nazi refugees H. A. and Margret Rey make no mention of war in the Curious George books. See Gail Schmunk Murray, *American Children's Literature and the Construction of Childhood* (New York, 1998), 167.

[62] Mary Lystad, *From Dr. Mather to Dr. Seuss: 200 Years of American Books for Children* (Boston, 1980), Table 8.9, 223, Table 8.10, 225.

[63] Tuttle, "*Daddy's Gone to War,*" 106–11.

protection and child mobilization had blurred, perhaps disappeared altogether, even for those children most likely to be protected in a prewar setting. While this particular struggle resulted in the reevaluation and extension of the modern conception of childhood in many postwar societies, present-day alphabet books remind us that politicization of the very young continues apace.

Appendix

Text of Samuil Marshak's *Zhivye bukvy*, in English; words beginning with the Russian letter being taught are italicized (author's translation)

A – *Alik* is an *aviator*, a real pilot – He flies a *crimson* plane in the *Arctic*.

B – *Borya* is a *drummer*.

V – *Vlas* is a *plumber*.

G – *Gleb* is a *grenade-thrower*. He is off to fight.

D – *Dima* is a *pediatrician*. He works in a hospital.

Ye – *Eva rides* horseback at the circus.

Zh – *Zhenya* is a *reaper* in the field. She *reaps* wheat.

Z – *Zinaida* is an *architect*. She *knows* how to build a house.

I – *Igor* is a *famous railway engineer*. He digs a tunnel *from* Moscow to Odessa.

K – *Kostya* is a *Red Navy* sailor, *Klim* is a *Red Army* soldier. *Which* of them more truly judges the target?

L – *Lyonya* is the *best skipper*. He leads *boats* and ships through the rapids to the river.

M – *Misha* is an *engine driver* on the tracks, *racing* day and night on a steam engine.

N – *Nikolai* is a *typesetter*. Letter by letter, he *places* them in a line with an experienced hand.

O – *Osip* is a *gardener, he* digs up rutabagas.

P – *Pavel* is a *border guard*, a fighting *guy*.

R – *Rodion* is a *worker*, a *miner* in the Donbass.

S – *Sonya* is a *nurse*.

T – *Tolya* is a *tractor driver*.

U – *Smart Yuliana teaches* kids in class.

F – *Fedya* is an *athlete*, the best *soccer player*.

Kh – *Khariton* is an *artist*. He is able to draw *good* pictures for you.

Ts – *Tsezar*, our *engraver*, can make *figures* and pictures in print by corroding *zinc*.

Ch – *Black-eyed Charlie*, our common friend, *Charlie Chaplin*, famous in film. *Charlie* plays in the yard and at home. *Slightly* he turns – and all is already silly.

Sh – *Shura* is a glorious *explorer*. *He stormed* ice floes. The *snow* is not terrible to him, in the cold he is not freezing.

Shch – Hooves *click*. This is Ukraine. *Shchors* sweeps on, riding – the real *Shchors*!

E – *Eduard* is an *electrician*. He fixes the switch.

Iu – *Iurii* is an experienced *naturalist* at the zoo. *Iurii* is the best friend and caregiver of *young* crocodiles and *nimble* frogs.

Ia – *Iakov* became a linguist from childhood. In our home, *Iakov* is very famous. *Iakov* speaks *Yakut* with the neighbors. I do not understand what he is saying!

Text of Samuel Lowe alphabets featuring professions: Unless otherwise noted, jobs are represented as male

Alphabet 1: aviator, barber, carpenter, dentist, engineer, fireman, glass blower, hackman, iceman, junkman, key-maker, lumberjack, mechanic, nurse (female), opera singers (male and female), policeman, quilt-maker (female), riveter, shoemaker, tailor, upholsterer, valet, wood carver, x-ray operator, yeoman, zinc worker

ALPHABET 2

A was an Archer, who shot a frog
B was a Butcher, who had a little dog
C was a Captain, covered with lace
D was a Dunce, with a funny face
E was an Esquire, with pride on his brow
F was a Farmer, and followed the plow
G was a Gamester, and had ill luck
H was a Hunter, who hunted a buck
I was an Innkeeper, who loved a good grouse
J was a Joiner, who built himself a house
K was a King, so mighty and grand
L was a Lady, who had a white hand
M was a Miser, who hoarded up gold

N was a Nobleman, gallant and bold
O was an Oboe player, who went about town
P was a Parson, who wore a black gown
Q was a Quaker, who would not bow down
R was a Robber, whose end will be sad
S was a Sailor, a fine jolly lad
T was a Tinker, who mended a pan
U was an Usher, a wee little man
V was a Vendor, a very good man
W was a Watchman, who guarded the door
X was Expensive, and so became poor
Y was a Youth, who did not love school
Z was a Zany, a poor harmless fool.

Alphabet 3: admiral, bombs, commando, dive bomber, engineer, flyer, general, howitzer, infantry, jeep, kitchen police, lieutenant, machinegunner, navy, observation balloon, paratrooper, quartermaster, reveille, sergeant, tank, U-boat, victor, wireless, "x marks the objective," Y Gun, zero hour

6

Boys and Girls in the Service of Total War: Defense Service Training in Swedish Schools During World War II

Esbjörn Larsson

In late 1943, as Sweden was still encircled by the German troops who were occupying Denmark and Norway, the Wahlström publishing house issued Gustaf Lindwall's *Sven i hemvärnet (Sven in the Home Guard)* in its series of stories for boys. Sven is sixteen years old when the story begins, and his father has just been made squad leader in the Home Guard. The unrest in the outside world worries Sven's father, who believes that Swedish neutrality means that Sweden must be prepared to defend itself against any country that violates Swedish borders. Sven also wants to be Home Guardsman, but, on account of his age, he can serve only as a reservist in the Home Guard. Still, Sven experiences a range of adventures. He puts out fires, participates in military exercises with real guns and grenades, finds a crashed British aircraft along with his father, discovers and stops an attempt to blow up a power line, finds and reports naval mines, and almost single-handedly apprehends the crew of a crashed German bomber.[1]

What makes *Sven i hemvärnet* so interesting is that it was not simply a made-up adventure story. During most of World War II, pupils in Swedish secondary schools were trained in putting out fires, scouting for enemies, handling army rifles, and throwing hand grenades. Moreover, a total of about 20 percent of boys in secondary schools participated in the two Home Guard organizations. Among secondary school girls, 12 percent served in the Red Cross, 9 percent in the Scout Corps, 9 percent as air surveillance personnel, 7 percent in the Women's Voluntary Defense

---

[1] Gustaf Lindwall, *Sven i hemvärnet: berättelse för pojkar* (Stockholm, 1943).

(Lotta Corps).[2] This chapter will examine the practice of defense service training within the Swedish secondary school system and the debates that preceded its introduction in order to show how the threat of war made lines of conflict in the perception of children visible during World War II.

Children's living conditions and adult perceptions of children in the West have changed dramatically during the past century. In addition to a decline in the number of children in the average family and the exclusion of children from the working world as schooling was gradually extended, there was also a change in children's status in society. Children's value came to depend less on their economic contributions and more on their emotional relationships with their parents.[3] Studies of Swedish conditions at the beginning of the twentieth century have pointed to a somewhat different trend, however. Increased schooling in rural areas did not automatically mean that Swedish children stopped working, and children did not lose their economic value in Sweden to the same extent as in the United States during the first decades of the twentieth century.[4] Similar results have also been presented for Great Britain, where a change in the perception of children during the interwar period, toward greater concern and the idea that childhood is a period of vulnerability, did not significantly affect children of the working class.[5] The first part of the century thus appears to have been a period when perceptions of childhood began to change even though children's living conditions remained unchanged in many places.

Another area that went through major changes during the twentieth century was gender relations. During World War II, opinions about women's place in the workforce changed dramatically.[6] Women in Sweden came to assume men's tasks in a number of spheres during

---

[2] Gunnar Richardson, *Hitler-jugend i svensk skol- och ungdomspolitik: beredskapspedagogik och demokratifostran i Sverige under andra världskriget* (Uppsala, 2003), 114–15.

[3] Hugh Cunningham, *Children and Childhood in Western Society Since 1500* (London, 2005), 172–74, 187; Colin Heywood, *Growing Up in France: From the Ancien Régime to the Third Republic* (Cambridge, 2007), 251; Viviana A. Zelizer, *Pricing the Priceless Child: The Changing Social Value of Children* (Princeton, [1985] 1994), 209–11.

[4] Mats Sjöberg, *Att säkra framtidens skördar: barndom, skola och arbete i agrar miljö. Bolstad pastorat 1860–1930* (Linköping, 1996), 259–60; Johanna Sköld, *Fosterbarnsindustri eller människokärlek: barn, familjer och utackorderingsbyrån i Stockholm 1890–1925* (Stockholm, 2006).

[5] Berry Mayall and Virginia Morrow, *You Can Help Your Country: English Children's Work During the Second World War* (London, 2011), 54, 79–81, 108, 237–38.

[6] See for example Lucy Noakes, "Women and World War II," in George Kassimeris and John Buckley, eds., *Ashgate Research Companion to Modern Warfare* (Farnham, 2010), 223–40.

World War II.[7] One task that had seemed unthinkable for women just a few years earlier was scouting for enemy aircraft from air surveillance towers. In 1943, no fewer than 5,600 Swedish women were serving as air surveillance personnel and had learned how to handle weapons. Interestingly, this shift in women's sphere of activity was accompanied by a redefinition of air surveillance. The often monotonous activity of scouting was described as a chore that was particularly suitable for women.[8]

In her analysis of this shift, Fia Sundevall emphasizes the importance of the changing nature of warfare. Advances in military aviation contributed to the extension of warfare beyond clearly defined fronts and the emergence of what has been described as "total war." In such a war, there were no longer protected areas. Suddenly, the entire population became involved in warfare, which redefined what were seen as female tasks.[9]

In the light of these developments, it is useful to examine phenomena such as defense service training in schools that aimed to prepare both girls and boys for the event of war. This training has been studied previously, but not in order to examine children's perceptions and the activities they actually engaged in during this training. Moreover, although girls were included in the training, scholars have not considered the category of gender in examining the exercises.[10]

Sweden was never involved in acts of war during World War II, although the whole of Swedish society was organized for war and the country's armed forces were periodically fully mobilized. It is impossible to say to what extent children and young people would have been involved in the event of war, but it is possible to examine what role was anticipated for children in the event of war as well as the other educational purposes the defense service training might have filled.

A broad range of source materials – government inquiries and regulations, consultation reports, training manuals, and reports from individual schools – makes clear that there was no consensus on the extent of defensive military training for children or children's participation in the event of war. Despite the lack of consensus, compulsory defense service training was introduced in Swedish secondary schools, and pupils were

[7] Johanna Overud, *I beredskap med fru Lojal: behovet av kvinnlig arbetskraft i Sverige under andra världskriget* (Stockholm, 2005).
[8] Fia Sundevall, *Det sista manliga yrkesmonopolet: genus och militärt arbete i Sverige 1865–1989* (Stockholm, 2011), 52–56, 63–65.
[9] Ibid., 61.
[10] Richardson, *Hitler-jugend i svensk skol- och ungdomspolitik*.

trained to take part in the country's defense. Moreover, the immediate threat of a total war led Swedish officials to regard girls as well as boys as potential participants in the war effort.

A BOLD PROPOSAL

The question of compulsory defense service training arose during late winter 1940, when a government commission was appointed to draft a plan for training activities.[11] Among the commission's members were several of Sweden's most distinguished teachers of physical education, including Colonel Bertil Gustafsson Uggla, an Olympic bronze medalist in the pole vault and the modern pentathlon.[12]

The report that the commission submitted in December 1940 proposed an extensive training program for Swedish schoolchildren on the grounds that "war has become a war machine and taken on a totalitarian character that does not leave any social function unaffected or any place within the country safely protected."[13] One distinct change from earlier training exercises in Swedish schools was that girls were to be included in compulsory defense service training.[14] Policymakers argued that the strain put on a society by modern war required the contributions of all members of society. In the event of war, women would be forced to take men's places in industry and, in turn, girls would be needed to take the place of women in civil defense.[15]

The commission recommended that children begin defense service training as early as the age of seven. Training would take the form of games, sports and athletics (e.g., swimming, skiing, ice skating), and road safety education. Terrain-oriented games such as hide-and-seek and various forms of tag would be added later. When the children reached the age of twelve, boys would do basic target practice and learn how to throw hand grenades. Girls at that age were to be educated in first aid; boys would receive that training a year later. At the age of thirteen, students of both sexes would be trained in what to do in the event of air raids and gas

---

[11] Ibid., 19–20; *Betänkande och förslag angående värntjänstutbildning för skolungdom* (Stockholm, 1940), v–vii.

[12] *Betänkande och förslag angående värntjänstutbildning för skolungdom*, v.

[13] Ibid., 7.

[14] Arms exercises for boys had been conducted in Swedish schools between 1863 and 1917: Henrik Meinander, *Towards a Bourgeois Manhood: Boys' Physical Education in Nordic Secondary Schools 1880–1940* (Helsinki, 1994), 173–81.

[15] Ibid., 6–8.

attacks, how to scout for enemy targets, how to report enemy troop movements, and how to serve as dispatch messengers.[16]

During the air raid exercises, the commission recommended, school-children should be given information about aerial bombing and air sur-veillance and also engage in practical exercises in how they could be of service in case of an air raid. They might, for instance, deliver dispatches on bicycle if telephone service were disrupted by bombing. The description of the exercises in scouting for targets made clear how the commission members imagined that this skill would help the young people defend their country. They pointed out that the training in scouting for targets would help prepare boys for their future military service as conscripts, and they also noted it was intended "to impart to students the requisite attention and perception for monitoring services (in air surveil-lance towers, guarding service at camps, etc.)." Scouting for targets was also presented as developing masculine traits, as it would help to "pre-serve and develop the natural 'hunting instinct.'" The training in first aid focused on dressing wounds, a skill that might be useful in any emergency. The only references to war in this part of the training program would come in the lessons on poison gas attacks.[17]

Target practice and weapons training would be limited to boys. The commission's members argued that boys could very well start learn-ing how to shoot at the age of eleven or twelve. At first, the boys would engage in short-range shooting (10–30 meters) using air guns or .22 caliber rifles. They would later progress to shooting range practice with army rifles at distances between 200 and 300 meters. At the age of sixteen, the boys would move on to shooting under field conditions. Boys seven-teen and older would be organized into military-style units for shooting drill.[18]

The plans for weapons training clearly indicate that the commission's members were advocating an activity that would prepare youngsters for combat, but they also emphasized that the training was not adequate for turning school boys into soldiers. The ultimate aim of the training becomes evident in one of the more advanced field practice exercises. Squads of students armed with loaded rifles practiced advancing in orderly formation on bicycle to confront enemy paratroopers.[19]

---

[16] Ibid., 21, 48–49.
[17] Ibid., 30–35, Appendix A; quotations, 32.
[18] Ibid., 35–36.
[19] Ibid., 142.

The report also suggested special exercises for girls such as "home and camp service," which trained girls to be helpers in evacuation camps. Another element in the training for girls was home healthcare. That was to include instruction in basic nursing tasks, emergency care, and the administration of medication. In addition to this, the girls would also be trained in childcare, above all the care of infants.[20]

The proposal for compulsory defense service training in schools led to a lively debate. According to Gunnar Richardson, the leftist press generally expressed harsh criticism, and conservative newspapers were positive. Critics charged that the proposed training program had been modeled on the Hitler Youth, that the country did not have enough qualified teachers to carry out the program, and that the program was simply too costly. Moreover, they targeted the fact that training would begin while students were still children.[21]

The Ministry of Education and Ecclesiastical Affairs asked a broad range of individuals and organizations – including schools and teacher training institutions, school boards, school inspectors, church officials, civil servants, and interest groups – for their views on the compulsory defense service training proposal. Their responses reveal that the most controversial proposal by far was the introduction of target practice and hand-grenade training for boys at the age of twelve.[22] Even the board of the Swedish Shooting Federation, which was otherwise strongly in favor of fire arms training, emphasized that, "on the basis of its experience in its own domain, it strongly questioned the appropriateness of beginning target practice at such an early age."[23]

Although there was broad agreement that twelve was too young to start target practice, there was no consensus on what age would be appropriate or, indeed, whether schools should be involved in teaching children how to shoot. Most who responded to the ministry did not offer specific recommendations; those who did proposed ages ranging from thirteen to seventeen.[24] Furthermore, it is difficult to see any clear pattern among the

---

[20] Ibid., 36–40.

[21] Richardson, *Hitler-jugend i svensk skol- och ungdomspolitik*, 25–32.

[22] More than 300 responses from a range of different bodies were submitted: No. 68, Ministry of Education and Ecclesiastical Affairs' Cabinet Meeting Documents, March 21, 1941, Swedish National Archives (no. 68, Ecklesiastikdepartementets konseljhandlingar 21/3 1941, Riksarkivet) (hereafter MEEA/CMD). Of these, only a few were fully in favor of the proposal. Among them can be mentioned the right-wing youth movement the Young Swedes, the Committee for School Sports, and the Association for the Promotion of Weapons Exercises Among School Youth.

[23] The board of the Shooting Federation, MEEA/CMD.

[24] This is based on a review of the submitted consultation responses: MEEA/CMD.

various bodies consulted, and in some cases there was clear disagreement within organizations and institutions. The faculty of a secondary school for boys in the Södermalm district of Stockholm, for example, recommend that weapons training be introduced at the age of fifteen; the school's headmaster and physical education teacher, on the other hand, saw no problem in starting such training as early as age thirteen.[25]

Practical as well as ethical and physiological reasons were given in the responses for completely rejecting firearms practice or postponing it until the children were older. Many of the responses pointed out that it would be extremely expensive to buy air guns or .22 caliber rifles so that the children could start learning to shoot at the age of twelve. The representatives of the elementary schools often questioned the benefit of target practice for elementary school students, as they would most likely have forgotten what they had learned by the time they came to do their military service as conscripts several years later.[26]

Those who rejected weapons training in schools entirely often did so on ethical grounds. Their main argument was that children should not be forced prematurely into the adult world. The elementary school inspector in Skaraborg's southern district argued that a people with highly developed cultural values "should to the very end be able to afford to show consideration and respect for the child and to let children be children throughout their childhood, to live and be engaged in things that are appropriate for them according to their nature and needs all through this phase of life."[27]

---

[25] The headmaster of the upper secondary school for boys at Södermalm: the faculty of the upper secondary school for boys at Södermalm, MEEA/CMD.

[26] The headmaster of the upper secondary school in Kristianstad; the faculty of the elementary school teacher training institute in Gothenburg; the elementary school inspectors for the districts of Roslagen, Södermanland (eastern), South Småland (western), Hälsingland northern, Halland northern, Älvsborg southern, Värmland western, Närke, Västerbotten (northern); the Gävle elementary school board; the Swedish YMCA; the Swedish Elementary School Teacher Association: MEEA/CMD.

[27] The elementary school inspector for the district of Skaraborg (southern), MEEA/CMD. For similar comments, see, for example, the faculty of the junior school teacher training institute in Landskrona; the headmaster at the elementary school teacher training institute in Falun; the faculty of the municipal middle school in Höör; the faculty of the Vasa municipal girls' school in Gothenburg; the elementary school inspector for Stockholm, Uppland, the districts of Östergötland (eastern), Northern Småland (central), South Skåne (western), Värmland (eastern), Hälsingland (southern), Norrbotten (southern); the Gothenburg school association; the central board of the Swedish Elementary School Female Teachers' Association; the board of the Swedish Junior School Female Teachers' Association: MEEA/CMD.

Others argued that military training in schools would in the long run teach children that war was a natural part of the world order and threaten peaceful coexistence between nations. This is evident in the response of the alliance of Swedish YMCAs, which stated that "an early initiation into military training may create a spirit of aggression and the delusion that violence and war are normal phenomena in human life. Young people ought instead to be brought up to be respectful of others and to show reverence for human life."[28]

Some opponents of the program focused on the issue of child development, especially children's physical development and intellectual maturity. The Karlstad secondary school, for example, warned that "the element of risk is too great when dealing with very lively and thoughtless little boys" in shooting practice.[29]

The element of the proposed program most heavily criticized according to the National Board of Education was hand-grenade training. Some sports organizations, by contrast, praised it for its athletic value. Some commentators warned that safely throwing grenades required greater muscular development than could be expected of twelve-year-olds.[30]

As for the girls' training, the respondents considered the home and camp services and healthcare training the most important aspects of the program. Several bodies were opposed to the introduction of childcare training because, they argued, it would not provide sufficient training to enable the girls to take care of babies.[31] Opinion was divided on training

---

[28] The Swedish YMCA: MEEA/CMD. See also the headmaster at the elementary school teacher seminar in Falun; the elementary school inspector in South Skåne western district; the central board of the Swedish Elementary School Female Teacher Association: MEEA/CMD.

[29] The upper secondary school in Karlstad: MEEA/CMD. For similar comments, see, for example, the National Board of Education; the upper secondary school in Uppsala; the faculty of the coeducational lower secondary school in Köping; the headmaster of the elementary school teacher training institute in Falun; the elementary school inspectors for the districts of Östergötland (eastern), Gästrikland, Ångermanland (southern); the central board of the Girls and Coeducational Schools' Association: MEEA/CMD.

[30] The upper secondary school in Karlstad; the Vasa secondary school; the coeducational lower secondary school in Klippan; the Association of Headmasters of State Secondary Schools; the central board of the Girls and Coeducational Schools Association; the National Board of Education; the Biology Teachers' Association: MEEA/CMD.

[31] The National Board of Education; the faculty of the upper secondary school for girls at Norrmalm (Stockholm); the faculties of the municipal girls' schools in Gävle, Majorna (Gothenburg), Vasa (Gothenburg), Hudiksvall, Kungsholmen (Stockholm); the coeducational lower secondary school and municipal upper secondary school in Kiruna; the central board of the Girls and Coeducational Schools Association; the Municipal Middle Schools Teachers' Association: MEEA/CMD.

girls to scout for targets, to write reports, and to serve as dispatch messengers.[32]

A MORE MODEST DEFENSE TRAINING PROGRAM

When the final form of the defense service education program was decided in the summer of 1941, it differed from the original proposal in several respects. The training was restricted to youth between sixteen and twenty years of age. However, the purpose of the program remained the same: "to prepare the pupils for the tasks that would come to be assigned to them in war or in the threat of war, and thus strengthen their sense of responsibility for the fatherland." The decree establishing the training program stressed in particular that the training would prepare young people not only for future military service as conscripts but also for immediate service in the Home Guard and similar bodies, such as the Red Cross.[33]

There were also some important changes to the substance of the training. Both boys and girls would be trained in air raid response, emergency care, and reporting service. Boys would also be taught how to shoot; girls would be given training in home and camp services and home healthcare. As for fire arms training, the decree emphasized that students would have the right to ask to be excused from participation.[34] Only 22 out of 6,932 boys opted out of target practice in the 1941/1942 academic year.[35]

The brief decree establishing defense service training was followed by series of short directives on specific parts of the training program. In May 1942, the National Board of Education issued detailed instruction manuals for boys and girls alike.[36] The analysis that follows draws on the

[32] Among those that were against such exercises for girls were the faculty of the upper secondary school for girls at Norrmalm (Stockholm); the faculty of the coeducational lower secondary school and municipal upper secondary school in Kiruna. Among those in favor were the headmaster of the higher secondary school in Kristianstad; the faculties of the municipal girls' schools in Kalmar, Kungsholmen (Stockholm). The scout corps of the Swedish YWCA was in favor of exercises in writing reports but against exercises in target reconnaissance and dispatch messenger services: MEEA/CMD.

[33] Swedish Code of Statutes: King-in-Council Decree Concerning Instruction in Compulsory Defense Service at Certain Educational Institutions (Sv. förf. saml. 1941:604: *Kungl. Maj:ts kungörelse angående utbildning i värntjänst vid vissa läroanstalter*) (hereafter Sv. förf. saml. 1941:604).

[34] Ibid.

[35] Richardson, *Hitler-jugend i svensk skol- och ungdomspolitik*, 114.

[36] *Anvisningar för den manliga skolungdomens värntjänstutbildning* (Stockholm, 1942); *Anvisningar för den kvinnliga skolungdomens värntjänstutbildning* (Stockholm, 1942); National Board of Education, July 31, 1941; August 8, 1941, F II:1, the Gymnastics

manuals as well as the exercises carried out during the 1941/1942 school year.

One area that is of particular interest for this study is the training for observation and reporting service, which prepared young people for assignments they were likely to be given in the event of war. Beyond the fact that exercises for boys in this area were twice as extensive as those for the girls, a clear difference in how the training was intended to be applied is evident. The introduction to the section on observation in the manual for training boys makes clear reference to the importance of observation skills when shooting; the instructions for girls make no mention of shooting. Similarly, the section of the manual on observation service for girls excludes mention of military targets almost entirely. Whereas boys practiced scouting for armed soldiers in combat situations, girls, according to the manual, were to search for "live targets" and "scouts." This difference in wording suggests that the training exercises for girls were not as clearly directed toward future combat situations as the exercises for boys were.[37]

A similar difference is evident in the exercises for reporting service even though boys and girls were taught essentially the same skills. Unlike the exercises for boys, the girls' exercises did not include practice in catching their breath after covering long distances on foot or in proper behavior when passing guards. This can be interpreted as a difference in how girls and boys were to be used as dispatch messengers. The boys were trained to carry reports between different units, whereas girls practiced conveying reports within a camp.[38]

Training exercises for boys and girls sometimes partially overlapped. Boys and girls alike learned camping skills and orienteering. The training for boys focused on survival in the forest, including erecting tents and building lean-to shelters. Girls' training focused on setting up tent camps and indoor camps. Boys learned to cook for themselves; girls learned how to cook for others.[39]

Maneuver exercises for boys and girls differed significantly. Girls practiced moving between two points in an organized manner. Boys' exercises in maneuvering were geared toward soldiers' behavior in the field. They learned how to move without being seen, for example, and the different

Section, the National Board of Education, Swedish National Archives (Gymnastiksektionen, Skolöverstyrelsen, Riksarkivet) (hereafter GS/NBE).

[37] *Betänkande och förslag angående värntjänstutbildning för skolungdom*, 33; *Anvisningar för den manliga*, 92–100; *Anvisningar för den kvinnliga*, 111–22.

[38] *Anvisningar för den manliga*, 106–19; *Anvisningar för den kvinnliga*, 126–35.

[39] *Anvisningar för den manliga*, 14, 165–75; *Anvisningar för den kvinnliga*, 12, 74, 83–110.

military squad maneuvers. Boys' and girls' exercises for finding people in the woods were more similar. Both boys and girls would be trained to move in a so-called hunters' chain. But whereas this exercise was cast largely as a game in the instruction manual for girls, it was presented to boys as practice in catching saboteurs.[40]

The authors of the manuals thought boys would be able to contribute in the event of war in other ways as well, as is clear from some of the other exercises. Acknowledging the possibility of attack from the air, the manual for boys pointed out that local communities might become the scene of combat. Airborne invasion was to be countered by modern mobile army units, but until they arrived it would be up to the Home Guard, with the help of schoolchildren, to delay the enemy's advance. That was to be achieved above all by erecting obstacles to prevent enemies from landing or to impede enemy units that had already landed.[41]

In the event of invasion, boys could serve in two different roles. If a boy was at least seventeen years old and was a skilled marksman, he could become a Home Guardsman (sixteen-year-olds could enroll as reservists in the Home Guard). Boys could also serve as civilian aides, who would be responsible for building barriers and reporting on enemy activity. The work of the civilian aides would allow the guardsmen to focus on defending the barriers. In training exercises to assist the Home Guard, boys did reconnaissance to locate suitable sites for barriers, erected barriers, and set up reporting chains to warn those defending barriers of enemy approach.[42] In the event of an enemy attack, in other words, schoolboys would find themselves between the enemy and the Home Guard.

In firearms training, there was no fundamental difference between the original proposal and the training set out in the instruction manual. Both emphasized that the training the boys received should lay a foundation for the training they later undergo as conscripts. The biggest difference between the original proposal and the exercises prescribed in the manual was that preliminary practice in short-range target shooting with air rifles or .22 caliber rifles was dropped. Target practice with army rifles was to begin at the age of sixteen, and the applied shooting had to wait until age eighteen. The most advanced arms exercise in the instruction manual was

---

[40] *Anvisningar för den manliga*, 25–36, 43; *Anvisningar för den kvinnliga*, 136, 141–46.
[41] *Anvisningar för den manliga*, 44–45.
[42] Ibid., 45–51.

to have boys advance one by one on the shooting range with loaded army rifles and fire at targets at distances up to 200 meters.[43]

One exercise proposed by the government commission but not mentioned in the decree on military training for schoolchildren was grenade training. Nevertheless, the instruction manual did include exercises on the use of hand grenades (only dummies were to be used). To make the exercises more vivid, the manual suggested that the boys could practice throwing grenades at cardboard human figures or that they could practice how to advance swiftly on the enemy by competing in getting up from a protected position and running toward the impact site just as the grenade detonated.[44]

Home healthcare was the only aspect of training for girls that was not also part of the boys' training. The instruction was not as comprehensive as the government commission had proposed. Home healthcare training lasted for one school year, not two as the commission had recommended, and it focused on nursing. No mention was made of medical training.[45]

Reports from schools provide additional information on boys' and girls' defense service training and how it was perceived. Training for girls usually started at the age of fifteen instead of sixteen. Otherwise the defense service training was organized very much in line with the instruction manuals issued in 1942. The municipal girls' school in Borås, for example, chose to organize a three-day training camp just before the start of the fall semester of 1941. The girls practiced using sheath knives and axes, pitching tents, estimating ranges, lifesaving, cooking outdoors, healthcare, terrain games with target reconnaissance, orientation, and writing reports. Similar training sessions were held for girls at other schools, albeit with some variation in the exercises. Most schools, for instance, allowed girls to engage in these exercises on target reconnaissance and messenger and reporting service, but there were some that did not.[46]

---

43 *Betänkande och förslag angående värntjänstutbildning för skolungdom*, 35–36, 134; *Anvisningar för den manliga*, 14, 52–53, 79–81.

44 *Betänkande och förslag angående värntjänstutbildning för skolungdom*, 16, 19, 25–26; Sv. förf. saml. 1941:604; *Anvisningar för den manliga*, 14, 120–29.

45 *Betänkande och förslag angående värntjänstutbildning för skolungdom*, 39; *Anvisningar för den kvinnliga*, 72–73.

46 Exercises in target reconnaissance and messenger and reporting services were conducted at the municipal girls' schools in Hudiksvall (December 5, 1941); Gothenburg upper coeducational school (June 11, 1942); Lund private elementary school (June 13, 1942); Saltsjöbaden coeducational school (June 11, 1942); the Sigtuna Foundation humanist secondary school (April 9, 1941); the Whitlock coeducational school (June 15, 1942); the

Schools generally followed the instructions on training exercises for boys issued by the National Board of Education very closely. Among the few exceptions were the Lundberg boarding school, which did not provide weapons training, and the Whitlock coeducational school, where boys were instructed in swimming but did not receive grenade training.[47] Some schools had ambitious training aspirations for boys. In the description of the exercises at Lund private school, the headmaster argued that the key objective of the military exercises had been for "the pupils to obtain the necessary knowledge and skills that were ultimately needed to be placed in the Home Guard, which is why the training was focused on the building of a certain self-confidence in pupils when it came to handling rifles and hand grenades and the use of these weapons as well as a map and compass in the field."[48] The upper secondary school in Norrköping emphasized the need to expand the exercises by including instruction in how "land mines were constructed and used in the ongoing war" and "exercises in hand-to-hand combat."[49]

BOYS AND GIRLS IN THE SERVICE OF TOTAL WAR

As demonstrated above, there was no consensus regarding the appropriateness of allowing children to be trained for national defense in Swedish schools during World War II. Although no one openly advocated the involvement of young children in direct combat as child soldiers, the members of the government commission suggested that defense service training should be made an integral part of education from the age of seven, and actual defense exercises started at the age of twelve.

When the commission's proposals were circulated for comment, they met with great resistance as being too extensive and far-reaching. Several

upper secondary schools in Gävle (January 22, 1942); Strängnäs (March 30, 1942); and Östersund (April 25, 1942); but not in the municipal girls' schools in Majorna (Gothenburg) (December 4, 1941); Vasa (Gothenburg) (December 5, 1941); Halmstad (December 2, 1941); or the New elementary school for girls (June 14, 1942). Exercises in target reconnaissance and writing reports but not messenger services were reported from the municipal girls' schools in Borås (December 5, 1941), Jönköping (December 5, 1941), and Gävle (December 6, 1941). Exercises in messenger and reporting services but not target reconnaissance were reported from the municipal girls' schools in Härnösand (December 7, 1941) and Varberg's secondary school for girls (June 8, 1942), F II:4, GS/NBE.

[47] Lundsberg boarding school (March 31, 1942); the Whitlock coeducational school (June 15, 1942), F II:4: GS/NBE.

[48] Lund private elementary school (June 13, 1942), F II:4: GS/NBE.

[49] The upper secondary school in Norrköping (March 31, 1942), F II:4: GS/NBE.

critics focused in particular on how training activities would affect the children. Despite the imminent threat of war, some stressed the right of children to be children, arguing that they should be kept out of the adults' menacing world. The proposed training was also believed to pose a threat to the peaceful coexistence of nations, as children might learn that war was a natural part of the world order. Deploying developmental arguments, some critics claimed that children were not mature enough for weapons training and lacked the physical capacity to learn how to shoot and throw hand grenades. There was no consensus about the age at which a person would be mature enough for such training, but most who commented on the commission's proposals agreed that children needed to be at least a few years older than the commission had suggested. In the end, the compromise between the different opinions on defense service training resulted in training being introduced at the age of sixteen instead of twelve.

A basic division between training for males and females can be observed. Boys learned to shoot and throw hand grenades, while the girls were instructed in healthcare and camp services. Although target reconnaissance, reporting, and dispatch messenger service were sometimes described as male activities, both girls and boys received training in these skills.

Target reconnaissance is especially interesting in this context, as it was an activity that can be said to have pushed the boundaries of what were perceived as female tasks during World War II. That this was not an uncontested change is evident in both the responses to the ministry, where some voiced opposition to target reconnaissance training for girls, and in the reports from individual schools, which indicate that some schools did not arrange such exercises for girls. Moreover, there is a clear difference in how the National Board of Education presented the exercises in target reconnaissance for boys and for girls in the instruction manuals. This activity was clearly linked to soldiers' tasks in the boys' exercises but was given a less specific form in the girls' training program, which made it unclear what the girls were supposed to scout for.

In looking at the defense service program, it becomes apparent that the program had a mainly instrumental purpose. The different exercises were put forward to fill the need for new skills in the event of war. During the late 1800s and early 1900s, by contrast, military exercises in elementary and secondary schools were mainly put forward as a tool to strengthen the male population's patriotic spirit.[50]

---

[50] Meinander, *Towards a Bourgeois Manhood*, 173–81.

As Sweden never entered World War II, it remains a hypothetical question how far children might have actually been able to contribute to the country's defense. It is often difficult to determine exactly which exercises were regarded as preliminary training and which were directly intended to make young people useful in the event of war, particularly in the case of the exercises for boys. However, the fact that boys could enter the Home Guard as early as at the age of sixteen made all exercises both preparation for military service and training for participation in the defense of their home district.

In addition to service in the Home Guard, there were other tasks that were considered suitable for adolescents. As mentioned above, girls were used as air surveillance personnel, and the commission's proposal pointed out that young people could be useful as dispatch messengers in the event that telephone lines were downed during air raids. The most far-reaching training of boys for noncombat service was undoubtedly the manual's exercises for defense against invasion by air. Those exercises envisioned placing young boys between Home Guard units and an advancing enemy and thus bordered on using minors in combat.

Thus, although many Swedish educators and nongovernmental organizations advocated keeping minors out of the preparations for war, Sweden was in fact prepared to let at least adolescents contribute to the country's defense in the event of war. The main reason behind this decision seems to have been the belief that, in the end, no one would escape the demands of a total war.

7

Good Soldiers All? Democracy and Discrimination in the Boy Scouts of America, 1941–1945

Mischa Honeck

The world wars were good to the Boy Scouts of America (BSA). Anyone strolling through the exhibition halls of the National Scouting Museum in Irving, Texas, will find it hard to resist that conclusion. Located just a few miles outside Dallas, the organization's memory palace is replete with images and objects suggesting that the nation's triumph over Nazi Germany and imperial Japan owed a great deal to the triumphant performance of boys wearing the Scout uniform. In early 1942, Boy Scouts began roaming through American towns and cities in support of the war effort. Some of their contributions became iconic symbols of the home front war effort – so iconic that Ken Burns featured them in his 2007 documentary on the United States during World War II. There were quite a few: the paper drive, the scrap metal drive, the aluminum drive, the rubber drive, the milkweed drive, and the grease drive (Figure 7.1). When the Scouts were not collecting resources for the war effort, they were handing out pamphlets, distributing government posters, planting victory gardens, receiving training in first aid, practicing air raid drills, or parading the Stars and Stripes. The statistics command respect: In 1942 alone, the Boy Scouts put up 1,607,500 informative and patriotic posters, gathered at least 50 million pounds of waste paper, and hauled in more than 80 percent of all the aluminum collected throughout the nation, 10.5 million pounds.[1] Their enthusiasm led to an outpouring of

Parts of this chapter draw on my book, *Our Frontier Is the World: The Boy Scouts in the Age of American Ascendancy* (Ithaca, 2018). I am grateful to Cornell University Press for permission to reproduce excerpts of it here.
[1] These figures are taken from the 1944 annual report of the Boy Scouts of America submitted to Congress: BSA, *Thirty-Fourth Annual Report of the Boy Scouts of America: Scouting in Wartime, 1943* (Washington, DC, 1944), 227.

FIGURE 7.1 Scouts collecting scrap metal.

praise from men in high places. Speaking like a father to his sons, President Franklin D. Roosevelt declared, "I am proud of what you have done, and I am proud of what you are doing."[2] Both world wars increased the BSA's visibility at home and abroad, resulting in the highest membership spikes since the organization's founding in 1910.[3]

It should come as no surprise that the United States' chief vehicle for the adult-directed socialization of boys attracted a wave of recruits after the Japanese attack on Pearl Harbor in December 1941. Few youth organizations offered a greater sense of masculine community, civic importance, and military preparedness for adolescent males in the wartime United

[2] "Once Again, We Have a Job to Do!" *Boys' Life*, March 1942, 30.
[3] On the Progressive-era roots of the Boy Scouts in England and the United States, which bundled together white middle-class anxieties regarding industrialization, urbanization, demasculinization, and juvenile delinquency, see David I. Macleod, *Building Character in the American Boy: The Boy Scouts, YMCA, and Their Forerunners, 1870–1920* (Madison, 1983); Benjamin R. Jordan, "A Modest Manliness: The Boy Scouts of America and the Making of Modern Masculinity, 1910–1930" (Ph.D. diss., University of California, San Diego, 2009); and Robert MacDonald, *Sons of the Empire: The Frontier and the Boy Scout Movement, 1890–1918* (Toronto, 1993).

States. Yet the path taken by the BSA was neither unique nor exceptional. In the interwar period, youth organizations on a global scale had moved to the center of public debates about national resilience and the collective will to emerge stronger from crises. Studies conducted by the federal government and private citizens in the 1930s acquainted Americans with youth from all continents working, camping, playing, singing, and marching to remarkably similar rhythms.[4] Mass spectacles, pledges, uniforms, big rallies, and what historian Mary Nolan has called the "masculinist vision of taming nature" united young individuals into large collective bodies and created a common language of service and sacrifice for the public good.[5] In the wake of World War I, youth and childhood had become embattled resources domestically as well as internationally. As the French socialist leader Léon Blum remarked in 1934, "We live at a time when everyone assumes the right to speak in the name of youth, when everyone, at the same time, wants to grab hold of youth, when everyone is fighting over youth."[6] Ideological and political differences aside, all parties believed that youth had the potential to revitalize nations and rededicate societies to a common purpose.

Acknowledging this rapidly evolving global landscape of youth regimentation in the service of disparate political projects helps to debunk at least three myths about the BSA's contributions to the war effort. First, the boys and their adult superiors did not simply reenact the patriotic war work of 1917–1918. Responding to the rise of fascist and communist youth movements as well as to changing conceptions of boyhood and manhood, the BSA leadership engaged in a delicate balancing act that gave male youth a share in defending the nation while reinforcing the limits of engagement drawn by post-Enlightenment ideals of a sheltered childhood. Second, despite propaganda to the contrary, adults and boys never constituted a unified front. A closer look reveals that the motivations of boys to serve in Scouting's home front divisions could diverge conspicuously from their elders' expectations. Adults hoped that wartime

---

[4] See W. Thatcher Winslow, *Youth: A World Problem* (New York, 1938); Eleanor Roosevelt, "Facing the Problems of Youth," *Journal of Social Hygiene* 21 (October 1935), 393–94; Maxine Davis, *The Lost Generation: A Portrait of American Youth Today* (New York, 1936); and Homer P. Rainey, *How Fare American Youth?* (New York, 1938).

[5] Mary Nolan, *The Transatlantic Century: Europe and America, 1890–2010* (New York, 2012), 124.

[6] Blum is quoted in Susan Whitney, *Mobilizing Youth: Communists and Catholics in Interwar France* (Durham, 2009), 3.

Scouting would curb juvenile delinquency and maintain order in a society disrupted by war. The boys, on the other hand, were often discontented with the tedious home front tasks assigned to them, which made them feel infantilized rather than masculinized in comparison to their European peers, many of whom saw actual combat. Third, the war did not meld American boyhood into a homogeneous fighting force for democracy. Instead, the BSA upheld and created various regimes of racial discrimination, in particular toward African-American Scouts, whose war work was barely recognized by the national leadership, and toward Japanese-American Scouts, whose membership did not protect them from internment.

Exposing these myths about Scouting as they have seeped into to the "Greatest Generation" narrative is not meant to diminish the patriotic fervor displayed by Scouts across the country, nor is it meant to paper over the emotional stress caused by the fear of foreign invaders, frequent migration, and the disintegration of families examined by William Tuttle and Lisa Ossian.[7] The purpose of this chapter lies elsewhere – to identify the contradictions between ideology and practice, and to probe how old and young Americans grappled to define for themselves the meanings of boyhood and manhood even as the demands of war blurred the lines between the roles of boys and men.

PLAYING ON UNCLE SAM'S TEAM

The cover of the March 1942 issue of *Boys' Life*, the BSA's monthly magazine, provides a useful entry point into discussing the organization's ideologies of gender, national service, and childhood as they converged in the BSA's mobilization rhetoric. The creators of this illustration must have felt good about their artwork because they republished it as a recruitment poster shortly thereafter. In it, a young Miss Liberty, holding the allegorical torch of freedom in one hand and the Bill of Rights in the other, leads a procession of Scouts representing the four branches of their organization (Boy Scouts, Sea Scouts, Air Scouts, Cub Scouts) into battle. Their facial expressions bespeak their determination and their focus on the struggle ahead. The weapons they carry – a pitchfork, an iron bar, a utility pole,

---

[7] William M. Tuttle, Jr., *"Daddy's Gone to War": The Second World War in the Lives of America's Children* (New York, 1993); Lisa L. Ossian, *The Forgotten Generation: American Children and World War II* (Columbia, MO, 2011). See also Steven Mintz, *Huck's Raft: A History of American Childhood* (Cambridge, MA, 2004), 254–74.

and a seed bag – are not the weapons of soldiers sent into combat, however. They are the materiel of a home front army, representing some of the scouts' wartime activities, including gardening, farming, and collecting wood and scrap metal to make arms. "We, Too, Have a Job to Do," the caption underneath the illustration reads, signaling that America's Boy Scouts are performing their wartime roles with the same sense of duty as regular soldiers fighting the Germans or Japanese.[8]

One might think that the BSA's creation of a space of participation appropriate to boys in times of national crisis was a direct consequence of the war. But this was only partly the case. Rather, this form of boy mobilization took place against the backdrop of wider social, cultural, and political transformations hastened by the Great Depression. Gender historians have convincingly argued that the economic crisis of the 1930s disrupted the reigning individualistic ethos of manhood that had developed during the economic boom that preceded it. The dominant conception of masculinity in the 1920s was based on entrepreneurial success, represented by fathers and husbands providing their families with the amenities of modern consumerism.[9] Seeking to rescue the traditional patriarchal ideal of the man as breadwinner, the New Deal's recovery programs, most prominently the Civilian Conservation Corps (CCC) and the National Recovery Administration (NRA), emphasized that collective action and public service were no less masculine in character than the private sector. Likening the Depression to a foreign enemy that had to be defeated in battle, New Dealers told young men to locate their manhood in a form of participatory citizenship that fused loyalty to the state with a soldier-like ethos of service and shared sacrifice. A fraternity of citizens, not a loose assortment of self-made men, was what New Dealers envisioned when they spoke of democracy.[10]

Although the BSA, in contrast to the Hitler Youth or the Young Pioneers in the Soviet Union, remained independent of government control, the United States' largest boy organization both inspired and profited from the New Deal's identification of discipline, respect for authority, and work for the public good as the pathways to masculine citizenship.

---

[8] "We, Too, Have a Job to Do," *Boys' Life*, March 1942.

[9] See, for instance, Philip Abbott, "Titans/Planners, Bohemians/Revolutionaries: Male Empowerment in the 1930s," *Journal of American Studies* 40 (2006), 463–85.

[10] See also William E. Leuchtenburg, *The FDR Years: On Roosevelt and His Legacy* (New York, 1995), 35–75. On the CCC, youth, and masculinity, see Olaf Stieglitz, *100 Percent American Boys: Disziplinierungsdiskurse und Ideologie im Civilian Conservation Corps, 1933–1942* (Stuttgart, 1999).

Commercialist interpretations of Scout virtues such as resourcefulness and self-reliance were eclipsed by a new narrative in which BSA leaders compared the economic emergency of the early 1930s to the national emergency of World War I. In a report about Scout troops donating food and clothing, BSA Publicity Director Frank Robinson stated that "this splendid and quiet worthwhile service certainly approximates, if it does not equal, the national service rendered by Scouts during the period of . . . the World War."[11] In the flurry of propaganda, posters, and processions on behalf of numerous programs launched by the Roosevelt administration, Boy Scouts were drafted for street duty just as their predecessors had been mobilized for war. Home front analogies quickly came to mind as local Scout troops marched in support of the NRA, waving the Blue Eagle and pushing "I will cooperate" cards into the hands of bystanders.[12] Militarized collective action, not partisan debate, promised to overcome the emasculating effects of economic victimhood and nudge boys and men away from particular group loyalties toward an inclusive ideal of national service.

The emphasis on the mental and physical preparedness of its young members as they enlisted in the fight against the Depression and the Axis powers was an attribute the American branch of the Boy Scout movement shared with youth organizations across the globe. Like its rivals on the revolutionary left and the radical right, the BSA deployed images of patriotic boyhood to mitigate wartime fears about child deprivation and juvenile lawlessness – caused partly by the absence of fathers – and to shame those depicted as alleged slackers, cowards, and deserters into joining an imagined fraternity of citizen-soldiers. However, to avoid identifications of the BSA with the heavily militarized programs of radical European youth movements, US boy workers were careful to downplay the more martial features of Scouting during the war. This was achieved by making sure that the violent theme of initiating boys into the masculine sphere of soldiering was hedged in by a modern discourse of youth and childhood that presented underage people as innocent, vulnerable, and deserving of special protection.[13] A memorandum issued by BSA officials on the eve of the country's entry into the war illustrates this. War service opportunities, the memo instructed, should be assigned "according to age

---

[11] BSA, *Annual Report* (1932), 37.
[12] Ruth McKenney, *Industrial Valley* (New York, 1939), 107.
[13] See also Kriste Lindenmeyer, *The Greatest Generation Grows Up: American Childhood in the 1930s* (Chicago, 2005).

and ability," and "strenuous and responsible jobs" including first aid and
rescue work should be restricted to "Scouts 15 and older." Scoutmasters
should "watch out for the welfare of the Scouts" and see that the boys
were not overtaxed with chores unbefitting their age and developmental
stage.[14]

What sounds like a commonsense approach to mobilizing children and
adolescents for war became the main discursive tool for drawing lines of
demarcation between democratic and totalitarian youth. Representations
of Boy Scouts assuming gender- and age-appropriate roles in the struggle
against dictatorship were frequently contrasted with images of Axis and
Soviet youths being physically and psychologically abused by their tyr-
annical leaders. US Scouting was said to foster freedom and independence,
whereas fascism was said to initiate youth into a death cult. Children
growing up in Italy, Germany, and the Soviet Union, one BSA brochure
claimed, were raised on a "diet of hate and intolerance" and had to endure
in "a world of blood and guns."[15] Speaking on the radio in January 1941,
BSA executive and Governor of New York Thomas E. Dewey portrayed
Scouting as the last best hope of boyhood in an age when fanatics were
violating their parental responsibilities by throwing youths into the blaz-
ing furnace of revolution and war. "Let's look at what is happening
elsewhere in the world. The first step of every dictator is to kidnap the
youths of the nation," said Dewey. "Human kindness is laughed at. And
the only moral code they know is slavery, conquest, and more slavery."[16]
Similarly, a children's book published in the same year under the title
Youth Under Dictators depicted how political indoctrination and military
drill impoverished the lives of the German boy Kurt and his Russian
counterpart Valla.[17] Although US educators suspended criticism of the
Soviets after the war had welded the two states into an alliance of necessity, such condemnations of youth militarization in foreign countries
bolstered the assumption that the American way of childrearing was
superior because it was more affectionate and less hierarchical and kept
the young safe from the ugly realities of war.

---

[14] BSA, "National Defense and War Relief Service Opportunities for the Boy Scouts of
America in the Present and Possible Future Situations," October 15, 1940, in Daniel
Carter Beard Papers, Box 139, Manuscript Division, Library of Congress, Washington,
DC.
[15] Boy Scout Foundation of Greater New York, *America's Answer* (New York, 1938), 3, 6.
[16] Thomas E. Dewey, "In Step with Democracy," Daniel Carter Beard Papers, Box 139.
[17] Oril Brown, *Youth Under Dictators: A Study of the Lives of Fascist and Communist
Youth* (Evanston, 1941).

Even after the United States entered the war in December 1941, BSA organizers took advantage of their country's distance from the conflict to promote the illusion of war as a boyish adventure. Recruitment slogans such as "Playing on Uncle Sam's Team" or illustrations of happy Scouts participating cheerfully in every scrap drive, which were a common element of wartime Scout propaganda, decoupled war from suffering and death and turned it into a sporting event.[18] Most Americans agreed that war games were not only a natural part of childhood development but particularly conducive to the socialization of boys in wartime, whether as an outlet for stress or a healthy form of hero-worship. Scout leaders and government officials declared war play an instinctive boyish urge that was most productive under adult supervision, reinforcing adult authority in a world in which loosening family ties evoked the specter of juvenile delinquency. "At this time of unrest," asserted BSA Chief Executive James West in January 1942 in a pamphlet circulated nationally, "youth in particular needs the stabilizing influence of the Scout Oath and Law."[19] To this another brochure added, "Newspaper headlines, almost daily, tell of a new juvenile crime wave ... The Boy Scout Program is a combative force against these conditions. More Scouts mean fewer potential delinquents."[20]

And yet, as BSA officials explained that wartime Scouting kept boys away from crime and violence, they also admitted that it prepared male youth for taking on the responsibilities of military manhood. Adapting to the exigencies of war, West twisted the movement's nonmilitary message and conceded that there was "abundant evidence" that the "Boy Scout program ... does give the basic training for a good citizen or a good soldier."[21] After the outbreak of hostilities in Europe, the BSA put in place the Emergency Service Corps for First-Class Scouts fifteen and older, who got to wear special insignia to verify that they possessed the physical fitness and lifesaving skills required to participate in civil defense. In 1942, the organization introduced an honor roll for former Scouts in

---

[18] See, for example, "Once Again, We Have a Job to Do," *Boys' Life*, March 1942, 30; and "On Uncle Sam's Team," *Boys' Life*, December 1942, 49.

[19] BSA, "Boy Scouts and Civilian Defense," January 4, 1942, in World War II Collection, Box "World War II Items Removed from Official BSA Scrapbook," National Scouting Museum and BSA Archives, Irving, Texas.

[20] BSA, "Boy Scouts on the Homefront" (undated brochure), in World War II Collection, Box "World War II Items Removed from Official BSA Scrapbook," National Scouting Museum and BSA Archives, Irving, Texas. The contention that Scouting decreased wartime delinquency originated in World War I. See BSA, *Annual Report* (1918), 19.

[21] BSA, *Annual Report* (1942), 34.

the armed forces and began cooperating with the government-sponsored High School Victory Corps, which trained students for future war services.[22] Boasting that the US officer corps was disproportionately composed of former Scouts, the BSA leadership reprinted endorsements of army men who praised Scouting as "the most complete, all-around, pre-induction training that can be given at that age level."[23] The claim that US Scouting possessed the simultaneous ability to harness youth energy for the war effort and to protect underage youths from premature military involvement was of enormous propaganda value. It helped manufacture consent around the notion that the United States was fighting the good war – for civilization, humanity, and the rights of children everywhere.

DEVOTION AND DISCONTENT

Historians of youth and childhood have argued persuasively for viewing youth organizations as intergenerational bodies, not as products of adult ideas about youth and proper youthful behavior but as a tenuous social contract shaped by the interplay of adult prescriptions and youth practices. As Scout historian Jay Mechling contends, writing the history of a youth organization requires grasping its hybrid culture, which Mechling locates in the tacit struggle between "adult intentions and youth's desire to exercise as much autonomy and agency as possible."[24] Signs of this struggle are largely absent from official narratives, but evidence drawn from sources about the boys or from accounts produced by the boys themselves quickly muddles the uplifting spectacle of intergenerational harmony projected by BSA administrators during World War II.

On its surface, this spectacle seemed to reflect the motivations of boys and men alike. Wartime propaganda produced images of young Scouts scavenging for metals or growing food with beaming faces. The press relished reports of record-breaking forages such as the scrap iron hunt of twelve-year-old Scout Gerald Zirbel from Wisconsin, which "built up Uncle Sam's muscle as well as his own," or the story of thirteen-year-old

---

[22] BSA, *High School Victory Program and Scouting: Issued by the Boy Scouts of America in Cooperation with the Committee on Scouting in Schools* (New York, 1943). See also Edward L. Rowan, *To Do My Best: James E. West and the History of the Boy Scouts of America* (Exeter, NH, 2005), 186.

[23] BSA, *Annual Report* (1942), 35.

[24] Jay Mechling, "Children in Scouting and Other Organizations," in Paula Fass, ed., *The Routledge History of Childhood in the Western World* (New York, 2013), 428.

Pennsylvania Scout Daniel Flory, who gathered more than 9,000 pounds of paper with a little wagon he pulled through his neighborhood.[25] "We were good soldiers all," San Francisco's Richard "Dick" Meister reminisced, "marching off in proper Scout uniforms to collect whatever we could that was needed."[26] Gaining a sense of civic importance through service and play, the young Scouts cited here made the war their own, which allowed them to uphold imaginary bonds with their absent fathers, uncles, and brothers fighting in the military.

The problem with these examples is not that they were selective but that they conceal the fact that the same youthful enthusiasm that Scout leaders had hoped to muster for the war proved the most difficult to control. When boys felt that they were not making any meaningful contribution to the war effort, hopes of achieving glory in their own backyard fizzled out quickly. The dissatisfaction was greatest when boys became bored with the tasks they were asked to perform. The story of fifteen-year-old Theodore Petzold from New York is a case in point. A journalist writing for the *New Yorker* in July 1942 called Petzold a "typical Boy Scout" who was "enthusiastic" about his work. Yet Petzold did not spare his elders from criticism. The government, he complained, "[didn't] always seem to know what it [was] doing." After Petzold's troop collected 300,000 pounds of wastepaper, officials told the boys to stop with no explanation other than that they had run out of storage space. The Scouts "never hear what is being done with the stuff they collected," and seeing the aluminum they gathered piled up in backyards or left around in store windows for months without being processed "gave them moments of disillusionment."[27] Disappointed that their adult superiors were not taking them seriously, Petzold and his friends started having second thoughts about their service. Chasing waste paper and hunting scrap metal that nobody needed – was that what they had signed up for? It was conceivable, the journalist concluded, that Petzold's one and a half million fellow Scouts felt the same way.

Young people's desire for heroic action clashed with adult conceptions of childhood, and it obviously did so more frequently than the men in charge of Scouting were willing to admit. As one sociological study commissioned by the BSA in 1943 found out, there was little that Boy Scouts hated more than

---

[25] "Boy Scouts at War," *Time Magazine*, June 15, 1942.
[26] Richard "Dick" Meister, "Good Soldiers All," www.dickmeister.com/id229.html (accessed March 13, 2014).
[27] St. Clair McKelway, "Trustworthy, Loyal, Helpful, Friendly ...," *New Yorker*, July 25, 1942.

being infantilized by their superiors. Boys of all age groups, according to interviews the researchers conducted with Scouts and Scoutmasters across the country, felt that their jobs "weren't big enough" and exhibited a remarkable envy toward the kind of war service opportunities available to older youth and men. "We could learn to watch for airplanes if they would trust us" was a complaint typical of elementary school boys enrolled in the Cub Scouts, whereas Boy Scouts age twelve and older expressed wishes such as, "We could do home defense and learn to be guerillas" and "older Scouts should be used as messengers behind the lines."[28] In light of prewar anxieties that youth would enter the war "demoralized" and "devitalized" as a result of the Great Depression, adults were evidently taken aback by their children's lust for combat.[29] It was hard to satisfy boys eager to be warriors by assigning them tasks such as planting victory gardens or serving as couriers, especially when Girl Scouts were performing many of the same duties. With the possibility of soldiering legally foreclosed to males under eighteen (or seventeen with parental consent), underage boys created fantasy war zones where they could match the exploits of their British and Soviet peers and act out their dreams of battlefield heroism.

Just how conscious US Scouts were of their place in a wider world at war becomes evident in their constructions of the enemy as well as their responses to stories of boys in Allied nations who had stood their ground in combat. Expecting to find naïvely innocent boys who needed to be instructed about the nature of their adversaries in Germany and Japan, BSA executives discovered the opposite. Growing up in an atmosphere of national crisis and increased ideological polarization, as Tuttle and Ossian have suggested, American children had made the friend/foe paradigms of the adult world a preferred coping mechanism for the war. US Scouts held Germans accountable for "murder[ing] critics, enemies, and their hostages" and described the Japanese as "brutal torturers" and "sly, wily, and not to be trusted."[30] What troubled adult organizers most was that, in their zeal to destroy the enemy, the boys had adopted a racialized view of their opponents that made it difficult for

---

[28] BSA, "Boys in Wartime: Special Research Supplement," *Scouting for Facts: A Bulletin of Information and Interpretation*, June 1942, 6–8. The survey also contains the point of view of Scoutmasters who said that "the boys feel that older people don't consider them seriously enough."

[29] BSA, "Gearing Research to Wartime Needs," *Scouting for Facts: A Bulletin of Information and Interpretation*, March 1943, 1.

[30] BSA, "Boys in Wartime," 14. Another common Boy Scout statement laden with racist stereotypes was that "the Emperor ordered the [Japanese] army to sneak up on Pearl Harbor. We don't sneak up on anyone."

them to see Americans of Italian, German, or Japanese descent in a positive light. "The patriotic fervor of wartime tends to create intolerance towards the beliefs and practices of persons who are not in one's group," one BSA study stated. "Intolerance grows even though democratic nations try to prevent it."[31] This totalized rejection of supposedly disloyal groups was not unique to children, yet its prevalence among the nation's youth contrasted sharply with the BSA leadership's claim that its young volunteers were fighting for the democratic values of tolerance and difference.

BSA magazines and literature kept their young readers abreast of developments in the Pacific and Atlantic theaters, filled their columns with information about modern weapons technology, and published stories of boy valor in the fight against the Axis powers. Perhaps the greatest recognition was reserved for the British "Blitz Scouts" who had seen action during the German air raids of 1940 and 1941. Four of them – John Bethell, Roy Davis, Stanley Newton, and Hugh Bright – were sent on a six-week publicity tour through the United States in July 1942. Speaking on the radio and to sellout crowds in stadiums packed with Scouts of both sexes, the Blitz Scouts recounted how they had spotted planes, extinguished fires, and helped with the evacuation of civilians. Young Davis, noted a *New York Times* reporter, even left "a trail of broken Girl Scout hearts."[32] It is impossible to gauge the extent to which American boys identified with their British peers, but it is easy to imagine that their performance enhanced a boyish fascination for war as a rite of passage leading to chivalry, celebrity, and a sexually attractive masculinity.

Depicting Russian youth in the fight against Nazi Germany proved to be a more delicate subject for US propagandists. *Boys' Life* waited until September 1943 to publish a letter to its young readers from Konstantin Gregorivich Konstantinov, a seventeen-year-old Cossack youth who had joined the Russian army and was wounded four times in combat. Printed in part to inspire American boys to keep doing their part, Konstantin's letter opened, "I guess I don't look like a soldier. I weigh 152 pounds, and I'm only five feet four inches tall, but I already killed at least 74 Germans."[33] Another Soviet boy soldier who received press

---

[31] Ibid.
[32] "British 'Blitz' Scouts See the Sights with 'Dead-End' Friends as Guides," *New York Times*, July 7, 1942. See also "'Blitz Scouts' Arrive Today to See Capital," *Washington Post*, July 8, 1942.
[33] "Booth Tarkington Writes a Letter to Konstantin Gregorivich Konstantinov," *Boys' Life*, September 1943, 13. See also "Hero of Leningrad," *Edwardsville Intelligencer*, October 21, 1942, and the *Piqua Daily Call*, October 27, 1942.

coverage in the United States was the Pioneer Michail "Mischa" Nikolayev. Only fourteen years of age, Mischa made headlines for his daring exploits, which involved capturing enemy soldiers and stealing their horses.[34] But while the stories of Konstantin and Mischa might have captivated US Boy Scouts longing for similar experiences, the young Soviets remained less-than-perfect role models in the view of American educators. Though eighteen was the official call-up age for the Red Army, most Americans read the widespread military involvement of Soviet children as mine clearers or regular combatants not as an emergency measure but as proof of the communist disregard for the welfare of children.[35] Journalist Quentin Reynolds, who introduced Mischa to the readers of *Collier's*, an American middle-class magazine noted for its investigative journalism, remarked, "The duties of Pioneers are not nearly as pleasant as those of Boy Scouts," and their job was not "one which would appeal to an ordinary American boy."[36]

In trying to reassure American parents that their children were special and content with their work far behind the lines, people like Reynolds missed a deeper irony. Many American boys would have loved to trade places with Mischa, Konstantin, or the Blitz Scouts. It remains a matter of speculation how many Boy Scouts would have exchanged their Scout hat for a GI helmet had the age of enlistment been lowered to fifteen or sixteen, but new research has shown that the US Army too had its share of illegal underage soldiers during World War II. To get past recruitment officers, as many as 200,000 boys forged documents or simply lied about their age. Many likely did so to escape poverty.[37] It is hard to imagine that American educators, BSA officials included, were unaware of underage soldiering, although the boy soldiers generally came from backgrounds direr than the middle-class households most Boy Scouts called their home.

---

[34] Quentin Reynolds, "Children of Mars," *Collier's Weekly*, June 26, 1943.

[35] On Soviet child mobilization, see Olga Kucherenko, *Little Soldiers: How Soviet Children Went to War, 1941–1945* (New York, 2011), and Julie K. deGraffenried, *Sacrificing Childhood: Children and the Soviet State in the Great Patriotic War* (Lawrence, 2014), 48–76.

[36] Reynolds, "Children of Mars." An opposing view on the relationship between US and Russian youth was articulated by Rowan Meyer, an American relief worker who lived in Moscow during the German offensive in 1941. Meyers wrote that Russian and American youth were "alike" in their patriotism and noted how the humanitarian contributions of groups like the Boy and Girl Scouts had cemented "American–Soviet friendship." See Meyers, "Russian Youth at War," *Christian Science Monitor*, November 16, 1944.

[37] These numbers are drawn from a current research project by Rebecca Jo Plant and Frances Clark on underage youth in the US military during World War II.

BSA organizers probably chose to gloss over the number of boys who were joining the armed forces because they found the implications of this trend too troubling to deal with. At the very least, underage soldiering speaks to the fact that the boundaries separating patriotic boyhood and military manhood proved harder to enforce than the BSA's wartime propaganda led people to believe.

SCOUTING IN THE SHADOWS

Contrary to the BSA's rhetoric of universal brotherhood and democratic inclusiveness, wartime Scouting meant different things for Boy Scouts of white, African-American, and Japanese descent. Since the Progressive era, black boys had been treated as a subordinate group within the movement.[38] The unequal status of African-American Scouts was reflected in the Inter-Racial Service (IRS), a subdivision of the BSA founded in 1927 to promote the formation of racially segregated black troops throughout the United States and the South in particular, where white supremacists had been threatening to boycott the movement if it admitted black boys. Still, by 1941, African-American Scouting had made modest strides, with 38,402 Scouts registered in 2,099 (mostly segregated) troops across the nation. These figures nearly doubled during the war to 74,855 Scouts in 3,587 troops.[39] White BSA officials, who sought to enhance the organization's anti-totalitarian credentials, cited these growth rates to argue that US Scouting, unlike the Hitler Youth, fostered racial and religious tolerance. "Shoulder to shoulder in the Scout uniform you will find ... Catholics and Jews and Protestants ... boys of every race ... linked by common interests and by common ideals," one BSA pamphlet trumpeted after denouncing the anti-democratic character of fascist and communist youth organizations. Accompanying this statement was a group picture of six Scouts – four white, one Hispanic, and one black – smiling into the camera with their arms draped over one another's shoulders.[40] Similarly, an image titled "Americans All – United Under One Flag," which was reprinted in newspapers in early 1941, depicted

---

[38] On the BSA's early policies toward African Americans, see also Jordan, *A Modest Manliness*, 170–220; and Macleod, *Building Character*, 212–14.

[39] These figures are taken from BSA, "Interracial Bulletin 1947," October 31, 1947, in Division of Relationships Papers, unfiled, BSA National Archives, Irving, Texas.

[40] Boy Scout Foundation of Greater New York, *America's Answer*, 13.

a group of Scouts representing white, Native American, Mexican-American, and African-American youth saluting the Stars and Stripes.[41]

These images stood in an uneasy relationship with various discriminatory practices in the movement. The IRS's segregationist policies toward African Americans were reinforced with a BSA-wide media campaign that linked patriotic boyhood to whiteness. None of the major recruitment posters celebrating the home front contributions of Scouts diverged from the established practice of foregrounding the idealized bodies of white, Anglo-Saxon boys. The few instances in which the BSA leadership acknowledged the service of African-American Scouts were pictures showing black youth in auxiliary roles or as poster boys for white pretensions to racial tolerance. How far removed lofty affirmations of a racially inclusive Americanism were from the realities on the ground becomes evident in the reactions of an Alabama Supreme Court justice to a war bond rally headed by African-American Scouts in Montgomery in February 1943. After a coworker assured him that the parade was not a civil rights demonstration, the justice went on to explain to a Northern black journalist who was wondering why the war had occasioned no change in race relations, "I think the principle of separation of the races is not only a natural thing, but it is conducive to good order in the South."[42]

Scout pageants may have waxed lyrical about the possibilities forged through black–white friendships, but none of these anti-totalitarian gestures translated into serious efforts to remove the institutional barriers separating white from nonwhite boys. Not only were the BSA's race policies upheld – the IRS continued to operate until the early 1960s – but BSA leaders also agreed that certain programs should not be extended to all groups. For example, a special commission on "Inter-Racial Activities" decided in 1936 that the BSA's ambitious "10-year plan" to reach one in every four American boys by the end of the decade should not apply to black boys.[43] Reading the fact that African Americans were hit harder by the Great Depression than any other population group as a sign that black males were lacking in masculine resourcefulness, IRS workers recommended nationalizing the policy of white supervision of black

---

[41] "Americans All – United Under One Flag," *Chicago Defender*, April 19, 1941.
[42] "Ala. High Court Justice Tells Waters Race Relations Improving in Southland," *Chicago Defender*, February 27, 1943.
[43] BSA, "Executive Conference Report" (1926) 125, 518–32, BSA National Archives, unfiled.

Scouting in racially segregated areas. Decisions like these made the African-American poet Langston Hughes wonder whether the war would really shame white-led organizations like the BSA into acknowledging "their past record of segregation and Jim Crowism."[44]

If the participation of African-American Scouts in the war did not extend the realm of democracy, why did they pour as much energy into invigorating the home front as their white companions? Simply put, the vague hope of making some progress had a greater appeal to most African Americans than opting for disengagement and thus confirming the negative stereotype that black people were unfit for citizenship or, worse, running the risk of being branded un-American fifth columnists. The *Chicago Defender*, the nation's leading black newspaper, took pride in the fact that the war had boosted African-American membership in the BSA. It reported about black Scout troops in Mississippi and Indiana collecting aluminum and paper with the same verve as white Scouts. It issued a recruitment call from former heavyweight champion boxer Joe Louis, who had become a patron of Detroit's African-American Scouts. And it filled its columns with testimonials of former black Boy Scouts who had joined the armed forces, declaring that "good Scouts make good soldiers."[45] Evidently, African Americans invested in the Boy Scout movement because they viewed it as a corridor to a military masculinity that had the potential of narrowing the gap between the proclaimed ideals of democracy and the legacy of black disfranchisement.

A glaring contradiction of another sort was created by the forced evacuation and internment of Japanese Americans after the attack on Pearl Harbor. Of the more than 112,000 citizens and noncitizens of Japanese descent who were forced to leave their homes and spent the remainder of the war incarcerated in government detention centers, many had embraced Scouting as an institution that would testify to their loyalty to the United States and the reigning ideology of Americanism. Since the early 1920s, Scout officials and federal administrators had praised Japanese Americans as a model minority for exactly that reason.[46] That American-born children of these immigrants had been enthusiastic Scouts, however, did not shield them from racial

---

[44] Langston Hughes, "Here to Yonder," *Chicago Defender*, May 22, 1943.

[45] "Collects Aluminum for Defense," *Chicago Defender*, August 30, 1941; "Cub Scouts Aid Nation's Defense: 2,800 Lbs. Paper," *Chicago Defender*, January 31, 1942; "Bud Gives Timely Hints to Kiddies," *Chicago Defender*, March 14, 1942; "Boy Scout Good Soldier," *Chicago Defender*, April 17, 1943.

[46] House of Representatives, *Japanese Immigration: Hearings Before the Committee on Japanese Immigration and Naturalization, Part 1* (Washington, DC, 1921), 710.

profiling and imprisonment after President Roosevelt signed Executive Order 9066 on February 19, 1942, consigning them and their parents to miserable lives in concentration camps. A photograph showing two Japanese-American Boy Scouts in Los Angeles posting a notice that unnaturalized Japanese, Italian, and German immigrants had been declared "enemy aliens" by the US government captures this bitter irony. They were among the Boy Scouts who soon would have to do their daily good turns behind barbed wire.[47]

Loyal to the federal government, BSA officials actively endorsed the jarring spectacle of Japanese-American Scouting in what contemporaries euphemistically referred to as "evacuee" or "relocation" centers. In an agreement with the War Relocation Authority (WRA) signed in June 1942, the BSA pledged itself to lend its staff and expertise to monitoring Japanese Americans who were forming Boy Scout troops in the camps on their own initiative (Figure 7.2). The lack of mobility, money, and material notwithstanding, the internees had to abide by all rules and regulations of the Scout program, including wearing uniforms and paying membership fees.[48] Although the BSA paid lip service to the fraternity of Scouts and requested that the WRA permit Japanese-American Scouts to go on supervised camping trips, the organizers' actions spoke otherwise. Racializing Japanese American youths as insufficiently American, national headquarters put IRS chief Stanley Harris in charge of the surveillance of Scouting in the detention centers. Harris's recommendation to "emphasize Caucasian leadership" of these troops reflected an ideological disposition to mistrust Japanese Americans because of their race, even as administrators hoped that "Oriental" boys who had been thoroughly Americanized could help US authorities separate loyal from disloyal internees.[49] For supporters of the program, this policy bore fruit in December 1942 when a group of interned Japanese Scouts at Camp Manzanar, California, reportedly prevented rioting inmates from tearing down the US flag in front of the administrative building.[50]

One must be careful not to overgeneralize Japanese-American attitudes toward Scouting. But the altercation at Manzanar suggests that detainees

[47] This photograph is reprinted in David M. Kenney, Lizabeth Cohen, and Thomas A. Bailey, *The American Pageant*, vol. II (Boston, 2010), 876.

[48] "Statement of Joint Policy for Japanese Relocation Centers: Boy Scouts of America – War Relocation Authority," June 15, 1942, Records of the War Relocation Authority (RG 210), Box 325, National Archives, College Park, Maryland.

[49] Stanley A. Harris to Edward B. Marks, July 21, 1943, and Harris to Marshall Stalley, April 25, 1944, Records of the War Relocation Authority, Box 325.

[50] "Japanese Boy Scouts Save Flag from Mob at Relocation Center," *Christian Science Monitor*, December 10, 1942; "Japanese Boy Scouts Save Flag in Riot," *New York Times*, December 10, 1942.

FIGURE 7.2 Japanese-American Boy Scouts conduct a flag-raising ceremony at the Heart Mountain Relocation Center, Wyoming.

were divided on the issue, and it is easy to imagine that some inmates regarded the pro-United States Scouts as stooges of the federal government taught to spy on and betray their own people. At the same time, it would be misleading to think that Japanese-American Scouts were merely carrying out the organizers' designs. Anecdotal evidence reveals at least two reasons why internees banded together in troops. First, for many parents in the camps, allowing their boys to become Scouts created a semblance of normalcy and mitigated the impression that the country to which they had pledged allegiance was imprisoning them. With the exception of sports, Scouting was just about the only recreational opportunity available to young internees. Second, being a good, loyal Scout held out some strategic benefits, such as the possibility to leave the detention centers temporarily for Scout activities at a time when most internees did not have the freedom to go anywhere.[51]

---

[51] Robert H. Lamott (BSA) to H. M. Coverley (WAR), February 22, 1943, and "Statement of Relationships: Boy Scouts of America and War Relocation Authority," Records of the War Relocation Authority, Box 325.

FROM WORLD WAR TO COLD WAR

A sober look at the BSA's record during World War II raises substantial doubts about claims that the organization's outlook on childhood, youth, and war was governed purely by democratic ideals and thus fundamentally different from that of its international rivals. Its vision of young masculine citizenship that gave (white) male youth a share in defending the nation without transgressing the cultural limits dictated by the white middle-class ideal of a sheltered childhood was not the product of abstract ideology. This "mobilization lite" was possible because America's children were never victimized and brutalized to the extent that the youths of other nations were during World War II. At the same time, the BSA had to grapple with many of the same problems faced by other youth organizations: assuaging concerns about juvenile softness and lawlessness, creating spaces of participation for boys too young to serve in the military, maintaining patriarchal order in a society disrupted by war, and including and excluding children along the lines of gender, age, and race. To state these points is not to imply a false moral equivalency. It is simply to caution against perpetuating an exceptionalist narrative of the BSA that conceals more about the places and practices of US boys during World War II than it tends to reveal.

Ultimately, the BSA's methods of rallying youth behind a militarized ideal of national service yielded long-term dividends. As the United States was seeking to shed the image of a warrior nation and refashion itself as the benign "leader of the free world," the BSA contributed to this process by drawing on wartime precedents. Simultaneously, the ideological fault lines of the early Cold War period gave the Boy Scouts a democratic veneer and muted accusations that the organization was no less militaristic and hierarchical than its illiberal adversaries. Campaigns such as the "World Friendship Fund," started in 1944 to revive Boy Scouting and combat communism in Europe and Asia, or the "Crusade to Strengthen the Arm of Liberty," which led to a membership increase of 33 percent between 1950 and 1953, continued the traditions of service and patriotism that had helped Uncle Sam defeat Germany and Japan.[52]

---

[52] On Cold War Scouting, see also Margaret Peacock, *Innocent Weapons: The Soviet and American Politics of Childhood in the Cold War* (Chapel Hill, 2014), 105–17.

By that time, the BSA's wartime service had been enshrined, and complaints about youth's lack of preparedness had largely faded, only to be raised again by conservative educators worrying about youth's frivolous consumption during the 1950s and the countercultural revolts of the 1960s.

PART II

ADAPTING AND SURVIVING

Every aspect of society bends before the forces unleashed by war, including the lives of children and youth. Yet even as destruction, hardship, and despair gnaw away at the assumptions and possibilities of families experiencing war, a semblance of normality remains. Children play, draw, make up stories, and read books; they go to school, squabble with siblings, and sulk after being scolded; they seek to engage with the adult world and are constantly seen by adults as portents and harbingers of their families' and their societies' futures.

The chapters in this section sample three forms of adaptation and survival: (1) ways in which prewar institutions – the British military, Ottoman orphanages, and the early twentieth-century German youth movement – adapted to World War I; (2) ways in which children and youth used self-expression to illustrate the Great War as they saw it, to cope somehow with the horrors of concentration camps during the Second, and to try to explain their contributions to the war effort; and (3) and ways that the American military and American media wrestled with the presence of children in the narrative of the ghastly aftermath of the deployment of atomic weapons against Japan.

The historians contributing to this section have taken advantage of the unfortunate fact that wars provide opportunities to examine in high relief a number of issues central to understanding the lives of children and youth: masculinity and gender, social welfare policy, politicization and socialization, literature and art, and generational conflict.

Although it is always a challenge to capture the experiences of children, wars provide a chance to see them at their most vulnerable, their most frightened, their most adaptable, their most responsible, their most resourceful. In some circumstances, war makes them seem utterly childlike and helpless, but in others war forces, even encourages, them to display courage, wisdom, and responsibility far beyond their years. Indeed, the chapters in Part II are based on sources that show not only how governments and institutions saw children, but also how children saw themselves. Some of those children experienced the sharp end of war on battleships, in death camps, or in bombed-out cities, while others viewed it from afar, in schoolrooms or orphanages. Yet all had to find ways to adapt and to survive in a world at war.

8

Combatant Children: Ideologies and Experiences of Childhood in the Royal Navy and British Army, 1902–1918

Kate James

It was not until the exploits of Boy First Class John Travers Cornwell were published in an Admiralty Dispatch that his mother, Alice, became aware of the true extent of her son's heroism during the Battle of Jutland on May 31, 1916. The Commander of the First Battlecruiser Squadron, Vice-Admiral Beatty, reported that:

Boy First Class John Travers Cornwell of "Chester" was mortally wounded early in the action. He nevertheless remained standing alone at a most exposed post, quietly awaiting orders till the end of the action, with the gun's crew dead and wounded all around him. His age was under sixteen and a half years. I regret that since he has died, but I recommend his case for special recognition in justice to his memory, and as an acknowledgment of the high example set by him.[1]

Cornwell volunteered for the Royal Navy on July 31, 1915, aged fifteen years and seven months. By May 1, 1916, he had completed his naval training. The following day he joined HMS *Chester*. One month later, he was dead. Cornwell's death captivated the nation's sensibilities and his courage was celebrated nationwide. He was posthumously awarded the Victoria Cross, the United Kingdom's highest military decoration for valor. In September 1916, a "Jack Cornwell Day" took place in elementary schools, while Frank O. Salisbury's painting of Cornwell at his battle station was given pride of place up and down the country. A welfare ward and housing for injured sailors, naval scholarships for "deserving boys," and a "suitable monument on Cornwell's grave" collectively made up his national memorial. Cornwell's family had buried their son and brother in

---

[1] Imperial War Museum (hereafter IWM): Research Papers Concerning Boy J. T. Cornwell VC, collated by Mrs. Marilda Knippel-Yuyama for Japanese TV documentary, 1993.

a quiet ceremony on June 8, 1916, but his body was later exhumed at public expense so that he could be accorded a funeral with full naval honors.[2]

Cornwell is remembered as the boy hero of Jutland; yet he was also one of thousands of boys who had joined the military and were knowingly sent into combat during World War I. Boy service was the military employment of boys under the age of eighteen. The Royal Navy recruited boys aged between fifteen and seventeen. After their initial seamanship training, boys with an adequate level of academic ability chose a trade such as advanced gunner, wireless operator, or signal boy. The other boys were trained as ordinary gunners. The British Army recruited boys between fourteen and sixteen years of age as bandsmen, trumpeters, drummers, buglers, pipers, clerks, tailors, shoemakers, and artificers. By 1914, the army's recruiting regulations set the establishment of boys at 4,829[3] while the Royal Navy estimates of the same year accounted for 4,479 boy sailors and another 6,192 undergoing training.[4] This chapter focuses on the experiences of these combatant boys by addressing their recruitment, training, and employment in both peace and war. Their experiences, recorded in a range of material including personal testimonies, government papers, and military records, show how these boys fared in a man's world and where allowances, if any, were made for their youth and inexperience. In doing so, this chapter considers how the concept of combatant children fits into contemporary notions of boyhood, manhood, and militarism, and how British society regarded their contribution to the war.

BOY COMBATANTS

At the turn of the twentieth century, childhood was little more than a period of development prior to entering the labor force. For many children, labor was an intrinsic part of their lives. Indeed, the school syllabus supported the child's development into adulthood by focusing on preparing them for the labor market. In 1909, the curriculum for boys prepared them for "manual trades together with masculine domestic

---

[2] "The Boy Cornwell," *The Times*, July 31, 1916.
[3] War Office, Regulations for Recruiting for the Regular Army and the Special Reserve 1912, reprinted with Amendments to 31 August 1914, 33.
[4] House of Commons Parliamentary Papers (hereafter HCPP), Navy estimates for the year 1914–1915, with explanations of differences.

duties,"[5] thus both inspiring them to become men and preparing them for their subsequent manhood. Boy service encapsulated the manual and masculine ethos of the time and was one of many apprenticeships available in the labor force.

The British military set eighteen as the demarcation between boyhood and manhood as boy service officially ended on reaching one's eighteenth birthday. When considering these boys as combatants, the distinction between boyhood and manhood is blurred. The use of the official rank "boy" in both services exemplifies their youth. Boy soldiers and sailors were trained separately from those joining the military as men, and they were billeted away from the men both on land and at sea. However, the ability to apply the distinction between boy and man is not so evident when examining their combatant status. The laws of war gave no regard for the age of a combatant, and boys were employed in combat roles. Many personal accounts of boy combatants' war experiences do not dwell on their youth. Those that do address them often make the point that being a boy made no difference and that they did not consider their age to distinguish them from the men. This lack of distinction was more pertinent during war. It is also interesting to note how in some circumstances the military, notably the navy, saw boys as a necessary pool of manpower for wartime roles. Thus, the distinction between boyhood and manhood was often negated through military policy in order to meet wartime requirements.

For some boys, their notion of manhood on joining the military was often at odds with the reality of the military men they encountered on joining up. The sharp difference with the reality of manhood can be best understood through Graham Dawson's definition of boy culture as an "idealized form of masculinity" in which military virtues are perceived as the "natural and inherent qualities of manhood, whose apogee is attainable only in battle."[6] This notion encapsulates the desire of these boys to both join the military and take part in battle. The "idealized" aspect of Dawson's definition is apparent in many memoirs that attest to the fact that military life, in particular once at war, was far from what they imagined. What is particularly interesting is despite the shattering of their idealized notions, many boys were accepting of the situation they found themselves in. Boy Allen recalled that his motivations to join the navy were to "see the world, free of charge, and mix and live with men,

---

[5] Joanna Bourke, *Dismembering the Male* (London, 1996), 13.
[6] Graham Dawson, *Soldier Heroes: British Adventure, Empire and the Imaginings of Masculinities* (Oxford, 1994), 1.

real men, similar to those I had read about in my adventure books." For Allen, the image of the fatherly sailor he had encountered at the recruiting office was shattered on his first night in the navy. The boys were sleeping when a drunken Petty Officer entered their dormitory. He ordered the boys out of their beds and made them run round the room. As they passed the Petty Officer, he hit them with a broom handle. Allen recounted that this individual gave him "a rough start to service life."[7] Allen's reference to literature is an example of the saturation of British popular culture with imperial and martial notions, which in turn defined masculinity through a militaristic lens in the period leading up to World War I. It is important not to overplay British imperialism and militarism when considering the motivations of the boys who joined the military at this time. For Britain's youth, these ideals were most visible in children's literature, through the significant growth in uniformed youth groups such as the Boys Brigade, Boy Scouts, or the Church Lads Brigade, and within the new education system.[8] It was normal for children to be involved in military-style activities at this time, mainly in the guise of youth groups or the cadets. In her review of representations of boy soldiers in children's literature during the period, Elizabeth Galway recognizes how youth organizations prepared future soldiers and that "childhood is clearly conceptualized as a training-ground not just for adulthood but for war itself."[9] Age was also not regarded as a barrier to being employed in wartime roles. Boys had long been recruited to fill shortages in times of war, but by the Edwardian period boys were no longer seen purely as a means to plug manpower gaps. These youth were considered a worthwhile investment, and they were regarded as future leaders within the ranks. For the boys themselves, the military offered a path to attain their idealized form of masculinity.

BOY RECRUITMENT

Boys joined the military for a variety of reasons. It was their military experiences, and not their backgrounds, which bonded these boys. Boy Cole joined the navy because of the uniform, whereas for Arthur Adams it was due to "economic upsets at home."[10] Some boys had been to

---

[7] IWM: Private Papers (hereafter PP) of C. F. Allen.

[8] John Mackenzie, *Imperialism and Popular Culture* (Manchester, 1994), 3.

[9] Elizabeth A. Galway, "Competing Representations of Boy Soldiers in WWI Children's Literature," *Peace Review: A Journal of Social Justice* 24(3) (2012), 302.

[10] IWM: forty-six questionnaires completed by men who served in the 'Lower Deck' of the Royal Navy, 1900–1939, at the request of researchers at the University of Sussex in 1972,

a military school, and others had spent time in detention at an industrial school or on a training ship. Some boys, having grown up on a diet of military adventure through popular literature or having spent time in one of the many youth organizations at this time, yearned for adventure and hoped to fulfill this through a military career. However, because many of the boys joining the military came from the poorest working-class backgrounds, the cost of periodicals and subscribing to such organizations may have prevented them from taking part. Thus, for the most disadvantaged boys, the military represented an attainable alternative to the uniformed youth movements of the day. For some boys, the military offered a route out of poverty, while providing orphans with a sense of family. However, although many of the boys did join the military to avoid the urban slums, memoirs show that we cannot assume that all of these boys were from such backgrounds. Boy service was not the sole domain of the lower working-class boy. The opportunity of career progression, supported by an academic and physical syllabus, as well as the chance to travel, set the military in a different light to other apprenticeships.

Many boys chose to continue the family tradition. Charles Ditcham spent the majority of his childhood in India and Africa, following his father's career in the Argyll and Sutherland Highlanders. As a son of the regiment, he felt he lacked any knowledge of the wider world and decided to remain in the only environment in which he felt at home, the army. Ditcham joined the army as a drummer and bugle boy, aged fourteen and a half. He believed there was neither advantage nor disadvantage in being a son of the regiment because there were so many of them, with some families having four or five brothers in uniform. The British Army regarded boy service as a way to develop future leaders. Indeed, this attitude has been a constant in the British Army since the eighteenth century. An 1876 report looking into the issue of boy enlistment encapsulates this approach stating that that boy soldiers are "looked upon as a source from which trained non-commissioned officers and sappers of the very best class can be procured."[11]

Some of the sons of sailors and soldiers who joined boy service had already experienced a semblance of a military life by attending a military

and covering the training and conditions for boy seamen, discipline and punishment in the navy, the relationship between the Lower Deck and officers, gambling, drinking, Naval Chaplains, Lower Deck conditions, and pay.

[11] The National Archives (hereafter TNA): WO 32/6881 (Enlistment of Boys under 16 into "Boys Regiments" to supplement recruiting, 1876).

school. The Royal Hospital School in Greenwich, the oldest of the military schools, was established by King William and Queen Mary in 1712 for the "maintenance and education of the children of seamen happening to be slain or disabled in such service."[12] The Duke of York's Royal Military School, the Royal Hibernian Military School, Ireland, and Queen Victoria School, Dunblane, formed a recognized part of the British Army at this time.[13] These schools were all founded on philanthropic grounds, but they were also a recruiting ground for the military. There was a significant military element to the school curriculum, with many of the staff being retired military personnel.

The British Army in India also formed a steady recruiting ground. Jack Callaway, the son of a soldier, had spent his childhood in India. In 1912, aged fourteen, he too joined the army. He was trained at the Royal Artillery's trumpet depot at Kirkee, Puna. It was a mounted unit, and he recalled that he was very small and scared of horses.[14] For many of these boys, both in India and Britain, their first taste of being away from home was the train journey to the training depot. Dudley Meneaud-Lissenburg recalled how on joining the army as a boy he was required to travel across India on his own from Madras to Secunderabad – a journey of nearly 600 kilometers. Of joining as a boy he wrote, "Starting life in the British Army as a boy, the lowest category certainly had its advantages. Here I found myself amongst boys of around my own age, all keen, idealistic, and determined as I to climb the steep ascent to the top."[15]

Frederick Wynne, a boy musician in the First Battalion, East Surrey Regiment, recalled that most of the band boys were reticent about their pasts. However, he remembered one boy who joined the army from Ardwick Industrial School. This boy's parents could not afford to buy him boots for everyday use. Apart from Sundays and attendance at school, he went barefoot. One day, he was caught stealing a pair of boots and sent to an industrial school.[16] During this period, juvenile delinquency was viewed as being a product of the environment in which a child lived, and it was believed that the removal of the child from this environment was necessary. Training ships, industrial schools, and reform schools formed a significant part of the process of rehabilitation. These institutions were

---

[12] H. D. T. Turner, *The Cradle of the Navy: The Story of the Royal Hospital School at Greenwich and Holbrook* (York, 1990), 1.

[13] War Office: The King's Regulations and Orders for the Army, 1912, 1.

[14] IWM: Interview with Jack Callaway, 1984.

[15] IWM: PP of Captain D. N. Meneaud Lissenburg.

[16] IWM: PP of F. C. Wynne.

a rich source of recruits, provided that a boy attained a certificate of "good character." Industrial schools were for boys up to the age of fourteen who may not have actually committed an offense but "whose circumstances are such that if left in their surroundings they are likely to join the delinquent population."[17] The managers of these schools and ships were able to give permission, in place of parents, for boys to join the military, but in all cases boys had to consent to joining. However, evidence suggests that this practice was sometimes open to abuse. For instance, in 1913, the Inspector of Industrial Schools informed the War Office that Regimental Bands were paying a bounty to the superintendent of industrial schools.

The different routes into the military represent the diversity of the boys' backgrounds. For some boys, becoming a boy soldier was a rite of passage based on family traditions, whereas for others the military presented an escape from a life of hardship. Class did not differentiate once boy service training commenced. Educational levels presented a demarcation of these boys' former lives, but the military provided an opportunity for those from more disadvantaged backgrounds to attain qualifications to put them on a more equal footing with boys from upper working-class or lower middle-class backgrounds.

MILITARY LIFE

The period 1902–1914 saw significant organizational change in both services, and the war brought in yet further change. The pre-1914 changes were largely shaped by the reaction to the inefficiencies and failures of the army during the Second Boer War. The Strachey Committee was established in 1911 to "enquire into the whole question of boy enlistment and to formulate proposals, in the light of recent discussions on the subject, regarding the terms of service on which musicians and tradesmen boys should be enlisted and the number of each class to be allowed."[18] The "terms of service" were the twelve years a boy would be required to serve in the military. In the army, the time was divided between full-time soldiering, known as "colour service," and part-time soldiering as a member of the reserve. Interestingly, any time spent in boy service did not count toward the twelve-year commitment – the prominent belief at the time being that boys, having been trained and paid by the army, should

[17] Home Office, *Memorandum Giving Some Account of the Reformatory and Industrial School of Great Britain* (London, 1904), 5.
[18] TNA: WO 32/6897 (Terms of Service for Boy Recruits, 1912).

give something back to the military through their service. This was even the case for boys who served on the battlegrounds of World War I despite the fact that they faced the same dangers as their adult comrades.

There was concern that, if tested, the Royal Navy might find itself as unprepared as the army had been during the Boer War, and the boys who joined the navy after 1902 had a very different experience from those who had joined in the nineteenth century. The most prominent change for boys was the modernization of boy sailor training. The Royal Navy's 1902 committee decided to abolish sail training and move boys from sail training vessels to shore-based establishments. The living conditions of shore-based training establishments were viewed as being better for the physical development of boys.[19] The conditions for boys on training ships had come under public scrutiny with incidents of disease and unsanitary living conditions being raised in public debate.[20] While there were also changes to the conditions on ship, such as improved ventilation, heating, and sanitary conditions, this was not the experience of all boys. Signal Boy Allen recalled that on HMS *Vengeance* in 1913, "The lack of fresh air, the limited light from the port holes, made this, my new home, comparable with my imaginative description of the black hole of Calcutta, short of suffocating."[21]

In the period leading up to World War I, the Royal Navy recognized that "the moulding of our future seamen depends very largely on the manner in which boys and youths are handled during their first year in service, and the impressions they receive whilst under training in harbour and afloat."[22] Despite this acknowledgement, the experiences of boy sailors varied quite significantly during this period. Some of the training methods recorded were brutal. Passing the navy's swimming assessment was a terrifying ordeal for some. Boy Adams recalled how the instructor's method was "very rough and forthright; you swam or else." Boy Cole recalled how he was "held under water by a boat hook for not learning fast enough until I was unconscious."[23] In Parliament, the navy's swimming training was discussed as it was revealed that in some instances boys

---

[19] *Parliamentary Debates*, fourth series, House of Commons, March 30, 1903, Navy Estimates 1903–1904.

[20] *Parliamentary Debates*, fourth series, House of Commons, April 29, 1902, Training Ship Impregnable, and April 2, 1903, The "Caledonia" Training Ship.

[21] IWM: PP of C. F. Allen.

[22] TNA: ADM 1/8373/82 (Difficulty in obtaining satisfactory Petty Officer instructors, 1914).

[23] IWM: Lower deck 1900–1939.

were birched and caned for not being able to swim properly.[24] In relation to these and other incidents, the navy was aware of the need to attract and employ suitable instructors at boy training establishments. A March 1913 report by the Inspecting Captain of Boys Training Establishments acknowledged that "instances of undesirable Petty Officers and others being sent to these ships have not been infrequent. Much has been done by vigilance to prevent disorder and impropriety, but one can never say they do not exist."[25] The employment of retired naval personnel became more widespread during World War I as able-bodied seamen were required to leave their instructor posts and join the fleet. Boy Roberts remembered that most of these men were helpful and understanding but that some instructors felt that the boys should be treated as they had been forty or fifty years before.[26]

The army did not centralize their boy training, although most boy soldiers recall a similar pattern of daily activity that included cleaning, a one-hour session in the gymnasium, and an education class, while the remainder of the day was dedicated to trade training. Unlike their counterparts in the navy, boy soldiers' military training was limited to learning to march, known as drill. Boy soldiers did not receive weapons training until they were eighteen years of age. Ditcham remembered how boys could pay to take part in shooting on Wednesday afternoon, but that for many boys, like him, this activity was prohibitively expensive. For most boys, their pay did not stretch beyond the odd bun and a cup of tea once they had paid their fines and the seemingly endless bills from the clothing store.

It is often on the topic of food that the memoirs of former boy soldiers and sailors provide the most detail. Despite a Royal Navy recruitment article in the *Boy's Own Paper* claiming that "The boys live a splendidly healthy life under training, and are well fed,"[27] Signal Boy Allen remembered that on joining the navy "food had become number one priority." Many boys attributed their insatiable appetites to the fact they were still growing into men. Indeed, Boy Musician Wynne recalled how they would at times eat the men's leftovers. He stated how at dinner, "I was hungry before I started eating the dinner and still hungry when I had finished," and that "it is sad to think that the British Empire, so wealthy, so

[24] *Parliamentary Debates*, fourth series, House of Commons, March 15, 1905, Navy Estimates 1905–6.

[25] Ibid.

[26] IWM: PP of W. G. Roberts.

[27] H. C. Ferraby, "From Ship's Boy to Lieutenant: Chances for Lads of England in the Royal Navy," *The Boy's Own Annual Volume 39, 1916–1917* (London, 1917), 366.

powerful, could not afford to give its soldiers sufficient food."[28] When stationed in Fort George in northern Scotland, Ditcham recalled how they would catch rabbits to supplement their rations. The boys' fixation with food is understandable in light of the physical nature of military life, together with their working-class backgrounds.

In most circumstances, both in barracks and at sea, the boys' sleeping areas were separated from the men. Any sexual relationships with other boys or men would result in all concerned being made to leave the military. The boys in both services were not allowed to smoke, drink, or swear. In this period (1902–1918), physical punishment was a constant of military life regardless of age, but changes did occur. Restrictions on the types of punishment became more constraining 1906, the navy's practice of flogging boys was abolished, with Parliament declaring that birching was "no longer essential to the preservation of discipline, nor consonant with public opinion."[29] Boys were still liable to caning, but this could happen only on the orders of the captain. In the army, birching had been abolished twenty years earlier than in the navy. Boys could be flogged for serious offenses. The adoption of physical punishment as a means of discipline emulated the methods used to punish adults. Boys were inculcated into the culture of discipline through violence from the outset, and there was little differentiation between boy service and adult service in how discipline was conceived and enforced. Thus, physical punishment blurred distinctions of age.

Another prominent aspect of the boys' preparation for the rigors of military life was their physical training. The focus on physical development was reflective of wider societal concerns regarding the physical state of the nation, a hangover from the debates on the bodily strength of male recruits during the Boer War and subsequent investigations into the physical state of the nation. The army at this time was one that marched from place to place. Boy Musician Wynne's battalion would march a distance of some thirty miles to their summer camp. For his first summer camp, Wynne recalled, "I and a few others were not considered suitable for marching that distance and went by train." Four months later, on the Battalion's return to Dublin, Wynne marched the distance with the band feeling "none the worse for this, my first long route march, taking my full share of the physical music effort, although perhaps it was not of a very

---

[28] IWM: PP of F. C. Wynne.
[29] *Parliamentary Debates*, fourth series, House of Commons, February 21, 1906, King's
      Speech (Motion for an address).

high quality."[30] In the early days of World War I, the British Expeditionary Force's marching endurance was tested to the full during the retreat from Mons. In circumstances such as these, there was no opportunity to make concessions for the young. Within the Royal Navy, allowances were not practical on a ship. Signal Boy Allen recalled that "Being only a boy made no difference to the routine of the navy," and this lack of distinction between boys and men was brought to the fore with the outbreak of war in 1914. The very nature of military life was physical, and this recognition that they needed to be able to meet the physical rigors of military life was a constant from their early days in training. Consideration of their youth was often made by a particular individual within a boy's unit, but once at war these opportunities became scarce.

BOYS AT WAR

The *Army's Regulations for Mobilization 1914* stated that, for service abroad, the requirement for a soldier to be at least nineteen years of age "may be waived in the case of trumpeters, buglers and drummers at the discretion of the O.C. [Officer Commanding] the unit and of the medical officer concerned."[31] In 1914, there were sixteen drummers and buglers per infantry battalion, although only some of these would be aged eighteen and under. These boys were not part of the band. For those boys who were not drummers or buglers, the thought of missing out on the war was devastating. On finding out they were not to be sent abroad on mobilization, the band boys of the First Battalion East Surrey Regiment paraded in front of the orderly room and requested to see the Adjutant. The Regimental Sergeant Major appeared stating that, "The Adjutant is pleased to know you have volunteered but King's Regulations are against it."[32] The boys who were left behind became part of the war effort at home.

When Charles Ditcham's battalion was mobilized for France, he remembered that two or three of the full drummers were sixteen years of age and that initially it was uncertain whether they would deploy to France. A boy who was a full drummer received the same pay as a man doing this job. Eventually "somebody decided that yes these people were getting man's pay and they needed to go and fight." Describing the

[30] IWM: PP of F. C. Wynne.
[31] The National Army Museum Archives: Regulations for Mobilization 1914, 44.
[32] IWM: PP of F. C. Wynne.

first day of the Battle of Le Cateau (August 26, 1914), Ditcham recalled, "what I shall never understand is what I was supposed to do with a bugle in the front line ... I couldn't blow a ceasefire because it didn't mean a thing." During the fighting, he was sent to retrieve some ammunition, but on arriving back at the front he was told to "get out of it as he thought I was doing no good with a bugle up there." After this battle, only five out of an initial sixteen drummers were left. Soon after, the drummers in the battalion became company runners. This would require them to take messages from the battalion headquarters to the frontline trenches. It was not without its dangers, and Ditcham recalled how on one occasion he was shot in the back, the bullet piercing his reserve rations but thankfully going no further. Not all drummers were so lucky, and Ditcham remembered that it was on October 23, 1914, that the Germans captured Drummer Boy McTavish. McTavish was aged sixteen and a half.

In 1915, the medal expert W. Augustus Steward recounted how, "Ruddy cheeked British Boys have taken part in most British battles and our painters have often depicted the brave little lads who, with their drums and pipes, have inspired elders with martial aims."[33] Indeed, in September 1914, *The Times* reported that, "I heard of a very plucky act on the part of a drummer boy, who, having been shot in the foot and being taken back for treatment, eluded the Red Cross, seized a rifle and went back to the firing line."[34] The role of these boys had not markedly changed since the Boer War, but as Ditcham recalled, the nature of the battlefields upon which they found themselves from 1914 onwards meant that their primary purpose of sounding bugle calls had become largely redundant. The character of World War I battles, together with the issue of underage boys joining the New Armies, contributed to the War Office's decision on February 21, 1915, to formally end the tradition of drummers and buglers going to war. The minimum combat age of drummers and buglers was set at eighteen years of age.[35] Eighteen was still one year younger than the rest of the army for service abroad at this time. Boy soldiers were assigned to Category A (iv) for the duration of the war, meaning they were too young for service overseas, but that they would be physically and mentally fit for active service when they came of age.

---

[33] W. Augustus Steward, "War Medals Won by Boys," *Boys Own Annual* (1915–1916), 330.
[34] "Shelled in a Wood," *The Times*, September 24, 1914.
[35] TNA: WO 293/2 (Army Council Instruction Jan.–Jul. 1915).

For some boys, the changes to the regulations for mobilization came too late. Boy Trumpeter Jack Callaway was sixteen years of age when the war broke out. Fresh out of training, he had been at his unit for three months. In October 1914, he left India by ship for Mesopotamia. His parents, living in Bombay at the time, had no idea that their son had gone to war as he was forbidden to tell them. Callaway was a Captain's Trumpeter and Signaller during the war, but he noted that "overseas the last thing you did was blow a trumpet or a bugle" as sound traveled easily in the desert, especially at night. His musical duties were limited to playing the Last Post when burying bodies after battle. In December, he had his first experience of battle. He recalled "a sort of excitement" during the battle, but he was mindful that his feeling would have been different if he had been in the infantry and thus in the midst of the fighting. Callaway was not directly caught up in the action. During battle he acted as a horse orderly for his Captain and the Signallers. He would take their horses, usually three of them, and his own to the rear until the guns ceased firing. Conditions in the desert were trying for all the troops, never more so than Callaway's time during the siege and eventual surrender at Kut-el-Amara. This was followed by three years as a prisoner of war. During this time, he turned eighteen years of age. His youth would have been apparent to the captors for there were no shaving facilities, and Callaway recalled that, "I was lucky as I didn't have to shave in those days." Of his time in captivity, Callaway concluded that as a young man he "took my lot as it came." The emotions of his war experience were largely left out of his memoirs.[36]

Boy sailor Alfred Fright was fifteen when war broke out, and he remembered how "we looked forward to this war to do something." His main employment was as a lookout, and he recalled that on the eve of battle he "stood on the bridge sometimes and cried with being scared" and how up the masthead he "froze to death and was crying," and that he always had the fear of drowning. For him, these emotions were not due to his youth, for he claimed to be speaking on behalf of most of the ship's company. This shows that Fright, like other boys, did not consider his age as a distinguishing feature of his wartime experience. Of the hardships of war, Fright's view was that "that's the sort of life it was in them days." On remembering the death of some of the crew, he stated that he had no sympathy for the Master of Arms who had died, for this individual was the "worst bloke I ever know."[37] Many boys like Fright witnessed death in

---

[36] IWM: Interview with Jack Callaway, 1984.
[37] IWM: Interview with Alfred Fright, 1975.

the course of their duties. Indeed, for boys like Callaway, their musical duties required them to play the Last Post at burials, and they would have seen at first hand the multitude of casualties that the battles of World War I amassed. The witnessing of death and destruction seems to mark a paradigm shift in the eagerness to take part in the war and the reality of what war entails. Indeed, Fright surmised that the war "turned out not to be a novelty."

The outbreak of war brought further opportunities for Britain's youth to engage in wartime duties. Major-General Sir Robert Baden-Powell, the Chief Scout, broke with his organization's declared non-military tradition by forming the Scouts' Defense Corps, open to boys aged between fifteen and seventeen. It is estimated that some 50,000 Boy Scouts supported the war in their role as scouts. Boy Scouts were equipped with better military skills than boy soldiers. Unlike boy soldiers, Boy Scouts took part in military training such as rifle shooting, judging distance, and first aid.[38] They were also employed in duties of military value, such as guarding strategic points and acting as messengers. Boys who were in the Cadet Corps were also employed on military duties. Senior Cadets aged between fifteen and eighteen were armed with rifles and bayonets and became guards at Territorial Force battalion depots. In comparison, the enlisted boy soldiers mobilized for duties at home were sent to depots, where they would take part in recruitment rallies and provide music for route marches and the drafts of men leaving for France. Norman Lesley Jacques was one of these boys. He joined the Eighth Battalion Durham Light Infantry in 1915, aged fifteen and a half, and spent his war in Britain. He played the bugle in the band, but he was also a drummer and remembered playing music on the route marches for the troops as they prepared to go to France. Another such boy was Boy Musician Wynne. On the outbreak of war, he was sent to learn the clarinet for a year. On finishing this course, he was sent to his regiment's training depot in Kingston where "About three times a week we marched them [the soldiers] to Kingston Station playing Auld Lang Syne and marched ourselves back again."

In September 1914, Arthur Cain tried to enlist in Kitchener's Army as a boy bugler, but there were no trumpeters, drummers, or buglers recruited into the New Armies. He decided to join the Territorial Army,

---

[38] F. J. Collett, "British Boys' Work in War Time," *The Boy's Own Annual Volume 39, 1916–1917* (London, 1916), 712.

which was still recruiting boys from age seventeen at this time.[39] In 1915, when Cain was recovering from a circumcision at Brighton General Hospital, his fellow patients falsely mentioned to some visitors that he had been to France. The story spread and Cain subsequently received more than 100 visitors with him recounting, "Now patriotism in 1915 ran very high."[40] Many other boys were successful in joining the New Armies but only through lying about their age to secure their place. As the reports of fighting reached the press, parents and members of Parliament (MPs) increasingly petitioned for their return. The government and the army did not automatically return these underage boys, and some were retained in theater. The pressures of war saw these boys become a valuable source of future manpower despite the protestations of their families.

The Army Council Instruction of December 23, 1914, stated that, "Complaints have been received that untrained and immature lads have been allowed to proceed overseas with certain T.F. [Territorial Force] units." Units were subsequently encouraged to return these boys.[41] Nevertheless, petitions for the return of underage soldiers from families persisted, and the order was reissued on numerous occasions. The army made a distinction between boys who were seventeen years old and those who were younger. The army was mindful that the former would soon be eligible to fight. From July 1915, boys under seventeen years of age were to be sent home, but if a boy aged seventeen was not willing to leave the operational theater, he could be employed behind the firing line. Those aged eighteen and over were automatically sent to a unit behind the firing line. Regarding the applications for discharge, the army confirmed that, while these were to be dealt with by the soldier's unit, "The age given by a soldier on enlistment is his official age, and battalion and company commanders should not make promises to parents that their sons will not be included in drafts for service overseas until they are nineteen (real age)."[42] Thus the army did not consider these boys to be too young to be held responsible for their decision to provide false ages to recruiting sergeants.

In June 1915, the liberal MP Barnet Kenyon first raised the topic of underage soldiers in Parliament. He argued that the War Office was knowingly permitting underage boys to join the army and fight.

---

[39] TNA: WO 293/3 (Army Council Instruction Jul.–Dec. 1915).
[40] IWM: PP of C. A. Cain.
[41] TNA: WO 293/1 (Army Council Instruction Aug.–Dec. 1914).
[42] TNA: WO 293/3 (Army Council Instruction Jul.–Dec. 1915).

The Under-Secretary for State for War, Harold Tennant, explained that it was impractical for all recruits to produce birth certificates on enlisting and as a result many underage boys continued to serve in the New Armies. In September 1915, Parliament was told that the army's policy was to retain immature soldiers aged seventeen and over and that if a medical officer deemed them to be of the physical standard of eighteen-and-a-half-year-olds they could be sent overseas, for "A man's age is not always a true measure of his physical efficiency."[43] The focus on the physical was at the expense of any consideration given to the emotional maturity of these boys. The following month Tennant confirmed that, "it is a deliberate policy of the War Office only to take those who are of proper age. If boys under proper age have been enlisted it is their fault for making a false declaration."[44] The removal of immature soldiers from the fighting front was largely a result of external pressure from families and MPs, but contemporary press coverage and juvenile literature show a widespread admiration for young boys who went off to fight.

The *Boy's Own Paper* regularly hailed these deeds of the young and kept their eager readers abreast of the boys and young men who had been recognized for their bravery. An example of this is the reports concerning the awarding of the Distinguished Conduct Medal to both Boy First Class F. G. H. Bamford and Boy First Class J. F. Rogers on HMS *Tiger* during the Battle of Dogger Bank on January 24, 1915. Bamford was selected to clean the sighting apparatus on one of *Tiger*'s turrets. This task, which required him to climb the turret and wipe the glass clean, was made all the more perilous when the gunners began to fire before he had climbed down. Of this incident, it was said that "He was not one to lose his head at this strange and dangerous predicament."[45]

Unlike the army, the Royal Navy relied heavily on boys as a source of manpower during the war. In April 1915, the Admiral of the Training Services wrote of the need to increase the output of wireless telegraphy (WT) boys to meet the war's demands. In July that year, the Captain of HMS *Actaeon* emphasized the importance of the WT boys by giving a number of examples from the previous three weeks when ships had been warned or saved by the boys' actions.[46] Questions were raised in the House of Commons about the age of boy sailors. In November 1914, the

[43] *Parliamentary Debates*, fifth series, 1915, 74, c711.
[44] Ibid., cc1173–7.
[45] Collett, "British Boys' Work in War Time," 714.
[46] TNA: ADM 1/8413/61 (Transfer of entire WT boys to Shotley, 1915).

First Lord of the Admiralty was asked "if he is aware that a number of very young boys are carried on His Majesty's ships; and if, in view of the loss of life which has already taken place in the Navy, he will arrange that very young boys shall be employed ashore?" In response, the Parliamentary and Financial Secretary to the Admiralty, Thomas Macnamara, made it very clear that boys were to remain part of the fleet, responding, "Boys are not less than sixteen years old when drafted to ships on completion of their harbour training, and the majority of them are well over that age."[47] The fact that boy sailors were among the growing casualties of this war was not considered a reason for them to be removed from the fleet.

After the Battle of Jutland, the Captain of HMS *Chester* highlighted the dangerous predicament in which boy sailors found themselves on his class of ship. He reported that the comparatively shallow gun shields permitted large numbers of splinters to "cause havoc among her gun crew" when fired on by the Germans. Forty-seven gun crew had become casualties out of a possible one hundred.[48] A significant number of these casualties were boys, and the captain wrote that "I feel it is my duty to represent strongly to you the deplorable lack of experienced ratings in the ships company drafted to this ship." HMS *Chester* had a complement of fifty-one boys. It should have had only thirty. The captain argued that boys should be sent to armored ships for, on this type of ship, "such a mass of casualties can hardly occur in such a short space of time and in full view of many other men." In addition to the threat from torpedoes and enemy guns, there was the ever-present threat from mines. As a signal boy on HMS *Audacious*, Signal Boy Perry filled a dual role as lookout and signaler. There were twelve signal boys, and he remembered how they struggled to stay awake at times. His service on HMS *Audacious* was brought to a swift close on the morning of October 27, 1914, when she hit a mine. On this occasion, the crew were rescued, but not all crews were so fortunate. The sinking of HMS *Aboukir*, HMS *Hogue*, and HMS *Cressy* on September 22, 1914, saw many boys number among the 1,327 enlisted men lost at sea. When a German submarine torpedoed HMS *Hawke* on October 15, 1915, it resulted in the death of more than sixty boys. Despite these losses, boys remained an intrinsic part of a ship's war establishment for the duration and beyond World War I.

---

[47] *Parliamentary Debates*, fifth series, 1914, 68, cc195–6.
[48] IWM: Letter from Ministry of Defense to Mrs. M. Y. Knippel dated November 24, 1993.

The experiences of the enlisted British boy soldier and sailor do not dominate Britain's collective memory of the Great War. This can in part be attributed to modern opinions that regard child combatants as victims. This notion suppresses the value of combatant children as historical agents. Boy soldiers and sailors provide another representation of this war, despite many of their memoirs omitting any reference to the significance of their youth. Dan Todman's work on myth and memory provides insight into understanding the context within which many of these memoirs were gathered. He recognizes that "veterans' versions of the war were reconciled with the way the war was being talked about around them" and that often the purpose of collating eyewitness accounts was "to describe for viewers what the war had been like, not what it had meant."[49] Despite many former boy soldiers and sailors not giving significance to their youth, the historian is able to do so and thus guarantee their agency.

CONCLUSION

Testimonies from World War I show that age did not preclude boys from taking part in combat and, in turn, that age did not figure decisively in former boy combatants' recollection of their wartime experiences. Boys were required, like men, to carry out their duties, and for some this had fatal consequences. Indeed, boys had been a constant in British battles at war and sea for more than a century, and this tradition continued into World War II. During World War I, the popular press hailed these boys as heroes, and their youth contributed to the adulation bestowed upon them. It was civilian children and those who lied about their age to join as adults who were portrayed as innocent victims. The families and MPs of boys who provided a false age in order to join Britain's volunteer armies dominated the opposition to boy combatants. Boy service was not perceived in the same way, and these boys had required parental consent to commence their military careers. The government's response to criticism of the employment of boys in the military shows that it did not believe that their age prevented them from making a useful contribution to the war effort. As for the boys themselves, they wanted to take part in the war. Records attest to the fact that in some cases their roles were largely redundant, as in the case of the army's drummer and buglers, but the memoirs of boy sailors tell of the vital role that they played. What is

[49] Dan Todman, *The Great War: Myth and Memory* (London, 2014), 187 and 200.

missing from boys' personal testimonies is the significance of their youth in the context of their war experience. As far as these boys were concerned, their war was no different from that of their adult comrades. In truth, this was not the case. For child combatants, the war accelerated the journey from boy to man. They were catapulted into a man's world where childhood notions of manhood were often shattered as they became culturally immersed into military life, faced the same dangers, and witnessed the same horrors. The nature of life on the battlegrounds of World War I meant that they quickly became men in all but age.

9

Drawing the Great War: Children's Representations of War and Violence in France, Russia, and Germany

Manon Pignot
Translated by David H. Pickering

"How do we talk about a group that doesn't talk?" asks the French historian Olivier Faron in the introduction to his work on French war orphans.[1] The question of sources plagues all historians of childhood,[2] but those focusing on wartime, and the world wars in particular, are perhaps even more preoccupied by it, given the place youth occupies in the belligerents' propaganda.[3] In the last ten years, as part of a wider trend in the study of the cultural and social histories of the world wars, children have been treated as full-fledged actors on the home front and have thus come into their own as a subject of study.[4] The challenge for the historian is to try to capture childhood *experience* in all its complexity. The term "experience" relates to the lived dimension of the event, to an everyday relationship to the conflict, but also to the modes by which war, its practices and its codes, are understood. This change of outlook

---

[1] Olivier Faron, *Les enfants du deuil. Orphelins et pupilles de la nation de la Première Guerre mondiale (1914–1941)* (Paris, 2001), 17.

[2] See in particular Quinto Antonelli and Egle Becchi, *Scritture bambine. Testi infantili tra passato e presente* (Rome, 1995).

[3] For World War I, see Stéphane Audoin-Rouzeau, *La guerre des enfants 1914–1918. Essai d'histoire culturelle* (Paris, [1993] 2004); Antonio Gibelli, *Il popolo bambino. Infanzia e nazione dalla Grande Guerra a Salò* (Turin, 2005); Susan Fisher, *Boys and Girls in No Man's Land: English-Canadian Children and the First World War* (Toronto, 2011). See also the author's survey article: Manon Pignot, "Children," in Jay Winter and the Editorial Committee of the International Research Centre of the Historial de la Grande Guerre, eds., *The Cambridge History of the First World War*, vol. III (Cambridge, 2014), 29–45 (text) and 645–48 (bibliographical essay).

[4] Andrew Donson, *Youth in the Fatherless Land: War Pedagogy, Nationalism and Authority in Germany, 1914–1918* (Cambridge, MA, 2010); Manon Pignot, *Allons enfants de la patrie. Génération Grande Guerre* (Paris, 2012).

requires a rethinking of archival research. Alternative sources, produced by children rather than for or about them, are essential if the historian wants to try to see through a child's eye by taking a microhistory approach to the subject. If this is "history at ground level," as Jacques Revel defined it,[5] the historian must stoop down to a child's height and try to achieve what Philippe Artières and Dominique Kalifa so aptly called the "infra-ordinary."[6] Letters, diaries, and school notebooks are all outlets for a child's thoughts about a conflict. To these personal sources, another, perhaps more eloquent, body of evidence can be added: their drawings. Drawing represents "one of the young child's preferred modes of expression[7] and an alternative to words, particularly for the youngest who have not yet mastered writing. Long used by psychologists and educators[8] – already at the time of the Great War – children's drawings also represent a *historical* source in their own right.

Of course, the ideas expressed in children's drawing are no "truer" or "purer" than those expressed in their diaries or school essays. Like any childhood source, drawings must adhere to guidelines and are thus subject to adult scrutiny. They give us insight, first of all, into the content of war discourse and the ability of children to reproduce it. However, the constraints placed on young artists appear to have been less stringent, in terms of both form and content, than those for written compositions. For a given essay topic, one often finds, from one paper to the next, the same stock phrases, identical figures of speech, and formulaic or even clichéd images, intended to satisfy the teacher. Though recurring visual representations are present in classroom art assignments, pupils appear to have been given greater freedom in their handling of the subject matter, which often resulted in less conformist and thus more personal work. Given the ubiquity of war discourse in children's lives, these childhood representations of conflict are obviously not spontaneous: They should be seen more

[5] Jacques Revel, "L'histoire au ras du sol," in Giovanni Levi, *Le pouvoir au village. Histoire d'un exorciste dans le Piémont du XVIIe siècle* (Paris, 1989).

[6] Philippe Artières and Dominique Kalifa, "L'historien et les archives personnelles: pas à pas," *Sociétés et Représentations* 13 (2002), 7–15.

[7] Alfred Brauner, *J'ai dessiné la guerre. Le dessin d'enfant dans la guerre* (Paris, 1991). Françoise and Alfred Brauner have compiled the largest collection of children's drawings pertaining to twentieth-century wars. Having served in International Brigades alongside the Spanish Republicans in 1936, they are considered pioneers in using drawing as therapy as well as in the use of children's drawings as historical source materials.

[8] Georges-Henri Luquet, *Le dessin d'enfant* (Paris, 1927; reprint, 1977).

as *autonomous* representations inspired by the general climate of mobilization.

Drawings are therefore one of the best places to observe childhood experiences of World War I. They tell us a great deal about children's day-to-day existence and family relationships as well as about their lives at school and the impact of the ideological instruction dispensed in all the belligerent countries during the war. In his 1993 study of war discourse aimed at children, Stéphane Audoin-Rouzeau noted that "the key problem is obviously children's receptiveness to what was offered, suggested, required of them. It is nevertheless difficult to measure what impact this propaganda had on the realm of childhood: cultural history is more comfortable analyzing the tools of control than their effectiveness."[9] The eminently visual character of propaganda for children makes drawings an ideal place to observe not only the internalization of European war discourses and their potential efficacy but also their limitations. Additionally, the historiography of childhood in wartime to this day is largely framed in national terms. This is easily explained by the fragmentary and scattered nature of sources, which makes them difficult for foreign researchers to collect, and by the need for an in-depth knowledge of local cultural, educational, and family systems. Thus drawings, intelligible even without a mastery of the young artist's tongue, also constitute a medium favorable to a comparative history of children's war experiences.

The graphic sources at our disposal are not nearly as rare as one might fear given their seeming fragility. Most drawings have reached us in the form of books published during the Great War. Drawings by Russian children were published in 1915 by G. E. Afanas'ev;[10] by German children in 1915 by Colestin Kik;[11] and by French children in 1917 by Charles Chabot.[12] However, given printing conditions at the time, these precious

[9] Stéphane Audoin-Rouzeau, "L'enfance mobilisée: un 'vécu' méconnu de la guerre 1914–1918," in Maria-Cristina Giuntella and Isabella Nardi, *La guerra dei bambini* (Naples, 1993), 79–100; quotation, 81.

[10] *Deti i voina. Sbornik statei* (Kiev, 1915). I warmly thank the historian Irina Mironenko for her invaluable assistance in the research on Russian drawings. The texts accompanying the drawings were translated by Masha Cerovic.

[11] Colestin Kik, *Kriegszeichnungen des Knaben und Mädchen, Beifete zur Zeitschrift für angewanddte Psychologie* 12 (Leipzig, 1915). All quotations translated by Thomas Schröter.

[12] Charles Chabot, *Nos enfants et la guerre. Enquête de la société libre pour l'étude psychologique de l'enfant* (Paris, 1917). It appears that no equivalent British work was ever published.

works deprive us of the added benefit that color represents in the original drawings. In this regard, the Sainte-Isaure collection at the Musée du Vieux Montmartre in Paris is priceless. It comprises 1,146 color drawings made in two boys' schools in Paris's 18th arrondissement, collected during the war by a teacher and secretary of the Association du Vieux Montmartre.[13]

Analyzing these drawings is complicated by the limited information at our disposal. In most cases, we know when the drawing was made and the name and age of the artist. Sometimes, the child's city of origin is given. Rarely, though, is anything more known about them. The issue of age is absolutely central to any historical analysis of children's visual representations: While children of all ages represent the same themes, they do so in very different ways. To the older children's preoccupation with verisimilitude and realism, the younger children respond with representations that are less "repressed" – to borrow from the psychoanalytic lexicon. Along with age-based variations, gender differences must also be examined: Children's representations do not always vary according to the gender of the artist. But we generally know nothing about the children's family life or social standing. Although comparing these collections reveals variations, it also brings to light the numerous links, recurrences, and similarities that exist between them – including what it might be tempting to call "constants" of childhood during wartime. By the time the war broke out, drawing had become part of elementary school curricula across Europe. In France, Britain, and Germany, the "geometric method," which was in vogue in the 1880s, came under criticism after 1900 from proponents of a new "intuitive" method. This method was defended in particular at the international congresses on the teaching of drawing held in Paris in 1900 and in Berne in 1904. European pedagogues overwhelmingly supported the idea that "free" drawing encouraged "raw" expression. As Gaston Quénioux explained in 1911: "Important works (*Arte dei Bambini*, Corrado Ricci, Bologna, 1887, the works of James Sully, *Studies of Childhood*; *Kinder-zeichnungen* of Levinstein; *A Study on Children's Drawings in the Early Years* by Lukens, Pedagogical Seminary, 1896) show that true laws govern how children draw. And these are the same laws that determined the same designs or

---

[13] A few drawings were published by the museum during the war: "La vie à Montmartre pendant la guerre racontée par les écoliers montmartrois de la rue Sainte-Isaure," *Bulletin de guerre du Vieux Montmartre* 18 (1915). For an extensive selection of drawings reproduced in color accompanied by commentary, see Manon Pignot, ed., *La guerre des crayons. Quand les petits Parisiens dessinaient la Grande Guerre* (Paris, 2004).

similar drawings from prehistoric man among primitive or savage peoples in our time."[14] If each country had its own national particularities, there was in Europe, on the eve of the Great War, a common pedagogy for teaching drawing, which would explain, at least partially, the parallels the historian finds between children's drawings from different countries.

Given the nature of this type of source, this chapter uses a microhistorical approach. Taken together, children's drawings enter into dialogue with one another and create a genuine "graphic community."[15] This chapter examines the interaction between the internalization of propaganda and the child's own personal self-expression through three of the most common themes in drawings: the figure of the enemy, representations of combat, and gender roles.

THE ENEMY

From the beginning of the war, the enemy was singled out to children as the embodiment of evil. The conflict was presented not only as a clash of nations but also as a just war, a war of civilization against barbarism. In all the belligerent nations, the enemy was portrayed as a barbarian. Classrooms, magazines, novels, and play all served as forums in which moral and racial superiority over the enemy was affirmed. French germanophobic discourse, for example, relied on simple devices such as animalization and bodily stigmatization (odor, filth, gluttony).[16] The enemy can thus be identified in children's drawings by certain distinctive signs. All childhood war cultures base their discourses of stigmatizing the enemy on

---

[14] Gaston Quénioux, "Dessin," in Ferdinand Buisson, ed., *Nouveau dictionnaire de pédagogie et d'instruction publique* (Paris, 1911), www.inrp.fr/edition-electronique/lod el/dictionnaire-ferdinand-buisson/document.php?id=2539 (accessed August 10, 2016).

[15] I have adapted the term "textual community," coined by Philippe Artières and Dominique Kalifa to describe personal archives, for analyzing children's drawings. Artières and Kalifa write, "We should doubtless recognize that this opposition between the singular and collective, the individual and society, is illusory after all is said and done. First, because, as the work of Philippe Lejeune points out, the world of autobiography is only rarely one of singularity. On the contrary, the act of speaking or writing that leads to a personal archive, often stems from an injunction, and therefore a social act ... But, above all, personal archives function for the most part in series, networks, in a continuum. They form 'textual communities.' The individual and the society, far from butting heads, emerge like two complementary abstractions": Artières and Kalifa, "L'historien et les archives personnelles," 13.

[16] To be sure, the enmity toward Germans in French discourse was particularly virulent, fueled no doubt by the bitter defeat of 1870 and the shock of the invasion of August 1914.

FIGURE 9.1 "All I have left to eat is my own head": student drawing from the Sainte-Isaure collection, Musée de Vieux Montmartre.

highly stereotypical literary and graphic representations, the influence of which is clearly evident in children's drawings.

This is most apparent in drawings of the "comic" sort. Directly inspired by the press, caricatures drawn by schoolchildren hinge overwhelmingly on the stigmatization of the enemy's body, notably those of its leaders. Wilhelm II is the most popular character in the Sainte-Isaure collection. "All I have left to eat is my own head," reads the caption to the drawing by a pupil at Prud'homme that shows the Kaiser sitting down to dine on a pig's head – a clear reference to the Allied strategy of "starving the enemy" through a naval blockade (Figure 9.1).[17] In a similar vein, a drawing by a slightly older middle-school student at the Ecole Alsacienne depicts the German emperor casting the shadow of a vulture on the wall. A drawing by a young German uses the same techniques. Entitled "United we stand," it represents Germany's enemies standing

[17] Pignot, *La guerre des crayons*, 46.

arm in arm: The Briton carries a toy boat under his arm and wears a Scottish kilt that reveals his hairy calves; the much smaller Frenchman has a pointed beard; the Russian is a one-legged Cossack: and the Japanese is depicted as a monkey in uniform. In these three examples, the direct influence of propaganda, the humorous codes of which were easy for young audiences to grasp, is obvious. Caricatures targeting enemy leaders are also present among the Russian drawings. One, for example, depicts Wilhelm II and his handlebar moustache, an old Franz Joseph with whiskers that look like drooping jowls, and Empress Augusta Victoria, whose nose and umbrella are both gigantic. "She wears the German soldiers' blue jacket with a bright yellow skirt. She wears boots with spurs. This character's outfit causes an involuntary smile," comments the author of the Russian study.[18] This mockery of the adversary's alleged physical defects should be understood as a direct effect of war propaganda. Stigmatization of the enemy went beyond military considerations alone. Customs, eating habits, and the body also invited denigration.

The internalization of propaganda codes by children is visible in the care young artists take to single out the enemy. It is not only leaders who are ridiculed; the rank-and-file soldier (or officer) is also made to bear all the flaws of his people. There is a set of "visual guidelines" in children's drawings that systematically equates the enemy with a distinguishing characteristic. In the French and Russian drawings, the sign of the enemy is quite obviously the spiked helmet. "Oh, those German helmets! You could do a whole study on them: The younger child focuses all his attention on this new detail, which takes on giant proportions, and at the same time extraordinary shapes," notes one educator.[19] A six-year-old schoolgirl chooses to portray Wilhelm II wearing a helmet as big as his torso and crowned with a spike of oversized proportions.[20] In their drawings, younger children, for whom realism is not a primary concern, scale things according to the importance they attribute to them. In the drawing "Boches doing 'kamarad,'" the rudimentary quality of the four-year-old artist's line does not stop her from trying her hardest to crown each stick figure's helmet with an immediately recognizable spike.[21] The drawing by pupil H., aged four and a half, is probably the most representative: beneath the title "Boches and Their Helmets," the little boy drew

---

[18] *Deti i voina. Sbornik statei*, 110.
[19] Chabot, *Nos enfants et la guerre*, 22.
[20] Ibid., 37.
[21] Ibid., 23.

triangular characters endowed with legs – in other words, German soldiers whose bodies have become helmets.[22]

The spiked helmet plays an equally crucial role in drawings made by Russian children. In the drawing "The attack of Koz'ma Kriuchkov on the German officers," in the opinion of the (anonymous) author of the article in which it was published, the little boy "successfully captured the likeness of a typical German officer with his 'Wilhelm whiskers' pointing upward."[23] But even more than the moustache, it is the officer's headgear that immediately catches the eye and that ensures that the enemy is clearly identifiable to artist and reader alike. Germany's allies also have their own distinctive signs. The Ottomans, for example, are often represented armed with a sort of scimitar, doubtless inspired by the Turkish *kilij*. In "The attack of Koz'ma Kriuchkov," the Ottomans' uniforms are depicted quite realistically but their swords suggest a medieval fantasy.[24] Set in contrast to the modern weapons used by Russian troops (who are identifiable thanks to the helmet worn by a soldier firing a cannon), the scimitar is clearly a reference to the enemy's savage character, to the barbarism decried in propaganda. The French drawing is even less realistic: Dressed in a purple uniform, the enemy carries a shield in addition to a scimitar, giving him the appearance of an eighth-century Saracen.[25] In drawings by German children too, the enemy is identified by his headgear: French prisoners of war are shown wearing kepis, which was characteristic of the 1914 uniform. In another, very dark drawing, Russian soldiers can be made out thanks to their flat caps and beards, giving them all a vague resemblance to Tsar Nicholas II.[26] Thus even when the drawings are reproduced in black and white, the enemy is always identifiable. Additionally, there is no observable gender difference in the modes of representing the adversary.

This easy identification of the enemy was absolutely necessary. The chaos in children's drawings of war and its terrible consequences is only surface-deep. The enemy must be immediately identifiable, for he must not be confused with one's own side. The distinctive features of the enemy serve an obvious function: to emphasize the clear-cut opposition between the good side and the bad in the conflict. It was not unusual for

[22] Ibid., 19.
[23] *Deti i voina. Sbornik statei.*
[24] Ibid.
[25] Pignot, *La guerre des crayons*, 91.
[26] Kik, *Kriegszeichnungen des Knaben und Mädchen.*

young French artists to write "Bosch" over a German soldier or camp, as if to reinforce the distinction and imply that no confusion with the French side is possible. This is apparent in another drawing by an anonymous student at rue Lepic. The black-and-white flags offer no clue as to which side is which, and the soldiers are tangled in a confusing mêlée. The only distinguishing feature is their headgear: spiked helmets versus kepis.[27] These young children reproduced the battle between good and evil in their own way: They did what their school demanded by showing the "good guys" (the French) killing the "bad guys" (the Germans). Identifying the figure of the enemy thus contributes to the justification for war. These visual signs, which are sufficient to conjure up the figure of the enemy all by themselves, have an almost totemic function. As Alfred Brauner writes, "when the enemy is remote, the child can assemble several anxiety-inducing elements to compose the figure of the enemy."[28]

For children on the home front who had no direct experience of the enemy, the spiked helmet functioned as a distillation of all the enemy's murderous potential and the fear it caused. In a drawing entitled "Combat," a twelve-year-old boy created a particularly interesting scene.[29] The author of the article in which the drawing is reproduced analyzes it in these terms: "A Russian cemetery has fallen in the line of fire; the Russians have already been wiped out, with the exception of a poor soldier who stands miraculously on one leg: His other leg and arm have been ripped off. The planes have apparently inflicted heavy enemy losses: German helmets and weapons are strewn everywhere."[30] However, this interpretation is flawed. Upon closer inspection, the character in the middle of the cemetery appears very young; he looks more like a child than a Russian soldier. In addition, it is extremely doubtful that the young artist would have intentionally shown his country-men outnumbered by the enemy. The drawing should therefore be viewed as a scene not of combat but of desecration. The enemy, clearly recognizable by his helmet, shows no mercy, even in a cemetery, and spares no victim, not even a child. The same sacrilegious dimension can be seen in a German drawing in which an enemy plane is shown dropping a bomb on a German ambulance: A shell is about to hit a stretcher carried by two nurses (in skirts) near a tent symbolizing the hospital.[31] In the French case, the spiked helmet fits perfectly

---

[27] Anonymous drawing (number 8486), Fonds Sainte Isaure, Musée du Vieux Montmartre.
[28] Brauner, *J'ai dessiné la guerre.*
[29] *Deti i voina. Sbornik statei.*
[30] Ibid.
[31] Kik, *Kriegszeichnungen des Knaben und Mädchen*, 6.

into this role of "anxiety-inducing element" described by Brauner. When coupled with the soldier's giant arms, it helps complete the picture of a terrifying monster.[32] Likewise, in the drawing "Bosches robbing a house and stealing a child," the enemy is clearly associated with a fabled ogre; his pointy helmet is the concretization of both the threat and the fear it provoked.[33]

COMBAT

Representations of combat are another opportunity to examine the prevalence of war discourse in children's drawings by comparing the internalization of propaganda codes with more personal forms of expression. The Russian and German drawings studied in this chapter have been explicitly defined as "free drawings," that is to say the children were instructed simply to "draw a picture of the war."[34] In the Russian and German drawings, as in those in the Sainte-Isaure collection, size is an indication of importance. This can be seen, for example, in one colorful drawing of unknown authorship. A warship outfitted with cannons appears in the background; the foreground is dominated by a fortified castle with a dungeon and crenelated walls.[35] One wonders to what extent this drawing – made early on in the war, during the 1914–1915 school year – draws on familiar imagery to represent an as-yet unknown conflict. The existence of similar representations among Russian children confirms the idea of a "graphic community": the use, for example, of imaginary, even otherworldly landscapes, probably inspired by classic children's literature. The Carpathian Mountains, for instance, occupy an important place. In the drawing "Combat in the mountains," a fort bears a certain resemblance to the one drawn by the French schoolchild.[36] The importance given to strongholds and bastions underscores the weight of imagination and historical knowledge in these personal representations of war. As the drawing "Siege of a fort by German Zeppelins" shows, combat was still a matter of siege warfare in the minds of many schoolchildren.[37] The drawings of Cossacks, of which there are quite a few, serve as a final illustration of the role of personal imagination in

---

[32] Chabot, *Nos enfants et la guerre*, 23.
[33] Ibid., 40.
[34] Kik, *Kriegszeichnungen des Knaben und Mädchen*, 3.
[35] Pignot, *La guerre des crayons*, 89.
[36] *Deti i voina. Sbornik statei*, 108.
[37] Ibid., 103.

depictions of combat. These troops, though integrated into the imperial cavalry in the late eighteenth century, retain a medieval aura, a point the author makes in the article in which the drawing is reproduced: "Cossacks are generally very much appreciated by children. In their drawings, we often find Cossacks rushing to the aid of their comrades-in-arms at a crucial moment: Either they are shown in the foreground, or galloping in the distance, visible on the horizon with their characteristic silhouettes and lances on their back."[38]

The influence of war discourses on children is also evident in the division of battlefield deaths in their drawings of combat scenes. It is not unusual, especially among younger children, for casualties to be limited exclusively to enemy combatants: "Judging from the drawing, the author's sympathies lie entirely with the Russians: We have no dead, and the Austrians have several."[39] This sugarcoating of violence should come as no surprise; it stems from the same oversimplified reading of the front mentioned earlier. In a battle of good against evil, death can affect only the latter. Moreover, although propaganda aimed at the young did not downplay violence, it fostered the idea that the enemy always suffered more – be it from cold, hunger, wounds, or death. "Why, yes, on the front it is not uncommon for a shell to explode right next to you and cover you in dirt. Quick, a whisk of the brush, and it's all gone ... Look, a bird is doing its business on the Bosch soldiers ... No, it's actually a plane dropping a bomb. In other words, more or less the same thing."[40] In the three published collections of drawings, younger artists seem to have believed their troops were somehow invulnerable. This lack of verisimilitude struck observers at the time: "The boy was so engrossed in his work he did not realize the Russian cannons could hit their own planes."[41] But one must not forget that, for the youngest children, the importance of the drawing's meaning trumps any realism. Older students, by contrast, represent the dead and wounded in both camps. Still, the "good guys" always rout the "bad guys," even if it means risking serious injuries. Examples from the Sainte-Isaure collection allow us to illustrate this age-related difference. For first-graders, the color of war is blood-red. The older students also use red, but it does not saturate their pictures as

[38] Ibid., 104.
[39] Ibid., 102.
[40] Raymond Renefer, *Belle petite Monde, histoires de poilus racontées aux enfants* (Paris, 2006 [reprint]).
[41] *Deti i voina. Sbornik statei.*

it does in the younger children's drawings. In the older students' drawings, the pursuit of realism and attention to detail bring out many more nuances, not least in the colors of uniforms (blue for the French, brown for the British, and green for the Germans). The same tendency is evident in the work of German pupils: "The blood is flowing and the red color of the box of watercolors is very worn."[42]

While both younger and older children depict scenes of death and bodily injury in battle, they do so in very different fashion. Drawings by Cours supérieur students almost exclusively depict gunshot wounds to the head and limbs. A drawing from Jolivet shows a Franco-British attack. Amidst the glare of explosions, the Germans retreat, the French and British soldiers in pursuit.[43] In this scene, the dead are almost as numerous as the living. The depictions of wounds are precise: Three bodies have been shot in the head and spurt fountains of blood. One of the fallen has even been decapitated. The younger children do not portray the same types of wounds; in their drawings, soldiers are shot mainly in the stomach. The stomach is the earliest center of the body, the home of childhood aches and pains. Younger artists seem to lump together battle wounds and stomach wounds, often adding profuse blood (in fact, wounds to the stomach bled less than wounds to many other parts of the body). In a drawing by a student in a lower grade, all the wounds caused by the enormous machinegun are abdominal.[44] The machinegun's enormous size clearly corresponds not to reality but to the importance the child attributes to it. It is a tool of mass slaughter that enables a single French soldier to kill no fewer than five enemies at once.

Wounds inflicted by laceration are even more prevalent in children's drawings than those caused by bombs. For younger children of this era, the bayonet epitomizes war. Colestin Kik comments in his introduction, "boys like close combat, with bayonet and rifle butt ... Of all the instruments of murder that modern war science has invented, it is [the bayonet and rifle butt] that we see in action."[45] The stomach, blood, and knife (or in this case the bayonet) are analytical constants that reference a precise representation of war understood as conflict limited to two opponents, as in hand-to-hand combat. Age difference plays a major role in the way war is drawn.

[42] Kik, *Kriegszeichnungen des Knaben und Mädchen*, 7.
[43] Pignot, *La guerre des crayons*, 74.
[44] Ibid., 91.
[45] Kik, *Kriegszeichnungen des Knaben und Mädchen*, 7.

The freedom shown in the drawings by students at the Rue Lepic School constitute an entry point into what war might *signify* for very young children: combat characterized above all by interpersonal conflict. Fighting is most often depicted in their drawings as duel-like encounters. This is the case in the drawing entitled "La gaire"[46] reproduced in the 1917 survey. For the young kindergarten-age artist, war is conceived as a hand-to-hand fight between two men, separated by a cannon.[47] The drawing entitled "Hand-to-hand" shows a French soldier – identifiable by his kepi – running a German soldier in spiked helmet through with his bayonet.[48] As Brauner writes, "what the child of a world at war gains from understanding its realities, he loses creatively."[49] Here, that reality is the personal responsibility of a soldier engaged in the act of killing. The same kind of combat representations can be identified in the drawings in the Sainte-Isaure collection. The scaling-down of the conflict to a mere face-off implies lifting the anonymity from death. Children know and see that war involves killing, as in the drawing in which a French officer kills a German soldier by stabbing him in the face.[50] This vision runs counter to the adult discourse on modern warfare with its remoteness and anonymity.

Even in the scenes of collective combat, the drawings express the idea of personal responsibility. A charge depicted by a Russian schoolboy focuses on a pair of soldiers about to face off in a hand-to-hand combat. Astonishingly, two drawings – one by a French student, the other by a Russian – use the technique to represent a battlefield filled with miniature soldiers. The two boys took care to trace the trajectories of the bullets fired by French and Russian soldiers to show where they end up (Figure 9.2).[51] Each bullet hits its intended target, sometimes even in the back. In other words, death is always personal. And that is probably the most important thing these drawings say about their young creators: The children realize that war is fundamentally about killing.

---

[46] "Gaire" is a misspelling of "guerre" (war).
[47] Chabot, *Nos enfants et la guerre*, 18.
[48] Ibid., 41.
[49] Brauner, *J'ai dessiné la guerre*.
[50] Pignot, *La guerre des crayons*, 93.
[51] Ibid., 90; *Deti i voina. Sbornik statei*, 102: "It is interesting to note the child's desire to explain in his drawing whom the Russian killed. The child found a simple solution: With a dotted line, he indicated the trajectory of the bullet toward a wounded or dead soldier."

FIGURE 9.2 Battle scene drawn by a French student: from the Sainte-Isaure collection, Musée de Vieux Montmartre.

DRAWING AND GENDER

Drawings are a good place to look for potential gender differences in how children portray warfare. Educators writing about childhood during the conflict were unanimous on the subject. "Girls, who were less affected by the chaos, were more deeply moved by charity. Like our women, their task was more clearly mapped out than that of the boys," wrote Charles Chabot in 1917.[52] Similarly, the Russian work *Children and War* (1915) notes, "While boys are interested in military events and like to portray them, girls rarely address them in their drawings. The more one observes female students in all-girls' schools and co-educational settings, the more convinced of this fact one becomes. In drawings and in games alike, girls depict peaceful scenes: the wounded, the Sisters of Christian Charity, military nurses, etc."[53] A similar comment can be found on the German side: "Boys are better at the representation of shapes while girls have a sensitivity for colors and demonstrate better taste ... The boys are

[52] Chabot, *Nos enfants et la guerre*, 73.
[53] *Deti i voina. Sbornik statei*, 107.

not frightened by the novelty of the task and face the most difficult problems with great boldness, while girls attempt to observe the war in an everyday perspective."[54]

Taking their cue from peacetime, war discourses reinforce gender roles: Boys fight, girls heal and console. Girls are expected to be wiser. Whereas a little "unruliness" is acceptable in a future *poilu*, more is expected of future mothers and nurses. Their subordinate place in the social order is also one of internal indebtedness, as is evidenced by their sense of charity, which was markedly superior to that of boys. While girls and boys are both subjected to the continuous onslaught of patriotic propaganda, the logic behind the construction of war discourse is nevertheless deeply gendered.[55] There is a visible difference between the treatment of girls and boys, apparent from the roles they are given in the war effort, and which they shoulder more or less spontaneously.

Drawings convey the undeniable internalization of the codes of childhood war culture. It is very likely that educators favored certain types of subjects for girls, which suggests a bias that must be accounted for in our analysis. Whether we are dealing with a French, German, or Russian archive, girls overwhelmingly draw nurses, sisters of charity, and hospital rooms. The degree of accuracy depends on age; the youngest students are content to add a few distinguishing characteristics to their female outlines (red cross, coif, or apron), while older children, from about the age of ten, pay closer attention to details (hospital beds, medical instruments such as thermometers, bowls of soup) (Figure 9.3). The nurses care for and console soldiers who, in the sacrificial rhetoric of war discourse, are dying *for them*. "Even in our small and tiny girls appears the nature of Eve," Colestin Kik wrote of German schoolgirls.[56] Boys, on the other hand, were constantly urged to imagine themselves in their future roles as warriors and to think of themselves as soldiers-in-training, temporarily relieving them of feelings of indebtedness toward the combatants. Physical education lessons, for example, become veritable paramilitary training drills that echoed the righteous spirit of the school battalions of the 1880s. The drawings show the degree to which children subscribed to the idea of military preparedness: Some young artists labeled themselves the "*poilus* of the class of 1923 or 1924." No fewer than

---

[54] Kik, *Kriegszeichnungen des Knaben und Mädchen*, 3–4.
[55] That discourse was part of a preexisting cultural context of sexual differentiation that was renewed at the beginning of the war. It was manifested in publications for children, which had been divided along gender lines from the outset.
[56] Ibid., 16.

FIGURE 9.3 Drawing by a ten-year-old Russian girl, reproduced in *Deti i voina. Sbornik statei* (Kiev, 1915).

thirteen drawings in the Saint-Isaure collection revisit, in various configurations, the theme of "future *poilus* in training."[57] In the boys' drawings, a parallel is drawn between young and adult combatants: Like physical education in school, war games played in the street were presented as a form of training and the parks are transformed into training grounds for "the practice of future *poilus*."[58] Diptych forms were regularly used to show the parallel between the young boys and their warrior models, even in school work: "When my father kills a bosch, I win a victory [of my own]," the student Jolivet wrote in the caption for his drawing on his elementary school diploma.

Although war propaganda established a difference between girls and boys from a very young age, subtle variations dependent in large part on age are evident in the drawings. In *Nos enfants et la guerre*, Mlle. Rémy analyzes the vast collection of drawings donated by teachers from several French departments:

In kindergarten, there are no girls or boys, so the fact that it is almost impossible to tell their drawings apart is not surprising … In the later grades, we find a proliferation of different types of nurses [in the girls' drawings], but the strangest part is how much they stretch the nurse's role in their imaginations. Indeed, they are confused with visiting nurses or stretcher-bearers and attributed all of their duties; they are sent into the battlefield to carry away the wounded, and

[57] Pignot, *La guerre des crayons*, 16.
[58] Ibid., 122.

are shown captive or participating in attacks . . . And then suddenly, around twelve years old, a contrast: While the boys' preoccupations lead them to prefer combat, the female sex, in turn, shows all its sensitivity: The young girl musing on everything that suffers, she knows it is she who must love, console, encourage the maimed father or brother, and her thoughts turn to the wounded, the blind, the infirm or the amputees.[59]

Kik made the same argument, noting that "the graphic evolution" between girls and boys is visible "from the age of ten," "a twelve- to fourteen-year-old boy is quite another human being than a girl of the same age."[60] This educator's point about age differences is quite accurate: Until about age ten, nurses are not confined to drawings by girls. Boys, too, used this figure, as shown in the Russian drawing entitled "Country Hospital." The nurse serves as a filler in drawings, like an additional bit of scenery on the battlefield, but also as a preferred target for the enemy, a way of emphasizing his barbarism. Little girls, too, as shown in the 1917 French survey, prefered to show nurses in action on the battlefield: A concern with realism, once again, rarely shows up in children under ten. Girls also frequently drew soldiers, as in one picture in which an officer sports his medal.[61] They also give special attention to mutilated soldiers in the streets of cities far from the front lines.[62] Contrary to what Mlle. Rémy wrote in 1917, the presence of mutilated soldiers cannot be explained solely by the reflex of "feminine sensibility." Of eighty-one pictures showing soldiers on sick leave in the Sainte-Isaure collection, which is composed exclusively of boys' drawings, sixty-three depict the critically wounded and amputees. The boys of Sainte-Isaure represented injured lower appendages more frequently than any other type of wound. One-legged and legless soldiers occupy a central place in these drawings, both literally and figuratively. The schoolchildren seem to have been struck by the accessories of the wounded, which are often drawn with great care: Crutches, canes, and, in particular, wooden legs are scattered throughout. The schoolchildren also illustrate other types of wounds: A few drawings show arms in slings and bandaged faces – often tinged with red. Rarer are representations of multiple injuries, the blind, and the disfigured. Should this extreme attention to bodily alterations be seen as gender-specific? It would seem that age is the more important criterion

[59] Chabot, *Nos enfants et la guerre*, 22, 26, 28.
[60] Kik, *Kriegszeichnungen des Knaben und Mädchen*, 6.
[61] Chabot, *Nos enfants et la guerre*, 26.
[62] Didier Guyvarc'h, *Moi Marie Rocher écolière en guerre. Dessins d'enfants 1914–1919* (Nantes, 1993).

here. After age ten, girls and boys are old enough to be deeply attentive to the realism of their drawings. That concern with authenticity leads them, very logically, to represent what they see – most commonly wounds to the lower limbs and amputations.[63]

By drawing different types of wounds, schoolchildren show the effect the wounds have on the maimed person's position within society. Their compositions show a reversal of roles caused by wounds, amputations in particular. The physical impairment of a combatant diminishes his ability to perform his protective function. The first form of reversal is generational: The wounded soldier is demoted to the status of a minor, as we can gather from Miquel's drawing of a child on a scooter beside a maimed soldier. The child and the soldier are positioned symmetrically and on equal footing.[64] Likewise, a drawing by a Prud'homme student conveys the impression left on the schoolboy by the spectacle of a legless soldier being driven by his own son: The soldier, robbed of his legs and deprived of his masculinity, has returned to the state of childhood while the child, in an abnormal reversal of generations, finds himself responsible for his father.[65] The opposite could also be true, as illustrated in a drawing by student named Noël that shows an old man with a white beard guiding a blind soldier. Here again, a schoolboy has represented, perhaps unconsciously, one of the most disturbing social consequences of war: an inversion of generations whereby, against the natural order of things, the father buries the son.

***

For the historian of childhood, drawings are much more than mere illustrations of war propaganda. Studying them as components of a "graphic community" brings to light the devices at play in war discourse and their undeniable efficacy, regardless of nationality. But it also shows the large degree of autonomy these documents exhibit. Children's representations, by breaking free of grown-up constraints, convey the signs of

---

[63] In France, for example, the *gueules cassées* – the facially disfigured – numbered about 15,000, and soldiers who suffered severe facial wounds generally spent the remainder of the war in hospital. Amputation, on the other hand, was a veritable social phenomenon. It is estimated that 40 percent of all French soldiers were wounded during the course of the war and that 10 percent of the injuries they suffered were to their limbs. Many of the two million French soldiers wounded had to have limbs amputated.

[64] Pignot, *La guerre des crayons*, 81.

[65] Ibid.

a potential way out of the war culture and even lay the groundwork for its deconstruction. Surely, children's drawings do not tell us everything, but they are like snapshots that teach us as much about the climate children live in, and their internalization of the conflict and its codes, as they do about their personal relationship to war and its representations.

Bellicists, Feminists, and Deserters: Youth, War, and the German Youth Movement, 1914–1918

Antje Harms

In the summer of 1914, Peter Kollwitz, an eighteen-year-old student of arts and crafts and the second son of the artist Käthe Kollwitz, was spending his vacation in Norway together with his seventeen-year-old friend Hans Koch. Like many other members of the German youth movement, they were on a so-called great journey (*grosse Fahrt*), a multiweek hiking tour in the great outdoors. When they learned about the German declaration of war, they immediately interrupted their mountain hike and just managed to get on one of the last ferries back to Germany. Although Koch and Kollwitz were not yet old enough to be drafted, they were tremendously eager to go to war "because we absolutely wanted to help with the rescue of our fatherland, which was, as we believed, being attacked from everywhere around us." Volunteering for military service was not easy, however. Barracks were already overcrowded as volunteers rushed to enlist. Moreover, because the boys were underage, they would need their parents' written consent. Kollwitz's father was hesitant, but his wife urged him to sign the document. Only on account of the initiative of Koch's father, who was a high-ranking official in the War Department, were Koch and Kollwitz finally able to secure postings in a volunteer regiment near Berlin. After a training period of not even two months, they were sent to the front in Flanders on October 13, 1914. Just nine days later, Kollwitz was killed in action. Koch buried his friend right at the trenches. He continued to serve in combat and earned the Iron Cross. After being seriously wounded several times, Koch was dismissed from the army in 1916. Back in Berlin, emotionally stricken by the death of many friends, Koch founded the Berliner Kreis (Berlin Circle), a small group within the youth movement that soon started to campaign against the war and was eventually prosecuted for revolutionary machinations.[1]

Young men and women who participated in the German youth movement responded to the Great War in extremely different ways. The movement was not a single organization or approach. Rather, it consisted of numerous independent groups and associations that constantly dissolved and reorganized. While the majority of young Germans active in the movement fiercely supported the war, a minority was either quite skeptical from the outset or became so as the war progressed. Both sides, however, were inspired by values and ideals they had absorbed in the youth movement before 1914. This chapter offers an analysis of the often contrasting ways in which members of the movement envisioned the war at home and on the battlefront. Whether they enthusiastically embraced war or opposed it, their choices were characterized by a special notion of youth that was distinctive of the youth movement. The ideological nexus between war and youth contributed to a widespread enthusiasm for war that encouraged countless young men and women to join the army or sign up for volunteer work on the home front. At the same time, the movement's idealization of youth and of youthful values inspired an antagonism toward war among some young people, leading them to participate in pacifist and opposition political activities. In both cases, the idea of youth played a pivotal role in reinforcing the views and shaping the actions of both pro-war and antiwar activists within the youth movement. That idea, moreover, was central to the movement's conception of itself as a moral avant-garde in the building of a new Germany.

The following analysis of the different meanings and conceptions of "youth" and its connection to war focuses on the older members of the youth movement, those born between roughly 1890 and 1900. This cohort has often been described as the "front generation" or the "generation of 1914."[2] Even though most of the individuals who will be discussed

---

[1] Koch recounted his wartime experiences and involvement in the Berliner Kreis to the historian Ulrich Linse in a letter of February 26, 1972: Ulrich Linse, *Die Kommune der deutschen Jugendbewegung: ein Versuch zur Überwindung des Klassenkampfes aus dem Geiste der bürgerlichen Utopie: Die 'kommunistische Siedlung Blankenburg' bei Donauwörth 1919/20* (Munich, 1973), 71–72, 93; see also Käthe Kollwitz, *Die Tagebücher*, ed. *Jutta Bohnke-Kollwitz* (Berlin, 1989), 153–57, 174–75, 199, 321, 376, 789, 793.

[2] Richard Bessel, "The 'Front Generation' and the Politics of Weimar Germany," in Mark Roseman, ed., *Generations in Conflict: Youth Revolt and Generation Formation in Germany 1770–1968* (Cambridge, 1995), 121–36; Robert Wohl, *The Generation of 1914* (Cambridge, MA, 1979).

here were already in their twenties during the war, they saw and presented themselves as youths. This self-conception was in line with the movement's notion of youth, which was focused less on biological age than on youth or youthfulness as an attitude and lifestyle that was independent of age.

THE YOUTH MOVEMENT'S PREWAR IDEALS AND GOALS

The German youth movement emerged at the turn of the twentieth century. It was a predominantly bourgeois, Protestant, and urban phenomenon, and it attracted as many as 50,000 young women and men between the ages of twelve and thirty. Because there was not a single organization or ideology behind the movement, the political and social attitudes of the various groups involved ranged from rather liberal and progressive to nationalist and anti-Semitic. Despite the ideological diversity and the lack of a consistent policy within the movement, its members shared a set of common ideas, notably the principle of youthful freedom and a belief in the power of the spirit of the young (*Geist der Jugend*) to change the world for the better. Claiming the right of youth to self-determination, self-education, and self-development, the movement aimed to liberate young people from adult control and to create a sheltered space where the supposedly natural characteristics of youth – including truthfulness, idealism, and authenticity – could be developed as a means for the rejuvenation of Germany. Through initiatives such as hiking tours and gathering places for young people (*Sprechsäle*), the movement cultivated a unifying identity and a sense of youthful community independent of adult institutions such as the family, school, and the allegedly philistine conventions of Wilhelmine society. Similar to participants in reform movements in Germany at the time, many members of the youth movement adopted a reformist, educational approach that focused on moral, spiritual, and cultural renewal through improvement of the individual. The Wandervogel groups in particular promoted a new, healthy way of life that espoused vegetarianism and abstinence from alcohol and tobacco as means to counteract the decadence, artificiality, and physical degeneration associated with industrial modernity.[3] Other groups, such as the

---

[3] The Wandervogel was founded around 1900 and became one of the most important umbrella organizations of the prewar youth movement. The term means "bird of passage" or "wandering bird" and was often used to describe the movement as a whole. See Anna

Youth Culture Movement (Jugendkulturbewegung),[4] focused on educational and social reform and campaigned for free expression, student self-administration, and a change in gender relations.[5]

Even though there was a certain condemnation of public jingoism and governmental militarism, the youth movement largely supported the ideas of patriotism and "Germanness." Pledging "to be ready, in case of emergency, to defend their people's rights with their lives at any time," the youth movement repeatedly contrasted its genuine love of the nation to the "cheap patriotism" of the older generation and state-approved nationalistic displays such as military celebrations and parades. Nevertheless, marching drills, war games, and singing soldiers' songs were common youth movement activities long before 1914.[6] Only a minority of movement members offered fundamental criticism of nationalistic tendencies and premilitary training organizations or maintained contact with the peace movement.[7]

The prewar youth movement nonetheless considered itself apolitical and ideologically neutral. It did not give much attention to the political and diplomatic events leading up to the crisis of 1914, and the outbreak of war found most members of the youth movement utterly unprepared. The German declaration of war sparked widespread enthusiasm in the youth movement and triggered a collective drive for action. "Everybody had a task, the boys as soldiers, the girls in auxiliary service," wrote nineteen-year-old secondary school student Hedwig Rokicki. "[N]obody cared

Mageras, *Nesting the Nation: Youthful Conceptions of Nature, Culture, and Modernity in Wilhelmine Germany* (Middletown, 2010), 27–39.

[4] The Youth Culture Movement was founded around 1912 and denotes a radical minority within the broader German youth movement which claimed the youth's right to their own culture and realm: see Philip L. Utley, "Radical Youth: Generational Conflict in the Anfang Movement, 1912–January 1914," *History of Education Quarterly* 19(2) (1979), 207–28.

[5] Walter Laqueur, *Young Germany: A History of the German Youth Movement* (New Brunswick, 1984); John A. Williams, *Turning to Nature in Germany: Hiking, Nudism, and Conservation, 1900–1940* (Stanford, 2007), 123–37.

[6] "Einladung zum Freideutschen Jugendtag 1913," cited in Winfried Mogge, et al., eds., *Hoher Meissner 1913: Der Erste Freideutsche Jugendtag in Dokumenten, Deutungen und Bildern* (Cologne, 1988), 68; see also Mageras, *Nesting the Nation*, 50–51, 86–92; Christoph Schubert-Weller, "*Kein schönrer Tod ...*": *Die Militarisierung der männlichen Jugend und ihr Einsatz im Ersten Weltkrieg 1890–1918* (Weinheim and Munich, 1998), 205–15.

[7] Peter Dudek, *Fetisch Jugend. Walter Benjamin und Siegfried Bernfeld: Jugendprotest am Vorabend des Ersten Weltkrieges* (Bad Heilbrunn, 2002), 213–15; Erich Mohn, *Der logische Positivismus: Theorien und politische Praxis seiner Vertreter* (Frankfurt am Main and New York, 1978), 78–97.

about themselves and their small private interests. Everything seemed insignificant, money and property did not matter anymore ... Throughout the entire nation [*das ganze Volk*], from the worker to the ruler, there was this huge desire to serve the nation [*dem Volksganzen*]."[8] Many members of the youth movement probably experienced August 1914 similarly. At home and at the front, most young women and men welcomed the German call to arms and were eager to support the war effort.[9]

YOUTH CONTRIBUTIONS TO THE WAR EFFORT

Like Koch and Kollwitz, most male members of the youth movement tried to enlist immediately after the outbreak of war. Eager to fight on the front lines, fearing the war might end before they could be deployed, they volunteered for military service in disproportionately high numbers. In November 1914, the Wandervogel boasted about the fact that nearly all of its members over seventeen years of age had enlisted "not only as a matter of duty but also enthusiastically." The volunteers were idolized within the movement as heroic, tenacious, and devoted "victors and fighters" who had been granted the privilege to sacrifice themselves for the German cause.[10]

When they arrived at the front, these idealistic young men quickly had to face the reality of modern mechanized warfare, a form of warfare that did not coincide with their notion of war as a proof of one's valor, toughness, and manhood. Many letters from soldiers who had been active in the youth movement convey their disillusionment with the day-to-day

---

[8] Hedwig Rokicki, "August 1914–November 1918: ein Beitrag zur Geschichte der Volksgesinnung," *Jungdeutsche Stimmen* 1(12/13) (1919), 84–86.

[9] Jakob Feldner, *Deutsche Jugend und Weltkrieg* (Zürich, 1918); Thomas Fenske, "Der Verlust des Jugendreiches: Die bürgerliche Jugendbewegung und die Herausforderung des Ersten Weltkriegs," *Jahrbuch des Archivs der deutschen Jugendbewegung* 16 (1986/87), 197–228; Gudrun Fiedler, *Jugend im Krieg: Bürgerliche Jugendbewegung, Erster Weltkrieg und sozialer Wandel 1914–1923* (Cologne, 1989).

[10] Walter Fischer, "Wandervogel und Krieg," *Wandervogel: Monatsschrift für deutsches Jugendwandern* 9(11/12) (1914), cited in Werner Kindt, ed., *Die Wandervogelzeit: Quellenschriften zur deutschen Jugendbewegung 1896–1919* (Düsseldorf and Cologne, 1968), 314; Christian Krauss, "Ein Ostergruss," *Kriegsfahrtenblatt der Fahrenden Gesellen* 2 (1915), 10; see also Mageras, *Nesting the Nation*, 86–87. The secondary sources disagree on the number of war volunteers and soldiers from the youth movement: see Williams, *Turning to Nature*, 299 n. 116. According to the Wandervogel itself, a full two-thirds of the 6,000 Wandervogel to enter the army in the first year of the conflict did so voluntarily, and 3,000 more entered the army either voluntarily or by compulsion before the end of the war. Two thousand soldiers were killed in action: see Alfred Odin, "Die Soldaten," *Wandervogel. Monatsschrift für deutsches Jugendwandern* 14(4) (1919), 111–12.

reality of war and their traumatic experience in combat. For example, Fritz Klatt, a 26-year-old student of art history from Berlin, wrote about lack of sleep, hunger, cold, and the "countless horrific scenes" he encountered on the eastern front. "Combat is not the place where an individual can prove his courage in an attack," he conceded. "This may have been the case once. Now the only form of great heroism for everyone lies in enduring what seems unbearable to mind and heart alike."[11] Even Friedrich Wilhelm Fulda, a thirty-year-old Wandervogel leader from Jena and a highly decorated lieutenant who advocated the propagation of "German thought throughout the world," had to admit as early as November 1914 that he had "had no premonition of how dreadful the war is."[12] Despite their growing feelings of frustration and longing for peace, the majority of the young combatants did not question the war per se. Even if the excitement and the spirit of 1914 had disappeared, most of them kept supporting the fight for a German victory and had the will to persevere. Over the course of war, they increasingly made rallying cries and invoked the soldiers' steadfastness and dutifulness as debts owed to their "brothers killed in action." The deaths of their comrades, idealized as a sacrifice and the "birth pang of something new that is greater than us," imposed the duty that they continue to endure the horrific realities of the war.[13]

On the home front, too, the youth movement was ardently committed to the war effort. Women's and girls' groups went to great lengths over the course of the war "to dedicate our energy to the service of the public good alongside the boys." The war offered them a chance to step out of their marginalized position in both Wilhelmine society and the youth movement. They could take on new responsibilities and take advantage of new opportunities for personal development.

[11] Letter from Fritz Klatt on October 16, 1914, cited in Philipp Witkop, ed., *Kriegsbriefe deutscher Studenten* (Gotha, 1916), 72; see also 60–66, 69–70, 71–80; concerning the biography of Klatt, see Ullrich Amlung, et al., eds., *Adolf Reichwein und Fritz Klatt: Ein Studien- und Quellenband zu Erwachsenenbildung und Reformpädagogik in der Weimarer Republik* (Weinheim, 2008).

[12] Friedrich Wilhelm Fulda, "Aus Vergangenheit, Gegenwart und Zukunft," *Wandervogelführerzeitung* 2(12) (1914), 222; Friedrich Wilhelm Fulda, *Wandervogelführerzeitung* 2(11) (1914), 211; concerning the biography of Fulda, see Hinrich Jantzen, *Namen und Werke: Biographien und Beiträge zur Soziologie der Jugendbewegung*, 5 vols. (Frankfurt am Main, 1972–82), vol. V, 85–90.

[13] Otger Gräff, "Die freideutsche Jugend (1917)," Archiv der deutschen Jugendbewegung A 2-104/8:7; see also Martin Deckart, cited in Knud Ahlborn, ed., *Krieg, Revolution und Freideutsche Zukunft: Die Reden und Aussprachen der Jenaer Tagung 1919* (Hamburg, 1919), 12–14; Fiedler, *Jugend im Krieg*, 52–58; Laqueur, *Young Germany*, 89–91.

Many women from the youth movement volunteered in agriculture, nursing, or social welfare programs for the young. They knitted socks for the soldiers, organized song recitals in the military hospitals, and participated in the National Women's Service (Nationaler Frauendienst) while simultaneously maintaining local groups of the youth movement and keeping in touch with male Wandervogel companions serving at the front. These patriotic young women were firmly convinced that the war effort was not exclusively a matter of men on the front line and had to be actively supported on the home front through a particular female contribution.[14]

That also held true for men who had been wounded or exempted from military service. Like their female counterparts, young men on the home front engaged in volunteer work, and they also took an active part in organizing military training for the young. They considered their work as the "less exhilarating part" of the war effort and thus probably as a threat to their virility. Failing to live up to the prevailing ideal of soldierly masculinity, these men at the home front apparently felt the need to compensate for their supposed emasculation by emphasizing the significance of their nonmilitary contribution toward a German victory. They repeatedly stressed that the fight "for the outward existence of our empire" was not the only task at hand. The "soul of the empire [*Reichesseele*]" also had to be protected, and it was necessary to fight against everything "un-German" to keep up morale on the home front.[15]

AFFIRMATIVE READINGS OF THE WAR

Regardless of gender or whether they were at home or at the front, most members of the youth movement committed themselves to the war effort. Of course, their enthusiasm is not surprising given the initial outpouring

---

[14] Gertrud Radel, "Jugendpflege: Aus dem Bericht einer freideutschen Gruppe," *Freideutsche Jugend* 1(3) (1915), 65–66; see Marion E. P. de Ras, *Body, Femininity and Nationalism: Girls in the German Youth Movement 1900–1935* (New York, 2008), 36–40.

[15] Krauss, "Ein Ostergruss," 10; Walther Lambach, "Am Sonnwendfeuer 1915," *Kriegsfahrtenblatt der Fahrenden Gesellen* 4 (1915), 42; see also Antje Harms, "'Den kämpfenden Freunden da draussen die Treue halten': Zur Mobilisierung jugendbewegter Frauen und Männer an der 'Heimatfront,'" in Aibe-Marlene Gerdes and Michael Fischer, eds., *Der Krieg und die Frauen: Geschlecht und populäre Literatur im Ersten Weltkrieg* (Münster, 2016), 149–60.

of support for the war among Germany's middle classes. The "Spirit of 1914" was primarily a bourgeois phenomenon propagated by the government, the media, and the educated elite. It received performative expression preeminently in rallies of secondary school pupils and university students in the cities, and it was reinforced by the rhetoric of national mobilization. That rhetoric portrayed Germany as surrounded by enemies, justified the German call to arms as a defensive and thus legitimate reaction to that encirclement, and cast the war as a means to unify German society.[16]

The youth movement adopted these ideas but at the same time transformed them for its own purposes. The popular notion of a new "national community [*Volksgemeinschaft*]" set out in the emperor's famous proclamation of August 4, 1914, for example, called to mind the sense of community that had emerged within the youth movement long before the war and had helped prepare for national unity at the start of the war.[17] In the summer of 1914, one observer later recalled, it seemed as if "the entire German nation [*Volk*]" had become one giant Wandervogel club with "[w]illingness to make sacrifices, fraternal solidarity among Germans, and camp spirit [*Fahrtenleben*] on all fronts."[18] In line with the idea of a *Volksgemeinschaft* that would surmount all social antagonisms, the youth movement made an effort to reach out beyond its bourgeois base and to include young people from the working class. Activities such as hiking, athletics, folk dancing, and classes in cooking and sewing were regarded as means to unite German youth of all classes in a youthful *Volksgemeinschaft*.[19]

The youth movement also developed its own readings of the war that invoked its prewar ideals while at the same radicalizing and politicizing them. When volunteering for military service, male youth movement activists wanted not only to prove their heroic masculinity as fierce fighters and patriotic Germans. They also yearned for adventure and wished to break free from the conventions of a bourgeois society they saw as

---

[16] Jeffrey Verhey, *The Spirit of 1914: Militarism, Myth and Mobilization in Germany* (Cambridge and New York, 2000).

[17] Paul Natorp, "Die grosse Stunde," *Freideutsche Jugend* 1(2) (1915), 29; see also Knud Ahlborn, "Erinnerung," *Freideutsche Jugend* 1 (1915–12), 244–45.

[18] Dankwart Gerlach, "Walter Fischers Verdienste um die deutsche Jugendbewegung und den Kronacher Bund [1924]," cited in Jantzen, *Namen und Werke*, vol. I, 58–59.

[19] Erna Behne, "Über die Arbeit Freideutscher Mädchen in der Jugendpflege," *Freideutsche Jugend* 1(6) (1915), 127; Walter Lempelius, "Die Hamburger freideutsche Jugend," *Freideutsche Jugend* 1(1) (1914), 18; Albrecht Meyen, "Für unsere Volksschuljugend!," *Wandervogelführerzeitung* 3(5/6) (1915), 67–68.

superficial and narrow-minded. The perceived contrast between the "the momentous events" taking place outside and the "dull and vapid life at home," together with the idea that war was a "struggle against daily routines that wear you down much more than days in icy wind and wet clothes," was a common motive for volunteering.[20]

It is thus not surprising that young men in the youth movement imagined war as an adventure similar to their annual hiking trips. In their understanding of war, the outdoor skills they had acquired in the Wandervogel were key qualifications for military service. "Prowess in marching, resilience, and experience in orienteering" are the "best foundations" that the youth movement can provide its members with regard to war, claimed 28-year-old Wandervogel leader Walter Fischer, who was fit only for garrison duty after having been severely wounded in Russia in 1915. With the outdoor expertise they had acquired, Wandervogel members would meet the requirements for frontline duty. "Then you only have to give him a gun, teach him how to shoot and move, and the soldier is ready for service."[21]

Young women and men on the home front also interpreted the war along the lines of the movement's goals. They were convinced that they were fighting an ideological battle for the German cause and the German soul (*deutsches Wesen*), complementing the external fight at the front line. During a gathering of the Deutscher Mädchen-Wanderbund, a hiking association for girls, and the Fahrende Gesellen (Wayfarers), a youth organization for boys, in 1917, Luise Walbrodt, a 27-year-old leader in the hiking group, proclaimed the movement's resistance against "the enemy that lurks inside" and warned that "if all young people do not

---

[20] Karl Bernhard Ritter [1914], cited in Christoph Cornelissen, *Gerhard Ritter: Geschichtswissenschaft und Politik im 20. Jahrhundert* (Düsseldorf, 2001), 76; Letter from Carl Boesch on September 18, 1914, *Wandervogelführerzeitung* 2(11) (1914), cited in Michael Fritz, et al., eds., " ... *und fahr'n wir ohne Wiederkehr": Ein Lesebuch zur Kriegsbegeisterung junger Männer. Der Wandervogel* (Frankfurt am Main, 1990), 53; see also Mageras, *Nesting the Nation*, 92–102; Andreas Gestrich, "Jugend und Krieg: Kriegsverarbeitung bei Jugendlichen in und nach dem ersten Weltkrieg," in Martin Kintzinger, et al., eds., *Das andere Wahrnehmen: Beiträge zur europäischen Geschichte: August Nitschke zum 65. Geburtstag gewidmet* (Cologne, Weimar, and Vienna, 1991), 633–52.

[21] Walter Fischer, "Wandervogel und militärische Jugenderziehung," *Wandervogelführerzeitung* 3(4) (1915), 60; see also Charlotte Heymel, *Touristen an der Front: Das Kriegserlebnis 1914–1918 als Reiseerfahrung in zeitgenössischen Reiseberichten* (Berlin and Münster, 2007), 40–52. Concerning the biography of Fischer, see Jantzen, *Namen und Werke* vol. I, 55–60.

rise up with iron will to expel the enemy, the German nation [*Volk*] will perish and no external power will be able to protect it."[22]

The youth movement thus thought it had a special task to perform on the home front. In fighting the "enemy within," it was not enough to oppose Jews, Social Democrats, and war profiteers, the alleged opponents of the *Volksgemeinschaft*. Equally important was the struggle against selfish and un-German behavior, in particular indulgence in the "metropolitan pleasures [*Grossstadtvergnügungen*]" responsible for the German people's moral and physical decline. Members of the youth movement attacked motion pictures, dance events, and theater as well as French fashion, the consumption of alcohol, and sexual excesses. Such critiques opened up a field of activity that could be easily linked to the youth movement's prewar values and pursuits. Before the war, *Lebensreform* (literally "life reform") was seen as a means of self-improvement and a way to dissociate oneself from the bourgeois conventions of the older generation. During the war, measures such as dress reform, sexual abstinence, and giving up alcohol, tobacco, and meat were increasingly seen as means to head off decay on the home front and became politicized. By identifying these practices and ideas with the youth movement, young women and men were able to display their patriotic stance as a youthful attitude and to portray the movement's commitment as a particular contribution by youth to the war effort.[23]

That firm belief was supported by the positive connotation that the term "youth" had acquired in Germany since the turn of the century. According to Jürgen Reulecke, "'[y]outhfulness' or 'youth' became popular labels, applied to all kinds of proposals. Indeed, 'youth' came to represent a vision of society in its own right. Instead of denoting merely a biological phase between childhood and adulthood . . . it came to encapsulate a life-style independent of age. Youth was thus the code-word for a renaissance, for the forging of a new, more healthy world." The educated bourgeoisie was especially responsive to this cult of youth. Confronted by the sweeping social and economic changes that had accompanied industrialization and by the growing influence of specialized, technologically oriented knowledge, upper-middle-class Germans were apprehensive about their loss of cultural hegemony and social status, which rested more on educational attainment than material wealth. The ideal of

[22] Luise Walbrodt, "Kraft und Freude," *Der Landfahrer* 3(4) (1917), 5.
[23] "Liebe Frau N.," Der Landfahrer 4(6) (1918), 6; see also Harms, "'Den kämpfenden Freunden da draussen die Treue halten.'"

youth thus became a screen onto which they projected their hopes for the moral and spiritual restoration of German society. Accordingly, the bourgeois youth movement could be identified as the agent of cultural renewal, and it was enthusiastically supported by liberal-minded parents and the reform movements.[24]

The idealization of youth as a force for national renewal thus became a popular part of German propaganda during the war. Novels portrayed girls and boys who endured wartime privation as selfless patriots, thus ensuring Germany's victory. Newspapers floated myths such as the legend of Langemarck, the self-sacrifice of 13,000 young volunteers who went to their deaths in the battle of Ypres (November 1914) while singing the national anthem. Teachers and intellectuals praised the steadfastness, dutifulness, and readiness of German youth to submit to the collective struggle as a shining example for the entire nation. The youth movement seemed to represent the ideal of a German youth that "joyfully embraces the opportunity to unsheathe its idealism and to prove its true will to greatness and heroism" and that "cheeringly welcomes the chance to fulfill its true duty," as the educational reformer Gustav Wyneken enthusiastically declared in a speech to young activists in November 1914.[25]

Given the exaltation of the patriotism of the young, it is not surprising that the youth movement was convinced it was making a deep impact on German society. The war allowed the movement to appoint itself as a moral avant-garde and offered a unique opportunity for it to fulfill its self-declared mission. According to Christian Krauss, deputy leader of the Fahrende Gesellen, the war had made the public realize "that German youth, with their longing for an economically, spiritually, and morally great unified Germany, have already found the right ways ... to lead our people to the inner greatness for which it is destined." The war thus fulfilled "the ideals of the German youth."[26]

---

[24] Jürgen Reulecke, "The Battle for the Young: Mobilising Young People in Wilhelmine Germany," in Roseman, ed., *Generations in Conflict*, 97; see also Frank Trommler, "Mission ohne Ziel: Über den Kult der Jugend im modernen Deutschland," in Thomas Koebner, et al., eds., *"Mit uns zieht die neue Zeit": Der Mythos Jugend* (Frankfurt am Main, 1985), 14–49.

[25] Gustav Wyneken, *Der Krieg und die Jugend* (Munich, 1915), 20, cited in Hans-Ulrich Wipf, *Studentische Politik und Kulturreform: Geschichte der Freistudenten-Bewegung 1896–1918* (Schwalbach, 2004), 238; see also Andrew Donson, *Youth in the Fatherless Land: War Pedagogy, Nationalism, and Authority in Germany, 1914–1918* (Cambridge, MA, 2010); Wohl, *The Generation*, 42–84.

[26] Krauss, "Ein Ostergruss," 10–11; see also Fiedler, *Jugend im Krieg*, 40–42; concerning the biography of Krauss, see Kindt, *Die Wandervogelzeit*, 695–98.

Ultimately, "youth" and "war" seemed to belong in both official and youth movement rhetoric. Because war could be seen as the beginning of a broad socio-cultural renewal, as a "great cleansing storm that would wash away everything rotting and decadent,"[27] it fit perfectly with youth on a symbolic level. The youth movement used the ideological ties between war and youth for its own purposes. Ideas of community, cultural rejuvenation, and *Lebensreform* were adopted by the youth movement and invested with distinctive meanings of its own. Reading the war as a mission of the young gave more significance to the movement's prewar principles and contributed greatly to the widespread enthusiasm for war.

YOUTH AGAINST WAR

The youth movement's commitment to the war effort was not an end in itself. It was seen, rather, as part of the fight for the movement's ideals. However, the same values inspired an alternative perception of war in a minority of participants in the movement. Coming predominantly out of the Jugendkulturbewegung, which later became the left wing of the youth movement, these young men and women articulated a more critical position toward the war. Defying the authorities, they launched several campaigns against the war. Nonetheless, much like their pro-war peers, these young pacifists had been deeply influenced by the ideology they had absorbed in the youth movement.

Most of these skeptical youths did not initially oppose the war. Like their pro-war comrades, they at first welcomed the call to arms and acceded to the widespread vision of war as a unifying force and the beginning of a new era. Karl Bittel, who was dedicated to cooperative socialism early on and later became a staunch communist, remembered experiencing the outbreak of the war as a time of "nationalist intoxication, not of war fever and bloodthirstiness, as we were pacifists and without any hatred in our hearts. We felt the immense urgency of the moment that made people close ranks. The experience of the *Volksgemeinschaft* delighted those of us who longed for human solidarity more than for anything else. And then this anticipation: Finally the last act of world history was about to start, after the previous one had been unbearably boring and without a solution."[28]

---

[27] Arnold Bronnen, cited in Mageras, *Nesting the Nation*, 97.
[28] Karl Bittel, cited in Ahlborn, *Krieg*, 20; concerning the biography of Bittel, see Manfred Bosch, "Bittel, Karl," in Bernd Ottnad, ed., *Baden-Württembergische Biographien*, 5 vols. (Stuttgart, 1994–2013), vol. II, 46–48.

Consequently, many male activists from the movement's pacifist wing volunteered for military service. Much more frequently than other young men from the youth movement, however, they volunteered with a skeptical attitude and for tactical reasons. Unlike draftees, volunteers could choose their place of military training and thus stay close to family and friends.[29] During the course of the war, and not least due to their frontline experiences, quite a few of these young war volunteers turned in opponents of the war. Alfred Kurella, a twenty-year-old Wandervogel leader from Bonn who would later become a prominent member of the Communist Party, increasingly spoke about the bitter experiences of war and the "futility of this reciprocal killing" in his letters from the front. He became even more frustrated when he witnessed the officers' corrupt and unfair treatment of low-ranking soldiers. On the front line, the bourgeois young man came in contact with members of the working class for the first time. He noticed that the war did not improve their social position at all. He began to read anti-war books and journals. After being buried alive during a battle in 1916, Kurella feigned a speech disorder, was dismissed from military service, and returned home, where he campaigned against the war together with Hans Koch, the veteran turned anti-war campaigner quoted at the beginning of this chapter.[30]

Some pacifists in the youth movement tried hard to avoid being drafted. For instance, 23-year-old Walter Benjamin, then a student spokesman of the Youth Culture Movement in Berlin, famously stayed up the whole night before his medical exam, consuming alcohol and huge amounts of black coffee so he could fake a heart condition. Through such ruses, he managed to secure deferment from military service several times and did not become a soldier until the end of war.[31] A considerable number of young men also deserted from the army. Some of them fled abroad to neutral countries, where they met anti-war activists from all over Europe. Jakob Feldner, a twenty-year-old student from Berlin and member of the Freideutsche Jugend (Free German Youth), escaped in 1916 just before

---

[29] Momme Brodersen, *Walter Benjamin: A Biography* (London, New York, 1996), 68–70; Rudolf Carnap, "Intellectual Autobiography," in Paul A. Schilpp, ed., *The Philosophy of Rudolf Carnap* (La Salle, IL, and London, 1963), 3–84.

[30] Letter from Alfred Kurella to Gustav Wyneken on April 30, 1915, Archiv der deutschen Jugendbewegung N 35 Sig. 683; see also Alfred Kurella, *Unterwegs zu Lenin: Erinnerungen* (Berlin, 1967), 14–35; Evelyn Lacina, "Kurella, Alfred," *Neue Deutsche Biographie* 13 (1982), 321–33.

[31] Gershom Scholem, *Walter Benjamin: The Story of a Friendship* (Philadelphia, 1981), 17; Brodersen, *Walter Benjamin*, 69, 93.

being drafted. He joined the leftist intellectual milieu in Geneva, worked together with leading figures of the international peace movement, and probably even obtained British support for plans to instigate a revolution in Germany during a stay in London in 1917.[32] Other young deserters went underground in Germany and participated in illegal political activities such as distributing pacifist pamphlets and attending secret meetings of communist revolutionaries.[33]

Young women from the youth movement also campaigned against the war. Instead of engaging in self-sacrificing service to the nation, they revolted against traditional gender roles and female duties at the home front. Susanne Leonhard, a nineteen-year-old student from Leipzig who later became a communist writer, refused to complete her high school studies ahead of time to earn the accelerated wartime "emergency diploma [*Notabitur*]." Declaring her "fundamental opposition to war," she also declined to volunteer as a nurse, as many of her schoolmates did. In 1915, she began to study at the University of Göttingen, where she came into contact with the Youth Culture Movement as well as with pacifist and socialist circles. She founded a communist group and started to fight for women's rights. Because of her provocative speeches, she received a severe reprimand from the university. Leonhard was also involved in illegal political activities such as hiding deserters; she was eventually charged with high treason in June 1918.[34]

SKEPTICAL READINGS OF WAR

One of the most important concerns behind pacifism in the youth movement was the fear that the war would curtail young people's freedom and autonomy. Accordingly, one of the main fields of action was a campaign against the government's plan to implement mandatory military training

---

[32] Hermann Müller, "Friedensbotschafter der Jugendbewegung: Jakob Feldner (1896–?)," in Eckard Holler, ed., *100 Jahre Hoher Meissner 1913–2013: Kritische Rückblicke auf 100 Jahre Meissner-Formel der freien bürgerlichen Jugendbewegung* (Ebersdorf, 2013), 49–57; Sean McMeekin, *The Red Millionaire: A Political Biography of Willi Münzenberg, Moscow's Secret Propaganda Tsar in the West* (New Haven, 2005), 49, 317.

[33] Linse, *Die Kommune*, 77–80, 92–97.

[34] Susanne Leonhard, *Unterirdische Literatur im revolutionären Deutschland während des Weltkrieges* (Frankfurt am Main, 1968 [1920]), i–xvi; Elisabeth Ittershagen, "Sophie Liebknecht (1884–1964): Susanne Leonhard (1895–1984)," in Günter Benser, et al., eds., *Bewahren – Verbreiten – Aufklären: Archivare, Bibliothekare und Sammler der Quellen der deutschsprachigen Arbeiterbewegung* (Bonn, 2009), 162–67.

for boys starting at the age of sixteen. Unlike their pro-war compeers who saw participation in the training program as an opportunity to spread the youth movement's ideals and to gain influence with the state, the young pacifists firmly opposed the government's plans. Championing "the sanctity and liberty of the young," they criticized the military training program not only as a "grave threat to youthful life [*schwere Bedrohung jugendlichen Lebens*]" and to "impulses of a free spirit in the young" but also as an instrument by which the older generation was seeking to implant its nationalistic and militaristic ideas.[35]

The young pacifists likewise rejected the vision of war as a symbol of rejuvenation and as an affair of the young that was widespread within the youth movement, portraying war instead as a matter for the old and as a result of Wilhelmine Germany's obsolete social conditions. Increasingly skeptical of official propaganda praising "the holy power of war," the pacifist youth movement held up capitalism, consumerism, and rationalism as the actual reasons for the war. They identified the present "unnatural, unhealthy era" with the past and their parents, and they blamed the "old generation" and its "materialistic romanticism and corrupt lifestyle habits" for having caused "catastrophes" like the war.[36]

Gustav Wyneken, a mentor of the prewar Youth Culture Movement and a supporter of its radical call for complete emancipation of youth from adult control, was heavily criticized by his former adherents. They regarded Wyneken's view of war as an "ethical experience" and as a superb performance test for young people – a view that found a sympathetic hearing from the majority in the youth movement – as a great betrayal of young people.[37] Wyneken was repudiated along with the rest of his generation in an open letter in 1915 by Hans Reichenbach, a 23-year-old member of the Youth

---

[35] Feldner, *Deutsche Jugend*, 23; "Resolution der Berliner Freien Studentenschaft zum Reichsjugendwehrgesetz," cited in Fiedler, *Jugend im Krieg*, 258 n. 90; Gerhard Fils, "Amtlicher Bericht über den ausserordentlichen Vertretertag der FJ in Göttingen am Pfingstsonntag 1916," Freideutsche Jugend 2(8/9) (1916), 258; cf. Fiedler, *Jugend im Krieg*, 84–95.

[36] Harald Schultz-Hencke, "'Andere' Ursachen des Krieges," *Freideutsche Jugend* 4(1) (1918), 25; letter from Margret Arends to Rudolph Carnap on June 21, 1918, in University of Pittsburgh, Special Collections Department, ASP.1974.01, Rudolf Carnap Papers, Series VIII, Box 81, Folder 14; Georg Gretor [Georges Barbizon], "Die Ideologie der entschiedenen Jugend," *Neue Schweizer Rundschau* 12(1) (1918), 11–12.

[37] Wyneken, *Der Krieg*, 20, cited in Wipf, *Studentische Politik*, 238; see also Fritz Jöde, "Der Krieg und die Jugend: Ein Vortrag, gehalten am 25. November 1914 in der Münchener freien Studentenschaft von Dr. Gustav Wyneken," *Freideutsche Jugend* 1 (3) (1915), 55–59; Gershom Scholem, et al., eds., *The Correspondence of Walter Benjamin, 1910–1940* (Chicago, 1994), 76; Dudek, *Fetisch Jugend*, 36–38, 48–50.

Culture Movement who had criticized German militarism even before the start of the war: "You, the older generation whom we have to thank for this wretched catastrophe, how can you still dare to speak to us of ethics and set us goals for our lives? . . . [Y]ou have forfeited the right to be our leaders. We despise you and your magnificent epoch."[38]

The young anti-war activists shared the youth movement's common conviction that the young generation had a mission to overcome the decrepit structures of Wilhelmine society and to build a new Germany. In contrast to their pro-war comrades, however, the pacifists believed that goal could be realized only by ending the war. As Jakob Feldner clearly stated, "The upcoming Germany will be liberated by us, by German youth, by the defiantly remaining few who have not been shot dead. May the world remember: This youth is strong enough! There are still people who know how to fight for their liberty, their independence, and their free education. To fight without the Iron Cross, without the Legion of Honor, but to fight in the light of better times to come. Struggle against the war: This is what we want and preach."[39]

CONCLUSION

The youth movement's experience and reading of World War I were significantly shaped by different meanings and uses of the term "youth." As an ideal, "youth" was invoked both by pro- and anti-war activists, female as well as male, in promoting their particular objectives. The majority within the youth movement appropriated the central ideas of the official war propaganda, tailored them to the movement's values, and created their own interpretations of war. The war could thus be regarded as a "great journey," hiking as a key military qualification, or an abstemious lifestyle as an expression of patriotism. Self-sacrifice, a sense of duty, and community spirit were seen as intrinsic attributes of the movement. A minority within the youth movement rejected those ideals,

[38] Letter from Hans Reichenbach to Gustav Wyneken on February 18, 1915, cited in Brodersen, *Walter Benjamin*, 72; see also Hans-Ulrich Wipf, "'Es war das Gefühl, dass die Universitätsbildung in irgend einem Punkte versagte . . . ': Hans Reichenbach als Freistudent 1910 bis 1916," in Lutz Danneberg, et al., eds., *Hans Reichenbach und die Berliner Gruppe* (Braunschweig, 1994), 161–81; concerning the biography of Reichenbach, see Andreas Kamlah, "Hans Reichenbach," in Sahotra Sarkar, et al., eds., *The Philosophy of Science: An Encyclopedia*, 2 vols. (New York, 2006), vol. II, 703–12.

[39] Letter from Jakob Feldner to Romain Rolland on September 1916, cited in Romain Rolland, *Zwischen den Völkern: Aufzeichnungen und Dokumente aus den Jahren 1914–1919*, 2 vols. (Stuttgart, 1955), vol. II, 52–53.

however. From their perspective, the war thwarted the movement's pursuit of its goals and threatened the principle of youthful freedom and autonomy that was so crucial to the prewar movement's self-conception. Instead of reading the war as the beginning of a new era, young pacifists associated it with the past and saw it as the doing of their parents' generation.

Nonetheless, both groups within the youth movement saw their wartime engagement as part of the struggle on behalf of the movement's ideals. As the war radicalized and politicized their shared vision, youth movement members felt increasingly compelled to create a new Germany and to break up the old, corrupt structures over which the older generation presided. Both supporters and opponents of the war developed a distinct sense of mission (*Sendungsbewusstsein*) based on the belief in youth as the agent of socio-cultural change. Ultimately, "youth" turned out to be a fluid and ambiguous term that served as an ideal concept to mobilize young people for as well as against the war.

11

Boys Without a Country: Ottoman Orphan Apprentices in Germany During World War I

Nazan Maksudyan

Ahmed Talib was born in Istanbul in 1901. His mother passed away when he was three years old. His father soon married again, but Ahmed was not at all satisfied with this situation. He constantly complained to his brother about their stepmother. Before the war, the family's economic standing was not bad. The father had a shoeshine shop in Kadıköy, and he was also an ice dealer. The fate of the family changed dramatically with the explosion of World War I. Ahmed's father was drafted in late 1914 and was killed the next year in Gallipoli. As an "orphan of a martyr," Ahmed Talib was entitled by the Ministry of Education to admittance to the state orphanage (darüleytam) in Kadıköy, a facility housing about 1,000 boys that was located on the campus of the famous French College of St. Joseph.

In the crowded orphanage, Ahmed was assigned to the trades department and started training in shoemaking. When he heard in early 1917 that a large number of volunteers would be sent by the orphanage administration to Germany for further training, he applied immediately. Sixteen-year-old Ahmed was among the first group of 314 "craft apprentices" who arrived in Berlin in late April 1917. He was transferred first to Frankfurt an der Oder and then to Fürstenwalde, where he stayed in the household of Albert Pöthke as an apprentice cobbler. In the following years, he learned German. Ahmed passed the journeyman exam (Gesellenprüfung) in shoemaking on April 30, 1921, and worked at Pöthke's shop until February 10, 1923. He worked at a number of workshops and factories in Berlin before opening his own shop in Fürstenwalde in late 1927. He married a young German woman and became a father. In 1935, Ahmed Talib was certified as a master by the Chamber of Trade in Frankfurt an der Oder and started to have apprentices of his own. He remained in Fürstenwalde for the rest of his life. A well-known figure in his neighborhood, Ahmed was described as a "typical shoemaker from Fürstenwalde."[1] He was among the few wartime orphan apprentices, however, who succeeded in making a new life in Germany. After years of homelessness and orphanhood, he had a well-established business and a family.

Ahmed Talib's life story, situated in the context of sending of Ottoman orphans to Germany for apprenticeships during World War I, differs substantially from those of most of the almost 1,000 other orphan apprentices in terms of earning a livelihood and integrating into German society. Many of the orphans sent to Germany endured poverty, felt excluded as foreigners, and thought that they had been deceived.

The idea of sending Ottoman orphan boys to Germany in the middle of the war to work as apprentices in craft trades, mining, and agriculture came from the leading figure in the Committee of Union and Progress (CUP), Minister of War Enver Pasha. He made it clear to the German military attaché, Otto von Lossow, in late 1916 that the government was willing to send between 5,000 and 10,000 orphan boys to Germany.[2] The German–Turkish Association, DTV (Deutsch-Türkische Vereinigung), the sole organization responsible for carrying out the project, decided to begin with roughly 300 apprentices for craft trades, 200 for the mining industry, and 200 for agriculture.[3] There was discussion of sending girls as well as boys, but no decision could be reached before the program was ended and thus only boys participated in the program.

Relying on German and Ottoman archival sources together with contemporary press and personal narratives, this chapter sheds light on a forgotten episode in the history of the Ottoman–German alliance during World War I. In an attempt to bring forward the voices and experiences of the orphan boys, it focuses on how this long-distance child displacement policy changed the lives of the children involved. This first section begins with the crowded orphanages that they longed to leave. The second section describes the details of their long and uncomfortable but also hope-filled journeys to Berlin on military trains and of the welcome they

---

[1] Börte Sagaster, *Achmed Talib: Stationen des Lebens eines türkischen Schuhmachermeisters in Deutschland von 1917–1983* (Cologne, 1997).

[2] Mustafa Gencer, *Nationale Bildungspolitik, Modernisierung und kulturelle Interaktion: Deutsch-türkische Beziehungen (1908–1918)* (Münster, 2002), 268–69.

[3] The association was led by Ernst Jäckh, Dr. Hans Hermann Russack and Dr. Gerhard Ryll.

received. The third section of the chapter is devoted to the orphan apprentices' bittersweet lives in the households of German masters. The attempt to reconstruct the personal experiences of the boys will also help to delineate the motives, engagement, and expectations of the Ottomans and Germans involved in this project. Finally, the chapter considers the children who returned to the Ottoman Empire and discusses some of the trajectories that their lives took.

OTTOMAN STATE WELFARE POLICIES FOR ORPHANS

The Ottoman state traditionally did not have centralized and institutional care mechanisms for needy children. In accordance with the rulings of Islamic jurists, the state treasury financially supported both individual households and religious foundations that agreed to provide for orphaned, poor, and destitute children. This customary policy of noninvolvement on the part of the state changed substantially during and after the *Tanzimat* era, the era of Ottoman modernization (1839–1876), which ushered in a range of reforms in the penal code, property and personal rights, the tax system, and education.[4] In this period, the state introduced a wide range of new institutions targeting the welfare and education of orphans and destitute children. These included a large imperial network of orphanages (*ıslahhanes*) providing serious vocational education, a foundling asylum (*ırzahane*), a children's hospital (Hamidiye Etfal Hastanesi), and the poorhouse (Darülaceze) with special children's wards.[5] Despite all these promising new undertakings, Ottoman state welfare could accommodate only a few thousand destitute children, a tiny minority of those in need.

Larger and more organized orphanages were opened during World War I in response to the orphan crisis created by the war. They owed their existence to educational institutions that had been established by the Entente powers and had then been abandoned as a result of the unilateral abolition of the Capitulations.[6] These institutions, including buildings

---

[4] For further information, see Roderic Davison, *Reform in the Ottoman Empire: 1856–1876* (Princeton, 1963).

[5] For a detailed analysis of provisions for needy children in the Ottoman Empire during the nineteenth century, see Nazan Maksudyan, *Orphans and Destitute Children in the Late Ottoman Empire* (Syracuse, 2014).

[6] The capitulations of the Ottoman Empire were contracts between the Ottoman Empire and European powers, particularly France, that regulated how each party would treat the other's subjects. Under the terms of the capitulations, traders entering the Ottoman Empire were exempt from local prosecution, local taxation, local conscription, and searches of their residences.

and staff, had been either taken over or confiscated from foreign relief agencies, mostly missionary bodies.[7] In addition, many Armenian schools, churches, and even monasteries that had been abandoned with the expulsion and massacre of Ottoman Armenians were occupied and used as orphanages. The new network of state orphanages (*darüleytam*) was run by the Directorate of Orphanages (Darüleytam Müdüriyeti) established in November 1914. In December, twenty of the new orphanages were already admitting orphans. Especially after the Gallipoli campaign, which led to the deaths of 60,000 Ottoman soldiers and the Armenian Genocide, which left behind hundreds of thousands of orphans, these "emergency orphanages" were incapable of dealing with the ever-increasing number of orphans.

The directorate kept taking over buildings and opening additional orphanages. In 1916, there were sixty-nine orphanages that covered almost the entire territory of the empire. Toward the end of the war, the number rose to eighty-five. In 1917, based on data from each institution, the directorate declared that it was providing for almost 11,000 needy orphans in the country.[8] That figure suggests that, in proposing the apprenticeship program to Lossow, Enver was in effect planning to empty the orphanages to create space for new arrivals. They were drastically overfilled, and the orphanage administrators were forced to refuse new admissions. The Ottoman archives are full of petitions to have children admitted to orphanages from relatives or district officials who had been told by orphanage administrators that there were no vacancies.[9] Moreover, the budgets allocated to the orphanage administration constantly proved to be inadequate to cover expenditures.[10] It was in this context that German master craftsmen and mine-owners appeared as an option for providing for the orphans.

It is not difficult to imagine why so many orphans volunteered to be sent away into the unknown. For one thing, state orphanages were

---

[7] Yasemin Okur, "Darüleytamlar" (MA thesis, Ondokuz Mayıs Üniversitesi Sosyal Bilimler Enstitüsü, Samsun, 1996).

[8] The table prepared by the Directorate in mid 1917 gives the total number of orphans as 10,870: Ottoman Archives of the Prime Minister's Office (hereafter BOA), MF.EYT, 7/51, 1/Tm/1333 (September 1, 1917).

[9] For example, BOA, MF.MKT., 1215/63, 04/B/1334 (May 7, 1916); BOA, DH. KMS., 38/3, 29/Ca/1334 (April 3, 1916); BOA, MF.MKT., 1229/46, 24/Za/1335 (September 12, 1917).

[10] BOA, İ.MMS., 198/1333-N-10, 06/N/1333 (July 19, 1915); BOA, İ.MLU., 10/1334-S-34, 24/S/1334 (January 1, 1916); BOA, MF.MKT., 1227/20, 19/Ş/1335 (June 9, 1917).

incredibly crowded. Many orphanages housed more than a thousand boys even though most had the capacity for no more than a few hundred. Tight living quarters often provoked fights among children. Dormitories were far from being warm and comfortable. The lucky children slept between three and six to a bed without sheets or pillows.[11] Most had to sleep on the floor, holding one another for warmth.[12] Diseases spread quickly because there was no space in the wards to separate the sick from the healthy.[13]

Hygiene was a huge problem in the orphanages. Most of the buildings did not have their own water source, and the toilets were in deplorable condition. Children had to wear dirty underwear for a long time, and they could bathe only during occasional visits to public baths in nearby towns or cities.[14] These conditions resulted in numerous cases of chiragra and frequent outbreaks of rashes.[15]

Hunger was the other great problem the orphans, like the rest of population, faced. They were constantly fed soup made from few ingredients and of little nutritional value. Orphan memoirs are full of sad descriptions of never-ending hunger.[16] The orphans lacked proper clothing as well. Many of them went barefoot, and they did not have coats. These deficiencies in shelter, nutrition, and clothing led to serious widespread illness. There were innumerable cases of malaria and pneumonia.[17] It was reported that 20 percent of the children in Edirne Orphanage had pneumonia.[18] More than a thousand children had trachoma, and three hundred lost their sight for lack of treatment.[19]

Despite the lamentable conditions in the orphanages, the Orphanage Administration's 1919 report claimed that children were generally happy and showing promising signs that they would grow up to be sensible and

---

[11] Minutes of the Grand National Assembly, 2nd Parliament, 1st Legislative Year (August 11, 1923–February 28, 1924), 15th Session (September 8, 13398 [1923]) (hereafter TBMM ZC), 448–79, www.tbmm.gov.tr/tutanaklar/TUTANAK/TBMM/d02/co0 1/tbmm02001015.pdf, 461; BOA, MF.EYT., 6/131 (report) cited in Safiye Kıranlar and Aynur Soydan Erdemir, "Köyün Modernleştirilmesine Dair Bir Uygulama ve Proje: Kimsesiz Köy Çocuklarının Köyde Eğitimi," *Yakın Dönem Türkiye Araştırmaları*, no. 8, 2005, 94–113.

[12] Hasan İzzettin Dinamo, *Öksüz Musa* (Istanbul, 2005), 14–16.

[13] TBMM ZC, 448–479.

[14] BOA, MF.EYT., 6/131 (report), cited in Kıranlar and Erdemir, "Köyün Modernleştirilmesine Dair Bir Uygulama ve Proje," 98–99.

[15] Dinamo, *Öksüz Musa*, 18–20.

[16] Nissim M. Benezra, *Une enfance juive à Istanbul, 1911–1929* (Istanbul, 1996).

[17] BOA, MF.MKT., 1225/98, 10/B/1335 (May 2, 1917).

[18] TBMM ZC, 461.

[19] TBMM ZC, 453.

responsible individuals.[20] Officials were definitely exaggerating about the orphans' happiness and their good character since many of them applied to go to Germany in 1917. Poorly informed about their country of destination, they assumed they would enjoy much better living conditions there than in the Ottoman Empire. It is clear from DTV reports that a large number of orphans assumed that they would become factory workers and earn a good salary.[21] What awaited them in Germany was quite different, however.

By and large, Ottoman authorities treated orphan boys as state property over which the state had an unrestricted right of disposal. The opportunities offered to the boys or the trades they were trained in were neither problematized nor scrutinized. The bankrupt Orphanage Administration tried to send as many orphans as possible abroad to relieve itself of the high cost of providing for them. As the entire financial burden of the project was borne by the DTV and the German masters, the project was free of cost to the Ottoman government.[22] That bargain, however, came at the expense of the young apprentices, who were not entitled to any form of financial compensation. The exchange between the two countries looked a lot like a fosterage agreement concluded between two households: A child would be transferred to a foreign household because his natural parents were no longer alive or unable to provide for him, and in exchange he would be asked to help with the chores.

WAR ORPHANS ON MILITARY TRAINS

Educational collaboration between imperial Germany and the Ottoman Empire started prior to World War I. However, when the Ottoman Empire entered the war, the policies of sending Ottoman youth to Germany changed significantly. Pupils and apprentices, together with workers and university students, were sent to Germany in much greater numbers during the war. In negotiating and carrying out the orphan transfer project, the DTV played the leading role. Ernst Jäckh, Paul

---

[20] BOA, MF.EYT., 6/131 (report), cited in Kıranlar and Erdemir, "Köyün Modernleştirilmesine Dair Bir Uygulama ve Proje," 98–99.

[21] Dr. Hans Hermann Russack, "Die türkischen Lehrlinge," in *Türkische Jugend in Deutschland: Jahresbericht der Schülerabteilung der Deutsch-Türkischen Vereinigung* (Berlin, 1918), 60.

[22] "The training of skilled trades and mining apprentices ended up being completely free of charge for Turkey through the German skilled trades and mining [industries]": "Tätigkeitsbericht der DTV (für das Jahr 1917)," Auswärtiges Amt Archives, R63454.

Rohrbach, Hjalmar Schacht, and Franz Schmidt were important actors on the German side. On the Ottoman side, the Türkisch-Deutsche Vereinigung, which was run by the most powerful Young Turks such as Talat Paşa, Enver Paşa, and Nazım Bey, was in charge.

The sending of Ottoman orphans to Germany was one of the boldest and most interesting joint educational undertakings of the two empires. Both sides were hoping to foster cultural understanding and to gain mutual economic benefit by giving large numbers of Ottoman boys direct contact with German culture and the German language. As Germany increasingly overshadowed France as a model and ideal, there was a change in educational philosophy among Ottoman educators, public officials, and politicians. German proficiency in technical education has been frequently stressed, and some technicians, apprentices, and vocational school students had been sent to Germany before the war. In sending students and trainees to Germany for vocational training, the Young Turks were hoping to train pioneers for a national bourgeoisie who would play a key role in helping the empire achieve economic independence from Europe.[23] Once the Ottomans entered the war, the German Military Supreme Command and Foreign Office pursued good relations with the Ottoman government and sought to build channels of German cultural influence. German businesspeople and Turcophiles, most prominently Ernst Jäckh and the DTV, wasted no time in forging ambitious plans for the "economic development of the Sultan's lands."[24] A growing labor shortage in Germany was also a determining factor. The mobilization of eleven million men left millions of job vacancies in German industry that needed to be filled.[25] The labor shortage provided new job opportunities for women and minorities – and apparently for immigrants as well. Immigrants were also seen as a way to circumvent labor unrest. Plagued by hunger and rising living costs, and frustrated by the continuation of the war, hundreds of thousands of long-suffering German workers participated in a total of 561 strikes in 1917.[26] In this context, it is understandable that German trade masters and mining authorities volunteered to take in Ottoman boys as

[23] Gencer, *Nationale Bildungspolitik*, 265.
[24] Ulrich Trumpener, *Germany and the Ottoman Empire, 1914–1918* (Princeton, 1968), 319.
[25] Colin Nicholson, *The Longman Companion to the First World War* (London, 2001), 248.
[26] On January 28, 1918, there was a massive strike in Berlin, in which 100,000 workers took to the streets, demanding an end to the war on all fronts. Within a few days, the number of strikers was up to 400,000. See Gerald D. Feldman, *Army, Industry and Labour in Germany, 1914–1918* (Princeton, 1966), 326–36.

apprentices. They probably hoped that the children would be quiet, obedient, and hard-working laborers.

Although economic considerations played their part, the reason why Germany accepted the heavy burden of educating and feeding Ottoman orphans lies in what Malte Fuhrmann has called a "semicolonial mentality."[27] The key figures at the head of the DTV, such as Rohrbach and Jäckh, were critical of German policy toward the Ottoman Empire. In their view, Berlin was obsessed with numerically calculable benefits of major investments such as the Baghdad Railway or the posting of technocratic advisors. They, in contrast, underscored the importance of the "moral conquest" of the hearts and minds of the Ottoman public to build sympathy for Germany and German political aims.[28]

The apprenticeship program for Ottoman orphans was finally able to get under way in February 1917 after the German Chambers of Trade and Industry agreed to arrange accommodation and work for the apprentices. The selection committee, made up of Jäckh and representatives of the Ottoman Ministry of Education and the Orphanage Administration, quickly decided on the first group of craft apprentices. They were all declared to be "orphans of martyrs" chosen from Istanbul orphanages. They were between fourteen and sixteen years old, with the exception of one seven-year-old, Ibrahim.[29] The Orphanage Administration prepared special passports for the boys.[30] The passports gave detailed personal information (age, family background, physical traits) about the boys, and they also included pages where masters were to write comments every third month.[31] The passports were thus intended to make it possible to track the orphans' vocational and educational development to a certain extent (Figure 11.1).[32]

---

[27] For further information on the concept of "semicolonial mentality," see Malte Fuhrmann, "Germany's Adventures in the Orient: A History of Ambivalent Semicolonial Entanglements," in Volker Max Langbehn and Mohammad Salama, eds., *German Colonialism: Race, the Holocaust, and Postwar Germany* (New York, 2011), 123–45.

[28] Ibid., 133.

[29] "Türkische Jugend in Berlin," *Berliner Tageblatt*, May 6, 1917.

[30] There is a copy of the passport of Mehmet, the son of Yusuf Efendi, in the Ottoman Archives: BOA, MF.EYT, 2/117, 8/Hz/1332 (June 21, 1916).

[31] Hakan Aytekin, "1914–1924 Yılları arasında Korunmaya Muhtaç Çocuklar ve Eğitimleri" (Marmara Üniversitesi, Türkiyat Enstitüsü, unpublished MA thesis, 2006), 108–10.

[32] Nurdan Şafak, "Darüleytam'da Çocuk Olmak: On Çocuk On Portre," *FSM İlmi Araştırmalar İnsan ve Toplum Bilimleri Dergisi*, no. 2 (2013), 261–84.

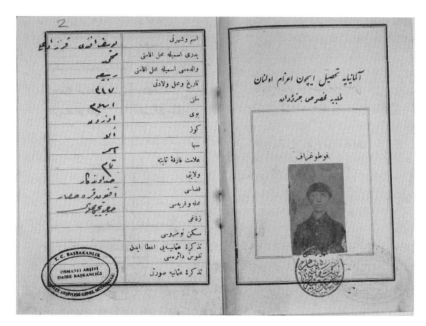

FIGURE 11.1 Passport of an Ottoman orphan apprentice. Ottoman Archives of the Prime Minister's Office (BOA), MF.EYT, 2/117, 8/Hz/1332 (June 21, 1916).

The first group of boys, 314 in all, departed from Sirkeci Train Station in Istanbul in April 1917. The passenger train between Istanbul and Berlin, which made the trip in three days, was deemed to be too expensive.[33] The boys, lacking warm clothing and shoes, thus had to spend ten days in a military freight train. Many contracted lung diseases along the way and were sent back a few months after their arrival in Germany.

In Berlin, the orphans were housed in a residence belonging to the city council in Sophienstraße 34. Soon after their arrival, they were assembled in the courtyard of an elementary school at Koppenplatz and were greeted by Major Ramsen of the Ministry of War, the Privy Cleff and Göhmann from the Ministry of Commerce, Dr. Glock from Ministry of Agriculture, and Vice Consul Tahir Bey from the Ottoman Embassy. The boys were given European-style shirts and trousers, with a blue pelerine as a coat and a blue fez-like cap (Figure 11.2).[34] From Berlin, the boys were sent to their posts in Augsburg, Breslau, Bromberg, Dusseldorf, Frankfurt an der Oder,

[33] Russack, "Die türkische Lehrlinge."
[34] "Türkische Jugend in Berlin," *Berliner Tageblatt*, May 6, 1917.

FIGURE 11.2 Ottoman orphan apprentices in Berlin. Photo from *Berliner Tageblatt*, May 6, 1917.

Mannheim, Oldenburg, Schwerin, Weimar, and Ulm. The master craftsmen and the Chambers of Trade and Industry committed themselves to paying for the boys' board but not for their return journeys.[35]

A second group of 200 Ottoman boys, who were to fill mining apprenticeships, arrived in June 1917.[36] In contrast to the first group, these boys had been chosen from orphanages in the provinces – from Maraş, Antep, Kilis, Ankara, Söğüd, Niğde, Konya, Bursa, Manisa, Karahisar, and Edirne. For boys from the eastern provinces, the journey lasted thirty days: twenty days on the Anatolian railway and ten on the military train from Istanbul to Berlin. In Berlin, they were housed at an inn at Hasenheide 52/53. As with the first group, a ceremony to welcome the boys was planned, and Dr. Russack of the DTV invited Dr. Söhring of the Foreign Office to visit the boys before they were sent off to their apprenticeships in various mines.[37] There is no evidence, however, that the

---

[35] This was to be paid either by the Ottoman government or by the boys themselves.
[36] DTV to Dr. Söhring, Auswärtiges Amt, June 13, 1917, Auswärtiges Amt Archives, R63063.
[37] DTV to Dr. Söhring, Auswärtiges Amt, June 13, 1917, Auswärtiges Amt Archives, R63063.

invitation was accepted. According to the plan prepared by the Ministry of Trade and Industry, representatives of the various mine administrations took the boys from Berlin to the places where they would be working. Roughly half the boys were sent to the western mining regions near Dortmund, Bonn, and Saarbrücken and half to the mining districts of Halle and Clausthal in central Germany. A small group went to Upper Silesia. Most of the boys worked in ore mining (iron, zinc, lead, and copper) and the coal industry; a small number were employed in lignite and cement production.[38]

Sending the last group of apprentices, the boys who would be working in agriculture, took much longer than expected. In May 1917, a memorandum sent by the DTV to the German Chamber of Agriculture made approximately 500 agricultural positions available for Ottoman boys. The boys were to be dispatched from two centers: Those to be placed in the southwest were to arrive at Karlsruhe, and those heading northeast were to arrive in Berlin. However, official business was moving slowly in the Ottoman Empire. A large number of prospective agricultural apprentices were taken to Istanbul from the provinces but then had to wait in crowded Istanbul orphanages for the preparations to be finalized.[39] Travel permits for boys born in 1315 (1899–1900) and 1316 (1900–1901)[40] could not be obtained from the Ministry of War until October.[41] As the boys waited in Istanbul, their behavior was criticized by the orphanage directors as inappropriate. Administrators voiced concern that the Istanbul orphans might be negatively influenced and insisted that the boys from the provinces be transferred to Germany immediately.[42]

In the autumn of 1917, the Ottoman Ministry of Education, again in collaboration with the Orphanage Administration, conducted a selection and sent a list of the chosen boys to Germany. However, the DTV officers in Berlin objected, pointing out that only about 100 of the 500 boys had a rural background.[43] Acceding to the demands of the DTV

---

[38] Russack, "Die türkische Lehrlinge," 54.

[39] BOA, MF.MKT., 1229/46, 24/Za/1335 (September 12, 1917).

[40] Birth dates based on the Rumi calendar, a specific calendar based on the Julian calendar but starting with the year of Muhammad's emigration (Hijra) in 622 AD. It was officially used by the Ottoman Empire after *Tanzimat* (1839).

[41] BOA, MF.MKT., 1230/82, 28/Z/1335 (October 16, 1917). In late October, the Ministry of Education was still sending orders for the completion of necessary documentation: BOA, MF.MKT., 1231/7, 09/M/1336 (October 26, 1917).

[42] BOA, MF.EYT., 7/ 57, 1/Ağ/1333 (October 1, 1917).

[43] "Sitzung des Ausschusses für türkische Schüler und Lehrlinge der DTV," September 17, 1917, Auswärtiges Amt Archives, R63063.

administrators, Dr. Nazım, a prominent figure in the CUP central committee and a member of the TDV, promised to arrange a new selection and to send a large number of Anatolian "farmers' sons [*Bauernsöhne*]" rather than "orphans from the city [*Waisenkinder aus der Stadt*]" to serve as agricultural apprentices.[44] In the end, only about 150 agricultural apprentices were sent to Germany in two convoys in June and July 1918.[45] The boys were assigned to positions mainly in northern and eastern Germany.

Each apprentice had an identity card that listed his profession, workplace, assignment number, and the Chamber of Trade to which he was attached. Administrators also intended to add photographs of the boys to their cards.[46] Judging by the names recorded in documents in the German and Ottoman archives – lists of apprentices, for example, and correspondence regarding complaints and other matters – all of the boys were Muslims. However, an article in the *Berliner Tageblatt*, which included a photograph of the first group of 314 boys, noted that the boys came "from various ethnic groups [*Völkerstämme*]." Referring to the photograph, the reporter claimed that "one can see both the white faces of the Armenians and Jews, Anatolian types, and also Arabs and Negroes among them."[47]

FOREIGN BOYS IN FOREIGN HOMES

Based on the training contract signed by the Chambers of Trade and Industry and a representative of the Ottoman embassy, the apprentices agreed to perform an unpaid three-year apprenticeship and to work for a year as a journeyman at journeyman's wages at the same workplace. In return, the master craftsmen would provide shelter, board, and, over time, some clothing (excluding underwear and shoes). The DTV considered it desirable to have the apprentices study German. Some attended part-time or night classes to improve their language skills.[48] Those who completed their apprenticeships were given certificates. A few certificates that apprentices submitted

---

[44] "30. Vorstandsitzung der DTV," October 29, 1917, Auswärtiges Amt Archives, R63064.
[45] "37. Vorstandsitzung der DTV," August 3, 1918, Auswärtiges Amt Archives, R63454.
[46] "Türkische Jugend in Berlin," *Berliner Tageblatt*, May 6, 1917.
[47] Ibid.
[48] In the future, those willing could even attend other classes (for example, maths) or even attend a vocational school: RUSSACK, "Die türkischen Lehrlinge," 62.

to governmental bodies for the purpose of accreditation or translation are preserved in the Ottoman archives.[49]

The DTV chose the master craftsmen after thorough examination of their households and families. In a leaflet for German households accepting Ottoman boys, the DTV underlined the program's two main goals. The boys were to become accustomed to German morals, ethics, honesty, thoroughness, and industriousness. To facilitate this kind of cultural transfer, the mining apprentices were lodged with experienced miners' families. The boys' religious and national identities were not to be threatened. They were to be allowed to perform their daily prayers and to observe Islamic religious holidays. The masters were also told not to offer them pork or alcoholic beverages.[50]

On paper, the rules and responsibilities of both sides were well defined and consistent with standard procedures. In practice, however, each side had many complaints. The most recurrent conflict in the first months after the arrival of craft apprentices was the "insufficient preparation" on the part of the Ottoman organizers. German masters repeatedly complained that they had to provide clothing beyond the terms agreed because the clothing the boys had brought was inadequate. The Chambers of Trade and Industry emphasized that the contract Professor Jäckh had prepared stipulated that each boy would bring two sets of clothing, underwear, and shoes so that his master would not have to make outlays for clothing costs for at least a couple of months, by which time the boy's productivity would offset the cost of supporting him. However, the clothing many boys had when they first arrived "could not be poorer." This is not hard to believe, given the circumstances in Istanbul orphanages. Some masters claimed that they had to spend as much as 100 marks to clothe their apprentices because they were ashamed to let the boys – members of their households – be seen on the street dressed in the clothes they had brought with them.[51]

The same complaints about the boys' clothing (particularly their shoes and underwear) were heard again after the 200 mining apprentices arrived in Germany. There was a long-lasting "shoe controversy'" that pitted the

---

[49] BOA, MF.MKT., 1238/91, 05/N/1337 (June 4, 1919).

[50] "An die Königlichen Provinzialschulkollegien, Der Minister der geistlichen un Unterrichts," October 14, 1916, Auswärtiges Amt Archives, R63062; "Maarif Şuunu," *Muallim*, 15 Kanunuevvel 1332 (December 28, 1916), 190–92.

[51] "[Report] Deutscher Handwerks- und Gewerbekammertag (e.V.): Unterbringung von jugenlichen Türken in deutschen Handwerksbetrieben," June 25, 1917, Auswärtiges Amt Archives, R63063.

masters and the DTV against Ottoman representatives. Apparently, many of the orphan boys arrived in Berlin without shoes. Several institutions and masters were forced to provide shoes for their apprentices out of their own pocket and later applied to the Foreign Office for compensation.[52] The DTV subsequently demanded that the Ottoman Ministry of Education cover the cost of its "blunders."[53]

For the boys, clothing was a very serious issue. Three mining apprentices from Frankleben, Necdet, Hüseyin, and Süleyman, turned to the DTV with the complaint that their clothing was not warm enough and that they were constantly cold.[54] The work in the mines, coupled with uncongenial temperatures, proved to be a health hazard. One apprentice died of a lung disease at the Charité Hospital in Berlin, and many boys were sent back to the Ottoman Empire after having fallen ill.[55]

Another source of discontent among the boys was food. Many of them acknowledged that the bread was much better in Germany. At the same time, however, they were never sure whether the meals they were served contained pork. They were constantly fed dark-colored soups that tasted unfamiliar to them.[56] Some boys also complained that they received only one meal each day and nothing else to eat.[57] Four mine apprentices from Altenberg and Eschbach escaped, complaining that the food was bad.[58]

For their part, German masters occasionally reported that their orphan apprentices had been "wrongly selected." It is obvious that the Ottoman authorities had been concerned solely with numbers in making the selections, hoping to send as many boys as possible to Germany. This process did not result in a group of candidates with skills appropriate to the vacant positions. The DTV also claimed that the Ottomans sent essentially all

---

[52] Reichsbekleidungsstelle to Auswärtiges Amt, September 27, 1917, Auswärtiges Amt Archives, R63063.

[53] "28. Vorstandsitzung der Deutsch-Türkischen Verein," June 26, 1917, Auswärtiges Amt Archives, R63063.

[54] "Sitzung des Ausschusses für türkische Schüler und Lehrlinge der DTV," September 17, 1917, Auswärtiges Amt Archives, R63063.

[55] "Sitzung des Ausschusses für türkische Schüler und Lehrlinge der DTV," August 2, 1917, Auswärtiges Amt Archives, R63063.

[56] Although Muammer Tuksavul was among the relatively rich students who had enough money to stay in boarding houses, he was unable to eat the soup served by his host. See Muammer Tuksavul, *Eine bittere Freundschaft: Erinnerung eines türkischen Jahrhundertzeugen* (Düsseldorf, 1985), 162–63.

[57] "Sitzung des Ausschusses für türkische Schüler und Lehrlinge der DTV," July 20, 1917, Auswärtiges Amt Archives, R63063.

[58] "Sitzung des Ausschusses für türkische Schüler und Lehrlinge der DTV," August 2, 1917, Auswärtiges Amt Archives, R63063.

who volunteered and did not give them proper medical examination or test their intellectual or moral qualities. Masters complained the boys were in poor health and, in some cases, too young for the work expected of them. To "get rid of unsuitable elements entirely [*den ungeeigneten Elementen gründlich aufzuräumen*]," as a result, 25 percent of the boys were sent back.[59]

Moreover, the selection committee in Istanbul was accused of disregarding the boys' previous training. A large number of the boys – about 50 per cent – were placed in apprenticeships in trades different from those in which they had previously been trained. Mining apprentices frequently voiced the grievance to the DTV that they had been trained in other fields and that they did not want to work where they were assigned. When possible, discontented boys were assigned to another, related trade. If that was not possible, they had to remain in their assigned positions. This is why many were unhappy at their workplaces and why several of them fled or showed signs of disobedience. For instance, a mining apprentice named Mazhar and a trade apprentice named Mustafa Osman escaped from their posts in Fürstenwalde because they were dissatisfied with their jobs. Having earlier received two years of training as lathe operators, they found their apprenticeships in Germany incompatible with their vocational qualifications. The German Chamber of Trade and Industry responded that it was not possible at that time to accommodate them as lathe operators.[60] The chamber was also unhappy about the timing of the boys' arrival and the problems that were created due to making reassignments. German apprentices traditionally began their apprenticeships at Easter, but the transfer of the Ottoman boys to their posts was delayed until mid or late May, which caused additional difficulty in trying to accommodate boys who wanted to change their training positions.[61]

In accordance with the demands of the Ottoman government, most of the boys were assigned to workshops in small and medium-sized towns to facilitate their integration in a foreign society and to allow them to get together occasionally. That also made it easier to monitor them. Although the DTV was convinced that integration would enable the boys to become envoys of German culture and values, integration remained an unachieved goal.

---

[59] Russack, "Die türkische Lehrlinge," 49.
[60] "Sitzung des Ausschusses für türkische Schüler und Lehrlinge der DTV," August 2, 1917, Auswärtiges Amt Archives, R63063.
[61] "[Report] Deutscher Handwerks- und Gewerbekammertag (e.V.): Unterbringung von jugenlichen Türken in deutschen Handverksbetrieben," June 25, 1917, Auswärtiges Amt Archives, R63063.

Language was an obstacle that made everyday life difficult for the boys. They received no language training and thus arrived at their posts with literally no knowledge of German. Some tried to attend German classes, but, as the reports of the Chambers of Trade and Mining Administrations indicate, most of the boys made little if any progress in mastering German. To facilitate the communication between masters and apprentices, a 700-word dictionary was prepared on commission from the Chamber of Trade.[62] It was of no use to the boys, however, as it provided only German-to-Turkish listings and definitions. Moreover, it was written in the Latin alphabet; even if literate, the boys knew how to read and write only Arabic script. As a pilot integration project, the Ottoman boys in the mines near Eisleben lived together with German apprentices. The administration assumed this would facilitate the Ottoman boys' linguistic progress and foster interaction between them and their German counterparts. There were, however, serious problems, ranging from verbal harassment to physical disturbances and fights. The German and Ottoman boys were eventually separated during work hours and assigned to separate wards in their residence.[63]

The surviving records give only spotty accounts of boys running away and of other acts of disobedience. We know for certain that, by November 1918, only 140 of the 200 mining apprentices and 181 of the 314 trades apprentices were still in Germany.[64] These figures suggest that the conditions the Ottoman boys encountered abroad were far from idyllic. They definitely dreamed of a better work environment with more opportunities. They were hoping to earn some money and to share in the promise of European prosperity. When the reality of poor living and working conditions shattered those dreams, some of the orphans began to resist or even revolt. The Chamber of Trade and Industry was worried that only a few masters gave positive feedback about well-behaved and modest apprentices who met German standards and fulfilled German expectations. Many masters regretted that they had agreed to having Ottoman boys who were demanding monetary compensation and free time.[65] Both were considered incompatible with the rights and

---

[62] "Ein kleines Wörterbuch, das wir auf Wunsch des deutschen Handwerks- und Gewerbekammertags für die Handwerkslehrlinge herausgegeben haben," July 24, 1917, Auswärtiges Amt Archives, R63063.

[63] Russack, "Die türkische Lehrlinge," 59–60.

[64] "Jahresbericht des Schülerheims," November 1, 1918, Auswärtiges Amt Archives, R63065.

[65] Captain Hüsni tells of a report by the Turkish supervisor Hasan in Mülheim that four apprentices employed by the Altenberg firm in Unter-Eschbach had asked for pocket money

responsibilities of an apprentice in Germany.[66] The boys were supposedly behaving very arrogantly and overconfidently. They insisted that they were promised and entitled to factory employment and handsome monthly salaries.[67] No matter how futile it was, orphan boys kept asking for time and money to remedy their situation, to empower themselves, and, possibly, to move elsewhere.

The main problem was the children's misinformed image of Germany and what they could expect there. Most of the boys arrived assuming that they would be employed in positions in line with their previous training. Those assigned to apprenticeships in mining had had no idea that was what awaited them in Germany. The boys at the coal mines in Breslau were openly resistant. They were rude to their coworkers, and they frequently refused to perform the tasks they were ordered to. Claiming that they were being exploited, they quit the premises.[68] Four mining apprentices from Altenberg and Eschbach ran away because they had no pocket money and were treated badly.[69] Orphan boys in the Rammelsberg mine administration reportedly escaped their duties and clearly had no interest in the work.[70] Apprentices, on the other hand, complained that they were not learning anything apart from transporting stones.[71]

There was a serious uprising at the Oberharzer Berg- und Hüttenwerke (Upper Harz Mining and Metallurgical Works). Fourteen Ottoman boys, supposedly under the leadership of the "Negro Mehmed Tevfik," refused to perform their tasks and disrupted the work discipline. Mehmed Tevfik was accused of discouraging his countrymen from working with "threats and ill treatment."[72] What turned minor cases of resistance into an open revolt was the employment of several boys in the same workplace. Group feeling bolstered the boys and encouraged them to take action. Eight of the ten apprentices at the Royal Mining Inspectorate at Rüdersdorf fled the

---

and ran away when their request was denied: "Sitzung des Ausschusses für türkische Schüler und Lehrlinge der DTV," August 2, 1917, Auswärtiges Amt Archives, R63063.

[66] "[Report] Deutscher Handwerks- und Gewerbekammertag (e.V.): Unterbringung von jugenlichen Türken in deutschen Handverksbetrieben," June 25, 1917, Auswärtiges Amt Archives, R63063.

[67] Ibid.

[68] Russack, "Die türkische Lehrlinge," 59.

[69] "Sitzung des Ausschusses für türkische Schüler und Lehrlinge der DTV," August 2, 1917, Auswärtiges Amt Archives, R63063.

[70] Russack, "Die türkische Lehrlinge," 60.

[71] "Sitzung des Ausschusses für türkische Schüler und Lehrlinge der DTV," September 17, 1917, Auswärtiges Amt Archives, R63063.

[72] "Sitzung des Ausschusses für türkische Schüler und Lehrlinge der DTV," July 20, 1917, Auswärtiges Amt Archives, R63063.

mines shortly after their arrival and did not come back. A few weeks later, five of the runaways were found at the Friedrichstraße train station and were sent back to their posts at Rüdersdorf by the DTV. However, the other three were never found.[73]

The source materials used for this study – reports prepared by either local DTV administrators or central DTV supervisors – are absolutely biased in terms of putting all the blame in cases of conflict on the apprenticed boys. According to the reports, the boys were ill prepared, they were not accustomed to workplace discipline, they were rude, they incited one another, and so on. The boys' disobedience was viewed with a more or less manifest "colonial gaze."[74] Russack argued that the difficulty in teaching them discipline and obedience stemmed from their untamed nature. They were "children of nature [*Naturkinder*]" who lacked the basic social training of civilized manners to adapt to German standards of hard work.[75] Social historians, informed by postcolonial theory, have underlined the difficulty of hearing the voices of the subaltern and of the importance of rereading the sources for traces of the agency of the disempowered, be they colonial subjects or children. In the complaints recorded in the DTV reports and the accounts of runaway apprentices, we can make out the boys' voices. Keeping their living and working conditions in mind, it is not so hard to reconfigure the narrative of the boys' experiences in Germany from their perspective.

HOME SWEET HOME?

The pressures and demands of the war facilitated rather than impeded the policy of child displacement between the two empires. The apprenticeship project was initiated in the middle of the war (1916), and, for all intents and purposes, it came to an end with the end of the war. The defeat of the Central powers led to the collapse of the German and Ottoman Empires, and made the continuation of educational collaboration projects impossible on account of financial difficulties and organizational breakdowns.

In April 1919, the DTV reported that it had a total of 800 Ottoman boys under its supervision as students or orphan apprentices.

---

[73] Ibid.
[74] As we learn from many works on the "colonial gaze," it was not uncommon for "civilized" Westerners to see the less developed colonies as "barbarians," "savages," or "untamed" (animals). See Pramod K. Nayar, *Colonial Voices: The Discourses of Empire* (Malden, 2012).
[75] Russack, "Die türkischen Lehrlinge," 61.

The expenses of some of the students were paid by their family members. Others had full or half scholarships from the DTV. As communications between the two empires were cut off with the conclusion of the Armistice, money transfers from Istanbul were interrupted. The DTV thus had to pay the expenses of all of the Ottoman students it was sponsoring in Germany. The organization was running out of money, however, and it began to consider the option of repatriation.[76] The Entente agreed on April 20 that the Ottoman ship *Akdeniz*, which had carried German troops back from Istanbul, could take Ottoman citizens living in Germany on board on its return voyage. As the *Akdeniz* was set to depart on April 30, there was little time to make arrangements to bring the orphan apprentices from across Germany to Hamburg. Nonetheless, complying with the demand of the Ottoman embassy, the DTV informed the masters and mine authorities that Ottoman orphan apprentices were supposed to return home.

The steamers *Akdeniz*, *Reşid Paşa*, and *Gülcemal* departed in late April, June, and August 1919, respectively, carrying Ottoman soldiers, officials, and students.[77] The DTV did not insist, however, that the Ottoman orphan apprentices and students be sent back. On the contrary, the organization stressed that it would be "politically valuable" to help Ottoman students continue their education without interruption and to have them return to their homeland only after their graduation or when their parents called them back.[78] It acted on the belief that Ottoman young people educated or trained in Germany would sustain and promote the country's reputation in the Middle East, which would in turn translate to economic gain.[79] Therefore, students who could cover their expenses and apprentices whose masters agreed to provide for them were allowed to stay.[80] Ahmed Talib, for instance, had an exemplary master–apprentice relationship with Albert Pöthke and was able to stay with him despite the termination of the official agreement.[81] In late 1919, about half of the DTV-sponsored students and apprentices were sent back – 320 young

---

[76] "Die gesamten Kosten für türkische Schüler," April 24, 1919, Auswärtiges Amt Archives, R14044.

[77] "Dank türkischer Untertanen an Deutschland," *Hamburger Fremdenblattes*, no. 113, August 9, 1919.

[78] "Die gesamten Kosten für türkische Schüler," April 24, 1919, Auswärtiges Amt Archives, R14044.

[79] Ibid.

[80] As noted earlier, Muammer Tuksavul was among the relatively rich students. In order to pass his *Abitur* exam and also to study chemistry in the technical high school in Darmstadt, he remained in Germany. See Tuksavul, *Eine bittere Freundschaft*, 162–63.

[81] Sagaster, *Achmed Talib*.

people in all – but the DTV still had 250 orphan apprentices and 230 students under its supervision.[82]

***

We, the Turkish students, do not want to miss this moment, as we leave German soil, to express our deepest gratitude for the hospitality and helpfulness that we were granted here at great expense.

We are well aware that we owe much to German culture, which helped us become competent.

We are happy to have spent our best years in this glorious land and we will always remember it with heartfelt pleasure.[83]

Thus one of the returning students bade farewell to Germany at a ceremony shortly before the steamer *Gülcemal* departed from Hamburg in August 1919. Like the other speaker that day, Ottoman military liaison Zeki Paşa, the student underscored the "sincere helpfulness" of Germany and voiced Ottomans' high opinion of German culture and German hospitality. In other words, despite numerous crises, regrets, and disappointments on both sides, formal declarations tended to emphasize the gains and accomplishments. Most of the Ottoman orphan apprentices definitely did not share that opinion.

Returnee orphan apprentices arrived in Istanbul just as needy as they had been when they left the city for Germany. The most serious problem for Ottoman officials was to find lodging for the destitute boys because many of the orphanages in the city were no longer in operation. After the Allied occupation of the country, buildings that had been confiscated were repossessed by their rightful owners.[84] Most of the state orphanages had to be shut down because their buildings were no longer under government control and the government was unable to offer alternative facilities. Sixty-one orphanages in Anatolia were closed, and their charges were asked to leave and find family members to take care of them. Only children without family who were reluctant to leave the orphanage system were sent to Istanbul.[85] In total, probably 10 percent of the Anatolian orphan population ended up in Istanbul. In 1923, there were

---

[82] "Jahresbericht der DTV für 1918[–1919], 11.Dezember.1919," Auswärtiges Amt Archives, R63443.

[83] "Dank türkischer Untertanen an Deutschland," *Hamburger Fremdenblattes*, no. 113, August 9, 1919.

[84] Abdurrahman Şeref recounts that French priests themselves threw the orphans out of Kadıköy Orphanage, the Collège de Saint Joseph: TBMM ZC, 465.

[85] Dinamo, *Öksüz Musa*, 13–30.

approximately 3,500 orphans residing in six state orphanages in the city.[86] Living conditions were very poor, with food and clothing in short supply.[87]

The orphan boys who came back from Germany could not easily be accommodated in Istanbul's downsized and crowded orphanages. For instance, Mehmed Fikri and İshak Namık, who had previously been training as tailors at the orphanage in Kadıköy, returned from Germany to find the orphanage closed. Petitioning the Ministry of Education, they asked to be admitted to the Yedikule Orphanage.[88] Almost all of the orphans who came back from Germany were put there because of its proximity to state-owned factories. The returnees were about five years older than the rest of the boys in the institution, and they were employed in Zeytinburnu iron works (Zeytinburnu Fabrika-i Hümayunu). They had a three-kilometer walk to and from their workplace each day. A younger resident of the orphanage complained in his memoirs that these older boys talked and made rude jokes all night.[89]

Returning mine apprentices who were originally brought from the orphanages in Anatolia were in particularly dire straits. Not only were their orphanages closed, but they were also hundreds of miles away from their hometowns with no means to return there. Some orphans were "temporarily" sheltered in the Poorhouse (Darülaceze), in various hospitals, and orphanages. However, this supposedly limited residence lasted longer than expected. They were sent back as late as March 1922.[90]

CONCLUSION

After the CUP came to power, the number of Ottoman admirers of Germany grew markedly. Educational journals were filled with articles on German proficiency in technical education and German economic and industrial success. This admiration had an impact on the educational policies of the CUP as Germany supplanted France as a role model. Technicians, apprentices, and vocational school students were sent to Germany. The goal, as the government often stated, was to produce a group of expertly trained specialists in the skilled trades who, on their

---

[86] These were in Validebağ (for girls), Çağlayan (for girls), Halıcıoğlu, Yedikule, Balmumcu, and Beykoz: TBMM ZC, 452–53.
[87] TBMM ZC, 458–59.
[88] BOA, DH.UMVM., 119/15, 16/N/1337 (June 15, 1919).
[89] Dinamo, *Öksüz Musa*, 37–38.
[90] BOA, DH.UMVM., 119/26, 12/B/1340 (March 11, 1922).

return, would be fully equipped to train new generations of workers.[91] Though it made sense on a theoretical basis, this explanation was only partially true and was valid only for the high school and university students sent to Germany, not for the hundreds of orphan boys. For those boys, the exchange program's economic goals went largely unfulfilled.

The Ottoman administration did not have the imagination for long-term economic planning. Officials were more interested in solving pressing current problems than in investing for a better future. The simple reason behind the idea of sending as many as 10,000 orphans to Germany was the difficulty of sheltering, feeding, and educating so many needy children and young people. Given the hastily made plans and preparations for the transfer of the children and the lack of care in selecting children for the program,[92] we can safely argue that the Ottoman government was concerned only with the number of children involved. Officials wanted to *get rid of* as many orphan boys as possible, regardless of whatever opportunities might be available to them. Orphan boys were sent off without any date set for their return. The way the boys were treated upon their unexpectedly early return suggests that they were not really expected to come back, at least not in the near future.

Why the Ottoman government was not able to utilize such a large labor force at home can be understood only by looking closely at the logic of foster-care arrangements. Poor households were not able to benefit from their child's labor as much as rich households could. Sending a child away helped save scarce resources and could even increase the household's disposable income. Orphans in the Ottoman Empire were in that situation. The state was in a very weak organizational situation, plagued by a financial crisis and low agricultural and industrial output during the war. It was thus unable to turn this army of boys into a real workforce.

The boys' qualifications and the quality of the training they were offered were not an issue for the Young Turk government. The DTV and German foreign policy makers accepted the heavy burden of educating and feeding Ottoman orphans only because of the promise that they

---

[91] Gencer, *Nationale Bildungspolitik*, 265.

[92] The Ottoman Ministry of Education acted as if the German educational outlets were banishment centers for unsatisfactory students, together with burdensome orphans. In October 1917, the ministry ruled that those who failed to pass their final exams more than once and those who did not have any chance of graduation would be sent to Germany to be trained as apprentices in crafts and agriculture: BOA, MF.MKT., 1230/54, 20/Z/1335 (October 8, 1917).

would receive "the sons and daughters of the best families of the country."[93] Because there were so few German-educated Ottomans, educating the orphans in Germany was a great opportunity to create a new generation of "friends of Germany."[94] In that respect, the Germans' educational aspirations had a quasi-colonial character and were driven by a long-term vision. Success would be dependent on being able to mold the boys. Dr. Ryll, the DTV's inspector for the Ottoman youth in Germany, described the issue in his report entitled "Quantity or Quality?" (July 1918):

Those who know and support our work – on both the Turkish and the German sides – increasingly recognize that our success does not depend on whether the number of Turkish youth studying in Germany is increasing every year by several hundreds. It depends more on the arrival of "the best minds of Turkish schools" (as it says in our guidelines) and to educate and train in our country those who could alone be the bearers of a better Turkish future. Therefore one might at first think of the "best families," i.e. the social elite of Turkish society, who have previously played the leading political role and who are also likely to continue to play that role for the time being.[95]

Squeezed between Ottoman demands for quantity and German demands for quality, orphan boys were expected to accomplish a mission impossible. The orphans thus felt betrayed on two fronts. On the one hand, their hopes to lead more prosperous lives in Germany were shattered. On the other, they were not welcomed back in their country as qualified workers to help rejuvenate the economy. They were still being treated as needy orphans that the state had a hard time providing for. Despite the miles they traveled and the hardships they endured, they had been unable to remedy their situation as destitute children.

[93] "Türkische Schüler in deutschen Familien," *Tägliche Rundschau*, July 3, 1916.
[94] "An die Königlichen Provinzialschulkollegien, Der Minister der geistlichen un Unterrichts," October 14, 1916, Auswärtiges Amt Archives, R63062.
[95] "Dr. Ryll, Quantität oder Qualität? Kritische Bemerkungen zur dritten Schülerentsendung," July 31, 1918, Auswärtiges Amt Archives, R63065.

12

In Their Own Words: Children in the World of the Holocaust

Patricia Heberer Rice

Young Yitskhok Rudashevski lived in the Vilna ghetto from the time of its inception until its final liquidation in the autumn of 1943.[1] An only child, Rudashevski was born in Vilna (Vilnius) on December 10, 1927, and before the war resided in the Lithuanian capital with his parents and maternal grandmother. His father was a typesetter for *Vilner Tog*, the city's most prominent Yiddish newspaper, and it was perhaps this influence that spurred young Yitskhok's interest in writing. In September 1941, when he and his family were forced to settle in the newly established Vilna ghetto, the fourteen-year-old began to keep a diary. Written in Yiddish, the thick journal brims with vivid descriptions of the ghetto surroundings and lively caricatures of its diverse and colorful inhabitants. Featured prominently in the pages of the narrative are the efforts of Rudashevski and like-minded youngsters to forge a cultural and intellectual life for the youth of the Vilna ghetto. In addition to his studies and independent writings, the teenager dedicated himself to the activities of two youth organizations; the first endeavored to compile a history of the ghetto and its inhabitants, while the second collected ghetto folklore: its stories and myths, jokes and curses, songs and literature.[2] Describing a club holiday on December 11, 1942, Rudashevski exclaimed:

This is the happiest evening I have spent in the ghetto . . . Many, many guests came. And here we sit crowded together. I look around at the crowd, all of our kind teachers, friends, intimates. It is so cozy, so warm so pleasant. This evening we

---

[1] See Yitskhok Rudashevski, *The Diary of the Vilna Ghetto, June 1941–April 1943*, transl. Percy Matenko (Tel Aviv, 1973).
[2] Ibid., 80.

demonstrated what we are and what we can accomplish. Club members came with songs, recitations ... Song after song resounded. It is already 12 o'clock. We are, as it were, intoxicated with the joy of youth ... We have demonstrated that we are young – "within the walls, yet young, forever young."[3]

For Rudashevski, such cultural endeavors were a way to escape the moral and material barrenness of the ghetto and to create a space and time in which beauty and enlightenment could continue to exist. "Our youth works and does not perish," Rudashevski wrote on October 22, 1942, suggesting that his activities and those of his colleagues represented a means of transcending the narrow limitations of their confinement and of defying both the physical and spiritual repression which persecution embodied.

Surviving the liquidation of the Vilna ghetto, Rudashevski and his parents fled to a hiding place (*maline*) at his uncle's home on Disne Street. In early October 1943, the teenager and all those concealed with him were discovered and transported to Ponary Woods (Paneriai), where they were shot and killed. Yitskhok Rudashevski was just one of the one and a half million Jewish children and juveniles murdered in the Holocaust. His story – their story – is the history of the Shoah in microcosm: a chronicle of genocide seen through the eyes and the fates of its youngest victims.

IN THE BACKGROUND

With notable exceptions, the contours and chronology of Nazi racial policy were parallel for children and adults. Jewish youngsters, just as their parents, were victims of discrimination, ghettoization, deportation, and mass murder. For scholars, the temptation is strong to frame their experiences as if children were a subset of the adult population. Unless they are the focal point of the story, children's experiences are often cast across the arc of the adult narrative. They are painted onto the backdrop, while their parents and caretakers squarely occupy the colorful central foreground.

Yet if adults and youngsters generally faced the same cycle of discrimination and violence during the Holocaust, children and juveniles confronted and contended with the Nazis' persecutory policies in markedly different ways. Their experiences were profoundly different from those of

---

[3] Ibid., 104–05. "Within the walls, yet young, forever young" was the name of the youth newspaper produced by Rudashevski and fellow club members.

their adult contemporaries. The challenge for historians is to represent these experiences in a meaningful and authentic way. The ever-expanding body of work on genocide during World War II leaves us in little doubt about what happened to the young during the Holocaust, but there is a relative scarcity of manuscripts that attempt to articulate the range of their experiences, especially in their own voices. In the many excellent works that feature the history of children during the Holocaust, the testimony of adults still often frame the conversation. They are the narrators – parents, caretakers, teachers, perpetrators, rescuers – who relate the fates and experiences of children.

One obvious remedy for this imbalance is to incorporate the postwar memories of child survivors into scholarly research and writing. As adults, child Holocaust survivors share their experiences, filtering the memories of their extraordinary childhoods with perspectives they have gained as adults. For them, the lapse of time allows for the contemplation and recollection of details perhaps omitted in initial testimonies and facilitates the interweaving of historical and factual knowledge with personal experiences. It is not uncommon for a survivor's in situ accounts – or recollections articulated in the immediate aftermath of the Shoah – to differ appreciably from testimonies given decades later, if not in detail, then in emphasis and perspective. This is particularly true of the testimonies of child survivors, for whom the passage into adulthood may fundamentally alter perceptions of persons and events. The passing of time obscures certain aspects of the past, while others stand out in sharp relief. Intellectual understanding and emotional maturity sharpen the lens and bring once inexplicable incidents into clearer focus.[4] A child may feel only anger and bitterness toward parents who "abandoned" her to utter strangers during the war years; now grown with children of her own, the adult survivor may at last comprehend the deed that ultimately saved her life and the tremendous personal sacrifice her parents made in undertaking such an action.

And yet the best way to understand the experiences of children during the Holocaust is to let the youngsters speak for themselves. In situ documentation created by young people lends not only an immediacy to events but also best captures youngsters' Holocaust experiences. It illustrates most profoundly how children framed their wartime circumstances and contended with the unusual challenges they faced. Using such sources as a primary frame of reference, however, presents its own set of

---

[4] See Patricia Heberer, *Children During the Holocaust* (Lanham, 2011), 409–20.

difficulties. Most significantly, there is a dearth of material. While scholars possess a wealth of first-hand documentation from the Shoah, only a fraction of these contemporary sources were actually created by children. There are many reasons for this. In part, the physical circumstances of persecutees and victims of war are responsible for this relative poverty of sources. Resettlement, deportation, and incarceration in concentration or forced-labor camp settings imposed formidable obstacles for both adults and children who wished to record accounts of their experiences. The lack of writing instruments and especially paper hampered children's efforts to depict what happened to them and their parents. Other reasons for this lack of children's sources lie in the very nature of childhood and young adolescence. Children generally did not, and do not, generate as much "copy" as their adult contemporaries. With certain exceptions, children do not engage in the same volume of private and public correspondence as their parents do; they do not commonly write studies, monographs, or letters to newspaper editors, nor do they author administrative files or legal documents. Furthermore, anti-Jewish policies in German- and Axis-occupied countries often prevented school-age youngsters from acquiring the education necessary to read and write, and thus deprived them of the technical capacity to record their experiences. Moreover, there is a marked imbalance between sources created by young children and those stemming from older youngsters and adolescents. Most of the childhood diaries, letters, and drawings available to us from the Holocaust period come from young people in their preteen or teenage years. Of course, very young children without the appropriate skill sets to write or draw had no chance to document their thoughts and feelings. Particularly for these youngsters, accounts by adult parents, relatives, or caretakers are the only sources we have to testify to their young lives. These voices often restrict our insight, for not even the most sensitive or perceptive adult can capture the full range of a child's experiences, hopes, and anxieties.[5]

Yet using in situ sources created by children as a primary focal point for discussion has its advantages, for it allows us to view the world from their vantage point. By examining how children coped with the events of the Holocaust through their own eyes and words, and through their elemental daily activities, we learn how young people were able to transcend the

---

[5] See, e.g., Bela Weicherz, *In Her Father's Eyes: A Childhood Extinguished by the Holocaust*, ed. and transl. Daniel Magilow (New Brunswick, 2008).

physical and emotional traumas they experienced and cling to their hopes for survival.

ESCAPE INTO LEARNING

Learning is an essential and indispensable feature of childhood, the school years a part of a youngster's rite of passage to adulthood. Yet, during the war years in German-occupied Europe, a majority of Jewish children were denied the possibility of a formal education. In November 1939, just weeks after the capitulation of the Polish army, German officials in the General Government banned Jewish children from all public and private schools. In the Polish capital alone, 40,000 Jewish youngsters of school age were barred from attending classes.[6] With very few exceptions, as in the case of the Łódź ghetto,[7] which boasted an impressive array of officially sanctioned educational institutions, prohibitions or severe restrictions upon formal instruction for Jewish children remained in effect when Jewish populations were ghettoized in Poland and other German-occupied territories in Eastern Europe.[8] Yet thousands of school-aged children defied such bans by attending a network of clandestine schools organized by education and welfare agencies in many ghetto communities. Many underground classrooms gathered in soup kitchens, orphanages, and care institutions for young people. In these instances, instructors and administrators pursued the dual goal of feeding hungry children and providing a basic education. Other less formally organized "schools" met secretly in the private homes of instructors or their pupils. Fifteen-year-old Miriam Wattenberg, the daughter of an American citizen incarcerated in the Warsaw ghetto, described in her diary how the clandestine nature of the instruction inspired a renewed dedication to learning among both students and teachers:

Twice a week the courses are given at our home, which is a relatively safe spot because of my mother's American citizenship. We study all the regular subjects, and have even organized a chemical and physics laboratory using glasses and pots from our kitchen … The teachers put their whole heart and soul into their

---

[6] Barbara Engelking and Jacek Leociak, *The Warsaw Ghetto: A Guide to a Perished City*, transl. Emma Harris (New Haven, 2009), 343.

[7] See Andrea Löw, *Juden in Getto Litzmannstadt: Lebensbedingungen, Selbstwahrnehmung, Verhalten* (Göttingen, 2006).

[8] Barbara Engelking-Boni, "Childhood in the Warsaw Ghetto," in *Children and the Holocaust: Symposium Presentations of the Center for Advanced Holocaust Studies* (Washington, DC, 2004), 34–35.

teaching, and all the pupils study with exemplary diligence. There are no bad pupils. The illegal character of the teaching, the danger that threatens us every minute, fills us all with a strange earnestness. The old distance between teachers and pupils has vanished, we feel like comrades-in-arms, responsible to each other.[9]

Clandestine classes for very young children incorporated lessons through stories, songs, and games. Parents and educators often described such gatherings as "play groups" in order to conceal covert learning activities and to prevent youngsters from inadvertently revealing their illicit schooling to others. Teachers stressed the importance of engagement in useful activity (*Beschäftigung*) as a way to combat boredom and delinquency among young children and to prepare them for the proficiency necessary from primary education.[10] For elementary school children, educators emphasized reading and writing, fearing that such skill sets might be lost to a generation of Jewish youth.[11] For older children, clandestine *gymnasia* and secondary schools also thrived in ghetto communities. The first underground *gymnasium* in Warsaw, established under the auspices of the Dror youth organization, sheltered seventy-two pupils in its first year and employed as its teachers intellectuals such as the famed Jewish writer Isaac Katzenelson.[12] Covert secondary schools in the ghetto maintained high standards, devising enrollment criteria for prospective pupils, offering advanced courses in literature, the arts, and the sciences, and issuing degrees. As secrecy was an important issue, students did not receive certificates on graduation; examination records were preserved in hiding and legitimized by a special education commission after the war.[13]

According to calculations made by chroniclers of the Oneg Shabbat archive, some 10,000 children and adolescents attended clandestine classes in the Warsaw ghetto between 1940 and 1942. For Warsaw ghetto youngster Pola Rotszyld, meeting with her secret study group gave her a sense of identity and purpose. Teenagers like Pola came to feel that

[9] Diary/memoir entry of Miriam Wattenberg, July 12, 1940, published in Mary Berg, *Warsaw Ghetto: A Diary by Mary Berg*, ed. S. L. Shneiderman, transl. Norbert Guterman and Sylvia Glass (New York, 1945), 32–33. Miriam Wattenberg and her family reached the United States in 1944. Published in February 1945, Miriam's diary appeared under the pseudonym "Mary Berg" in order to protect friends and relatives still at risk of Nazi violence.

[10] See Lisa Anne Plante, "Transition and Resistance: Schooling Efforts for Jewish Children and Youth in Hiding, Ghettos, and Camps," in *Children and the Holocaust*, 45–46.

[11] Ibid, 45–48.

[12] Engelking and Leociak, *The Warsaw Ghetto*, 346.

[13] Ibid., 349.

emotional and intellectual survival was integral to their physical survival. Clandestine learning provided a sense of fellowship and camaraderie, which had evaporated elsewhere among a desperate community, and allowed young students, at least temporarily, to transcend the deprivation and miseries of ghetto life. Such secret study was quite literally an escape into learning. "These lessons were our happiness," Rotszyld recounted, "our oblivion":

Outside there was a war storm, the groans of people dying of hunger ... And somewhere in the corner of the room on Pawia or Nowolipki Street, some girls between thirteen to fifteen years of age were sitting around the table with a teacher, engaged in studying. They all forgot about the whole world, even about the fact that they were a bit hungry, maybe more than a bit.[14]

In many instances, youngsters used learning to expand their intellectual and cultural horizons beyond the impoverishing walls of the camp or ghetto. Art, literature, and scholarly study provided a means to confront the confining bounds of their existence and to create an alternate universe that they could cultivate themselves. Siblings Petr Ginz and Eva Ginzová were born in Prague to a prosperous middle-class family. Their father, Otto Ginz, stemmed from a liberal Jewish family and worked as a manager at a large textile concern. Their mother, Maria, had been raised as a Catholic but kept a kosher household for her husband and insisted on a Jewish education for her children. Because the Ginzes were children of a mixed marriage and were themselves practicing Jews, they were categorized as *Geltungsjuden*[15] according to the tenets of the Nuremberg Laws and were dispatched to the Theresienstadt ghetto at age fourteen, Petr in October 1942 and Eva in May 1944. Both children kept diaries during their confinement. Eva's journal, begun on June 24, 1944, is a chronicle of daily ghetto life. Many entries were written as correspondence to her absent parents, as if the written word could form a bridge between her desolate existence and the happy family life she had once known. If Eva's writings mirrored the terrible conditions of the Terezin ghetto and revealed a narrative of loss and despair, her brother Petr's diary took a decisively

---

[14] Diary entry of Pola Rotszyld, published in Engelking-Boni, "Childhood in the Warsaw Ghetto," 35.

[15] An unofficial term for a "half Jew," or *Mischling* of the first degree, who legally qualified as a "full Jew" under German law. *Geltungsjuden* were persons with two fully Jewish grandparents who, in addition, were married to a Jewish spouse or practiced the Jewish faith.

different tack.[16] Petr Ginz refrained from recording daily occurrences or experiences in his journal. Rather his entries were plans for the immediate future: lists of readings and projects and goals yet to be accomplished. He itemized books he had read, creative projects, and scholarly interests. In August 1944, Ginz wrote:

> I've read: Dickens: [*A Christmas*] *Carol*; Hloucha: *The Sun Vehicle*; [Nyklíček]: *Miracles on Every Step; Fight in the Settlement*; Trojan: *Little People in Court; Boy Scouts of the Good* [part of line illegible]; Flammarion and Scheiner: *Is There Life on Stars?* ...
>
> I work in the Lithography Department half a day and the other half I attend the program. I have a lot of catching up to do in Latin and math. I do stenography and I also do a bit of English and zoology every so often. I have spent most of my time on drawing and [linoleum cuts]: two flowers ... and various small sketches. Five-sixths of the the map of the world is colored in.[17]

If Petr Ginz was "whistling past the graveyard," his strategy of study and learning certainly seemed to divert him from the daily horrors that found their way into his sister's diary entries. Amidst the geography of Arabia, the history of the Phoenicians, and the exploration of the moon, the tragedies of Terezin became a backdrop, a more distant and separate reality.[18]

CHILD'S PLAY

Like learning, play proved a powerful outlet, and children used both to adapt to their difficult circumstances and to restore a sense of normalcy to their disordered lives. The juxtaposition of child's play with the tragic events of the Holocaust presents us with a striking contradiction. Instinctively, we balk at the suggestion that mass murder and the games of childhood could exist side by side. And, yet, scores of contemporary documents and the vivid recollections of survivors and bystanders make it plain that they did.[19]

---

[16] Alexandra Zapruder, ed., *Salvaged Pages: Young Writers' Diaries of the Holocaust* (New Haven, 2002), 122–89.

[17] Diary entry of Petr Ginz, dated August 1944, reprinted ibid., 174.

[18] While Eva Ginzová survived Theresienstadt, Petr Ginz was deported to Auschwitz in the fall of 1944 and was gassed shortly after his arrival.

[19] While play has long been a component in the history of childhood, there are few scholarly works on children's play during the Holocaust. The seminal work is George Eisen's *Children and Play in the Holocaust: Games Among the Shadows* (Amherst, 1988). See also Catherine Wheeler, "Representing Children at Play in the Literature of the Shoah" (Ph.D thesis, University of Massachusetts, Amherst, 2003), and Yad Vashem, ed., *No Child's Play* (Jerusalem, 2004). Nicholas Stargardt also addresses the issue in his excellent study *Witnesses of War: Children's Lives under the Nazis* (New York, 2006).

Youngsters in camp and ghetto settings lived in a kind of exile from child-hood. With the loss of their homes and belongings, young children felt the absence of their favorite playthings acutely. With forced ghettoization, families took to their cramped quarters only what they could carry; and personal items, among them children's toys and games, were necessarily limited. Material goods were even more severely circumscribed with an individual's transfer to a concentration or forced labor camp; and where young children survived in these circumstances, as in the so-called Theresienstadt family camp in Auschwitz, playthings were a rare commodity among young deportees. With a creativity and ingenuity that often impressed their adult contemporaries, young people forged new toys from cardboard, bits of wood, scraps of metal and cloth – the refuse of the captive society which surrounded them. Children played with what was at hand. For those children fortunate enough to retain a cherished toy or childhood possession, a doll or stuffed animal might figure as the center of the youngster's existence. Playthings were rare and precious, and their young owners often clung to them with a fierce possessiveness. Such toys offered not only an opportunity for amusement but also a source of emotional stability and security. In a menacing world of upheaval and change, material items remained stead-fast and unchanging. Toys were good listeners in the way that harried and exhausted adults were not. Even broken and damaged playthings retained their currency; they did not wither away from hunger or face deportation as parents or siblings did. A toy might also transport its small owner into an imaginary world, far away from the charnel surroundings of the camp or ghetto.

In the formative years of the Theresienstadt ghetto, a prisoner employed as a carpenter in a joiner's workshop in the Small Fortress created a remarkable pull toy in the shape of a butterfly. Affixed to a wheeled base, the brightly painted butterfly "takes flight," fluttering its wooden wings when it is rolled across the floor or flat surface. The butterfly motif has long been associated with the children of Theresienstadt, thanks largely to the discovery and widespread publication of Pavel Friedman's poem, "I Never Saw Another Butterfly," written shortly after the young man's arrival in the Theresienstadt ghetto in April 1942.[20] The butterfly is an evocative symbol, not only because it represents an element of natural beauty long inaccessible to Theresienstadt's incarcerated community, but also because the winged creature had the ability

---

[20] Pavel Friedman, "I Never Saw Another Butterfly," in Hana Volavková, ed., *I Never Saw Another Butterfly: Children's Drawings and Poems from Terezin Concentration Camp, 1942–44*, expanded 2nd edn. (New York, 1993), 39.

literally to transcend the confining walls of the ghetto and to escape the barrenness and despair of the prisoner's existence. Of course the craftsman who constructed the pull-toy in question is unlikely to have been aware of Friedman's poem, and it is doubtful that a concrete connection lies between the artifact and the young writer's famous verse. The maker of the small wooden toy is unknown, as are the identity and fate of its young recipient. But the object is a poignant reminder of children's need for the tangible vestiges of childhood in the harrowing world of the Holocaust.

Children often invented new modes of play in order to accommodate their difficult circumstances and the limited resources available to them. Sometimes, too, youngsters adapted traditional children's games to incorporate their radically altered environment. To the horror of their adult contemporaries, children's "new" games often accurately depicted the dramas and tragedies of ghetto or camp life. Many Jewish youngsters had never known a park or a playground or owned a doll or stuffed animal. Thus, they constructed their make-believe worlds from the only existence they knew. Starvation and deprivation were a part of their quotidian lives. Words from the ghetto or camp vernacular – "*Aktion*," "deportation," and "transport" – became a part of their daily vocabulary. While play that incorporated camp or ghetto life was unconventional and shocked adult observers, such activities presumably helped young children to process the perplexing circumstances in which they found themselves and offered youngsters a kind of "buffered learning," as George Eisen suggests – a way to rehearse a dangerous situation within a secure sphere, as within the parameters of a game or play activity.[21]

Children's games incorporated the harrowing reality of the camp or ghetto environment. This kind of play was not an escape into fantasy or imagination but a way of assimilating the dangerous world that surrounded them. Here, role playing in particular represented a creative means of accommodating and coping with the tremendous challenges youngsters confronted.

Of course, such play grew in part from children's natural impulse to emulate the actions of adults. As in the normal realm of childhood, enacting adult behaviors often divided along gender lines. Predictably, as in other places and times, young boys' play frequently took the shape of war games. Ghetto lads of six or seven engaged in make-believe combat as "Germans" and "Russians" or pretended to join in the adventures of the partisans of whom they had heard so much. Closer to their own

---

[21] Eisen, *Children and Play in the Holocaust*, 73–75.

experience, pre-teenaged boys in Vilna or Warsaw played "Going Through the Gate" in which young "Gestapo men" searched returning "forced laborers" for smuggled food and contraband.[22] Girls could and did participate in such games, but their play more often embraced female roles in the ghetto. Small girls who had perhaps once nursed their dolls now imitated their mothers in a eerily realistic game of "Playing House." Standing in queues before an imaginary shop window, little girls clutched make-believe ration cards, jostling their neighbors and bickering with the shopkeeper over goods and wares. The young "housewives" could be heard to wonder aloud where their next piece of bread would come from or how with their few rotten potatoes they might manage to feed their hungry families.[23]

A favorite game of both genders was "Germans and Jews," play that wed aspects of "Cops and Robbers" with the traditional "Hide and Seek." An eight-year-old inhabitant of the Vilna ghetto explained to onlookers how young children emulated a roundup for deportation:

Part of the children became "policemen" and part "Germans." The third group was comprised of "Jews" who were to hide in make-believe bunkers; that is under chairs, tables, in barrels and garbage cans. The highest distinction went to the child who played *Kommandant* Kitel [*sic*], the head of the Gestapo.[24] He was always the strongest boy or girl. If a dressed-up "policeman" happened to find "Jewish" children, he handed them over to the "Germans."[25]

INNOCENCE AND KNOWLEDGE

Like learning and play, innocence is another element closely associated with childhood. In a conventional sense, innocence stems from the ignorance of evil and an absence of worldliness and guile. Yet, living in the upside-down world of the ghetto or concentration camp, many children had become well acquainted with evil und understood from their own limited experience that guilelessness and naïveté could prove a deadly combination. Here youngsters grew up quickly. At a tender age, many had witnessed unspeakable horrors and shouldered adult responsibilities.

[22] Testimony of Dr. Aharon Peretz, May 4, 1961, *The Trial of Adolf Eichmann: Record of Proceedings in the District Court of Jerusalem*, vol. I (Jerusalem, 1992–1995), 478.

[23] See Eisen, *Children and Play in the Holocaust*, 79.

[24] Oberscharführer (Technical Sergeant) Bruno Kittel was a member of the German Security Police and was later responsible for the liquidation of Vilna ghetto.

[25] Eight-year-old resident of the Vilna Ghetto, Genia Silkes Collection, YIVO, quoted in Eisen, *Children and Play in the Holocaust*, 72.

Teenagers in particular harbored few illusions of the grim fate that might await them at the next roundup or selection.

Helga Weissová began to sketch her observations of ghetto life shortly after her arrival in Theresienstadt in December 1941.[26] Helga was born in Prague in 1929 to a middle-class family; from an early age, she occupied much of her time with drawing and painting. Exactly one month after her twelfth birthday, Helga arrived with her parents with one of the first transports of Czech Jews to Theresienstadt. In the three years before her deportation from Terezin to Auschwitz, she completed more than 100 drawings and illustrations.

Helga began to ply her artistic talents in Terezin shortly after settling in one of the ghetto's homes for young girls – Mädchenheim L-410 – in December 1941. Using art supplies that she had packed with her at the time of her deportation, Weissová initially sought to ease her loneliness by drawing upon the happy images of her girlhood in Prague. Painting a nostalgic winter scene in which small children built a snowman, she persuaded fellow prisoners to smuggle the picture to her father in the men's barracks. Otto Weiss, who had constantly championed his daughter's artistic endeavors, admonished Helga instead to depict what she observed around her. "Draw what you see!" he advised her.

"That snowman was actually my last genuine drawing as a child," Weissová later recalled. "Through this sentence of my father's, and through my own inner motivation, I felt called from now on to capture in my drawings the everyday life of the ghetto. The impressions that from this point in time would affect me ended my childhood."[27]

Helga comprehended the dangers of her new environment and resolved to record them on paper and canvas. With a candidness that unsettles, the young teenager faithfully portrayed the wrenching arrivals and departures of transports at Terezin, the unending lines to receive meagre rations, the colonies of workers going to forced labor. Weissová had an eye for the ironic, depicting with unvarnished candor the macabre and surreal aspects of ghetto culture. We feel for the aged German Jews who arrive at the "rest community for the elderly" that the Nazi government has promised them,

---

[26] For a more extensive view of Helga Weissová's life and Holocaust-era drawings, see Helga Weissová, "Zeichne, was Du siehst!": *Zeichnungen eines Kindes aus Theresienstadt/Terezin*, ed., Niedersächsischen Verein zur Förderung von Theresienstadt/Terezin, e.V. (Göttingen, 1998).

[27] Ibid., 13.

only to encounter the ugly and deadly reality of Theresienstadt. We are likewise amused at the farcical efforts of camp authorities to create from Terezin a "model ghetto" for the visit of International Committee of the Red Cross (ICRC) officials in 1944. Other illustrations capture the pathos and suffering of her fellow prisoners: the faces of deportees waiting for days in the cold or heat of the ghetto's dreaded "Sluice"[28] before their transport to Auschwitz or the solemn farewell of ghetto residents to their dead comrades, who were daily carried on sledges to a crematorium outside the ghetto.

Sometimes Weissová deployed her artistic gifts in a more traditional vein: to create a birthday greeting or a holiday card for friends and loved ones. In "Birthday Wish I" ("Přání k narozeninám I"), Helga transcends the hunger and deprivation of the ghetto by conjuring a delicious torte for the birthday honoree (Figure 12.1). Here, a childish yearning is fulfilled as a young boy and girl, clad in their summer best, wheel an enormous birthday cake from Prague to Theresienstadt. The fourteen-year-old artist drew her native city in gauzy contours; one can make out the prominent features of Prague Castle – the Hradschin – in its outlines. The well-dressed youngsters push the gigantic confection through the green landscape and up to the fortress walls of Terezin. On the surface, the composition is a dreamlike, innocent vision, like a fairytale from childhood. But the idyllic scene bristles with dark humor. The cart which carries the mighty cake is a hearse, a conveyance often used in Theresienstadt to transport items. In another stroke of wit, the wagon seems to bears the inscription "Entsorgung" (waste disposal). Even in the context of this youthful idyll, Helga Weissová grasped where she was and what danger she was in.

A third document concerning innocence and knowledge strikes out into different territory. Historians have recently taken note of the diary of Elisabeth Block, a Jewish teenager living in rural Bavaria. Elisabeth was "no Bavarian Anne Frank"[29] who described her experiences in vivid detail. Indeed what makes her diary so interesting to scholars is that even in the blackest moments of her personal history, Block appears almost pathologically unable to record unpleasant developments. It is

---

[28] "Slojska," Czech variant of the German "Schleuse," a slang term used in Theresienstadt for the collection point that held deportees arriving and departing upon transports.

[29] Peter Miesbach, quoted in Elisabeth Block, *Erinnerungszeichen: Die Tagebücher der Elisabeth Block*, ed. Haus der Bayerischen Geschichte and Historischer Verein Rosenheim (Rosenheim, 1993), 17.

FIGURE 12.1 Helga Weissová, "Birthday Wish I." United States Holocaust Memorial Museum Collections, WS# 60926.

true that in the village of Niedernburg, near Rosenheim, Elisabeth and her family felt closely integrated into the small community in which they lived and endured little discrimination at the hands of their neighbors, even as Nazi anti-Jewish policy escalated in the late 1930s. Elisabeth seemed loath to record those encroachments that the government's anti-Semitic measures made upon the Blocks' economic and social circumstances during these years. During Kristallnacht, for example, rampaging SA men had murdered Elisabeth's uncle, Dr. Leo Levy, in his apartment in Bad Polzin, an event the teenager referenced only in passing in her journal. Further disturbing developments – the exclusion of Jewish pupils from public schools, the loss of the family home and business, the compulsory sterilization of Elisabeth's father, Fritz Block – received similarly short shrift. It was as if the young girl failed to see herself and her family within the wider framework of Nazi persecution. In her diary, coincidentally begun in 1933, Block uses the terms "we Jews" just once, in the context of the September 1941 decree that required German Jews to wear the "yellow star" badge.[30]

<hr />

[30] Ibid., 25.

On March 8, 1942, Elisabeth Block wrote the last entry in her journal. As usual, she focused on her daily activities, on her interactions with friends and family members, on the weather, and on events that had transpired in her community. In this instance, the latest excitement was the birth of little Friedi, the newborn daughter of Elisabeth's friend Regina Zielke, in a little town two kilometers from her home. Elisabeth had been deployed to a farm in the vicinity in compliance with a March 1941 decree compelling all able-bodied Jews to undertake compulsory labor assignments. It is clear from all accounts that she was well treated on the farmstead and that she and her employers felt that she was part of the family there. This may explain in part why she makes so little mention of the summons by the local labor office dispatching her to agricultural work or of the fact that her service there, however agreeable, was essentially forced labor. Elisabeth pays little attention to her father's more strenuous compulsory service laying tracks for railway and commuter tram lines; in her March 1943 account she mentions only that the frostbite that Fritz Block contracted from his heavy work in frigid weather had fortunately occasioned him leave at a time when the family could spend the weekend together:

From January 18 until February 2, I was not at home; but it was so convenient that I could go home quickly within a few hours by sleigh by riding with Christl and Gina-Mouse because [their trip] coincided with a farmer's holiday. That was really fun, and it appeared to me as if [the scene] came out of a novel or a winter's tale, riding in a charming horse-drawn sleigh through the winter landscape, bundled warmly.[31]

Most notably missing from Elisabeth's March 1943 entry is the issue that the Blocks faced imminent deportation. The exact date upon which they received their summons is unknown, but it is clear as the teenager wrote of her winter sleigh ride with friends, the family had already begun packing up their household and distributing valuables with trusted neighbors. Block was eighteen years old when she wrote the last passage in her diary, and could scarcely have been in ignorance of the mass deportation of Jews from Germany or of the policy's significance for herself and her family. Was Elisabeth's silence on this point a matter of discretion or circumspection? Did her refusal to acknowledge menacing developments spring from denial or from a naïve belief that her family might be spared, even as her co-religionists went to their deaths? We will never know.

---

[31] Diary entry of Elisabeth Block, March 8, 1942, ibid., 266.

On April 3, 1942, the Blocks were deported with 989 fellow Bavarian Jews to the Piaski ghetto near Lublin. On an unknown date, Elisabeth and her family were transferred to a killing center, presumably Bełzec or Sobibor, and murdered there.

IN HOPES AND DREAMS

Children adopted many strategies to help them adapt to the horrors and deprivations of the Holocaust. Youngsters aged quickly and beyond their years under such conditions, and many of their responses to persecution were practical and pragmatic. Often powerless to shape their individual circumstances in the way that adults could, however, children frequently found highly creative ways to cope with the terrors they faced. Through imagination, young people were able to transcend the physical and emotional traumas they experienced.

Lvov ghetto survivor Nelly Toll used her interest in painting to escape the dangerous world in which she lived. She was born Nelly Landau in 1933, the only daughter of an affluent businessman who owned several apartment buildings. On November 8, 1941, the Germans established a ghetto in Lvov and by December 15 had forced all Jews in the municipal area into the sealed "Jewish quarter." After an ill-fated attempt to escape to Hungary, Sygmunt Landau succeeded in finding a hiding place outside the ghetto for his wife and daughter. Drawing on earlier loyalties – and proffering a handsome sum as compensation – he convinced his former Polish tenants, Michaj and Krysia Wojtek, to conceal Nelly and her mother in a hidden room in their apartment. Sygmunt planned to join them there as soon as he had found places for members of his extended family. Yet a short time after his wife and daughter went into hiding, Sygmunt Landau disappeared without a trace; Nelly and Rose Landau never saw him again.

For the next thirteen months, Nelly and her mother lived in their tiny room with its boarded window, their quarters sealed off from the Wojteks' flat by a door concealed behind a hanging tapestry. After a few long weeks in hiding, Rose Landau arranged for a Polish friend to procure a set of watercolors for her daughter. Over the next several months, ten-year-old Nelly amused herself by painting images on small note cards and writing in her diary. The youngster drew many of her miniature scenes from her imagination: from her readings in Leo Tolstoy and Jules Verne, from stories her mother told her to pass the time, or from memories of her happy childhood before the war. On other occasions, she incorporated the street scenes she witnessed through the boarded casement in their hiding place. Looking through her "secret window," Nelly often blended the reality of what she saw with her own fantasies and hopes for the future. In "Teachers with Children Wearing Black Uniforms," Nelly painted children she glimpsed on their way to class, imagining the time when she too could be out of doors and go to school. "I walked with them. I silently talked with them,"[32] Nelly Landau Toll recalled in a 1998 interview. Young Nelly's watercolors enabled her to reshape the perilous world around her into gentle tones and tranquil scenes. "My art was done in very dangerous times," Toll explained. "It gave me pleasure, it let me forget."[33]

Drawing served not only as means of escape and entertainment; for very young children, such as hidden child Ilona Goldman, it was sometimes the only means of communicating with absent family members. Separation from loved ones was a central experience for many young persecutees during the Holocaust. Whether divided by long distances or isolated in hiding, youngsters often bore the pain of separation in silence, either because they lacked a sympathetic environment to express their emotions or because doing so might endanger themselves or their rescuers. Very young children, such as Ilona, suffered doubly, for they had very few practical avenues to communicate with parents or family members or to convey their feelings of loneliness and abandonment. Ilona Goldman (today Alona Frankel) was born in Krakow on July 27, 1937.[34] She was two years old when German forces invaded her native Poland in September 1939. Like many Jewish families, the Goldmans decided to escape German-occupied Poland and fled to Lvov (today Lviv), then in Soviet territory. Following the German invasion of the Soviet Union in June 1941, the Goldman family found themselves incarcerated in the Lvov ghetto. The following spring, Salomon Goldman, fearing liquidation of the ghetto, escaped to the "Aryan" side and found a former employee who was willing to hide him and his wife, on one condition: that they find another place of concealment for their lively and voluble four-year-old daughter. In the end, Salomon and Gusta found a hiding place for young Ilona with a Polish peasant family in the countryside.

Ilona Goldman spent several months separated from her parents. Because the four-year-old had not yet learned to write, she could not converse with her

---

[32] Bruce Frankel, "Nelly's Secret," *People* 49(27) (July 13, 1998).
[33] Ibid.
[34] Concerning the story of Ilona Goldman and her family, see Alona Frankel, *A Girl*, transl. Sondra Silverston (Ramat Gan, 2009).

FIGURE 12.2 Drawing by Ilona Goldman (today Alona Frankel) for her parents in hiding, Marcinkowice, Poland, 1942. United States Holocaust Memorial Museum Collections, gift of Alona Goldman Frankel. Note the writing showing through the paper from the other side.

parents through notes or letters. Instead she communicated with them through a series of drawings sketched on the *reverse side* of her rescuer's weekly correspondence with the Goldmans. Now in the collection of the United States Holocaust Memorial Museum, Ilona Goldman's childhood drawings captured images of the village in which she hid: of peasants in the fields, animals ambling across green meadows, passenger trains traversing the Polish countryside. During her time in hiding, the little girl heard complaints from local farmers about the shortages of consumer items, especially cigarettes and smoking materials; in one drawing, Ilona rectified the situation (Figure 12.2). As the residents of her rescuer's household engage in hunting for mushrooms, a common family pastime in late summer and early autumn, the menfolk drag at their cigarettes. The farmers smoke, the house chimney smokes; yes, even the bird aloft in the sky seems to take a few puffs.[35]

[35] Drawing by Ilona (Alona) Goldman for her parents in hiding, Marcinkowice, Poland, 1942, United States Holocaust Memorial Museum Collections, Gift of Alona Goldman Frankel.

In Ilona's last months with her foster family, Gusta Goldman sacrificed a gold dental crown every week for her only child's continued safety, her husband prying each tooth from her mouth with the help of his Swiss Army knife. The Goldmans were careful to pay her caretakers on schedule, for they had learned that the rescuer had abandoned an earlier charge, a very young boy, to his death when the youngster's parents were unable to pay for his upkeep.[36] Thus, the Goldmans were doubly grateful to receive their daughter's tiny parcels. Besides the connection the pictures established between parents and child, Ilona's drawings served an additional important purpose: The pictures assured the Goldmans on a weekly basis that their daughter was still alive.

*** *** ***

For many youngsters, the escape into a world of imagination aided their survival. Whether through learning, art, play, or a flight into imagination, these means proved crucial avenues for coping with the miseries of hunger, fear, and deprivation and provided emotional insulation from the surrounding reality. Seen through their own eyes, these daily experiences of children present us a unique vantage point on the Shoah, as framed by the youngest witnesses of the Holocaust.

[36] Ibid., 16.

13

The Dark Side of the "Good War": Children and Medical Experimentation in the United States During World War II

Birgitte Søland

Lloyd Campbell had just turned twelve years old when Germany invaded Poland in the autumn of 1939, but the outbreak of war seemed to him an event that would hardly impact his life. "At first, when they started fighting over in Europe, we didn't think much of it. Of course, we didn't know that [the United States] would become involved in the war."[1] George Kline, born in 1930, agreed. "I don't remember much [about the war]. I remember we were over there fighting. Lots of people left. It didn't really affect us. We always had enough food and stuff. No, you can't say it really affected us."[2] Elmer Johnston remembered hearing about the Japanese attack on Pearl Harbor, but he recalled little else. "I was, what, fourteen [years old] at the time? Of course, we knew the war was going on, but I think I was more interested in baseball."[3] Lois Baker, another child who came of age during the war, had a friend whose older brother fought in the Pacific. "We worried about him," she recalled, "but other than that life was pretty normal."[4]

Given the current state of scholarship, it seems that the historical profession is largely in agreement with these narrators' claim that daily

The author wishes to thank all the former orphanage children who agreed to be interviewed for this project. To protect their privacy all names have been changed. The author also wishes to thank Susan Hartmann, Katherine Marino, Steve Conn, James Marten, and all the participants in the "War and Childhood Conference," sponsored by the German Historical Institute, Washington, DC, June 2014, as well as the anonymous reviewers for their insightful comments on the manuscript.

[1] Lloyd Campbell, oral history interview, Cincinnati, Ohio, May 12, 2010.
[2] George Kline, oral history interview, Dayton, Ohio, October 3, 2008.
[3] Elmer Johnston, oral history interview, Lancaster, Ohio, March 3, 2011.
[4] Lois Baker, oral history interview, Columbus, Ohio, April 11, 2011.

life during World War II remained fairly unchanged for American children. Perhaps this explains why remarkably little work has been published about the topic. Accounts of life on the home front have tended to leave children out of the story, and broader studies of American childhood have often paid only scant attention to World War II.[5] With the exceptions of Robert Kirk's slim volume *Earning Their Stripes*, William Tuttle's more substantial study *Daddy's Gone to War*, and Lisa Ossian's recently published work *The Forgotten Generation*, we have surprisingly few book-length studies of American childhood during World War II.[6] The explanation for this may lie in the fact that the history of American children during the war was not all that dramatic, and generally they were spared the horrors experienced by so many other children around the world. Collecting scrap metal for the war effort is hardly the same as suffering fear and hunger. Buying "Victory Stamps" and selling war bonds is not the equivalent of trying to procure desperately needed foodstuffs on the black market. And missing a father or a brother fighting overseas does not compare to losing one's family in the death camps.

Nonetheless, American children and American childhood were impacted by the war in myriad ways, and American war efforts depended on the contributions of children in more ways than typically appreciated. Most of these contributions were offered freely by patriotic youngsters eager to do their part for the war effort; others were coercively extracted from vulnerable kids with few available choices. The experiences of Lloyd Campbell, George Kline, Elmer Johnston, and Lois Baker provide just one example of this. Although they insisted that World War II did not really affect their lives, they were among the many children who in the 1940s became involuntary subjects of medical experimentation funded by the

---

[5] Studies of life on the American home front during World War II include John P. Resch, ed., *Americans at War: Society, Culture and the Homefront* (Detroit, 2005); and Allan Winkler, *Home Front USA: America During World War II* (Arlington Heights, IL, 1986). Neither of these studies includes much information about children. Histories of American childhood that largely leave out the World War II era include, for example, Harvey Graff, *Conflicting Paths: Growing Up in America* (Cambridge, MA, 1995); and Elliott West and Paula Petrik, eds., *Small Worlds: Children and Adolescents in America, 1850–1950* (Lawrence, 1992).

[6] Robert William Kirk, *Earning Their Stripes: The Mobilization of American Children in the Second World War* (New York, 1994); William M. Tuttle, Jr., *"Daddy's Gone to War": The Second World War in the Lives of America's Children* (New York, 1993); Lisa L. Ossian, *The Forgotten Generation: American Children and World War II* (Columbia, MO, 2011).

American government and designed to enhance American combat efficiency.[7]

This chapter examines the history of one such example of medical experimentation involving children, namely the testing of dysentery vaccines that was carried out between 1943 and 1945 at the Ohio Soldiers' and Sailors' Orphans' Home, home to the four narrators quoted above. It explores how medical researchers and physicians conducted experiments involving not just these four individuals but dozens of other poor, orphaned, and abandoned children, submitting them to repeated rounds of injections with an experimental vaccine not previously tested in humans. In addition, it investigates the memories of thirty-four individuals who, as teenagers, were part of these experiments. Their accounts, collected through oral history interviews, provide rare testimonies of the experiences of a group of involuntary research subjects, and it examines the ways in which these former orphanage children sought to come to terms with information about their early lives. Finally, this chapter highlights the involuntary participation of children in the history of medical experimentation in the United States. While numerous other historical studies have documented the practice of using marginalized, minority, and incarcerated (adult) populations as participants in scientific experiments, few have investigated the inclusion of children in medical research.[8] Yet children, and especially orphaned, hospitalized, and institutionalized children, were frequently targeted as research subjects.[9] Unable to grant voluntary and informed consent, children stand out among the populations subject to exploitation as an exceptionally vulnerable group, and their incorporation into medical research therefore seems a particularly egregious

---

[7] For an account of the scientific projects undertaken, see E. C. Andrus, et al., eds., *Advances in Military Medicine Made by American Investigators Working Under the Sponsorship of the Committee on Medical Research*, vols. I–II (Boston, 1948).

[8] Studies focusing primarily or exclusively on adult populations include Susan E. Lederer, *Subjected to Science: Human Experimentation in America Before the Second World War* (Baltimore, 1995); and Andrew Goliszek, *In the Name of Science: A History of Secret Programs, Medical Research, and Human Experimentation* (New York, 2003).

[9] Historical studies focusing on the use of children in medical experimentation include Allen M. Hornblum, Judith L. Newman, and Gregory J. Dober, *The Secret History of Medical Experimentation on Children in Cold War America* (New York, 2013); M. A. Grodin and J. J. Alpert, "Children as Participants in Medical Research," *Pediatric Clinics of North America* 35 (1988), 1389–1401; and Susan Lederer, "Orphans as Guinea Pigs: American Children and Medical Experimenters, 1890–1930," in Roger Cooter, ed., *In the Name of the Child: Health and Welfare, 1880–1940* (London, 1992), 96–123.

example of the disparities of race and class in American history and of the subjection of powerless populations to the interest of science.

THE OHIO SOLDIERS' AND SAILORS' ORPHANS' HOME

The Ohio Soldiers' and Sailors' Orphans' Home was founded in 1869 by members of the Grand Army of the Republic, a fraternal organization for Civil War veterans, to create a permanent home for children whose fathers had perished in the war. From modest beginnings, the orphanage quickly grew. Merely a decade after its founding, the institution was home to almost 600 children, and by the end of the 1880s more than 900 children were permanent residents. By the eve of World War II, the number of children had declined slightly, but the institution still cared for close to 700 children.[10]

By the standards of the day, this was an exceptionally large orphanage whose very existence ran counter to prevailing ideas about proper care for dependent children.[11] Yet, in the 1940s the Ohio Soldiers' and Sailors' Orphans' Home was generally known as "a good place for kids."[12] The food was nutritious, varied, and plentiful; the buildings were clean, centrally heated, and well lit; and, while discipline remained strict, the institution offered both general education and vocational training along with a variety of sports and other leisure activities.[13] The institution was known among struggling Ohio families as the best place to send children if necessity required it, and many former wards emphasized the comforts they had experienced there. Eleanor Lawson, for example, boasted that "rich people send their kids to boarding school. We always said that this was our boarding school; that's how nice it was."[14]

For all the facilities and opportunities available to its children, the Ohio Soldiers' and Sailors' Orphans' Home was, of course, not a boarding school. Neither was it an orphanage in the technical sense of that term. Most children who entered the institution were in fact not legally orphans.

[10] In 1940, the institution was home to 682 children: Edward Lentz, *A Home of Their Own: The Story of Ohio's Greatest Orphanage* (Wilmington, OH, 2010), 163.

[11] See Birgitte Søland, "'Never a Better Home': Growing Up in American Orphanages, 1920–1970," *Journal of the History of Childhood and Youth* 8(1) (2015), 34–54.

[12] Thomas Miller, oral history interview, Tallahassee, Florida, May 3, 2011 (interview conducted via telephone).

[13] Dorothy L. Fornia, "An Evaluation of the Physical Education and Recreation Programs of the Ohio Soldiers' and Sailors' Orphans' Home, Xenia, Ohio" (MA thesis, Ohio State University, 1944).

[14] Eleanor Lawson, oral history interview, Gahanna, Ohio, February 12, 2009.

In most cases, they had at least one living parent. More typically, it was poverty, illness, mental health problems, and/or alcoholism that forced parents to relinquish their offspring. But even when parents were alive and intellectually capable, for children to enter the institution, they had to relinquish their parental rights, making their children wards of the state of Ohio, which in turn granted guardianship of the children to the superintendent of the institution.

The consequences of this legal arrangement would prove detrimental to the children. Even though most of the residents at the Ohio Soldiers' and Sailors' Orphans' Home did in fact have living parents and/or relatives, the institution remained a relatively closed environment where children had little interaction with family members and the surrounding community. Though never surrounded by walls or fences, its physical location on the outskirts of Xenia, a small town in rural southwest Ohio, the onsite education of the institution's children, and orphanage rules limiting the physical freedoms of residents all functioned to confine its wards to the orphanage grounds. Though some parents attempted to keep in touch with their children through letters, all mail was subject to review by orphanage staff, and interactions with family members were limited to one monthly, Sunday-afternoon visit, annual Christmas vacations, and brief summer visits. In short, the many children who grew up at the Ohio Soldiers' and Sailors' Orphans' Home lived practically their entire lives within the confines of the institution, without parents able to look out for their best interests and deprived of family members with legal standing to intercede on their behalf. And thus many of them became human guinea pigs during World War II.[15]

MEDICAL RESEARCH AND THE QUESTION OF ETHICS

When the children at the Ohio Soldiers' and Sailors' Orphans' Home became subjects of medical experimentation in the mid twentieth century, the use of humans as participants in scientific research was hardly a new phenomenon. During the second half of the nineteenth century, the embrace of experimental science had transformed the medical profession, redefining "the ideal physician from a practitioner, whose authority stemmed from the exercise of clinically informed judgment, into

---

[15] The fact that many orphans were used as research subjects in the United States was first brought to public attention in 1921, when the writer and journalist Konrad Bercovici published the article "Orphans as Guinea Pigs" (*The Nation*, June 29, 1921).

a scientist [with] specialized knowledge gained from experimentation on animals and human beings."[16]

From the outset, many doctors had been concerned about the ethics of medical experimentation involving human subjects. Already in 1865, the influential French professor of medicine Claude Bernard had articulated the doctrine he believed should guide research practices. "The principle of medical and surgical morality," he wrote, "consists in never performing on man an experiment which might be harmful to him to any extent, even though the result might be highly advantageous to science."[17] American physicians generally embraced a similar stance. Echoing Bernard's maxim, the well-known clinician and medical researcher William Osler reminded attendees at the 1907 Congress of American Physicians and Surgeons that "we have no right to use patients entrusted to our care for the purpose of experimentation unless direct benefit to the individual is likely to follow."[18] Osler's dictum soon became the official stance of the American Medical Association: Only when preliminary animal research had established the safety of a new drug or procedure, and only if a patient was likely to experience immediate therapeutic benefits, were physicians justified in proceeding with experimental treatments.

Yet even as medical experts agreed that treating ailing patients remained their primary moral obligation, scientific research often required testing new substances and procedures on large numbers of individuals, not all of whom would necessarily benefit therapeutically. Determining the source of transmission of various diseases, for example, required the potential infection of otherwise healthy individuals, and the development of effective vaccines depended on clinical trials involving research subjects not previously exposed to the disease. Seeking to strike a balance between potentially beneficial new forms of patient treatment and medical research designed to enhance scientific knowledge, early twentieth-century physicians committed themselves to the ethical principle of informed consent.[19]

---

[16] Lederer, *Subjected to Science*, 1. See also David J. Rothman, *Strangers at the Bedside: A History of How Law and Bioethics Transformed Medical Decision Making* (New York, 1991).

[17] Claude Bernard, *An Introduction to the to the Study of Experimental Medicine* (1927), quoted here from Rothman, *Strangers at the Bedside*, 23.

[18] William Osler, "The Evolution of the Idea of Experiment in Medicine," *Transactions of the Congress of American Physicians and Surgeons* (1907), quoted here from Lederer, *Subjected to Science*, 1.

[19] Paul M. McNeill, *The Ethics and Politics of Human Experimentation* (New York, 1993); see also Rothman, *Strangers at the Bedside*, 15–29.

In principle, the commitment to informed consent should have excluded all children from any form of nontherapeutic experimentation, but pediatric research remained extensive throughout much of the twentieth century. Sometimes it was a commitment to child health that spurred physicians to undertake research involving children. Experiments in the 1950s with the Salk vaccine against polio, for example, involved large numbers of children who seemed particularly vulnerable to the virus. In other cases, it was the research problem that dictated the choice of children as human subjects. Given the ubiquity of tuberculosis infections in adults in the early twentieth century, some researchers seeking to develop a vaccine against the disease turned to (yet uninfected) children when they needed to test their prophylactic agents. Most often, though, it was more pragmatic considerations that led to the inclusion of children in medical experimentation. Hospitalized children, for example, constituted an easily accessible group of research subjects, and worried parents often found it difficult to decline a request for consent from the medical authorities on whom the wellbeing of their children seemed to depend. An even larger group of children subjected to medical experimentation were orphanage inmates, such as the children at the Ohio Soldiers' and Sailors' Orphans' Home. The existence of large groups of children, most of them healthy and fit, living in one location, without meddlesome parents present, proved a temptation that many researchers could not resist, especially when convinced that their work might ultimately benefit the greater good.

MEDICAL RESEARCH AT THE OHIO SOLDIERS' AND SAILORS' ORPHANS' HOME

The foundations for the medical experimentation carried out at the Ohio Soldiers' and Sailors' Orphans' Home were laid in the spring of 1941, when President Franklin D. Roosevelt ordered the creation of an executive body to coordinate American medical research needs in the event that the United States was drawn into the war. Named the Committee on Medical Research, and placed under the wartime Office of Scientific Research and Development, this body would oversee the most ambitious medical research program in the nation's history. By the end of the war, it had provided funding for a total of 638 medical studies undertaken by researchers at 135 universities, hospitals, clinics, and pharmaceutical firms around the country, at a cost of more than $25 million.[20]

---

[20] For a complete listing of the scientific projects undertaken, see *Advances in Military Medicine*.

The Committee on Medical Research allocated considerable funds to projects devoted to the treatment of wartime injuries, such as shock, physical trauma, wounds, and burns. Other monies were earmarked for secondary dangers confronting soldiers far from home, including gonorrhea and syphilis. Most of the research projects that received funding, however, were designed to alleviate more general health problems of American soldiers fighting overseas. Fear of debilitating illnesses such as malaria, dysentery, and typhus, and of their ability to undermine combat efficiency, loomed large. Research projects aimed at preventing, or finding quick, effective treatments for, these ailments received generous grants.[21]

For talented medical researchers, the prospect of taking part in the quest for scientific progress while simultaneously contributing to the war effort was enticing. At a time when clinical research was acquiring ever-greater importance as a marker of professional status among doctors, the fact that one was likely to advance one's career in the process probably did not hurt either. Applications for research funding poured into the offices of the Committee on Medical Research. Among the applicants was a group of doctors from the Cincinnati Children's Hospital under the leadership of the well-known pediatrician Dr. Merlin Cooper.[22]

Dr. Cooper and his team of researchers proposed to study the feasibility of developing an effective vaccine against dysentery. Hence, he focused on the administration of antigenic materials – i.e., a vaccine that would produce immunity to the disease. Injections of the *Shigella paradysentaria* bacteria in lab mice had already proved promising, but, as Cooper explained in his grant application, for this research to produce clinical payoff – an objective in the obvious interest of American troops overseas – time, money, and further experimentation were required. Most importantly, he added, such experimentation would need the participation of a substantial group of human subjects in the testing of a potential vaccine.[23]

Assembling a suitable group of individuals willing to serve as human subjects for medical experiments was often a challenge for researchers, but Dr. Cooper faced no such difficulty. As he noted in his application, he had

[21] Ibid.
[22] See Beatrice Katz, ed., *Images of America: Cincinnati Children's Hospital Medical Center* (Charleston, 2008).
[23] "Proposal for Contract in Medical Research Pertaining to National Defense," December 4, 1942: United States National Archives and Records Administration, Records of the Office of Scientific Research and Development, Record Group 227.6, Records of the Committee on Medical Research (CMR), 1940–1946.

"access to large numbers of normal children" who were inmates at a local orphanage.[24] Scientifically, this seemed close to an ideal situation: An orphanage offered a stable, confined, monitored population living in the same physical environment and exposed to similar environmental factors. Apparently, this swayed the Committee on Medical Research, and Cooper won his research grant.

The local orphanage, home to the "large numbers of normal children" to whom Dr. Cooper claimed "access," was the Ohio Soldiers' and Sailors' Orphans' Home, located just sixty miles northeast of Cincinnati. At the time, the Cincinnati Children's Hospital and the Ohio Soldiers' and Sailors' Orphans' Home had a longstanding connection. From its foundation, the orphanage had featured its own medical clinic, where newcomers to the institution were examined for communicable diseases and resident children were treated for minor accidents and illnesses. In 1928, the General J. Warren Keifer Hospital was built on the orphanage grounds, and during the following years the overwhelming majority of the orphanage inmates in need of medical attention would be treated there. Children with influenza and strep throat, measles and mumps, and the unfortunate few with broken limbs were all treated at the Keifer Hospital, while more complicated medical problems were referred to specialists at the Children's Hospital in Cincinnati, the closest urban center.[25]

The original orphanage clinic and the Keifer Hospital were staffed by trained nurses and supervised by local doctors. While nurses were part of the paid orphanage staff, the doctors were volunteers who, according to an article in the *Home Review*, the weekly orphanage paper, gave "both their talents and their time freely and without reserve, being paid only with the knowledge that their services have made [the orphanage] and some students better."[26] Until the early 1940s, this arrangement seems to have worked well, but as the United States entered the war and thousands of men departed for military service, the orphanage administrators found themselves struggling to cope with the consequences. Not only did many male employees leave their positions, but the local physician who had provided medical care for the orphanage children also joined the war effort.

At this critical moment, the connection between the orphanage and the Cincinnati Children's Hospital was formalized in new and important ways. According to the 1942 annual report of the orphanage's board of

[24] Ibid.
[25] Lenz, *A Home of Their Own*, 111–14.
[26] Ibid., 114.

trustees, "an arrangement was effected with Dr. A. A. Weech, Director of Children's Hospital, Cincinnati, whereby supervisory direction of the [orphanage] hospital was assured."[27] In June that same year, the report continued, "Dr. Jack Tepper, an intern at Children's Hospital, was sent to the [orphanage] by Dr. Weech to act in the capacity of resident physician."[28] In the coming years, Dr. Tepper would be the man "on the ground" who conducted the actual experiments.

According to the research reports that Cooper would later submit to the Committee on Medical Research, the experiments at the orphanage began in the spring of 1943. A total of 143 children between the ages of thirteen and seventeen were selected to take part. Over the following eighteen months, they were all given intravenous injections of a vaccine that contained varying dosages of *Shigella paradysentaria* bacteria that might render the host immune to dysentery. The object of the experiments was twofold. First, the researchers were eager to determine the dosage of bacteria that might produce immunity; second, they were intent on exploring the reactions of the human body to the injection of the bacteria.

RECALLING MEDICAL EXPERIMENTATION AT THE OHIO SOLDIERS' AND SAILORS' ORPHANS' HOME

The 143 children who participated in the experiments constituted practically the entire teenage population living at the orphanage in the final years of World War II. There is no written evidence to suggest that the children were asked to give their consent to take part in the experiments or that they were informed about the nature and purposes of the injections they received. On the contrary, evidence collected from oral history interviews indicates that children were given no such information, much less asked for their consent. Almost all of them told an identical story of how they came to be research subjects. At some point, typically during a Friday or Saturday lunch, a group of children would be told to report to the Keifer Hospital on the orphanage grounds after school. Once they arrived, they were informed that they were to get some shots. Dr. Tepper administered the shots, and for the rest of the weekend the children were kept at the hospital, where their symptoms were observed and recorded.

---

[27] Ohio Soldiers' and Sailors' Orphans' Home, Annual reports of the Board of Trustees, Ohio Historical Society, Columbus, Ohio, State Archives Series 4618, 74th Annual Report (1942).

[28] Ibid.

In retrospect, some of the former orphanage wards recalled finding the sudden requirement of the previously unannounced shots surprising. According to Geraldine Meyer, "we knew that we had to get certain shots at certain times, like when you became older," but, she added, "this was different. We hadn't heard of this before, and my older sisters hadn't gotten these shots when they were at the [orphanage]."[29] Wally McCourt, one of her classmates, was equally taken aback. "I asked what it was for, but I don't think I got an answer. I never did know what it was for."[30] When asked specifically whether he had agreed to get the shots, Arnold Johnson, another of the medical research subjects, was incredulous: "I was fourteen or fifteen years old! Of course, I wasn't asked! We weren't asked about anything. We were just told what to do. And that's what we did."[31]

Quite possibly because of the lack of information about the purpose of the shots, combined with the passage of time, the recollections of most of the former research subjects were fairly brief. John Evans, for example, recalled that he "was told to go to the hospital" where he "got some shots. I didn't know what for. I think I had to stay for a few days, but I can't remember how long."[32] Homer Miller recalled being sent to the hospital with one of his roommates. "We both got shots and then we had to stay. I remember playing cards with the nurse."[33] Eileen Collier's recollections were slightly more detailed. She remembered that "it was a Thursday, I think, or perhaps a Friday. Right after lunch [the house parent] told me to go to the hospital after school. So, I went to the hospital and I got some shots, but when I went to leave, the nurse told me that I would have to stay. I didn't understand that, and I was pretty mad because that meant I would miss the Saturday night movie."[34]

None of these informants recalled having had any adverse physical reactions to the shots. Many other children were not as fortunate. According to Charles Fisher, "the shots weren't bad, but boy, did I get sick after! I was sick as a dog . . . I don't remember how long [the sickness lasted], but I remember I went back to school again that Monday."[35] Fred Simonds had similar memories: "I have no idea what it was they gave us,

[29] Geraldine Meyer, oral history interview, Montpelier, Ohio, December 10, 2010.
[30] Wally McCourt, oral history interview, Pittsburgh, Pennsylvania, November 3, 2009 (interview conducted via telephone).
[31] Arnold Johnson, oral history interview, Toledo, Ohio, March 24, 2016.
[32] John Evans, oral history interview, Louisville, Kentucky, December 13, 2011.
[33] Homer Miller, oral history interview, Beaver Creek, Ohio, November 13, 2009.
[34] Eileen Collier, oral history interview, Dayton, Ohio, December 3, 2009.
[35] Charles Fisher, oral history interview, Beaver Creek, Ohio, September 1, 2010.

but it was bad. I was real sick."[36] Lucinda Brown also remembered "getting real sick" after the shots,[37] and Robert Bolton recalled "puking [his] guts out."[38] Emily Basan, aged seventeen when she received the injections, added that "I got so sick, so sick. Had to stay in the hospital for almost a week, throwing up, diarrhea. I got really weak. They gave me milk with honey – and to this day I can't stand the taste of honey." After a pause, she added, "my period didn't come back for a long time, and ... you know, I never did have any children, and I have always wondered if it was because of that. I mean, those injections. They really made me sick and my period ... it was never the same."[39]

Cooper's report about the experiments submitted to the Committee on Medical Research confirms these memories. In fact, they suggest that the vast majority of children responded adversely to the injections. He notes, for example, the reactions of ten boys who, on March 12, 1943, were each given a single intravenous injection of vaccine containing ten million bacteria. Their reactions were immediate and severe. Within thirty minutes, their skin turned "pale and ashy gray in color." Their temperature "sky-rocketed to 105 degrees Fahrenheit and up in spite of measures to counteract the rise. Severe pounding headache and a constricting type of backache were almost universal complaints ... Rapidly, nausea, vomiting and watery diarrhea ensued. Fever persisted for 24 hours and when it subsided the subjects were exhausted."[40] Injections with lower doses of bacteria also produced severe reactions, including medium-grade fevers, stomach cramps, aching muscles, dizziness, and physical exhaustion. Even injections containing fairly low bacteria counts sickened many children, and at the end of their lengthy experiments, Cooper and his research team had to conclude that the toxicity of the antigenic materials necessary to produce immunity to the disease was too virulent to facilitate an effective vaccine. To this day no effective vaccine against dysentery exists.[41]

[36] Fred Simonds, oral history interview, Circleville, Ohio, October 4, 2009.

[37] Lucinda Brown, oral history interview, Middletown, Ohio, April 1, 2009.

[38] Robert Bolton, oral history interview, Mount Vernon, Ohio, May 4, 2009.

[39] Emily Basan, oral history interview, Cincinnati, Ohio, April 3, 2009.

[40] Merlin Cooper, "Immunization Against Bacillary Dysentery. Contract OFMcmr-293. Final report," 26, United States National Archives and Records Administration, Records of the Office of Scientific Research and Development, Record Group 227.6, Records of the Committee on Medical Research (CMR), 1940–1946.

[41] Vaccine Resource Library. "*More about shigellosis and enterotoxigenic Escherichia coli (ETEC)*" (accessed March 3, 2014), http://www.path.org/vaccineresources/shigella-etec .php.

"I DON'T THINK I LIKE WHAT YOU ARE TELLING ME":
FORMER ORPHANAGE CHILDREN RESPOND TO
NEW KNOWLEDGE

After 1945, the history of the medical experiments at the Ohio Soldiers' and Sailors' Orphans' Home was buried for years. I came across this aspect of the past only while interviewing former residents about their experiences of growing up in an American orphanage.[42] Joe Hillenmann was the first of several informants to bring up the subject. At the end of a two-hour long interview, he suddenly asked, "Do you know about those experiments? I have always wondered about those."[43] Other narrators raised similar questions. Ellen Crawley was curious about "those shots they gave us,"[44] and Robert Bolton thought that he and his orphanage peers "were used for something. I don't know what it was, but they were doing something to us with those shots."[45] "I think it was the government," speculated Homer Miller. "They used us for something."[46]

Inquiries to the National Archives through the Freedom of Information Act about medical experimentation during World War II proved Homer Miller's suspicions correct. The records of the Office of Scientific Research and Development included remarkably detailed reports about the research undertaken at the Ohio Soldiers' and Sailors' Orphans' Home, including the full names of all the children involved. That made it possible to trace many of the former medical research subjects, including many who had never thought to question the injections or had long forgotten what seemed an insignificant event in their early lives.[47]

Being presented with information about the medical experimentation triggered a range of responses among the former research subjects. Some simply refused to believe the historical evidence. Though the research reports showed that Joseph Morrison, for example, had been injected twice with vaccines containing fairly high bacteria counts, both times resulting in

---

[42] See Birgitte Søland, *Other People's Kids: Orphanages, Foster Care and Child Welfare in Twentieth-Century America* (forthcoming).

[43] Joe Hillenmann, oral history interview, Xenia, Ohio, February 3, 2009.

[44] Ellen Crawley, oral history interview, Marietta, Ohio, October 9, 2009.

[45] Robert Bolton, oral history interview.

[46] Homer Miller, oral history interview.

[47] United States National Archives and Records Administration, Records of the Office of Scientific Research and Development, Record Group 227.6, Records of the Committee on Medical Research (CMR), 1940–1946.

significant fevers, he flatly denied that he had ever received any shots.[48] Others responded with anger. "I don't care [about the experiments]," declared an indignant Marlene Steele. "I loved that place and they treated me right."[49]

Other reactions were more ambivalent. "They were such good people. How could they do that?" asked a bewildered Lois Baker.[50] "I always knew there was something they didn't tell us and I didn't like that," said Rose Staunt, but "the [orphanage] saved my life. My father was a drunk and my mother died … but look at me now! I have all these nice things, and I had a nice husband. Life has been good to me."[51] It was Joe Hillenmann, the man who first asked me about the experiments, who articulated most clearly what many others seemed to feel. "So you found out what it was all about, huh? And now you are telling me that they used us as some sort of guinea pigs? I don't like that. I don't think I like what you are telling me … You know, [the orphanage] was a really good place, good for the kids. People were good to us. But that – that is not right. Are you sure?" Upon seeing his name listed in Cooper's research report, he quietly shook his head. "I don't know what to think; that's not right, but you know, they really were good to us."[52]

The differences in their individual reactions notwithstanding, the discomfort of the former orphanage children as they digested the information about the medical experiments was palpable. The recorded interviews include long pauses during which the only sounds to be heard are those of bodies shifting uncomfortably, coffee being sipped slowly, knuckles cracking softly, deep sighs escaping. Even for those individuals who had themselves raised the subject and wondered about what had happened to them in their youth, the difference between wanting to know and actually knowing was often great. The majority of informants had generally positive memories of their childhood at the orphanage, and the new knowledge about their past sat uncomfortably with settled perceptions. "I wish I hadn't come to know that. Now I don't know what to think," admitted Greg Wilson, who had previously delighted in telling stories about what he called "a really good childhood."[53] "I don't know. I just don't know … I don't know what to say," added Fred Simonds, a man otherwise never at

---

[48] Joseph Morrison, oral history interview, Washington Court House, Ohio, September 30, 2011.

[49] Marlene Steele, oral history interview, Cincinnati, Ohio, May 3, 2011.

[50] Lois Baker, oral history interview.

[51] Rose Staunt, oral history interview, Columbus, Ohio, September 4, 2010.

[52] Joe Hillenmann, oral history interview (follow-up), Xenia, Ohio, January 10, 2010.

[53] Greg Wilson, oral history interview, Bucyrus, Ohio, April 2, 2010.

a loss for words. "I loved that place," he continued, "I loved that place, but I don't know. That's just not right."[54]

None of the former research subjects labeled the experiments a moral wrong, but with only two exceptions they all declared the treatment they received "not right." This may seem a distinction without a difference, yet in this case semantics are significant. Even as they struggled to come to terms with the meaning of this new information about their lives, none of them raised ethical concerns about exposing children, such as themselves, to involuntary medical experiments, even as some recalled fairly violent physical reactions to the injections, and none criticized orphanage personnel for having permitted the experiments to take place. Rather, what they identified as "not right" was the silence surrounding the experiments, the intentional concealment of information. "I just don't understand why they didn't tell us," reflected Rose Staunt. "Why didn't they just say what was going on?"[55] George Kline agreed. "They should have told us," he insisted. "I mean, why didn't they?"[56] "That's what I can't understand," added Louella Knoblauch, "they should just have told us. We even asked [the house mother] and she didn't tell us anything."[57]

Discovering dishonesty on the part of adults in charge of one's upbringing can be a difficult experience for anyone, but for the former orphanage children it seemed to carry an especially heavy weight. Before arriving at the orphanage as young children, most of them had experienced a tumultuous existence, the causes of which were rarely discussed. Terminal illness of a parent, for example, was typically knowledge kept from young children, and mental illness went unexplained. Divorce and abandonment often struck children without much warning. And alcoholism, physical violence, emotional neglect, and poverty frequently meant that children were shuffled around among neighbors and relatives for weeks, months, or even years before they found a more permanent home at the Ohio Soldiers' and Sailors' Orphans' Home. In the routinized and highly regimented orphanage life, many institutionalized children found a source of comfort and stability, a place where adults could be trusted to be if not loving and affectionate, then at least reliable, and everyday life predictable.[58] Perhaps that is the reason why the

[54] Fred Simonds, oral history interview (follow-up), Circleville, Ohio, February 9, 2010.
[55] Rose Staunt, oral history interview.
[56] George Kline, oral history interview (follow-up), Dayton, Ohio, April 19, 2010.
[57] Louella Knoblauch, oral history interview, Tiffin, Ohio, November 4, 2010.
[58] Søland, "'Never a Better Home.'"

unexplained shots still lingered in the memories of so many former orphanage children more than a half-century later.

Moreover, having grown up in an environment where honesty topped the hierarchy of moral values, learning that their caretakers had been less than forthcoming, and sometimes directly untruthful, in their relationship with their charges took on additional meaning for many informants. Charles Fisher, for example, the man who recounted "being sick as a dog" after receiving the injections, went on to say that the shots were not "all that big of a deal. Yes, it took a few days, but I got over it, but what I don't like is that they didn't tell us. They should have told us. They knew, and they should have told us. That's the part I don't like."[59] As if she had listened in on the words of her former orphanage "brother," Eleanor McCoy declared, "they should have told us about it, not just said nothing. They should just have said it."[60] More than a violation of their bodily integrity and right to safety and protection, the former orphanage children generally interpreted the medical experiments that were permitted to take place as a breach of trust and a repudiation of the code of honesty they had been raised to respect.

"DOING THEIR BIT": FORMER ORPHANAGE CHILDREN COMING TO TERMS WITH THE PAST

Over the past decade, I have interviewed close to 200 people who grew up in American orphanages in the twentieth century. Certainly, this is a self-selected group of individuals willing to share personal stories of their non-normative childhoods. Almost by definition, they are the ones who "made it," who survived rough patches during their childhood and grew into competent, functional adults. Yet, almost to a person, they bristle at the idea of being described as "survivors."[61] "I am not 'damaged goods,'" one woman bluntly told me, clearly perceiving "survivor" as a patronizing term for people whose lives have been less than easy.[62] Echoing this sentiment, another woman scoffed at popular perceptions of "poor, pitiful orphans, Oliver Twist and all that. That's not how it was. They treated us well."[63] Emphasizing the same point Dolores Byers, one of the many

[59] Charles Fisher, oral history interview.
[60] Eleanor McCoy, oral history interview, Worthington, Ohio, April 15, 2011.
[61] Søland, "'Never a Better Home.'"
[62] Jeannine Harroway, oral history interview, Dayton, Ohio, May 28, 2009.
[63] Lois Brackston, oral history interview, Toledo, Ohio, December 12, 2010.

former wards of the Ohio Soldiers' and Sailors' Orphans' Home, insisted that "I can't imagine a better home. Really, I had the best childhood."[64]

Such life narratives, characterized by equal measures of resilience and defiance, may help explain the ultimate reaction to the story of their own past that most of the former research subjects ended up sharing. Seemingly endowed with a stubborn resolve to persevere in the face of hardship, to make the best of the hand they had been dealt, many of the former research subjects surprisingly quickly moved from discouraged reflections on the breach of trust they experienced as children to surprisingly positive assessments of the medical experiments to which they had been subjected. "So, it was for the war, was it? The soldiers?" Elmer Johnston asked me after a few minutes of pensive silence. "Well, that's good. I think that's good."[65] Lucinda Brown agreed. According to her, "so many of our boys went to war. I am glad that we did something to help them."[66] Similarly, Eileen Collier was delighted to hear about the purposes of the medical research. "That makes my heart proud," she admitted, humbly adding, "I know I didn't do anything, really, but I still feel a little bit proud."[67] Even Robert Bolton, the man who recalled "puking [his] guts out," was ultimately pleased to hear about the purpose of the experiments. "Really?" he commented with a smile; "So that's like, you know, like we did our bit?"[68] For most of the former wards of the Ohio Soldiers' and Sailors' Orphans' Home, all children of veterans, helping the American military in the war effort was a point of pride, even if that contribution came at the expense of their own distress.

Yet amidst these patriotic sentiments, other voices revealed more somber reactions. "My brother was killed in the war," Gertrud Blum told me. "If I had known that [the experiments] were for helping soldiers that would have been different. I would have felt different."[69] Ingrid Blumenfeld's brother returned safely from several tours of duty as a marine in the Pacific but, as she recalled it, he came home a changed man. "I don't know what happened, but after that he always had chips [*sic*] on his shoulders, like we were nothing and everything, and we were just nothings, having done nothing. I wish I could have told him [about the experiments]."[70]

[64] Dolores Byers, oral history interview, Dayton, Ohio, October 4, 2009.
[65] Elmer Johnston, oral history interview.
[66] Lucinda Brown, oral history interview.
[67] Eileen Collier, oral history interview.
[68] Robert Bolton, oral history interview.
[69] Gertrud Blum, oral history interview, Marion, Ohio, June 1, 2010.
[70] Ingrid Blumenfeld, oral history interview, Middletown, Ohio, August 22, 2009.

Other former orphanage inmates, without direct personal connections to those who fought in the war, also reflected on their participation in the experiments as an event with positive potential. "So," the buoyant Mike Himmelmann laughed, "does that mean I can say I helped win the war? My great-grandchildren will like that!"[71] More soberly, Elisabeth Faye commented, "at least we did something. I am glad to know that we offered something. Like we weren't just burdens on society. That has always been my thinking, like we were burdens on society."[72] The opportunity to substitute the shame of having grown up in public care at the expense of taxpayers for a sense of having made a valuable contribution to science and society during wartime turned the knowledge about having been exposed to unethical medical experimentation into a point of pride for many of the former orphanage children.

CONCLUSION

American medical research during World War II never approached the gross inhumanity of Nazi experiments, but the national interest and the desperate push for victory nevertheless allowed expediency to run roughshod over moral principles. Despite professional commitments to informed consent as a key principle when conducting scientific experiments involving human subjects, many American doctors – such as the ones who conducted experiments at the Ohio Soldiers' and Sailors' Orphans' Home – violated not only the Hippocratic oath of "doing no harm" but also the principles of ethical behavior articulated by the American Medical Association. As a result, some of the nation's most vulnerable children became victims of adult interests.

The former orphanage children who were involuntarily subjected to medical experiments with dramatic consequences for at least their short-term wellbeing saw things differently, however. More often than not, they embraced the knowledge, folding it into their life narratives in ways that strengthened their sense of self and boosted their personal and patriotic pride. "Wait, wait, wait!! What did you just say?" asked Dotty Lawson after learning the truth about the medical experiments. "Did you just say that those little shots were for the war? Really? Really?? That is amazing!"

---

[71] Mike Himmelmann, oral history interview, Massillion, Ohio, June 2, 2011.
[72] Elisabeth Faye, oral history interview, Kettering, Ohio, October 3, 2009.

Tearing up, she added, "if that means I helped my country, I couldn't be prouder!"[73]

Among historians, ethicists, and others, the fact that poor, vulnerable children, living outside the family without any protection by parents and relatives, were subjected to medical experimentation that compromised their safety and wellbeing, can only be condemned. Yet, as the memories of those subjected to these experiments remind us, childhood experiences during wartime often carry different meanings than anticipated, highlighting once again the importance of listening to the voices of the subjects we study.

[73] Dotty Lawson, oral history interview, Huber Heights, Ohio, July 19, 2010.

14

Attacking Children with Nuclear Weapons: The Centrality of Children in American Understandings of the Bombings of Hiroshima and Nagasaki

Robert Jacobs

About the matter of how the bomb looked to the children of Hiroshima, one can say with considerable truth: pretty much as it did to adults, only more so. This is not because children are psychologically the same as adults, but because the extremity of the experience reduced everyone's response to something akin to childlike awe and terror.[1]

Robert Jay Lifton

Within weeks of the Japanese surrender, American teams had arrived in Hiroshima and Nagasaki to assess the impact of the revolutionary nuclear weapons that had been used in the attacks against the two cities. As it was assumed that future wars would likely involve nuclear weapons, the United States was eager to gather as much data as possible about their effects and so had left six Japanese cities "un-bombed" for use as nuclear targets to allow for accurate postattack assessments. Based on existing "rice rationing" population data in Hiroshima, the November 1945 census data, and their own questionnaire of the surviving population, US analysts determined that 64,602 people had been killed in the initial nuclear attack on Hiroshima (these figures did not include a much smaller number of military casualties).[2]

However, buried in this dataset was a much grimmer accounting. The analysts had determined that the most effective way of measuring

---

[1] Robert Jay Lifton, introduction to "Atomic Bombed Children," in Lifton, *History and Human Survival* (New York, 1970), 187.

[2] Army Institute of Pathology, "Medical Effects of Atomic Bombs," in *The Report of the Joint Commission for the Investigation of the Effects of the Atomic Bomb in Japan*, Vol. VI (Washington, DC, 1951), 10.

casualties was by counting dead schoolchildren. The researchers found that, amidst the chaos of wartime Japan, better records had been kept of the names, numbers, and locations of schoolchildren than of any other cohort. This led them to prioritize the study of dead schoolchildren. The analysts scoured school records in Hiroshima and Nagasaki (where most school buildings had been destroyed) to establish the status of as many children as possible. These initial calculations determined that more than 3,000 children had been killed instantly by the nuclear attacks. These data were then extrapolated to calculate "distance–casualty curves" that could help estimate total fatalities.[3]

However, the ongoing triumphalism inspired by American power and influence, as represented by the victory over the Axis powers and the successful development of nuclear weapons, convinced the military that they needed to shroud behind a curtain of official secrecy not only the fact that so many children had been killed but also that their deaths were quantified for rather cold-blooded efforts to measure the effectiveness of the bombs. When the US government published its survey on the effects of the nuclear weapons in Hiroshima and Nagasaki several years later, the detailed section of their report assessing dead children school by school was removed and only tangentially referenced.[4]

In spite of this secrecy, Americans would increasingly come to understand that many of those killed by the bomb had been children. Some of the first images of *hibakusha* (the Japanese term for survivors of the bombs) seen in the American press in 1946 showed children and women rather than soldiers. Almost all of the *hibakusha* who would become known in the United States either were children or had been children at the time of the nuclear attack. This included a group of young women from Hiroshima, dubbed the "Hiroshima Maidens" by the American press, who would travel to the United States in the mid 1950s for reconstructive and cosmetic surgery. But the most important symbol of child victims was Sadako Sasaki, a young girl from Hiroshima who would die at the age of twelve from leukemia caused by her exposure to radiation when she was two years old. The widely published story of Sadako's plight, and the campaign to help her survive her disease by folding a thousand paper cranes, would eventually be taught in schools worldwide, and inspired children around the world to fold paper cranes and send them to

---

[3] Ibid., 21–39 (Table 6).
[4] Greg Herken, *Counsels of War* (New York, 1985), 15–17; "Medical Effects of Atomic Bombs."

Hiroshima. For many American schoolchildren, Sadako's story was their first encounter with the idea, and the history, of Hiroshima.

In both the cloaking of the value of an accurate count of dead school-children to military war planners and the emergence of children as the archetypal *hibakusha* in American media depictions, we can see that the "imaginary" of Hiroshima and Nagasaki in the United States pivoted around children. The foregrounding of children in depictions of *hibakusha* would seem to have been a conscious strategy on the part of those who had opposed the bombings, but in fact it mirrored the understanding of those who had assessed the attack. While nuclear weapons were used in warfare conducted by militaries, it was the presence of civilians, specifically children, that proved to be the key point around which both secret assessments and public narration would turn.[5]

This chapter charts a course through memories, cloaked accountings, and publicly constructed artifices concerning children affected by the nuclear attack on Hiroshima. It is primarily an examination of how the relationship of Americans to the children of Hiroshima took many postures for many different people, essentially reflecting the relationship each group of Americans had with nuclear weapons. It contrasts the hidden history of the accounting of dead schoolchildren with the media-driven public embrace of the Maidens and finally in the globalization of the story of one child, Sadako Sasaki. The stories of macabre number-crunching, the sensationalization of a small group of survivors, and the near-beatification of a single victim are bound together by the simple fact that they all involve young people. The children are almost entirely without agency in these American fixations: They are signifiers, in turn, of the power – the horror – and the vulnerability inspired by nuclear weapons.

---

[5] The idea of the "imaginary" of Hiroshima and Nagasaki is a traditional framing mechanism based in sociological theory about the social construction of ideas and beliefs about scientific paradigms and extant technologies. Rooted in the theories of Charles Taylor and John Searle, the concept of the "imaginary" has been extended into scholarship about the social construction of scientific and technological understandings. Discussing "technoscientific imaginaries," anthropologist George Marcus wrote, "the term *imaginary* emerged effortlessly and just seemed to fit the topic very well ... visualization has always been the defining aspect of Western scientific cognition." See George E. Marcus, "Introduction," in Marcus, ed., *Technoscientific Imaginaries: Conversations, Profiles and Memoirs* (Chicago, 1995), 3. See also Raminder Kaur, "The Nuclear Imaginary and Indian Popular Films," *Journal of South Asian Studies* 37 (2014), 539–52; Weston M. Eaton and Stephen P. Gasteyar, "Bioenergy Futures: Framing Sociotechnical Imaginaries in Local Places," *Rural Sociology* 79(2) (June 2014), 227–56; Christine Erica Wiley, "The Japanese Nuclear Imaginary: Representations of the Nuclear Age in Postwar Japanese Art" (Ph. D. dissertation, University of California at Irvine, 2011).

Useful as data points, as celebrity victims, or as martyrs, the children of Hiroshima were a screen on which Americans projected their own relations to the weapons almost as one more graft onto the keloid scars of the Hiroshima Maidens.[6] Through these various and contradictory invocations of the children of Hiroshima the children themselves, as actual human beings, remain as they were on August 6: relatively invisible.

Imaginations of the *omnicidal* nature of the weapon drove the nuclear imaginary from the start. Nuclear weapons were quickly understood to be an existential threat to the whole of civilization and stood in opposition to any coherent belief in the sustainability of human society through the health and welfare of future generations of children. While the use of nuclear weapons in Japan had originally occurred as an act of warfare between two nations, it was quickly repositioned by many American social thinkers as a warning for all humankind about the apocalyptic violence our species had conjured. The framing of this trope was woven with images of children. The study of children as both victims and actors in warfare provides a clearer focus for nuclear warfare and for the transnational, even transcendental, nature of the end of World War II.[7]

COUNTING AND HIDING DEAD SCHOOLCHILDREN

On August 6, 1945, the White House released a press statement from President Harry S. Truman announcing the existence and first use of a nuclear weapon. "Sixteen hours ago," began Truman's statement, "an American airplane dropped one bomb on Hiroshima, an important Japanese Army base." After the United States carried out a second nuclear attack on Nagasaki three days later, Truman remarked that, "The world will note that the first atomic bomb was dropped on Hiroshima, a military

---

[6] A keloid scar is the result of an excessive growth of scar tissue and collagen at the site of a burn or cut, typical of the kind of scarring formed over burns among *hibakusha* in Hiroshima and Nagasaki.

[7] Lisl Marburg Goodman and Lee Ann Hoff, *Omnicide: The Nuclear Dilemma* (New York, 1990); Robert Jay Lifton, "Imagining the End," in Robert Jay Lifton, *The Future of Immorality, and Other Essays for a Nuclear Age* (New York, 1987), 111–70; Robert Jacobs, "Whole Earth or No Earth: The Origin of the Whole Earth Icon in the Ashes of Hiroshima and Nagasaki," *Asia-Pacific Journal* 9(13) (March 2011), http:// japanfocus.org/-Robert-Jacobs/3505. For an examination of apocalyptic nature of the immediate post-Hiroshima discourse among prominent American thinkers, see Robert Jacobs, "Dodging Dystopia: The Role of Nuclear Narratives in Averting Global Thermonuclear Warfare," in Antony Adolf, ed., *Nonkilling History: Shaping Policy with Lessons from the Past* (Honolulu, 2010), 219–36, http://nonkilling.org/pdf/nkhistory.pdf.

base. That was because we wished in this first attack to avoid, in so far as possible, the killing of civilians." Within days of the nuclear attacks, the Western press was referring to both locations as cities and not as military bases and describing Hiroshima as roughly equivalent in population to Denver, Colorado. Maps showing the areas of devastation resulting from the bombs made it clear that the targets were urban areas: The notion that these nuclear weapons were used against Japanese soldiers was displaced by the awareness that the primary victims of the bomb were Japanese civilians.[8]

From its earliest days, World War II had been characterized by the shift from military engagements on battlefields to both ground and aerial attacks on cities and civilian populations. The tactic of fire-bombing had been used to ravage civilian-populated urban areas in both Britain and Germany since the beginning of the war and was used in a more systematic manner in Japan throughout 1945. The addition of industrial targets, and especially of the workers' housing areas around them, became known as "total war," which was intended to compel an enemy's surrender not only through defeating its military forces on the battlefield but also by eliminating the economic and human resources that supported the military. The United States initiated the tactic of using incendiary bombs in saturation bombing attacks in which planes would drop only incendiary bombs (previous attacks had been a mix of incendiary and explosive bombs) in a grid, starting thousands of small fires that would merge into an immense fire and burn whole cities. The first attack of this design, on Tokyo on March 9, 1945, resulted in more than 100,000 casualties in one night. After the use of saturation bombing to create firestorms capable of engulfing entire cities, it was not the targeting of cities that made the nuclear attacks on Hiroshima and Nagasaki so shocking to some Americans. Nor was it mass killing of Japanese civilians per se that aroused horror. Rather, it was the sheer capacity of the new weapon, its indiscriminate lethality, and its implications for the future of warfare that would become a source of anxiety and horror. Americans' triumphal pride during the Cold War of having produced a "super" weapon of

---

[8] "Text of Statements by Truman, Stimson on Development of Atomic Bomb," *New York Times*, August 7, 1945. The paper repeated this framing of Hiroshima as an army base in its reporting: see "Our Answer to Japan," *New York Times*, August 7, 1945; "President Truman's Report to the People on War Developments, Past and Future," *New York Times*, August 10, 1945; "Hiroshima Area That Sustained Damage from the First Atomic Bomb Attack," *New York Times*, August 10, 1945.

unprecedented power was soon tempered by a sense of vulnerability and the realization that nuclear weapons made all nations indefensible.[9]

In July 1951, the United States Atomic Energy Commission and Army Institute of Pathology published a classified report titled "Medical Effects of Atomic Bombs," which was declassified and made available to the public in December 1954. However, several sections of the original type-written and unpublished version (housed at the archives of the National Museum of Health and Medicine at Walter Reed Army Medical Center) were not declassified and not published.[10] The original report contained an extensive analysis of the mortality of schoolchildren throughout the blast area done on a school-by-school basis. Page after page of statistics and analysis documented the percentages of schoolchildren killed, injured, or left (seemingly) unharmed.

There are several reasons that the US military chose schools and school-children as a metric of the lethality of the new weapon. As the unpublished report explains, "An analysis of the casualty data of the school children yields a comparison of largely 'shielded' with largely 'exposed' groups at various distances . . . It was thought by the Commission . . . that an analysis of the effects on sizable groups distributed in known circumstances throughout the city would yield an approach to casualty–distance curve." Additionally, many schools were built of concrete and were more typical of the buildings that would experience nuclear attack in the United States, thus yielding data deemed useful for nuclear war fighting.[11]

It was the fact that groups of children were under the direct control and supervision of schools (and patriotic work parties) that made them useful to analysts. Their dependence put them in a position of being useful data points. "The schools seemed the most useful for this type of analysis," the unpublished report noted, "since it was expected that records were probably kept of the fate of the children . . . It was found not only that good records had been kept but that the headmasters in many instances

[9] Marilyn B. Young, "Bombing Civilians, from the Twentieth to the Twenty-First Century," in Yuki Tanaka and Marilyn B. Young, eds., *Bombing Civilians: A Twentieth-Century History* (New York, 2009), 154–74; Raymond Aron, *The Century of Total War* (Boston, 1955); Jacobs, "Dodging Dystopia."

[10] Both versions can be found online. For the published version, see https://ia700505.us.archive.org/16/items/MedicalEffectsOfAtomicBombsVol6Published/ReportOfTheJointCommissionAtomicBombV6Published.pdf. For the unpublished version, see https://ia700501.us.archive.org/20/items/MedicalReportOfTheJointCommissionForTheInvestigationOfTheEffectsOf_612/ReportOfTheJointCommissionAtomicBombV6Manuscript.pdf.

[11] "Medical Effects of Atomic Bombs," unpublished version, 20.

had made earnest efforts to trace families by letter, messenger or personal contact."[12]

The military personnel charged with declassifying the report clearly understood that such a practical, matter-of-fact analysis could turn the report into a political bombshell. In a letter dated August 10, 1950, Major Robert J. Coakley, the Acting Adjutant General of the Armed Forces Special Weapons Project, wrote on the subject of "declassification of documents" that, "Pages 36 through 40 of Volume VI contain references to the mortality of 'shielded' and 'unshielded' school children. For that reason, it is felt that a statement of policy from the Department of the Army should be obtained before release of this information to the public. This information may have political implications; i.e., children, etc."[13]

Frank Pace, Jr., the Secretary of the Army, determined that these sections should be "regraded restricted" as reported by L. L. Clayton, the Adjutant General of the Department of the Army. Clayton wrote that, "Volume VI of the report contains information on numbers and details of casualties to school children which is deemed to require RESTRICTED classification as a safeguard against exploitation as propaganda prejudicial to the security of the nation." The entire report was classified but the higher classification of restricted was applied specifically to the sections titled "Casualties Among School Children at Hiroshima" and "Casualty Study of Yasuda Girls' High School."[14]

When the report was declassified and made public, it did include some information about the effects of the weapon on a few schools, but it did not include the systematic school-by-school, full analysis of casualties among schoolchildren. One of the reasons is certainly that the "information may have political implications; i.e., children, etc." It is also likely officials feared that the long section of statistics and tables listing large numbers of dead children would erode the view held by the American public that Hiroshima was full of soldiers and not children. This can be seen by the types of maps of Hiroshima released by the US government after the bombing. The maps made available for public release identified the numerous military facilities located within the blast area. The restricted

[12] Ibid.

[13] Robert J. Coakley, letter to Chief, Technical Information Office, Office of the Surgeon General, Department of the Army, August 10, 1950: included in the unpublished version of "Medical Effects of Atomic Bombs."

[14] L. L. Clayton, letter to the Office of the Surgeon General, Department of the Army, October 19, 1950: included in the unpublished version of "Medical Effects of Atomic Bombs."

maps that were kept secret, by contrast, showed not only military facilities but also the locations of the many dozens of schoolchildren's patriotic work parties.[15]

In images of Hiroshima reproduced for American newspaper and magazine readers, the shots chosen were, first, the mushroom cloud and, second, aerial shots of the city showing an empty landscape with no people visible. Hundreds of thousands of people had been there, of course; but in the photos they are absent. This was analogous to the importance of schoolchildren to the American postwar assessment of the lethality of the nuclear detonation. It was built on statistics about schoolchildren, but in the published version of "Medical Effects of Atomic Bombs," they, like the people of Hiroshima in the photographs taken from the eye-of-God perspective, are conspicuous by their absence.

AWARENESS OF HIBAKUSHA IN THE UNITED STATES: THE HIROSHIMA MAIDENS AND SADAKO SASAKI

This absence began to be filled as the first stories about individual survivors appeared in American media outlets in 1946. John Hersey's *New Yorker* article about Hiroshima survivors (all adult civilians) appeared in August and was published in book form later that year. A bestseller, Hersey's *Hiroshima* was serialized in numerous newspapers and magazines, and enacted in radio dramas in several countries. In the summer of 1946, several newsreel companies presented stories showing footage of Hiroshima one year after the attack. Some of these included images of *hibakusha*, such as the famous image of a woman who suffered burns in the pattern of her summer dress (*yukata*), and of children being taught in a schoolroom without walls. These film clips included numerous shots of children standing in the midst of the rubble of Hiroshima before rebuilding had begun.[16]

---

[15] For an example of a map listing extensive military facilities, see "Hiroshima Area That Sustained Damage in First Atomic Bomb Attack," *New York Times*, August 10, 1945; most "targets" on the map were bridges. For an example of a map detailing the locations of schoolchildren's patriotic work parties in Hiroshima, see "Medical Effects of Atomic Bombs," 75 (figure 8) (unpublished version).

[16] John Hersey, "Hiroshima," *New Yorker*, August 31, 1946; John Hersey, Hiroshima (New York, 1946). See also Michael Yavenditti, "John Hersey and the American Conscience: The Reception of 'Hiroshima,'" *Pacific Historical Review* 43 (February 1974), 32–34; "Hiroshima Bombing and Crossroads Nuclear Weapons Test," *Universal Newsreel* 526 (August 5, 1945); "Hiroshima Anniversary," *British Movietone News* 897 (August 12, 1946).

Besides these film clips, the first photographic image of a child victim of the nuclear attack on Hiroshima appeared in the United States in an October 1946 *Popular Mechanics* article describing radiation as one of the "strangest" dangers in the world. What was most remarkable about the story was the accompanying picture of a disfigured Japanese boy, approximately six years old, who the story said was "scarred" by radiation. This was one of the first images of an actual human victim of the nuclear attacks ever seen in the United States, and it was the image of a child. A few months later, British Pathé released a short newsreel called "The Fifth Warning." It showed victims of the nuclear attack, many of whom were children, being treated in a Hiroshima hospital, surrounded by children presumably from their own families. The images counter the arguments of some historians such as Robert Lifton and Gregg Mitchell, who erroneously claim that, "it would be years until Americans saw – or were allowed to see – any Hiroshima images that put a human face on the consequences of the bombing." The examples cited above show that Americans did see the faces of individual *hibakusha* as early as 1946.[17]

Yet, despite these references during the first year after the war, additional representations of *hibakusha* did not appear in the United States until almost ten years later when twenty-five young, female Japanese *hibakusha* from Hiroshima were brought to the United States for medical treatment, funded by several religious and peace groups. The American mainstream media called them the "Hiroshima Maidens." These women were given reconstructive surgeries to repair burned and damaged limbs and appendages, and plastic surgery to repair scarring to their faces so that they might become wives. Many *hibakusha* had experienced widespread discrimination, including the reluctance of others to marry them as it was assumed that they were likely to have deformed or sickly children. This was compounded for those who had additionally been scarred or disfigured.

There was extensive discussion in the American press about the marital prospects of the Maidens and of how the skill of American doctors could "restore" their beauty. What was left unsaid but implied in this discourse was that, because all of these women were in their late teens or early twenties, they had been children when their bodies were burned and disfigured by the nuclear detonation ten years earlier. Publisher

---

[17] Carl Dreher, "The Weirdest Danger in the World," *Popular Science*, November 1946, 86; "The Fifth Warning," *British Pathé Newsreel* (December 8, 1946); Robert Jay Lifton and Gregg Mitchell, *Hiroshima in America: A Half Century of Denial* (New York, 1995), 60.

Norman Cousins and the others who arranged the visit and surgeries for the young women specifically chose only women to soften Americans' vision of the victims of Hiroshima and Nagasaki, and young women to evoke the sympathy of the American public for the *hibakusha*. It would have been impossible to win support for the *hibakusha* by bringing over Japanese men in their thirties or forties, who would likely have been received with hostility in the United States. Nonetheless, the presence of these young female victims of the nuclear attacks were an implicit reminder that many of the victims had been noncombatants and in fact had been children.

The visiting Japanese women were generally depicted as childlike, innocent, and grateful. They were uniformly spoken of as being "almost pathologically shy" and as "blossoming in the warmth they shared in the homes of American parents." While this childlike image was not atypical for depictions of Asian women in the American press, it had not been typical of depiction of Japanese women a decade earlier during the war. In anticipation of a possible American invasion of the Japanese home islands, Japanese women were frequently depicted as bamboo-spear-wielding warriors. The presentation of the Maidens as docile reflects the rehabilitation of a wartime trope rooted in colonial-era images of the childlike Asian woman. A *Time* magazine article claimed that Shigeko Niimoto was the "youngest and prettiest of Oyster-Fisherman Masayuki Niimoto's three daughters." Shigeko had been thirteen and on her way to high school on the morning of the attack. Standing on a bridge less than a mile from Ground Zero, she was one of a handful of people who survived despite having been so close to the blast and in the open. She suffered severe burns to her face, chin, and arm.

Much was made of the need to restore the beauty of the Japanese women, and newspaper coverage focused on the likelihood of their marriage prospects. "Of the 6,000 Hiroshimans who suffer lingering injury from fire or radiation," claimed one article, "the most poignant cases have been these girls who reach marrying age bearing the akuna no tsume ato – the Devil's claw marks – as the Japanese describe the Bomb scars." There is no record of keloid scars being called that in Japan, and in fact the expression *akuna no tsume ato* is an old expression meaning "nail marks of the Devil" that had long been used to describe the physical scarring left on the land by natural disasters such as typhoons, tsunamis, and earthquakes. The use of this phrase evoked the sense that the scarring of the women could be seen as the aftereffect of natural forces rather than the wounds inflicted by a deliberate act of warfare. This is similar to the frequently used description of the bomb having "dropped" on Hiroshima and Nagasaki as though this was not an aggressive act but something natural or accidental.[18]

The idea that the Japanese women "forgave" or held no animosity toward the United States for the use of the atomic bomb was a commonly repeated theme. Moviegoers learned this lesson from a Universal International Newsreel shown in movie theaters in November 1956. A report about the Maidens returning to Japan shows the women happily waving to friends and supporters from an airport tarmac as narrator Ed Herlihy informs the audience that "they say now that their sacrifice was worth it if only the atom is never used again in war." One woman, Tazuko Shibata, was quoted as saying that she loved being in New York City and that, "If it had not been for the atomic bomb I would never have gone to America." Suzue Oshima, another of the Maidens, remarked, "When I think about how kind everyone is, I'm glad I've never been bitter about the bomb."[19]

The Quaker peace activists who sponsored the Maidens' trip deliberately depicted them as childlike so that the American public would not find them threatening. That depiction also served to reinforce the impression that many of the victims of the nuclear attacks, and certainly the most sympathetic of them, had been children. The Maidens' status as children at the time of the attacks was the reason behind their selection as "representative" *hibakusha* and the core of their media identity in the United States.

The single most representative – and still the most famous – *hibakusha* was Sadako Sasaki, a young girl from Hiroshima. Sadako was two years old when, as noted earlier, she was exposed to radiation from the bomb. She was not burned and did not suffer serious radiation sickness, but nine years later she began to run a fever and developed swelling in her glands. She was soon diagnosed with leukemia. While receiving treatment in a hospital, Sadako and her friends began to fold the paper in which her powdered medicines were delivered into origami paper cranes. There is an old Japanese custom that if you fold 1,000 paper cranes, you will be granted one wish. Sadako died of her radiation-induced leukemia in the fall of

---

[18] Gloria Kalischer and Peter Kalischer, "Love Helped to Heal the 'Devil's Claw Marks,'" *Collier's*, October 26, 1956, 92; "Young Ladies of Japan," *Time*, October 24, 1955, 53.

[19] "News in Brief," *Universal International Newsreel* (November 8, 1956); Kalischer and Kalischer, "Love Helped to Heal," 94; Joy Miller, "A Blinding Flash, White Heat, Then Death: The First Atomic Bomb," *St. Petersburg [FL] Times*, July 31, 1955.

1955, ten years after her exposure to radiation and less than a year after her illness presented symptoms.

The actual history of Sadako and how her story came to prominence is, of course, much more complicated. After her death, Sadako's father moved the family away from Hiroshima and tried to hide the fact that they had been exposed to radiation in Hiroshima. He tried to keep the family's status as *hibakusha* out of the story of Sadako. During this period, the story spread outside Japan and became widely popularized, first in Germany and Austria. Robert Jungk briefly told the story of Sadako in his 1959 book *Strahlen aus der Asche* (published in English translation under the title *Children of the Ashes* in 1961). Two years later, Karl Bruckner published *Sadako will leben!*, which told the story in its full, heroic form. Dozens of biographies of Sadako, most aimed at young readers, have been published in numerous languages between the 1950s and today. Sadako's story spread the message of peace in a tangible form that has been integrated into school curricula around the world. It is because of the story of Sadako that children all around the world learn to fold paper cranes for peace.[20]

Sadako is the *hibakusha* most often identified by name in literary and memorial commemorations of Hiroshima. She is sometimes referred to as Japan's Anne Frank. A shrine to the child victims in Hiroshima that has a statue of Sadako was dedicated in 1958, and it is where many of the donated paper cranes are displayed in the Hiroshima Peace Park. As the most represented and narrated victim of the nuclear attack, Sadako again positions the archetypal *hibakusha* as a young female child. She is a powerful symbol both because of her creative response to her illness and also because of her innocence: There is no way that two-year-old Sadako – or any child – could be considered a legitimate target for a weapon of mass destruction.

In 1967, the American psychologist Robert Jay Lifton published a profound book that was the result of years of interviews with *hibakusha* in Hiroshima, *Death in Life*. The book, partly dedicated to "the world of my children," provided the first psychological assessments of the survivors of the nuclear attack, based on Western models of human consciousness and mental health. Lifton interviewed several dozen *hibakusha* in

[20] Robert Jungk, *Strahlen aus der Asche* (Bern, 1959); Karl Bruckner, *Sadako will leben!* (Vienna, 1961); Eleanor Coerr, *Sadako and the Thousand Paper Cranes* (New York, 1977); Masamoto Nasu, *Children of the Paper Crane: The Story of Sadako Sasaki and Her Struggle with the A-Bomb Disease* (Armonk, 1996).

Hiroshima about their experiences and memories of the attack and its aftermath. As Ran Zwigenberg has shown, Lifton's work was linked with concurrent studies of the survivors of the Holocaust and was fundamental in the establishment of a global memory culture of victimhood in the 1960s and 1970s. "Lifton transmitted and translated the Hiroshima survivors' political usage of their experience into a universal scientific knowledge," writes Zwigenberg, noting that a primary outcome of these efforts was the development and establishment of the diagnosis of post-traumatic stress disorder (PTSD) in later psychotherapeutic models, no matter the source of the trauma.[21]

Lifton's book would win the National Book Award for Science in 1969. Lifton's work introduced another cohort of *hibakusha* to a new generation of Americans immersed in the brutalities of the civil rights movement, the Vietnam War, and the terror of the nuclear arms race. Readers could extrapolate global truths about trauma and the suffering of victims in Hiroshima. However, this time, unlike in Hersey's 1946 book, many of the *hibakusha* interviewed had been children at the time of the nuclear attack. Lifton would later write, "these 'children of the A-bomb' are – psychologically, technologically, and ethically – the children of our era, our children, ourselves."[22]

CHILDREN AND NUCLEAR WEAPONS

While Americans were coming to identify specific victims of the nuclear attacks on Hiroshima and Nagasaki primarily as children, American children became the focus of the nuclear imaginary in the United States as well. The period of the first four years of the Atomic Age, when the United States was the sole nuclear-armed nation, nuclear discourse was typified by philosophical discussions that often focused on the possibility that such weapons would bring an end to civilization and that, in turn, the generation of children then alive might well be the last generation of children ever. However, the acquisition of nuclear weapons by the United States' adversary, the Soviet Union, led to an altogether different obsession with children: how to train them to survive a nuclear attack. US government-funded films aimed at schoolchildren such as *Duck and*

---

[21] Robert Jay Lifton, *Death in Life: Survivors of Hiroshima* (New York, 1967); Ran Zwigenberg, *Hiroshima: The Origins of Global Memory Culture* (Cambridge: 2014), 144–75.
[22] Lifton, introduction to "Atomic Bombed Children," 188.

Cover and *Atomic Alert* were designed to train children what to do in the case of a nuclear attack when no adults were around to guide them. Contrary to their intended purpose, these films expressed deeply existential counternarratives: Rather than assuring children of nuclear survivability, they instead communicated hopelessness and abandonment. Researchers would find that by the early 1960s large percentages of American children assumed a nuclear war in their lifetimes was inevitable.[23]

This mirrored the beliefs of their parents and of most adults. While there was widespread support for resisting the perceived Soviet threat, there was never support for fighting a nuclear war or for stockpiling tens of thousands of nuclear weapons, as would be the case for the United States by the end of the 1950s. These choices were made by political and military leaders and never placed before the public for debate, except as part of the discourse of presidential campaigns, such as when John F. Kennedy asserted that Republicans had allowed a "missile gap" to develop between the United States and the Soviet Union. Even then, Kennedy's aim was to build support not for the expansion of the American nuclear arsenal but rather for continuing the Cold War and increasing the defense budget generally. The public stance toward nuclear weapons in the Cold War was one of fatalism and inevitability. No opinion polls ever showed large majorities of Americans believing that a nuclear war would be winnable or even survivable. Although thousands of Civil Defense pamphlets, films, and booklets were produced to instruct citizens on the steps that would supposedly lead to survival, fewer than 5 percent of Americans ever prepared any kind of home shelter with the aim of surviving a nuclear war.[24]

---

[23] Anthony Rizzo (director) and Leo M. Langlois (producer), *Duck and Cover*, Archer Films, 1951; *Atomic Alert* (Elementary Version), Encyclopedia Britannica Films Inc., 1951 (made in collaboration with the Institute for Nuclear Studies at the University of Chicago); Robert Jacobs, "Atomic Kid: *Duck and Cover* and *Atomic Alert* Teach American Children to Survive an Atomic Attack," *Film and History* 40(1) (Spring 2010), 25–44; Milton Schwebel, "Nuclear Cold War: Student Opinions and Professional Responsibility," in Schwebel, ed., *Behavioral Science and Human Survival* (Palo Alto, 1965), 210; Sibylle K. Escalona, "Children and the Threat of Nuclear War," in Child Study Association of America, *Children and the Threat of Nuclear War* (New York, 1964), 3–24.

[24] B. Wayne Blanchard, *American Civil Defense, 1945–1984: The Evolution of Programs and Policies* (Emmitsburg, MD, 1986), 19–23; David Monteyne, *Fallout Shelter: Designing for Civil Defense in the Cold War* (Minneapolis, 2011), 42.

Children have always been casualties of warfare, both directly and through the social devastation warfare leaves in its wake. However, the twentieth century saw a dramatic shift from wars generally being fought on battlefields between armies to wars being waged against societies as a whole: total war. In this shift, civilians became a dramatically larger proportion of the casualties in war, and with that children also became significantly more victimized. With many of the young males in societies mobilized into militaries, cities were largely populated by women, the elderly, and children. During World War II, hundreds of thousands, even millions, of children were killed in the Holocaust, the V2 rocket attacks on Great Britain, the fire bombings of German and Japanese cities, conventional bombing of cities, and, finally, the nuclear attacks on Hiroshima and Nagasaki.

Because of the existential threat that the advent of nuclear weapons posed to the human race as a whole, public interest in the nature and effects of this new weapon was intense throughout the Cold War. Thousands of articles and books were published on the topic in just a few short years. While many thousands of children died in the first firebombing of Tokyo, this was not particularly noted at the time. However, when Americans learned about the existence of nuclear weapons and the attacks on Hiroshima and Nagasaki, their imaginations extended swiftly to their own homes, cities, and families, and they became plagued with a sense of vulnerability. Not specifically fearing firebombing, the victims in Hiroshima and Nagasaki would eventually be envisioned as more like "normal Americans" than would those killed in places such as Dresden or Tokyo. A 1948 reprinting of John Hersey's *Hiroshima* had a cover illustration that showed a typical American family fleeing a bombed Midwestern American city. Here, just three years after the nuclear attacks, we can already see the degree to which Americans imagined themselves as the victims of future Hiroshimas.[25]

The initial narrative presented Hiroshima as an army base and the victims of the bomb as soldiers, yet within ten years most stories in the mainstream Western media about the dead of Hiroshima and Nagasaki would be stories about children. There are two key reasons that children became identified not just as the victims in Hiroshima and Nagasaki but of

---

[25] John Hersey, *Hiroshima* (New York, 1948). See also Robert Jacobs and Mick Broderick, "Nuke York, New York: Nuclear Holocaust in the American Imagination from Hiroshima to 9/11," *Asia-Pacific Journal* 10(11) no. 6 (March 12, 2012), http://japanfocus.org/-Mick-Broderick/3726.

nuclear war in the abstract. First, because the cells of children's bodies divide more rapidly, the effects of radiation exposure on children are far worse than on adults. The second reason is that nuclear weapons came to pose an existential threat to the existence of human society as a whole. In the 1952 American film *The Atomic City*, the son of the protagonist asks his friend, "What do you want to be if you grow up?" demonstrating that nuclear weapons had rendered this question moot for children during the Cold War.[26]

[26] Jerry Hopper (director) and Joseph Sistrom (producer), *The Atomic City*, Paramount Pictures, 1952.

Index